LEARNER FEEDBACK for Language Growth

A Guidebook for Evaluating Learner Work Through Performance Domains and Indicators

by

Megan Budke • Karen Nickel • Sarah Strauss*

** All three authors share co-first authorship.*

ACTFL
Language Connects

1001 North Fairfax Street, Suite 200
Alexandria, VA 22314

ISBN: 978-1-961332-09-6 (Print)
ISBN: 978-1-961332-10-2 (ePub)

Table of Contents

Foreword

"We do not learn from experience; we learn from reflecting on experience." —John Dewey

How can educators become even more effective in providing feedback that guides language learners to higher levels of performance? *This* is the critical question that led Megan Budke, Karen Nickel, and Sarah Strauss to write this book. Not satisfied with the results that come from providing learners with a score, grade, highlighted errors, or corrections after they respond to a communicative task, these three co-authors used their own classrooms as learning labs to develop strategies to ensure that their feedback led to learners' improved performance. The authors developed their approach to providing feedback to language learners through their extensive experiences teaching, coordinating language programs, collaborating to present at conferences, researching language acquisition, and using various strategies to support their learners. Through these experiences and their shared, frequent, and extended discussions on issues around language learning, they identified how to help learners reflect on their performance in comparison to elements of language that are essential to strengthening language proficiency. The clear guidance these authors provide is ready to support language educators at all levels and in all types of programs.

The authors' framework for providing feedback to language learners is solidly grounded on the foundational documents for describing and assessing learners' language proficiency: the *ACTFL Proficiency Guidelines*, the *NCSSFL-ACTFL Can-Do Statements*, and the *ACTFL Performance Descriptors*, as well as the books on implementing integrated performance assessment. **This book is not a training manual for how to rate language samples: the authors are focused on what educators need to know to coach learners to move along the proficiency continuum.** They have isolated five performance domains—Language Use, Text Type, Intercultural Communication, Impact, and Communication Strategies—for educators to emphasize, so learners can make conscious choices in those domains to increase their effectiveness when performing real-world tasks. When learners are made aware of indicators of higher levels of proficiency, they can act intentionally on that knowledge and produce language (in Interpersonal or Presentational tasks) at that target level.

This book helps educators improve their feedback practices to benefit language learners. The authors provide examples of performance tasks and learners' responses from their own teaching, highlighting specific evidence of how learners demonstrate different ranges of proficiency in their performance. Through the description and examples of each of the five key language performance domains, Budke, Nickel, and Strauss help educators focus on what will yield faster growth for learners along the proficiency continuum. This guidance creates a mindset, not just for providing feedback, but for designing experiences to help learners reach higher levels of language proficiency. The authors also address head-on the challenging issue of how grades and reporting practices can better convey learners' growth toward stronger language performance.

Learner Feedback for Language Growth offers effective ways to provide feedback, with detailed tools and templates that guide learners to reflect on their performance, setting personal goals to focus their own journey to stronger language proficiency. The authors provide examples of specific tasks that help learners unpack each of the five critical domains of language performance, showcasing how to heighten learners' awareness and understanding of the criteria that they need to develop over time to reach higher levels of proficiency. The ultimate goal is for learners to take ownership of their learning, knowing what to do to improve and then doing it. For language learners that means reflecting on their performance in comparison to the indicators and identifying what they can do to improve (hint: it is not just producing more language, nor knowing more vocabulary or grammatical structures). Programs, departments, and individuals will benefit from applying this book's actionable steps, feedback tools, and specific strategies for heightening learners' awareness of what they can do to be more effective communicators in Interpersonal and Presentational tasks. What can be more powerful than seeing learners shine a light on what they can do to better express themselves and chart their own path to achieve their goal?

By Paul Sandrock

Author of *The Keys to Assessing Language Performance*

ACTFL Director of Education and Senior Advisor (2011-2023)

Acknowledgements

We are thankful for a variety of people who have supported this book. Thank you to the team at ACTFL, under the leadership of former Executive Director Howie Berman and former Senior Advisor for Language Learning Initiatives, Paul Sandrock. The work of NCSSFL and ACTFL have been pivotal in our professional lives, and it was such a privilege to work alongside professionals who have been role models to us throughout our careers. We would like to thank our reviewers—Donna Clementi, Judy Liskin-Gasparro, Meg Malone, and Ali Moeller—whose perspectives and suggestions helped inform the final version of this guidebook. We are especially grateful for Paul Sandrock, who championed this book from beginning to end and provided invaluable insights to shape the final manuscript. We are so grateful for your mentorship and your unending faith in us. It's an honor to have you write the foreword for this book.

For each of us, the ideas in this book represent our work with learners in our own classrooms. We want to thank learners, educators, and administrators we have worked with over the years, as they have supported, collaborated, mentored, and inspired us. In particular, this work would not be possible without our esteemed colleagues at Wayzata Public Schools, Minnetonka Public Schools, and St. Paul Public Schools. Your perspectives, questions, and contributions made us the educators that we are today. We are so proud to call you colleagues.

Thank you to the middle school Spanish team at Wayzata Public Schools (Samara Eugene, Teresa Jaeb, Lisa Rudolph, Alison Ryan, Patricia Simmons, and Angela Swanson) for the contribution of multiple learning experiences. Many colleagues provided us feedback on early drafts of this book, including Sheen Heng, Allison Jakucki, Barbara Melbye Janssen, Lisa Parra Staves, and Kara Parker. In addition, feedback from Davia Christiansen, Emily Nelson, Polly Patrick, and Chong Xiong helped with revisions. We appreciate your generosity and your insights.

To our education colleagues near and far, conference presenters and attendees, and all those we have had an opportunity to consult and learn from, thank you for your inspiration and widened field of experiences from which we draw.

We are indebted to our friends and families, including children and dogs, for their love, support, and unwavering encouragement throughout our writing process. Writing takes a village, and we are so grateful for ours.

CHAPTER 1 | INTRODUCTION

As co-authors, each of us has taken a different journey to get where we are today. We differ in the training we have received, the languages we teach, the levels we have taught, the districts we have worked within. Yet, our journeys intersected as we asked the same question: **How do we provide feedback that promotes language growth for our learners?**

To answer this question, we applied the *backward design* method from Wiggins and McTighe (2005) to a world language classroom:

1. *Identify desired results* = Target performance level
2. *Determine acceptable evidence* = Performance tasks evaluated by performance domains and indicators
3. *Plan learning experiences and instruction* = Strategies, activities, and formative tasks

In world language classrooms, the *desired learner result* around developing learners' language performance can be identified as a target performance level, for example Novice Mid, Intermediate High, or other levels from the *ACTFL Proficiency Guidelines* (ACTFL, 2012b). This book specifically targets language *performance*, or what learners can produce within the context of what was learned within the classroom, which is different from language proficiency, or what learners can do regardless of where, when, or who the language was learned (ACTFL, 2012a). The levels as outlined by the *ACTFL Proficiency Guidelines* (ACTFL, 2012b) are similarly used to identify target levels of language performance (Novice Mid, Intermediate High, Advanced Low…). For learners to achieve a target performance level, it is important that educators understand 1) what the different aspects of language performance are and 2) how they develop through language learning experiences. To *determine acceptable evidence*, educators must design performance tasks that elicit learner samples at the target performance level. Criteria is needed to evaluate learner performance across the levels (Novice, Intermediate, and Advanced). We outline a set of criteria by identifying specific domains of performance and developed performance indicators to describe learner work in each domain across various proficiency levels. In this book, we refer to these criteria as Performance Domain Indicators (PDIs), which we developed by cross-referencing multiple sources, including the *ACTFL Performance Descriptors for Language Learners* (ACTFL, 2012a), the *ACTFL Proficiency Guidelines* (ACTFL, 2012b), the *Implementing Integrated Performance Assessments* book (Adair-Hauck et al., 2013), *The Integrated Performance Assessment: Twenty Years and Counting* (Troyan et al., 2023), and the *NCSSFL-ACTFL Can-Do Statements: Performance Indicators for Language Learners* (NCSSFL-ACTFL, 2017). The intent is to create consistent criteria that can be used to evaluate learner performances throughout a course. With each performance, there is an opportunity to provide learners meaningful, actionable feedback to support language growth.

The final step is for educators to *plan learning experiences and instruction* that includes strategies, activities, and formative tasks for learners to develop their language skills within each performance domain. In this way, educators and learners can better identify where learners are, where they are going, and actionable steps that learners can take for language growth.

The ultimate goal of this book is to empower learners. Performance domains and performance domain indicators are tools to support learners to take control of their own learning and strategically adjust their performance for language growth. The framework presented here for evaluating performance and providing feedback is but one way to structure it. We recognize there are other models. It is our hope that the ideas expressed in this publication will enable educators to seek a deeper understanding of language development through performance and spark continued conversation and professional development.

Overview of This Book

Chapter 2 differentiates performance from proficiency and presents an overview of the performance domains. The focus of this book is how to develop learners' language performance in a classroom setting, through feedback and coaching from the educator.

Chapter 3 describes the key elements of designing an effective performance task. With the end in mind, the performance task is an important tool that helps elicit evidence of what learners can do with and through the language at a target performance level.

Chapter 4 focuses on feedback. The chapter presents key elements of effective feedback and models for educators the GLOW and GROW framework for providing feedback to learners. An assessment and feedback guide is presented, which highlights what learners can do to build learner efficacy and promote language growth.

Chapters 5-9 present each of the performance domains:

- **Chapter 5 | Language Use:** The choices a learner makes in how they use language in order to communicate and complete the functions of a performance task.
- **Chapter 6 | Text Type:** The various types of text (word, phrase, sentence...) and the ways in which a learner organizes text to communicate a message.
- **Chapter 7 | Intercultural Communication:** The socially and culturally responsive ways in which learners use language and behaviors to appropriately communicate their message.
- **Chapter 8 | Impact**: The ways a learner captures and maintains the attention of the audience through the use of organization, descriptive details, and/or originality. This performance domain is only evaluated in a presentational task.
- **Chapter 9 | Communication Strategies:** The ways in which a learner maintains and advances communication. This performance domain is only evaluated in an interpersonal task.

Each of the performance domain chapters follow the *backward design* method from Wiggins & McTighe (2005):

- **Identify desired results:** *I can* statements are included at the beginning of each chapter to describe for readers what they will be able to do as a result of engaging with the information, examples, and tasks to apply the learning.
- **Determine acceptable evidence:** The Performance Domain Indicators are presented by performance level (Novice, Intermediate, and Advanced). Learner samples are used to illustrate and describe the characteristics of language development across the sublevels (Low, Mid, High). An assessment and feedback guide demonstrates how to evaluate learner work and provide feedback.
- **Plan learning experiences and instruction:** Each domain chapter includes strategies, activities, and formative tasks that educators can use to design instruction that will help learners understand the performance domain, self-assess their performance, and take next steps towards language growth.

Chapter 10 presents a standards-based approach to grading and reporting practices using performance domains and their indicators. By transferring performance domain indicators to a scoring rubric, consistency is created: consistent expectations for learners, consistent scoring practices for educators, and consistent shared evaluation practices across languages and levels within a department.

Additionally, educators are invited to participate throughout the book by completing the **Your Turn!** sections in each chapter to check for understanding and apply the key concepts.

Distinguishing Features of This Book

1. This book focuses only on the interpersonal and presentational modes of communication. It does not address the interpretive mode. We chose to focus on providing feedback based on what language learners produce as output (interpersonal or presentational).
2. This book focuses on performance domains in which learners can take actionable steps for language growth. Additional performance domains, such as Comprehensibility (How well is a learner understood?) or Language Control (How accurate is the learner?) can be evaluated in learner work. The focus of this book is on performance domains that reflect what learners CAN do, even if some inaccuracies occur, and what the next steps might be on the learner's pathway to language growth.
3. Language function is highlighted as an element of performance task design, along with content and context.
4. The Language Use performance domain focuses on how learners use language; that is, the language choices they make with vocabulary, structures, and time frames in order to complete the functions required of a performance task.
5. The Intercultural Communication performance domain provides indicators to evaluate the *NCSSFL-ACTFL Can-Do Statements: Performance Indicators for Language Learners* (NCSSFL-ACTFL, 2017) "Interact" statements (not the "Investigate" statements). We are only evaluating the language and behaviors produced by the learner ("Interact" statements). We are not evaluating their ability to understand nor reflect upon cultural practices, products, and the perspectives behind them ("Investigate" statements). However, we hope the washback effect will help promote intercultural competency in our learners.
6. Each performance domain includes a set of indicators that are referred to as Performance Domain Indicators (PDIs). They include *I can* statements and learner-friendly language.
7. The PDIs intend to create a common language among educators as well as between educators and learners using terms found across ACTFL resources. In the final stages of publishing this book, the fourth edition of the *ACTFL Proficiency Guidelines* (2024) was released. After cross-referencing the 2012 and 2024 publications of the *ACTFL Proficiency Guidelines*, we found one update among the terms used within the PDIs: the term *linguistic forms* is used instead of *structures* throughout multiple levels. We maintain the use of the term *structures* within the PDIs as a learner-friendly term. The remaining terms used in the PDIs that are cited from the 2012 publication of the *ACTFL Proficiency Guidelines* can also be found in the 2024 publication. Having reviewed a 2024 draft version of the *NCSSFL-ACTFL Can-Do Statements*, we found that the suggested updates to the interpersonal and presentational performance indicators still reflect the PDIs in this book.
8. Learner samples are included in this book. These learner samples are not perfect. Some were translated versions of learner performance from our own classrooms, others were samples collected from English language learners. All learner samples are examples of learner work completed within or after a unit of study in which learners were familiar with the content, practiced it in a variety of

ways, and were coached and provided feedback. The samples are not meant to be reflective of any one classroom or proficiency level. Rather, the goal is to provide samples to practice determining acceptable evidence; that is, evaluate learner work using a range of indicators for each performance domain and provide feedback.

9. In accordance with the American Psychological Association (APA) bias-free language guidelines (2022), this book uses *they* and *their* for a generic person (the learner and *their* performance). In addition, we use the term *base language* and *target language* rather than the terms *L1 & L2* in recognition of our multilingual learners. The inclusive language in this book is by design.

How to Use This Book

There is no one way to use this book. Educators reading this book will be at various points in their journey to assess performance, provide feedback, and coach learners for language growth. As such, there may be various ways to enter into this book:

- Follow the given format of this book: learn about performance tasks and feedback first (Chapters 3-4), then explore the performance domains and evaluate the learner samples and provide feedback (Chapters 5-9), then identify a standards-based approach to grading and reporting practices using performance domains and their indicators (Chapter 10).
- Learn about the performance domains (Chapters 5-9) to deepen your knowledge of the performance domain indicators, then return to performance task development (Chapter 3) to better understand how to design performance tasks that elicit learner performance at the target performance level for your course(s).
- Understand the performance domains (Chapters 5-9) and work towards inter-rater reliability with the learner samples in this book, then identify a standards-based approach to grading and reporting practices using performance domains and their indicators (Chapter 10).
- Focus on the assessment and feedback matrix as well as the learning experiences within each performance domain (Chapters 5-9), in order to better coach learners for language growth.
- Use this book as a guide for ongoing professional development within a team, department, or district. A collective understanding of the performance domains can lead to alignment of assessment practices among professional learning communities. Collaborative evaluation of the learner samples in the appendix can lead to consistent inter-rater reliability and grading practices. Consistent application of the assessment and feedback matrix as well as the learning experiences for each performance domain can align a team's approach to coach learners for growth.

Overall, educators are encouraged to thoughtfully self-evaluate their own needs or that of their department/district to best determine a pathway for learning.

References

ACTFL. (2012a). *ACTFL performance descriptors for language learners.* https://www.actfl.org/educator-resources/actfl-performance-descriptors

ACTFL. (2012b). *ACTFL proficiency guidelines – Speaking, writing, listening, and reading* (3rd ed.). https://www.actfl.org/educator-resources/actfl-proficiency-guidelines

ACTFL. (2024). *ACTFL proficiency guidelines 2024* (4th ed.). https://www.actfl.org/uploads/files/general/Resources-Publications/ACTFL_Proficiency_Guidelines_2024.pdf

Adair-Hauck, B., Glisan, E. W., & Troyan, F. J. (2013). *Implementing integrated performance assessment.* ACTFL.

American Psychological Association (APA). (2022). *Bias-free language.* https://apastyle.apa.org/style-grammar-guidelines/bias-free-language

National Council of State Supervisors for Languages (NCSSFL) – ACTFL. (2017). *NCSSFL-ACTFL Can-Do Statements: Performance Indicators for Language Learners.* ACTFL. https://www.actfl.org/educator-resources/ncssfl-actfl-can-do-statements

Troyan, F. J., Adair-Hauck, B., & Glisan, E. W. (2023). *The integrated performance assessment: Twenty years and counting.* ACTFL.

Wiggins, G., & McTighe, J. (2005). *Understanding by design.* ASCD.

CHAPTER 2 | PERFORMANCE VS. PROFICIENCY

LEARNING TARGET:	
I can	☐ explain the difference between performance and proficiency.

As noted by the *ACTFL Performance Descriptors for Language Learners* (ACTFL, 2012a), the terms performance and proficiency can both be used to indicate what a learner can do with language. Both terms signify purposeful communication. The difference lies in the content, context, tasks, and evaluation of each.

Proficiency is independent of the learning process; that is, it describes what a learner can do with language regardless of where, when, or how language was learned (ACTFL, 2012a). As it is real-world, unrehearsed language, proficiency is not limited to content that a learner has practiced or a context with which a learner is familiar. Rather, it encompasses a broad range of content and context appropriate for a given level. Proficiency tasks are designed as unrehearsed situations, in which both the content and context may or may not be familiar to learners. When evaluating proficiency, a learner must demonstrate sufficient evidence of all the criteria of a given level (Novice, Intermediate, Advanced) to be rated as someone who can use language at that level. For example, when given a set of unrehearsed tasks, a learner must demonstrate every indicator of the Intermediate level all of the time in order to be rated at that level. This is a key point of proficiency: that learners demonstrate "sustained performance across the tasks and contexts for the level" (ACTFL, 2012a, p. 5).

Performance, in contrast, is based on instruction. As described in the *ACTFL Performance Descriptors for Language Learners* (ACTFL, 2012a), performance indicates what learners can do with language based on what they learned. Performance is limited to what a learner has **practiced**, **rehearsed**, or **experienced**: the content and context are based on what was learned in the classroom. Performance tasks are designed based upon practiced content and familiar contexts. That is, performance tasks provide learners an opportunity to apply their skills in a context that is similar, but not identical, to what they learned and practiced in the classroom.

Table 2.1 highlights the differences between performance and proficiency. To evaluate performance, a learner's performance is compared to "the description of the features of the domains of a given range" (ACTFL, 2012a, p. 4). That is, the features of a given proficiency level can be categorized into various domains of performance. These domains, aligned to the *ACTFL Proficiency Guidelines* (ACTFL, 2012b), help operationalize the features, or indicators of a given level.

Table 2.1
Performance vs. Proficiency

PERFORMANCE	PROFICIENCY
Definition: Describes what a language learner can do based on what was learned and/or what resulted from provided feedback	**Definition:** Describes what a language learner can do regardless of where, when, or how the language was acquired
Content: Based on what was learned and practiced	**Content:** Appropriate for the given level
Context: Similar, but not identical, to what was learned	**Context:** Appropriate for the given level
Tasks: Familiar, practiced situations based on content and context that was learned	**Tasks:** Spontaneous, unrehearsed situations that may or may not be familiar
Evaluation: Performance is compared to the indicators of the performance domains of a given range	**Evaluation:** Sustained performance across multiple tasks. The learner must meet all the criteria for a given level all of the time

Note: From *ACTFL Performance Descriptors for Language Learners* (ACTFL, 2012a).

It is important to understand that educators work with learner performance, not proficiency. Performance happens in the classroom, while proficiency occurs in real world, unrehearsed situations. Learners can *perform* at or within a proficiency level, but they may not necessarily be proficient at that level. However, performance paves the way for proficiency. While one learner's performance is not indicative of proficiency, how a learner performs on a variety of performance assessments throughout a course can point towards the proficiency level a learner might achieve. Each performance, then, provides an opportunity for learners to receive feedback on their path to proficiency. Feedback that is aligned to the performance domains and their indicators describes to learners where they are on the path to proficiency, where they are going, and what next steps they might take for language growth. Feedback on numerous and varied performances is critical, as multiple performances at a targeted level are needed before proficiency at that level is realized. Therefore, educators should view each interpersonal and presentational performance task as an opportunity for feedback on learner performance.

The focus of this book, then, is to provide educators a deep understanding of the performance domains and their indicators. These domains are drawn from a variety of sources. Some of the performance domains are derived from the *ACTFL Performance Descriptors for Language Learners* (ACTFL, 2012a), such as Language Use, Text Type, and Communication Strategies, but their Performance Domain Indicators (PDIs) reflect the updated indicators included in the *NCSSFL-ACTFL Can-Do Statements: Performance Indicators for Language Learners* (NCSSFL-ACTFL, 2017). The performance domain of Intercultural Communication is derived from both the *ACTFL Performance Indicators for Language Learners* (ACTFL, 2012a) and the *NCSSFL-ACTFL Can-Do Statements: Performance Indicators for Language Learners* (NCSSFL-ACTFL, 2017). The Impact domain is the one performance domain that is not derived from performance or proficiency documents, but rather the work of Wiggins (1998), of Adair-Hauck et al. (2013), and of Troyan et al. (2023). These same performance domains (illustrated in Table 2.2) can be used to evaluate learner performance, regardless of the level of the learner. The performance domains are constant across all levels of performance and describe the key features that distinguish a performance as Novice, Intermediate, and Advanced (ACTFL, 2012a).

Table 2.2
Performance Domains

PRESENTATIONAL PERFORMANCE DOMAINS	INTERPERSONAL PERFORMANCE DOMAINS
Language Use: How do I use language to complete the performance task?	**Language Use:** How do I use language to complete the performance task?
Text Type: How extensive and complex is the language I use and how do I organize it?	**Text Type:** How extensive and complex is the language I use and how do I organize it?
Intercultural Communication: How well do my language and behavior match the social and cultural context of the performance task?	**Intercultural Communication:** How well does my language and behavior match the social and cultural context of the performance task?
Impact: How do I present my ideas to maintain my audience's attention?	**Communication Strategies:** How do I maintain and advance communication?

Within each performance domain, the PDIs outline a continuum of performance for a given level (Novice, Intermediate, Advanced) and sublevel (Low, Mid, High). They describe the range of performance within which a learner is expected to perform. These PDIs can serve as overarching goals for learner performance within a course. Table 2.3 is an example from Chapter 6 of the targeted PDIs for Text Type used with each interpersonal and presentational performance throughout a course.

Table 2.3
Performance Domain Indicators (PDIs) by Performance Level

	NOVICE		
Sublevels	LOW	MID	HIGH
Context	familiar, informal, formal, predictable		
Content	very familiar	very familiar, everyday	familiar, everyday
Performance Domain Indicator	**I can use practiced** and **memorized words and phrases**.	**I can use practiced** and **memorized words and phrases**, and at times **use simple sentences**.	**I can use simple sentences most of the time**.

- The language in bold indicates the source is the *NCSSFL-ACTFL Can-Do Statements: Performance Indicators for Language Learners* (NCSSFL-ACTFL, 2017).
- Some language may appear in additional levels to provide scaffolding, consistency and/or clarity (*at times*).

	INTERMEDIATE		
Sublevels	**LOW**	**MID**	**HIGH**
Context	familiar, informal, formal, straight-forward		
Content	familiar	familiar, at times researched	familiar, concrete, at times researched
Performance Domain Indicator	**I can form simple sentences**, and at times **series of sentences**.	**I can form a series of connected sentences**, and at times complex sentences.	**I can form (a) series of connected** and complex **sentences that may combine to create a simple paragraph(s)** and/or *paragraph-length discourse.*

- The language in bold indicates the source is the *NCSSFL-ACTFL Can-Do Statements: Performance Indicators for Language Learners* (NCSSFL-ACTFL, 2017).
- The language in italics indicates that the source is the *ACTFL Proficiency Guidelines* (ACTFL, 2012b).
- Some language may appear in additional levels to provide scaffolding, consistency and/or clarity.

	ADVANCED		
Sublevels	**LOW**	**MID**	**HIGH**
Context	familiar, unfamiliar, informal, formal, complex		
Content	familiar, academic, social, concrete	academic, social, professional, concrete	academic, social, professional, concrete, abstract
Performance Domain Indicator	**I can** create **simple paragraphs** and/or *paragraph-length discourse.*	**I can** create **organized paragraphs** and/or *connected paragraph-length discourse.*	**I can create** organized paragraphs and/or *connected paragraph-length discourse,* and at times *cohesive extended discourse.*

- The language in bold indicates the source is the *NCSSFL-ACTFL Can-Do Statements: Performance Indicators for Language Learners* (NCSSFL-ACTFL, 2017).
- The language in italics indicates that the source is the *ACTFL Proficiency Guidelines* (ACTFL, 2012b).
- Some language may appear in additional levels to provide scaffolding, consistency and/or clarity.

In addition, the PDIs can be used to assess learner performance. To evaluate learner performance, the PDIs can be transferred to a rubric (see Table 2.4) which is distinguished by different levels of quality (*Exceeding, Meeting, Developing, Approaching*).

Table 2.4
Aligning Text Type Performance Domain Indicators (PDIs) in a Rubric

Target Performance Level: **Novice High** Context: familiar, informal, formal, predictable Content: very familiar, everyday				
	INTERMEDIATE LOW	**NOVICE HIGH**	**NOVICE MID**	**NOVICE LOW**
Performance level description	I can form simple sentences, and at times series of sentences.	I can use simple sentences most of the time.	I can use practiced and memorized words and phrases, and at times use simple sentences.	I can use practiced and memorized words and phrases.
	EXCEEDING	**MEETING**	**DEVELOPING**	**BEGINNING**
Performance assessment rubric	I can form simple sentences, and at times series of sentences.	I can use simple sentences most of the time.	I can use practiced and memorized words and phrases, and at times use simple sentences.	I can use practiced and memorized words and phrases.

The range of the PDIs within each performance domain is intended to guide both educators and learners about the expected level of learner performance for multiple units within a course; that is, the course's desired result, the starting point for *backward design*. They also serve as the criteria educators can use to evaluate learner performance across levels (Novice, Intermediate, and Advanced). When there is a clear purpose and explicit performance goals, educators can design and select the appropriate learning experiences to achieve the desired results (Wiggin & McTighe, 2005). In addition, criteria, such as the PDIs, can guide students to achieve mastery (Fisher et al., 2021). Learners can use the PDIs to self-assess their performance throughout a unit to achieve the targeted level of performance. Overall, the PDIs are a tool for both educators and learners to engage together in the process to elicit, evaluate, and provide feedback on a learner's performance to promote language growth.

YOUR TURN

LEARNING TARGET CHECK:	
I can	☐ explain the difference between performance and proficiency.

Pause and reflect:

How would you describe performance and proficiency to your learners? Consider any explanations, examples, and/or visuals you might use to describe performance vs. proficiency:

References

ACTFL. (2012a). *ACTFL performance descriptors for language learners.* https://www.actfl.org/educator-resources/actfl-performance-descriptors

ACTFL. (2012b). *ACTFL proficiency guidelines – Speaking, writing, listening, and reading* (3rd ed.). https://www.actfl.org/educator-resources/actfl-proficiency-guidelines

Adair-Hauck, B., Glisan, E. W., & Troyan, F. J. (2013). *Implementing integrated performance assessment.* ACTFL.

Fisher, D., Frey, N., & Almarode, J. (2021). *Student learning communities: A springboard for academic and social-emotional development.* ASCD.

National Council of State Supervisors for Languages (NCSSFL) – ACTFL. (2017). *NCSSFL-ACTFL Can-Do Statements: Performance Indicators for Language Learners.* ACTFL. https://www.actfl.org/educator-resources/ncssfl-actfl-can-do-statements

Troyan, F. J., Adair-Hauck, B., & Glisan, E. W. (2023). *The integrated performance assessment: Twenty years and counting.* ACTFL.

Wiggins, G. (1998). *Educative assessment.* Jossey-Bass.

Wiggins, G., & McTighe, J. (2005). *Understanding by design.* ASCD.

CHAPTER 3 | THE PERFORMANCE TASK

LEARNING TARGETS:	
I can	☐ describe a performance task. ☐ identify the mode of communication of a performance task. ☐ describe content and how it elicits a learner language sample with characteristics of the Novice, Intermediate, or Advanced level. ☐ describe context and how it elicits a learner language sample with characteristics of the Novice, Intermediate, or Advanced level. ☐ describe language functions and how they show up in performance tasks at various levels. ☐ write interpersonal and presentational performance tasks that elicit a learner language sample with characteristics of the Novice, Intermediate, or Advanced level.

To begin with the end in mind requires educators to determine what acceptable evidence will demonstrate that learners have met the goals of the units (Wiggins & McTighe, 2005). Within a unit of instruction, a performance task is needed to assess learner performance. A performance task is a real-world situation that elicits a learner language sample; it is in completion of a performance task that learners demonstrate they have met the goals of the unit, providing evidence of what they can do in a real-world scenario to communicate in the target language. By focusing on what a learner can do in the target language, learners are empowered to choose how to demonstrate their learning through language and behaviors.

To determine acceptable evidence, educators need criteria or indicators to evaluate learner performances and provide feedback. In a world language classroom, the Performance Domain Indicators (PDIs) can serve as the criteria to indicate the level of performance needed for learner success. Therefore, it is important that educators design tasks with the performance domains and their indicators in mind. A successful task elicits learner evidence of all the performance domains within the expected range of indicators. Educators must design tasks that are open-ended and appropriate to the language level, taking into account the PDIs by which a learner's performance is evaluated. The performance task should elicit the desired learner evidence by allowing learners to showcase what they *can do* with the language.

Performance tasks can be formative or summative. Formative performance tasks, or assessment for learning, occur during the learning process; that is, while learning is still taking place. Summative performance tasks, or assessment of learning, demonstrate if learners have met the goals of the unit (Earl & Katz, 2006). That is, they are designed to elicit evidence of how learners have met the unit's goals in each mode of communication. Any performance task can be formative or summative. The distinction lies in how the performance task is used. For example, feedback may be provided on formative performance tasks, while the learning is still taking place, so learners can make adjustments to their performance prior to the summative performance task, which marks the end of the learning sequence for that unit. Or, feedback may be provided on a summative assessment, which can be used by learners to make adjustments in a subsequent performance in the following unit. Additionally, summative performance tasks do not necessarily need to take place at the end of the unit. Rather, they can be integrated throughout a unit, occurring when learners are ready to demonstrate what they can do (Clementi and Terrill, 2017).

Every task operates within a mode of communication. This book focuses on how learners can demonstrate what they can do either in the interpersonal or presentational mode. An interpersonal performance task is characterized as two-way communication that is spoken, signed, or written where learners engage with others, not the educator. Learners must interact collaboratively with their partners to react and respond, guided by the performance task. Even though learners may have practiced elements of the performance task throughout the unit of instruction, engaging in an interpersonal performance task is designed to elicit practiced content in a spontaneous manner. Unlike a play, where scripted roles indicate the exact questions and responses, an interpersonal performance task requires learners to react and respond in the moment, applying what they have learned, practiced, or rehearsed to the performance task. The summative interpersonal performance task should be similar to what was practiced, but not identical. Adding unrehearsed elements to a performance task, such as not knowing in advance who one's partner will be or what picture will be discussed, help facilitate spontaneous communication on content that has been practiced but not rehearsed.

The presentational performance task is characterized as one-way communication that is spoken, signed, or written, where learners present information for audiences within and beyond the classroom. This requires learners to consider how to create an organized product with intentionally crafted information that maintains the attention of their intended audience. A presentational performance task could be *polished* or *on-demand* (Clementi & Terrill, 2017). *Polished* performance tasks allow learners the opportunity to draft, edit, and revise before submitting their final product. Or the performance task could be *on-demand*, in which the learner might have practiced elements of the task throughout the unit, but some aspect of the performance task is not known in advance, such as a corresponding picture, resource, or idea.

YOUR TURN

LEARNING TARGETS CHECK:	
I can	☐ describe a performance task. ☐ identify the mode of communication of a performance task.

Pause and reflect:

How would you describe a performance task to your learners? Consider any explanations, examples, and/or visuals you might use to describe a performance task:

Performance tasks and their mode of communication:

Read the following performance tasks and consider if they are interpersonal or presentational performance tasks.

Performance Tasks:

1. Talk with your partner to find an activity you both like to do.
2. Post a reply to your friend's breakfast photo message on social media and compare your breakfasts.
3. Create a podcast episode for your listeners that brings awareness to how nutrition impacts the human body.
4. After watching a news report about locally grown food, discuss with a friend if you think it is a sustainable option.
5. Write a note to your new instructor telling them about an activity you like to do.
6. You and a friend discuss and decide where to eat lunch together.

Next, write the number of the performance task in the appropriate mode of communication (interpersonal and/or presentational) and provide evidence of your reasoning. If a performance task can fit in more than one mode of communication, list it in both and explain why.

INTERPERSONAL	
Two-way communication in which learners engage with others	
Performance task number	Evidence of your reasoning

PRESENTATIONAL	
One-way communication in which learners present information for audiences within and beyond the classroom	
Performance task number	Evidence of your reasoning

Note: Answers can be found in Table 3.3.

To design effective interpersonal and presentational performance tasks, educators must attend to the content (Table 3.1) and context (Table 3.2), as seen in sample performance tasks in Table 3.3 and Table 3.4.

Table 3.1
Content

	NOVICE		
Sublevels	LOW	MID	HIGH
Content	very familiar	very familiar, everyday	familiar, everyday

Note: From *NCSSFL-ACTFL Can-Do Statements: Performance Indicators for Language Learners* (NCSSFL-ACTFL, 2017).

	INTERMEDIATE		
Sublevels	LOW	MID	HIGH
Content	familiar	familiar, at times researched	familiar, concrete, at times researched

Note: From *NCSSFL-ACTFL Can-Do Statements: Performance Indicators for Language Learners* (NCSSFL-ACTFL, 2017).

	ADVANCED		
Sublevels	LOW	MID	HIGH
Content	familiar, academic, social, concrete	academic, social, professional, concrete	academic, social, professional, concrete, abstract

Note: From *NCSSFL-ACTFL Can-Do Statements: Performance Indicators for Language Learners* (NCSSFL-ACTFL, 2017).

Content

In world language classrooms, content refers to the topics that learners discuss (ACTFL, 2012a). That is to say that content is *not* the language of study (Chinese, Hmong, German, etc.), *nor* is it the grammatical structures or vocabulary the learners will use. Rather, content is the ideas that learners communicate about in a performance task using the target language. Focusing performance task design on ideas, rather than vocabulary or grammatical structures, provides learners "opportunities to use language in meaningful ways" (Glynn & Spenader, 2020, p. 72). The content within which learners operate most successfully is influenced by their proficiency level. That is, learners may demonstrate what they can do most successfully with content that aligns to the proficiency level they are operating within. Learners performing within the Novice level can successfully engage with everyday, familiar topics (NCSSFL-ACTFL, 2017). Learners performing with the Intermediate level can communicate on familiar, concrete topics that are, at times, researched; that is, the topics that learners can successfully engage with expand beyond everyday content and may include researched topics. Learners performing within the Advanced level engage with familiar, concrete topics that range from social to academic and professional. When designing a performance task, the content of the task should reflect what learners have learned and practiced within a unit of instruction. The content within which learners operate most successfully is influenced by their performance level.

YOUR TURN

LEARNING TARGET CHECK:	
I can	☐ describe content and how it elicits a learner language sample with characteristics of the Novice, Intermediate, or Advanced level.

Pause and reflect:
How would you describe content to your learners? Consider any explanations, examples, and/or visuals you might use to describe content:

Content in a performance task:
Consider the content of the following performance tasks. Which performance task would best elicit a learner language sample with characteristics at the Novice, Intermediate, or Advanced performance level? Write your answers in the chart and provide evidence of your reasoning. If needed, refer to Table 3.1 for guidance.

Task 1
Based on the movie, write a diary entry from the perspective of one of the baseball players that includes their reflections of the recruiting practices of professional baseball leagues.

Task 2
For the hallway display, select one of the people we have studied in this unit. Create a descriptive writing in which you compare how you are similar to highlight what you have in common, and contrast how you are different in order to feature how you each make use of your attributes in our diverse world.

Task 3
As part of an Earth Day campaign in your community, write a formal letter to an influential leader advocating for change that would address an environmental issue that you have learned about.

PERFORMANCE LEVEL	TASK #	EVIDENCE OF REASONING
NOVICE Content: very familiar, familiar, everyday		
INTERMEDIATE Content: familiar, concrete, at times researched		
ADVANCED Content: familiar, academic, social, professional, concrete, abstract		

Note: Answers can be found in Table 3.6.

Table 3.2
Context

	NOVICE		
Sublevels	LOW	MID	HIGH
Content	very familiar	very familiar, everyday	familiar, everyday
Context	**familiar**, informal, formal, *predictable*		

- The language in bold indicates the source is the *NCSSFL-ACTFL Can-Do Statements: Performance Indicators for Language Learners* (NCSSFL-ACTFL, 2017).
- The language in italics indicates that the source is the *ACTFL Proficiency Guidelines* (ACTFL, 2012b).

	INTERMEDIATE		
Sublevels	LOW	MID	HIGH
Content	familiar	familiar, at times researched	familiar, concrete, at times researched
Context	**familiar**, informal, formal, *straight-forward*		

- The language in bold indicates the source is the *NCSSFL-ACTFL Can-Do Statements: Performance Indicators for Language Learners* (NCSSFL-ACTFL, 2017).
- The language in italics indicates that the source is the *ACTFL Proficiency Guidelines* (ACTFL, 2012b).

	ADVANCED		
Sublevels	LOW	MID	HIGH
Content	familiar, academic, social, concrete	academic, social, professional, concrete	academic, social, professional, concrete, abstract
Context	**familiar**, **unfamiliar**, *informal*, *formal*, **complex**		

- The language in bold indicates the source is the *NCSSFL-ACTFL Can-Do Statements: Performance Indicators for Language Learners* (NCSSFL-ACTFL, 2017).
- The language in italics indicates that the source is the *ACTFL Proficiency Guidelines* (ACTFL, 2012b).

Context

For learners to best display what they can do, the performance task should be designed with the appropriate context, or "situations within which the learner can function" (ACTFL, 2012a, p. 8), for their performance level. The context keeps learners within the boundaries of the performance level; that is, contexts are the situations where learners can showcase what they can do, while not requiring or forcing them beyond their language abilities. Contexts work on a continuum so that as learners continue to develop their language skills, they can engage effectively with a greater variety and complexity of topics and situations. It is important to note that contexts are permeable; learners are not limited within them. However, this may be where learners perform most successfully with the target language.

The content of a performance task is influenced by the context of the level that the learner is performing within. Learners performing within the Novice level can communicate within familiar, predictable situations (ACTFL, 2012a; NCSSFL-ACTFL, 2017). These learners function in a highly practiced and memorized way. For example, learners performing within the Novice level can discuss and compare what they like to eat for lunch at school with a friend. As learners progress towards performing within the Intermediate level, they can interact in familiar, straightforward situations. For example, learners can discuss and decide where to eat lunch together. Along the continuum, learners performing within the Advanced level can communicate in familiar, complex situations. So after watching a news report about locally grown food, learners can discuss the advantages and disadvantages of locally grown food to determine if it is a sustainable option.

Understanding how a performance level influences the context of a performance task is important. Performance tasks designed within the appropriate level in which a learner is performing enable that learner to demonstrate what they can do within a context. In fact, performance tasks that are designed outside the context of the appropriate level may negatively impact the learner's performance. Contexts that require language beyond a learner's abilities may cause the learner to avoid or abandon the message altogether. Contexts that do not offer opportunities for complex language may restrict the learner from using all their language resources to show what they can do. Having a broad view of the context for each performance level is necessary to design tasks that are appropriately situated within the range selected as the target for learners' performance.

Table 3.3
Sample Performance Tasks

	NOVICE		
Sublevels	LOW	MID	HIGH
Context	familiar, informal, formal, predictable		
Content	very familiar	very familiar, everyday	familiar, everyday
Interpersonal performance tasks	• Talk with your partner to find an activity you both like to do. • Discuss and compare what you and your friend prefer to eat for lunch at school.		
Presentational performance tasks	• Write a note to your new instructor telling about an activity you like to do. • Send your friend a status update on social media describing your Saturday morning breakfast experience.		

	INTERMEDIATE		
Sublevels	LOW	MID	HIGH
Context	familiar, informal, formal, straight-forward		
Content	familiar	familiar, at times researched	familiar, concrete, at times researched
Interpersonal performance tasks	• Persuade your friend to participate in an activity you like to do. • You and your friend discuss and decide where to eat lunch together.		
Presentational performance tasks	• Email a friend to describe what you did this past weekend. • Post a reply to your friend's breakfast photo message on social media and compare your breakfasts.		

	ADVANCED		
Sublevels	LOW	MID	HIGH
Context	familiar, unfamiliar, informal, formal, complex		
Content	familiar, academic, social, concrete	academic, social, professional, concrete	academic, social, professional, concrete, abstract
Interpersonal performance tasks	• Persuade your partner to join you in an activity you think they might like to do. • After watching a news report about locally grown food, discuss with a friend if you think it is a sustainable option.		
Presentational performance tasks	• Write a note to your coach reflecting on your journey and future goals of becoming a professional athlete. • Create a podcast episode for your listeners that brings awareness to how nutrition impacts the human body.		

Sociocultural Context

It is important to note that within a context, communication does not happen in a void. Rather, messages are influenced by social and cultural factors. The context of a performance task should encourage learners to analyze how culture influences their language and behavior. This is done by defining the sociocultural context of a performance task; that is, the social and cultural situation within which the learner functions. This is key to providing learners the opportunity to reflect on and use Intercultural Communication. In a performance task, the sociocultural context addresses three factors: the genre, the setting, and the audience.

With both interpersonal and presentational tasks, the genre must be made clear to learners. The genre communicates to learners the manner of speaking, signing, or writing through which they will complete the task. Genres offer a flexible pattern for learner interaction that is reflective of how people authentically communicate with each other (Johnson-Sheehan & Paine, 2016). That is, they do not dictate a rigid structure that learners must adhere to within a task. Rather, learners can make choices around the appropriate norms, behaviors, and conventions needed for the sociocultural context of the genre. The social purpose of the performance task, the cultural context within which the performance task takes place, and the participants involved will influence the pattern of interaction and the choices that learners make. There are many genres and ways of categorizing them. Specific to interpersonal communication, example genres could include an argument, conversation, debate, discussion, interview, meeting, online chat or discussion board, or role-playing. The type of genre taking place, its social purpose, and the culture it's operating within will determine the structure of communication. For example, a conversation versus a debate offers learners opportunities to make choices in their language and behaviors to best operate within the norms of each of these genres. Specific to presentational communication, example genres could include a blog, infographic, instructions, informational report, narrative, persuasive argument, social media post, speech, story, and video. With each genre, learners must consider what information should be included, how to organize it, and what language, behaviors, and norms would be appropriate. For example, an informational report versus a narrative offers two different structures that learners can work creatively within to make choices about the norms and conventions they should use. Overall, the genre of a task provides an opportunity for learners to make choices and select the language and behaviors that best reflect the sociocultural context.

The setting, or the place or surroundings within which the task is performed, helps create the sociocultural context. A learner's intercultural communication is dependent on *where* a task takes place. For example, a performance task could center around the experience of dining in a restaurant. The country, city, or region in which the restaurant is located influences learners' performances. Learners will need to consider how the setting influences the way they order food, what tools they use to eat, and what behaviors would indicate satisfaction. In this way, the learner must adapt their performance to account for the setting in which the performance task takes place. Therefore, the setting is an important factor of the sociocultural context within which the learner performs.

The audience, or participants involved in the task, is another factor to consider when creating the sociocultural context of a performance task. *Who* a learner is as well as with whom they interact influences a learner's performance. For example, a performance task could ask learners to advocate for change around an environmental issue they have learned about. If the audience for this performance task is another learner, the appropriate language and behaviors would be informal. However, if the audience is an influential leader who can enact change, learners would need to use formal language and behaviors to appropriately complete the performance task. Consideration of the audience, with whom the learner is communicating, influences the language and behaviors needed to complete a performance task.

A performance task that includes the genre, setting, and audience provides the needed sociocultural context so learners can determine what language and behaviors are appropriate to successfully complete the task. In this way, the sociocultural context of a performance task adds depth to the content being discussed. Clarifying the sociocultural context of a performance task allows learners to "understand that they have choices when using language and that those language choices are context-dependent and collaboratively constructed" (Glisan & Donato, 2021, p. 18) with the participants involved. Performance tasks that link content with its sociocultural context are launching points for learners to use language in truly meaningful ways. Thus, it is essential to consider the sociocultural context of each task that learners will undertake so they can effectively communicate with others.

Table 3.4
Context of Sample Performance Tasks

PERFORMANCE LEVEL	NOVICE	INTERMEDIATE	ADVANCED
Interpersonal performance task	Discuss and compare what you and your friend prefer to eat for lunch at school.	You and your friend discuss and decide where to eat lunch together.	After watching a news report about locally grown food, discuss with a friend if you think it is a sustainable option.
Context	Familiar, informal, predictable Genre: Conversation Setting: School in the United States Audience: Another learner	Familiar, informal Genre: Conversation Setting: City in the United States Audience: Another learner	Familiar, academic, social Genre: Conversation Setting: City in the United States Audience: Another learner

PERFORMANCE LEVEL	NOVICE	INTERMEDIATE	ADVANCED
Presentational performance task	Write a note to your new instructor telling them about an activity you like to do.	Email a friend to describe what you do on the weekend.	Create a podcast episode for your listeners that brings awareness to how nutrition impacts the human body.
Context	Familiar, formal, predictable Genre: Note Setting: School in the United States Audience: Instructor	Familiar, informal Genre: Email Setting: City in the United States Audience: Another learner	Familiar, academic, social Genre: Podcast Setting: City in the United States Audience: Adults and youth

YOUR TURN

LEARNING TARGET CHECK:	
I can	☐ describe context and how it elicits a learner language sample with characteristics of the Novice, Intermediate, or Advanced level.

Pause and reflect:
How would you describe context to your learners? Consider any explanations, examples, and/or visuals you might use to describe context:

Context in a performance task:
Consider the context of the following performance tasks. Which performance task would best elicit a learner language sample with characteristics at the Novice, Intermediate, and Advanced performance level? Write your answers in the chart and provide evidence of your reasoning. Then write what the sociocultural context of each performance task might be. If needed, refer to Tables 3.2 and 3.4 for guidance.

Task 1
After reading and viewing texts to learn about ways we can implement change, select an organization that works to better their community. Discuss your organization with a partner to learn more about the organizations you have each selected, why you selected yours, and how your organizations implement change for others.

Task 2
You and a friend discuss your reactions to learning about the monarch butterfly migrations and their sanctuaries in Mexico.

Task 3
Chat with your new classmate to find out how you both may be similar to and/or different from each other.

PERFORMANCE LEVEL	TASK #	EVIDENCE OF REASONING	SOCIOCULTURAL CONTEXT
NOVICE Context: familiar, informal, formal, predictable			Genre: Setting: Audience:
INTERMEDIATE Context: familiar, informal, formal, straight-forward			Genre: Setting: Audience:
ADVANCED Context: familiar, unfamiliar, informal, formal, complex			Genre: Setting: Audience:

Note: Answers can be found in Table 3.5.

Language Functions

Language functions describe what people can do with language. Within a performance task, the language functions indicate what a learner must be able to do in order to successfully complete the performance task within a given situation. Language functions focus on the goal of the communication—the communicative purpose—rather than on the use of specific vocabulary and/or grammatical structures. Identifying the communicative purpose of a performance task provides learners a reason to interact with others and/or communicate a message to an audience. Clementi and Terrill (2017) note that the numerous language functions fall into six overarching categories:

- Describing people, places, things, how (and how well) something is done
- Asking and responding to questions
- Expressing feelings and emotions
- Expressing advice, opinions, preferences
- Telling and retelling stories, and sequencing
- Expressing hopes, dreams, and future plans

All learners, regardless of the level they are performing within, are capable of completing performance tasks designed around these six categories of language functions. However, "within each category is a progression from simple to more complex" (Clementi & Terrill, 2017, p. 46). The performance level a learner is operating within may determine the progression of language choices a learner makes to express each function. For example, all learners can ask and respond to questions. However, learners performing within the Novice range communicate using highly practiced questions that follow a pattern (*Do you like…? Are you…?*). Learners performing within the Intermediate level can ask open-ended questions that demonstrate they are able to listen to their partner and can follow-up on mentioned ideas (*What do you think of …? Really? Why do you like it?*). Whereas learners performing within the Advanced level can ask probing questions, maintaining and advancing conversations by equally sharing the communicative load with their interlocutor (*What is your opinion about . . . ? I agree. I also wonder. . . Do you think it will influence . . . ? Could you give me some examples?*). Overall, all learners can perform all language functions; however, the performance level within which a learner is performing will determine what language a learner can use to complete the language function.

It is important to note that functions enable the use of specific language vocabulary and structures, but do not necessarily predetermine them. This allows for learner choices in how they show evidence of their learning. For example, a unit may indicate that learners must *ask and respond to questions about what all learners need to go to school*. This indicates the global function (*ask and respond to questions*) that can be repeated within multiple units as well as the descriptor (*about what all learners need to go to school*), which is specific to a unit theme and essential question. This particular function can indicate vocabulary and structures that may effectively lead to communicative success (*What do you need for math class? I need. . .*), but does not necessarily predispose learners to use only those vocabulary and structures. For example, a learner might ask *Is a pen important?* and respond with *Yes, or a pencil* to successfully achieve the same function. Thus, once the performance task functions are determined, educators will need to clarify possible vocabulary and grammatical structures, as appropriate for the performance level, that enable learners to successfully achieve the communicative goals. This places the vocabulary and grammar structures of the language functions within a communicative purpose.

YOUR TURN

LEARNING TARGET CHECK:	
I can	☐ describe language functions and how they show up in performance tasks at various levels.

Pause and reflect:
How would you describe language functions to your learners? Consider any explanations, examples, and/or visuals you might use to describe language functions:

Language functions in a performance task:
The following exercise includes a sample performance task for each of the performance levels. Write possible language functions for each performance task. Use the provided Intermediate sample to guide you.

PERFORMANCE LEVEL	PERFORMANCE TASK	LANGUAGE FUNCTIONS
NOVICE	Chat with your new classmate to find out how you both may be similar to and/or different from each other.	
INTERMEDIATE	After reading and viewing texts to learn about ways we can implement change, select an organization that works to better their community. Discuss your organization with a partner to learn more about the organizations you have each selected, why you selected yours, and how your organizations implement change for others.	I can ask and answer questions about an organization that works to better a community. I can describe my organization and give reasons why I selected it. I can explain how an organization implements change for others.
ADVANCED	After visiting a Monarch butterfly sanctuary, you and a friend discuss your reactions to learning about the monarch butterfly migrations and how it's being threatened.	

Note: Answers can be found in Table 3.5.

Performance Tasks for Learner Language Samples

In this book, performance tasks at each level (Novice, Intermediate, Advanced) are used to elicit learner language samples. These are summative assessments in the interpersonal and presentational modes of communication. That is, learners complete these performance tasks after multiple opportunities of formative practice within a unit of instruction. Each performance task addresses the content, context, and language functions, as outlined in Table 3.5 and Table 3.6. The performance tasks operate within different sociocultural contexts, which influence the language and behaviors that learners need to successfully complete the performance task.

Table 3.5
Sample Performance Task Outlines: ***Interpersonal***

INTERPERSONAL PERFORMANCE TASK	CONTENT	CONTEXT	LANGUAGE FUNCTIONS
PERFORMANCE LEVEL: NOVICE			
Chat with your new classmate to find out how you both may be similar to and/or different from each other.	Familiar, everyday	Familiar, informal, predictable Genre: Conversation Setting: School in the United States Audience: Two learners	I can ask and answer questions about likes and dislikes.
PERFORMANCE LEVEL: INTERMEDIATE			
After reading and viewing texts to learn about ways we can implement change, select an organization that works to better their community. Discuss your organization with a partner to learn more about the organizations you have each selected, why you selected yours, and how your organizations implement change for others.	Familiar, researched	Familiar, informal, straight-forward Genre: Conversation Setting: A community in the United States Audience: Two learners	I can ask and answer questions about an organization that works to better a community. I can describe my organization and give reasons why I selected it. I can explain how an organization implements change for others.
PERFORMANCE LEVEL: ADVANCED			
After visiting a Monarch butterfly sanctuary, you and a friend discuss your reactions to learning about the monarch butterfly migrations and how it's being threatened.	Familiar, academic, social, concrete	Familiar, informal, complex Genre: Conversation Setting: Anywhere in the United States Audience: Two learners	I can express my reaction about the monarch butterfly migration. I can describe environmental and cultural aspects of the butterfly migration and their sanctuaries. I can describe environmental impacts on the migration and sanctuaries of the butterflies. I can ask and respond to questions about butterfly migration and their sanctuaries. I can agree or disagree with the opinions of my partner(s).

Table 3.6
Sample Performance Task Outlines: ***Presentational***

PRESENTATIONAL PERFORMANCE TASK	CONTENT	CONTEXT	LANGUAGE FUNCTIONS
PERFORMANCE LEVEL: NOVICE			
For the hallway display, select one of the people we have studied in this unit. Create a descriptive writing in which you compare how you are similar in order to highlight what you have in common, and contrast how you are different in order to feature how you each make use of your attributes in our diverse world.	Familiar, everyday	Familiar, formal, predictable Genre: Compare/contrast Setting: School in the United States Audience: Learners and adults at school	I can describe what activities I like and don't like to do. I can describe activities that other people like and don't like to do. I can describe the personality of myself and others. I can describe how I am similar or different to another person.
PERFORMANCE LEVEL: INTERMEDIATE			
As part of an Earth Day campaign in your community, write a formal letter to an influential leader advocating for change that would address an environmental issue that you have learned about.	Familiar, researched	Familiar, formal, straight-forward Genre: Persuasive Argument Setting: United States Audience: A learner and a leader	I can describe an environmental issue. I can describe examples of my concerns. I can describe what groups are impacted by an environmental issue and how. I can express possibilities that diminish the threat of the environmental issue.
PERFORMANCE LEVEL: ADVANCED			
Based on the movie, write a diary entry from the perspective of one of the baseball players that includes their reflections of the recruitment practices of professional baseball leagues.	Familiar, social, professional, concrete	Familiar, informal, complex Genre: Diary entry Setting: Dominican Republic Audience: Self	I can describe the social and emotional impact of recruitment practices in a professional baseball league. I can retell a recruitment experience with a professional baseball league. I can express my opinion about the recruitment practices of a professional baseball league. I can express the needs, hopes and dreams of a baseball player.

Conclusion

Performance tasks are real-world situations that provide learners choices in how to demonstrate what they can do with the language. Performance tasks designed with the target performance level in mind elicit the desired language learner sample. An effective performance task describes the content, context, and language functions so learners have a reason to interact with others and/or communicate a message to an audience. Additionally, performance tasks that clearly indicate the sociocultural context within which a learner performs provides learners an opportunity to choose language and behaviors that are most appropriate to successfully complete the performance task.

This chapter focused on how to design effective performance tasks. The subsequent chapters will focus on:

- **Feedback:** What makes feedback effective? What might a feedback model look like for educators and language learners?
- **Performance Domains:** Once the performance tasks are designed, what are the criteria to evaluate learner work? How can educators use the Performance Domain Indicators to create effective feedback loops for learner language growth?
- **Grading and Reporting:** Once learners' work has been evaluated using the Performance Domain Indicators, how do educators report what learners can do in the form of grades?

A deep understanding of performance domains and indicators will enhance an educator's ability to design interpersonal and presentational performance tasks for learners.

YOUR TURN

LEARNING TARGET CHECK:	
I can	☐ write interpersonal and performance tasks that elicit a learner language sample with characteristics of the Novice, Intermediate, or Advanced level.

Creating interpersonal and presentational tasks:
Consider a current or developing unit of instruction. How would you design the performance tasks for the unit? Use the reflective questions as a guide to develop each performance task.

INTERPERSONAL Performance Task

INTERPERSONAL TASK *How will this task be spontaneous and encourage negotiation of meaning among learners?*	**CONTENT** *What ideas will learners say, sign, or write about in the task?* (Circle what best fits your task)	**CONTEXT** *What is the social and cultural situation within which the learner will function?* (Circle what best fits your task. Then write the genre, setting, and audience.)	**LANGUAGE FUNCTIONS** *What must a learner be able to do in order to successfully complete the performance task?*
PERFORMANCE LEVEL: NOVICE			
	Very familiar, familiar, everyday	Familiar, informal, formal, predictable Genre: Setting: Audience:	
PERFORMANCE LEVEL: INTERMEDIATE			
	Familiar, concrete, at times researched	Familiar, informal, formal, straight-forward Genre: Setting: Audience:	
PERFORMANCE LEVEL: ADVANCED			
	Familiar, academic, social, professional, concrete, abstract	Familiar, unfamiliar, informal, formal, complex Genre: Setting: Audience:	

PRESENTATIONAL Performance Task

PRESENTATIONAL TASK *How will learners present information: polished or on-demand?*	**CONTENT** *What ideas will learners say, sign, or write about in the task?* (Circle what best fits your task)	**CONTEXT** *What is the social and cultural situation within which the learner will function?* (Circle what best fits your task. Then write the genre, setting, and audience.)	**LANGUAGE FUNCTIONS** *What must a learner be able to do in order to successfully complete the performance task?*
PERFORMANCE LEVEL: NOVICE			
	Very familiar, familiar, everyday	Familiar, informal, formal predictable Genre: Setting: Audience:	
PERFORMANCE LEVEL: INTERMEDIATE			
	Familiar, concrete, at times researched	Familiar, informal, formal, straight-forward Genre: Setting: Audience:	
PERFORMANCE LEVEL: ADVANCED			
	Familiar, academic, social, professional, concrete, abstract	Familiar, unfamiliar, informal, formal, complex Genre: Setting: Audience:	

References

ACTFL. (2012a). *ACTFL performance descriptors for language learners*. https://www.actfl.org/educator-resources/actfl-performance-descriptors

ACTFL. (2012b). *ACTFL proficiency guidelines – Speaking, writing, listening, and reading* (3rd ed.). https://www.actfl.org/educator-resources/actfl-proficiency-guidelines

Clementi, D., & Terrill, L. (2017). *The keys to planning for learning* (2nd ed.). ACTFL.

Earl, L., & Katz, S. (2006). *Rethinking classroom assessment with purpose in mind: Assessment for learning, assessment as learning, assessment of learning*. Manitoba Education, Citizenship and Youth. https://www.edu.gov.mb.ca/k12/assess/wncp/full_doc.pdf

Glisan, E. W., & Donato, R. (2021). *Enacting the work of language instruction: High leverage teaching practices* (Vol. 2). ACTFL.

Glynn, C., & Spenader, A. (2020). Critical content based instruction for the transformation of world language classrooms. *L2 Journal*, *12*(2). https://doi.org/10.5070/l212246307

Johnson-Sheehan, & R. & Paine, C. (2016). *Writing today* (3rd ed.). Pearson.

National Council of State Supervisors for Languages (NCSSFL) – ACTFL. (2017). *NCSSFL-ACTFL Can-Do Statements: Performance Indicators for Language Learners*. ACTFL. https://www.actfl.org/educator-resources/ncssfl-actfl-can-do-statements

Wiggins, G., & McTighe, J. (2005). *Understanding by design*. ASCD.

CHAPTER 4 | FEEDBACK

LEARNING TARGETS:	
I can	☐ describe feedback: what it is and why it is important for language learners. ☐ identify elements of effective feedback. ☐ identify pitfalls to avoid when providing feedback to language learners. ☐ reflect on my own feedback practices and identify areas for growth.

What do we mean by feedback?

Feedback is information about a performance that is used for improvement towards achieving a goal (Fisher et al., 2021; Wiggins, 2012). The focus of this book is on the feedback provided to language learners about their performance after completion of a formative or summative task, as this performance demonstrates what the learner can do. This feedback provides information to learners about how they used language and behaviors to complete a performance task and can also provide information for how to improve towards achieving the target performance level for a course. Feedback may be provided by the teacher, but it is meant to be learner-driven. That is, the learner plays an active role in evaluating their own performances and makes choices in order to better achieve their goals.

Why is feedback important?

Feedback is considered critical for advancing learners' language proficiency (ACTFL, n.d.). Therefore, how educators respond to learners' performances is a significant opportunity for language growth. Brookhart (2008) notes that effective feedback does the following:

> gives students information they need so they can understand where they are in their learning and what to do next – the cognitive factor. Once they feel they understand what to do and why, most students develop a feeling that they have control over their own learning – the motivational factor. (p. 2)

That is, when feedback highlights what learners can do and indicates what to do next, it builds the learner's capacity and develops their efficacy.

What makes feedback effective?

Feedback is most effective when 1) it provides information about where the learner is at, 2) it provides information about where the learner is going, and 3) promotes learner thinking on how to take next steps (Brookhart, 2008; Fisher et al., 2021; Hammond, 2015; Wiggins, 2012). Information in all three of these areas is needed for feedback to be goal-referenced, actionable, tangible and transparent, and user-friendly (Wiggins, 2012). This type of feedback effectively encourages a *can-do* attitude, empowering learners to take action in the learning process to achieve their goals.

What does effective feedback look like after a learner's performance?

Table 4.1 shows a learner performance, a scoring rubric using the Performance Domain Indicators for the Text Type performance domain, and a variety of feedback. Both Wiggins (2012) and Hammond (2015) note that effective feedback is not advice, praise, judgment, or evaluation. Advice (*I think you should include more transitional words*) can indicate next steps for a learner, but it does not provide information about the current level of performance or the goals of the performance task. Praise (*Good job!*), judgment (*I don't think you included enough personality traits*), and evaluation (*Meets Expectations/B+*) all provide some information on the performance level of a learner, but none of these examples indicate to learners where to go next, nor do they promote learner thinking about how to get there. With all these examples, the power of the feedback resides with the educator; that is, the educator has done all the thinking to determine the current level of the learner's performance and any next steps for growth. When the educator owns the feedback, there are no opportunities for learners to think about their own level of performance, determine if they met the goals of the performance task, and consider next steps for growth.

In contrast, effective feedback states where the learner is (*You used simple sentences most of the time*), where the learner is going (*moving from the "Meeting" level of performance to the "Exceeding" level of performance in Text Type*), and promotes thinking on how to get there (*How might you write multiple sentences about one activity to create a series of sentences?, What coordinators (and, but, or, for, so) could you add to better connect your ideas?*). It is only when feedback is provided in all three of these key areas that learners are empowered; that is, they are equipped to take action (Fisher et al., 2021), applying their learning to adjust subsequent performances for improvement.

Table 4.1
Sample Learner Performance, Evaluation, and Feedback Possibilities

Target performance level: **Novice**
Context: familiar, informal, predictable
Content: familiar, everyday

Task	Write a digital post introducing yourself to the class.
Sample learner response	Hi, my name is Emerson. I is United States. I is 11. My birthday is February 6. I like to play sports. A lot summer. I don't like to sing. Sometimes dance. I is not funny. I like to draw. I like to run. I don't like to write stories. I like to read.

Evaluation: This sample learner response matches the description for the *Meeting* level of Text Type for learners performing within the Novice level.

TEXT TYPE				
	EXCEEDING	**MEETING**	**DEVELOPING**	**BEGINNING**
Performance Domain Indicators	I can form simple sentences, and at times series of sentences.	I can use simple sentences most of the time.	I can use practiced and memorized words and phrases, and at times use simple sentences.	I can use practiced and memorized words and phrases.

Which of these feedback possibilities will be most effective for learners?

- Good job!
- I think you should include more transitional words.
- You used simple sentences most of the time.
- What coordinators (and, but, or, for, so) could you add to better connect your ideas?
- Grade: B+
- I don't think you included enough personality traits!
- How might you write multiple sentences about one activity to create a series of sentences?
- You said *I is* multiple times. Correct each error by saying *I am*.

Note: Answers found in the following *Feedback Based on Performance Domain Indicators* section and in Table 4.2.

Feedback Based on Performance Domain Indicators

The Performance Domain Indicators (PDIs) in this book play a crucial role in how world language educators assess learner performance and provide effective feedback. Each performance domain focuses on different aspects of how a learner can perform within a given performance task. For example, Table 4.1 displays the PDIs for Text Type for learners performing within the Novice level. They display a continuum of language performance based on established criteria. Brookhart (2008) argues that comparing learner work to an established set of criteria is the primary kind of comparison to use for effective feedback, as it is this kind of feedback that "...helps the student decide what the next goal should be" (pp. 22-23). These PDIs allow language educators and learners to determine the current level of performance so that they can then identify next steps to further develop their language skills, revealing a pathway for language growth.

When providing feedback for language growth, the *how*, *when*, and *what* we say impacts our learners. Wiggins (2012) notes key elements to consider for effective feedback: Is it goal-referenced? Is it actionable, tangible, and transparent? Is it user-friendly? Is it timely, ongoing, and consistent? Let's consider how these elements of effective feedback apply to the PDIs, using the feedback examples from Table 4.1.

Is it goal-referenced?

The PDIs establish communicative goals for learners to work towards with each performance task. Feedback that incorporates the PDIs is goal-referenced because it directly references the communicative goals for the learner and describes the pathway to language growth. For example, the feedback *You used simple sentences most of the time* describes what the learner can do by directly referencing the *Meeting* level of the Text Type performance domain: *I can use simple sentences most of the time.* This feedback indicates where the learner is performing within the Text Type performance domain. The feedback *How might you write multiple sentences about one activity to create a series of sentences?* Is also goal-referenced, as it references the Exceeding level of the Text Type performance domain. It indicates a new goal for the learner, or where the learner is going next. The learner can now consider what adjustments or new learning might need to take place to reach this next goal.

Using the same PDIs to evaluate each performance task throughout multiple units of content shifts the focus to long-term communicative goals that can be achieved throughout a given level or even across multiple courses. When the same set of PDIs are referenced to learners throughout multiple units of varying content within a course, learners can see the overarching goals for a course. Learners then have multiple opportunities over time to self-assess, adjust, and demonstrate growth. For example, if the same PDIs serve as the long-term course goals through multiple units of content, then the learner who received the feedback *How might you write multiple sentences about one activity to create a series of sentences?* Will be able to make adjustments that can be applied to subsequent performance tasks within a course. With each performance task, regardless of the content, the learner can track their language growth within the Text Type performance domain.

Is it actionable, tangible, and transparent?

Empowering learners to take action upon receiving feedback requires careful consideration of the language used to provide feedback. Providing feedback on what a learner *can do* in reference to the PDIs articulates observable and tangible elements of learner success in their performance. The feedback *You used simple sentences most of the time* is transparent, directly referencing a concrete skill the learner can demonstrate when communicating their message. When considering how to spur learners to take action, Brookhart (2008) indicates that learners need sufficient guidance, but not so much that learners passively receive feedback and do not think for themselves. For example, if the learner received the feedback *I think you should include more transitional words*, the educator has done much of the thinking on behalf of the learner. However, when feedback is recast as an open-ended question—*What coordinators (and, but, or, for, so) could you add to better connect your ideas?* (see Table 4.2)—the learner is now invited to consider the possibilities of how they might approach a performance task differently and make choices in how they communicate their message. Providing feedback in the form of open-ended questions is actionable: it indicates where the learner is going while simultaneously promoting learner thinking on how to get there. When feedback is provided in the form of questions, the power shifts to the learner; the responsibility of reflecting and assessing belongs to the learner, and the learner gets to decide what the next steps will be.

Is it user-friendly?

According to Wiggins (2012), feedback is not effective if the learner cannot understand it or is overwhelmed by it. User-friendly feedback is jargon free: it avoids highly technical, abstract language, acronyms, or abbreviations. Instead, effective feedback uses learner-friendly language, or language that is descriptive, specific, and developmentally appropriate for learners (Moss & Brookhart, 2012). In addition, educators need to consider how much feedback to give. Educators can help guide learners by focusing feedback on one or two performance domains. For example, the feedback examples provided in Table 4.1 all focus on the Text Type performance domain. A balance of what went well and what could be improved is important. First, provide feedback that indicates a learner's current level of performance in reference to the PDIs. This aspect of feedback focuses on what the learner does well when communicating their message. For example, *You used simple sentences most of the time* directly references what the learner is able to do successfully within the Text Type performance domain. Second, provide feedback that indicates an area of improvement for the learner. This feedback should also indicate where the learner is going, or the next performance level in reference to the PDIs. The feedback *How might you write multiple sentences about one activity to create a series of sentences?* indicates a clear pathway of action for learner growth within the Text Type performance domain.

Is it timely, ongoing, and consistent?

Effective feedback needs to occur while learners are still working on the learning goal. Both Brookhart (2008) and Hammond (2015) indicate that feedback is timely when it is given on something that learners are still striving for, not something that learners have already done. Without prompt feedback, learners can become disconnected from the performance task and lose motivation to improve. Understandably one educator cannot promptly provide feedback on all tasks for all learners all the time. Therefore, educators must provide learners opportunities to self-assess and evaluate their own performances while they are still striving towards their goals. Fisher et al. (2021) note that "the ability to think about their own thinking promotes learners' self-awareness, and it enables them to problem-solve around the learning experience or task..." (p. 108). The PDIs can be used to guide learners to think about their own work and problem-solve through performance tasks as they strive towards their goals. Examples of learner self-assessments based on the PDIs can be found in Figure 4.2, Table 4.5, and Figure 4.3. Learners who self-assess using the PDIs are empowered to own their learning, play an active role in the feedback process, and adjust their performance to achieve their goals. When this happens during the learning process, it allows for timely, ongoing, and consistent feedback opportunities.

Table 4.2
Recasting Feedback

ORIGINAL FEEDBACK		RECAST TO MORE EFFECTIVE FEEDBACK
Praise Great job!	>>>	**Recast to goal-referenced feedback:** You met expectations by writing complete sentences most of the time.
Evaluative Grade: B+	>>>	**Recast to actionable feedback:** How might you write multiple sentences about one activity to create a series of sentences and exceed expectations?
Advice I think you should include more transitional words.	>>>	**Recast to user-friendly feedback:** What coordinators (and, but, or, for, so) could you add to better connect your ideas?

Note: The feedback possibilities from Table 4.1 at the beginning of this chapter have been recast to be more effective using some of the key elements from Wiggins (2012).

YOUR TURN

LEARNING TARGETS CHECK:	
I can	☐ describe feedback: what it is and why it is important for language learners. ☐ identify elements of effective feedback.

Pause and reflect:
How would you describe effective feedback to your learners? Consider any explanations, examples, and/or visuals you might use to describe effective feedback:

Evaluating feedback for effectiveness:
First, review the performance task, learner sample, and evaluation of Text Type using a range of the Performance Domain Indicators.

Target performance level: **Novice High** Context: familiar, informal, predictable Content: familiar, everyday	
Task	Write a digital post introducing yourself to the class
Sample learner response	Hi, my name is Payton. I from United States. 12 years. My birthday August 16. I like sing, draw, read, listen to music, and watch TV. Dance sometimes. No sports, ski, swim, and run. Not sport-minded, social, and impatient. I is reserved, artistic, and patient.

Evaluation: This sample learner response matches the description for the *Developing* level of Text Type for learners performing within the Novice level.

TEXT TYPE				
	EXCEEDING	**MEETING**	**DEVELOPING**	**BEGINNING**
Performance Domain Indicators	I can form simple sentences, and at times series of sentences.	I can use simple sentences most of the time.	I can use practiced and memorized words and phrases, and at times use simple sentences.	I can use practiced and memorized words and phrases.

Next, read the feedback possibilities in the chart below. For each example, answer each question by circling *Yes* or *No*. Then, write if the feedback is effective and include evidence of your reasoning.

Feedback example	Is it goal-referenced?	Is it actionable, tangible, and transparent?	Is it user-friendly?	Is the feedback effective? Include evidence of your reasoning
You wrote a lot!	Yes / No	Yes / No	Yes / No	
You should include more complete sentences.	Yes / No	Yes / No	Yes / No	
You used memorized words and phrases most of the time to express your thoughts.	Yes / No	Yes / No	Yes / No	
How might you combine some of your phrases to build complete sentences?	Yes / No	Yes / No	Yes / No	
You are still at the developing stage. You didn't use many complete sentences.	Yes / No	Yes / No	Yes / No	
You show evidence of using some simple sentences at times in your message.	Yes / No	Yes / No	Yes / No	

Note: Answers can be found at the end of this chapter on p. 63.

The Performance Domain Indicators (PDIs) Assessment and Feedback Guide

To harness each element of effective feedback, each performance domain chapter includes a PDI guide for assessment and feedback: *The Performance Domain Indicators (PDIs) Assessment and Feedback Guide.* This tool can help educators evaluate learner work and provide effective feedback to language learners. A sample of this guide can be viewed in Figure 4.1. The feedback in these assessment and feedback guides is not specific to any content or unit, but rather supports overarching communicative performance goals learners can work towards within multiple units of varying content in a given course or level. The feedback also focuses on what a learner *can do*, which promotes learner confidence and self-efficacy (Erkens et al., 2017). This positions educators as language coaches, providing feedback to help learners understand where they are, where they are going, and what adjustments they can make in future performances to show language growth.

Figure 4.1

A Sample From the Performance Domain Indicators (PDIs) Assessment and Feedback Guide for the Text Type Performance Domain

The PDI for the target performance level

What the learner can do in reference to the goal

TEXT TYPE Target performance level: **Novice High** Context: familiar, informal, formal, predictable Content: familiar, everyday			
Guiding questions	**Performance Domain Indicator**	**GLOW**	**GROW**
Novice Low Beginning Can the learner: • use words and/ or phrases to communicate their message?	I can use practiced and memorized words and phrases.	• You use words/phrases to communicate your message.	• Which words/phrases might you combine to make a more complete thought?What vocabulary could you add to express a more complete idea? • How might you use (*example sentence starter*) to create complete sentences?
Novice Mid Developing Can the learner: • use words and phrases to communicate their message? • at times use simple sentences?	I can use practiced and memorized words and phrases, and at times use simple sentences.	• You use words/phrases to communicate your message. • You are beginning to use simple sentences to communicate your message.	• How might you combine some of your phrases to build complete sentences? • What vocabulary/structures might you add to create complete sentences? • How might you use (*example sentence starter*) to create complete sentences?

What the learner can do without assistance

Novice High Meeting Can the learner: • use simple sentences most of the time throughout the performance?	I can use simple sentences most of the time.	• You use simple sentences most of the time throughout your performance.	• How might you group sentences on a related topic into a logical sequence to create a series of sentences? • How might you say/write multiple sentences on a related topic to create a series of sentences? • What coordinators (*and, but, or, for, so*) could you add to better connect your ideas?
Intermediate Low Exceeding Can the learner: • use simple sentences throughout the performance? • at times form multiple sentences on a related topic to create series of sentences?	I can form simple sentences, and at times series of sentences.	• You use simple sentences throughout your performance. • At times you say/write multiple sentences on a related topic to create series of sentences.	• How might you group sentences on a related topic into a logical sequence to create series of sentences throughout your performance? • What coordinators (*and, but, or, for, so*) could you add to better connect your ideas? • How might you add complexity? Consider using subordinating conjunctions (*once, while, when, where, before, after...*).

Questions to help the learner consider changes they can make for language growth

Below are the elements of the *Performance Domain Indicators (PDIs) Assessment and Feedback Guide* and how they work together to provide effective feedback to language learners:

Guiding Questions

To clarify each PDI, the assessment and feedback guide includes guiding questions to evaluate learner work for each sublevel (Novice Low, Novice Mid, Novice High, etc.). These are what Thorpe and Gallimore (1988) refer to as "assessing questions." These determine the level of a learner's performance: that is, what learners can do without assistance. They are specific, concrete questions based on the PDIs that focus on observable learner performance in each performance domain. These assessing questions are intended to be used by both educators and learners to guide assessment of and feedback on learner performance in each performance domain.

Performance Domain Indicators

The Performance Domain Indicators, which are also included in the assessment and feedback guides, allow both educators and learners to collectively identify and articulate the target performance levels in each unit of study. Consistent, ongoing use of these PDIs throughout multiple units of various content familiarizes learners with the language and level of performance associated with each PDI, thus creating a tangible and transparent pathway to language growth.

GLOW and GROW

Embedded in the *Performance Domain Indicators (PDIs) Assessment and Feedback Guide* are GLOW comments and GROW questions. The GLOW comments are what Tunstall and Gipps (1996) consider "achievement feedback" because it describes what learners can do well in reference to a standard or goal. Feedback provided through these descriptive, nonjudgmental comments demonstrates to learners how the PDIs align with their performance. The assessment and feedback guides also include GROW questions. These are "assistive questions" that help learners consider changes they might enact that will lead to improvement (Tunstall & Gipps, 1996). Each question promotes reflection through user-friendly feedback, which encourages learners to think about their next steps for language growth. Using achievement feedback and assistive questions, learners are invited to identify where they are, where they are going, and problem-solve how to get there (see Table 4.3). In this way, learners can see themselves as an active participant, capable of growth and change.

The Assessment and Feedback Guide

It is important to note that the *Performance Domain Indicators (PDIs) Assessment and Feedback Guide* in this book is designed to nurture learner growth at every level, not just for those learners who are not yet meeting expectations. All educators and learners can use these guides to provide ongoing feedback to unpack the PDIs and gain a deep understanding of the skills needed for language growth, regardless of the current level of achievement. For this reason, the guiding questions, GLOW achievement comments, and GROW assistive questions are aligned to each PDI. This creates a tangible, transparent, ongoing continuum of learner language growth.

Table 4.3
Evaluation and Feedback

Using the evaluation of the sample learner response from Table 4.1, below is a model of how to use a GLOW comment and GROW question from the *Performance Domain Indicators (PDIs) Assessment and Feedback Guide* to provide effective learner feedback.

Evaluation:

TEXT TYPE Target performance level: **Novice High** Context: familiar, informal, predictable Content: familiar, everyday				
	EXCEEDING	**MEETING**	**DEVELOPING**	**BEGINNING**
Performance Domain Indicators	I can form simple sentences, and at times series of sentences.	I can use simple sentences most of the time.	I can use practiced and memorized words and phrases, and at times use simple sentences.	I can use practiced and memorized words and phrases.

Feedback:

- GLOW: You use simple sentences most of the time.
- GROW: How might you write multiple sentences about one activity to create a series of sentences?

Feedback Pitfalls

Here are some common feedback pitfalls and how the *Performance Domain Indicators (PDIs) Assessment and Feedback Guide* can help educators recast these pitfalls to focus on more effective feedback practices (see Table 4.6).

Prioritizing Accuracy

Effective feedback focuses on what learners can do to promote learner language growth; that is, it focuses on the meaning of the message the learner is trying to communicate. In contrast, an overemphasis of feedback on form and accuracy can lead to learner demotivation (Reichelt, 2019). Feedback solely focused on accuracy does not value learners' efforts to express meaning. Research has shown mixed results when feedback focuses on error correction. When it comes to feedback on grammatical accuracy, the type of feedback provided (direct versus indirect error correction), who provides it (teacher or peers), and how it is provided (written, oral, or digital methods) all have varying degrees of impact (see Truscott (2007), Biber et al. (2011), Sippel & Jackson (2015), Glisan & Donato (2017), and Sánchez-Naranjo (2019)). Ultimately, no matter how it's done, feedback that focuses on grammatical accuracy is based on a deficit model, focusing on what learners cannot do. This does not motivate learners to act towards achieving their goal to communicate meaningful messages.

To avoid this feedback pitfall, this book focuses on using the PDIs as goal-referenced feedback that recognizes and builds upon learner assets. That is, feedback is focused on what learners *can do*, even if some inaccuracies occur, and what the next steps might be on the learner's pathway to language growth. Educators are encouraged to consider the comprehensibility of the learner's message, or how well their message is understood by their partner or audience. If the message is comprehensible, focus feedback on one or two performance domains that highlight what the learner can do (GLOW comment) and an area for growth (GROW question). When inaccuracies do interfere with the message the learner is trying to communicate, feedback can still focus on the goal-referenced PDIs that best support a learner to convey a comprehensible and appropriate message. Feedback should focus on the type of error that, if improved upon, would enhance communication. For additional guidance, review the types of communication breakdowns in Table 4.4 and the recommended performance domain the feedback should focus on to address each type of communicative breakdown.

Table 4.4
Types of Communication Breakdowns and How to Focus Feedback

A COMMUNICATION BREAKDOWN OCCURRED BECAUSE OF...	PROVIDE FEEDBACK IN THE PERFORMANCE DOMAIN OF...
How the learner was using language (vocabulary, structures, and/or time frames) to complete the performance task.	Language Use
The type of text the learner used (example: disconnected words, incomplete sentences) and/or how it was organized.	Text Type
The learner used language and/or behaviors that were inappropriate for the social or cultural context of the performance task.	Intercultural Communication
The way the learner presented their ideas did not maintain the attention of their audience (example: unorganized, not enough details).	Impact
The learner's inability to maintain or advance communication to overcome the breakdown.	Communication Strategies

Too Much Feedback

Too much feedback is overwhelming and will be counter-productive to learners (Wiggins, 2012). Instead, focus feedback on one or two performance domains. Strive for a balance of what the learner can do successfully and an area for improvement. Select one area of achievement that is reflective of what a learner can do well and provide feedback using a GLOW comment. Then, select one area that has potential for growth and provide feedback using a GROW assistive question.

Short-Term Goals

Short-term goals based on specific themes, vocabulary, and grammatical structures within a unit of study are limited to the content of that specific unit. That is, the goals will differ from unit to unit due to the varying content. For example, unit goals such as *I can compare and contrast school experiences in different countries, I can use adjectives to describe food*, or *I can use the present progressive* are limited to specific content covered within a unit. In contrast, the PDIs provide educators and learners the opportunity to remain focused on long-term, overarching communicative goals, such as the targeted level of performance for a course. For example, using the Text Type PDI *I can use simple sentences most of the time* serves as a long-term, overarching communicative goal throughout multiple units within a course that is targeting the Novice High performance level. Using the PDIs that align to the target performance level of a course ensures that the communicative goals remain consistent throughout multiple units of varying content. This consistency can lead learners to a deeper understanding of the performance domains and the expectations of performance, which form their pathway to language growth. It also allows learners multiple opportunities to meet expectations, over time, throughout different units of content. The implications are powerful – though the content, vocabulary, and structures may change throughout various units, learners will remain focused on the skills that contribute towards communicating a comprehensible and appropriate message.

Educator-Designed and Educator-Driven

Feedback is not meant to be educator-designed and educator-driven. That is, educators do not need to both design and provide all the feedback to learners all the time. Rather, learners can take an active part in the feedback process. The *Performance Domain Indicators (PDIs) Assessment and Feedback Guide* streamlines feedback so it is teacher-designed in a way that can be replicated, reproduced, and reused in every unit. Each performance domain chapter shares examples of how these guides can be used to provide feedback that is learner-driven. Learners can use the given feedback structures to self assess, shifting responsibility and ownership to learners. Learners might self-assess by:

- Using the *guiding questions* in the *Performance Domain Indicators (PDIs) Assessment and Feedback Guide* in each performance domain (see Figure 4.1).
- Circling, highlighting, underlining, using parentheses, or color-coding their work to make features of their performance more visible (see Figure 4.2).
- Reflecting on the *Meeting* PDI using the GLOW (*What are my strengths?*) and the *Exceeding* PDI using the GROW (*What can I do to improve?*) prompts (see Table 4.5).
- Using the guided self-assessments (see Figure 4.3), which provide scaffolded questions for learners to reflect upon before determining their level of performance in a performance domain as well as next steps for language growth.

Figure 4.2
Self-Assessment Using the "Make It Visible" Strategy

Directions: Read over your presentational work and mark it accordingly:

- Underline simple sentences.
- (Put parentheses) around series of sentences.
- Circle any coordinators (*and, but, or, for, so*) or subordinating conjunctions (*because*).

Example of how the learner, performing within the Novice level, completes this self-assessment:

Hi, my name is Emerson. I is United States. I is 11. My birthday is February 6. I like to play sports. A lot summer. I don't like to sing. I is not funny. I like to draw. I like to run. I don't like to write stories. I like to read.

Table 4.5
Example of How a Learner, Performing Within the Novice Level, Completes a Self-Assessment Using the GLOW and GROW Framework

TEXT TYPE Target performance level: **Novice High** Context: familiar, informal, formal, predictable Content: familiar, everyday		
Instructions: Complete the following reflection by writing where you GLOW and where you can GROW in each area. Make sure to include evidence from your work to support your reasoning.		
Where I GLOW: What are my strengths?	**Performance Domain Indicator**	**How can I GROW? What can I do to improve?**
I think I used simple sentences most of the time.	I can use simple sentences most of the time.	*I could write more than one sentence about one of the activities to create a series of sentences.*

GLOW IDEAS	**GROW IDEAS**
• Did you use simple sentences most of the time throughout your performance?	• How might you group sentences on a related topic into a logical sequence to create a series of sentences? • How might you say/write multiple sentences on a related topic to create a series of sentences? • What coordinators (*and, but, or, for, so*) could you add to better connect your ideas?

Figure 4.3

Example of How a Learner, Performing Within the Novice Level, Completes an Interpersonal/Presentational Guided Self-Assessment

TARGET PERFORMANCE LEVEL	Novice High	CONTEXT	Familiar, informal, formal, predictable
PERFORMANCE DOMAIN	Text Type	CONTENT	Familiar, everyday

What description best matches your performance today?

- ☐ Practiced or memorized words and phrases
- ☑ A mixture of practiced or memorized words, phrases, and simple sentences
- ☐ Simple sentences most of the time
- ☐ Simple sentences, and at times a series of sentences

Write or record an example of a complete sentence that you used today:

I am athlete.

Option 1: Select vocabulary/structures that helped you create complete sentences today:

- ☑ I like…
- ☐ I do not like…
- ☑ I am…
- ☐ I am not…

Option 2: What vocabulary/structures did you use to create complete sentences today?

How often did you use a series of sentences (*multiple sentences on a related topic*)?

- ☑ I did not use a series of sentences today.
- ☐ I used a series of sentences once today.
- ☐ I used a series of sentences multiple times today.

Option 1: If you used a series of sentences, write an example of a series of sentences that you used today:

Option 2: If you did not use a series of sentences today, think of one sentence you used today. How would you add or extend the sentence to create multiple sentences on a related topic?

People think I am weak. Not good on team.
I am athlete. I am strong.

Option 1: What coordinators did you use today to connect your ideas?

- ☐ also
- ☐ because
- ☐ but
- ☐ when
- ☐ Other: ____________________

Option 2: What coordinators could you add to better connect your ideas?

I red hair but I like my red hair.

Evaluate how you think you performed in your use of Text Type today:

- ☐ **Beginning:** I can use practiced and memorized words and phrases.
- ☐ **Developing:** I can use practiced and memorized words and phrases, and at times use simple sentences.
- ☑ **Meeting:** I can use simple sentences most of the time.
- ☐ **Exceeding:** I can form simple sentences, and at times series of sentences

Think about your own experience and what you have done to improve in Text Type. What advice would you give other learners to help them develop text type?

Write sentences. Then see if they go together. Maybe with coordinators.

These learner-driven strategies are designed to promote learner ownership and build learner confidence. Regular, ongoing, and consistent self-assessment can promote learner metacognition and self-regulation. That is, through self-questioning (assessing and assisting feedback questions) and self-reflection, learners can practice metacognition, or thinking about their thinking to become aware of their own learning (Fisher et al., 2021). As learners become more self-aware, they have a better understanding of how language helps them communicate a comprehensible and appropriate message to successfully complete performance tasks. They can own their learning, increasing their motivation and understanding. This leads to self-regulation: that is, learners who use and control their own thought processes (Brookhart, 2008). Learners who self-regulate are empowered, independent learners. They are able to decide on their next learning goals and have the tools to select and/or devise strategies to reach their goals. Language learners who self-regulate can determine their next steps on their pathway along the continuum of language proficiency.

Table 4.6
Recasting Feedback Pitfalls

PITFALL		RECAST
Prioritizing accuracy Mark every grammatical mistake a learner makes.	>>>	**Recast to GLOW feedback** Highlight what learners can do using GLOW feedback comments.
Too much feedback List multiple items for a learner to correct.	>>>	**Recast to GLOW & GROW feedback** Select one area of achievement (GLOW) and one area for improvement (GROW).
Short-term goals Separate, disconnected performance goals that differ with every unit.	>>>	**Recast to long-term performance goals** Consistent PDIs, based on the target performance level of a course, used throughout every unit.
Teacher-designed, teacher-driven The educator provides all the feedback to all learners all of the time.	>>>	**Recast to teacher-designed, learner-driven** The educator provides some feedback to learners at intentional points in the unit. Learners have multiple opportunities to self-assess, determine how well they are meeting the goals of the course, and select strategies for language growth.

YOUR TURN

LEARNING TARGET CHECK:	
I can	☐ identify pitfalls to avoid when providing feedback to language learners.

Pause and reflect:

Reflect on the feedback pitfalls in the chart below. What might be an area of growth for you? How might you recast this feedback pitfall to a more effective feedback practice for yourself and your learners?

FEEDBACK PITFALL	AREAS FOR GROWTH	NEXT STEPS I CAN TAKE TO CREATE MORE EFFECTIVE FEEDBACK PRACTICES INCLUDE...
Prioritizing accuracy		
Too much feedback		
Short-term goals		
Teacher-designed and teacher-driven		

Conclusion

To encourage a *can-do* attitude of confidence, feedback must describe where the learner is at, where the learner is going, and promote thinking on how to get there. This book is designed to provide educators with the needed tools to provide effective feedback to language learners: guiding questions to evaluate learner work, the PDIs, GLOW achievement comments, and GROW assistive questions. The tools are intended to empower both educators and learners.

Each performance domain chapter includes self-assessment ideas (*Make It Visible, Glow and Grow Self-Assessment, Guided Self-Assessments*) so learners can reflect upon and assess their own performance. These learner-driven strategies are designed to promote learner ownership and build learner confidence. As educators work towards supporting learners to self-assess, self-reflect, and self-regulate, learning experiences will be needed to further develop learner language skills. Each performance domain chapter includes a variety of learning experiences that can be used at Novice, Intermediate, or Advanced level to promote language growth. These learning experiences can be implemented by educators, throughout multiple lessons in a unit, to model expected performance as well as provide ideas for language growth.

Equally important, though, is that learners can self-select some of the strategies presented in the learning experiences to use as they work to self-regulate. Once learners have grasped feedback aligned to the PDIs, learners will seek strategies to use for language growth. For some learners, providing GROW feedback through the use of assisting questions will be sufficient to spark their thinking and personalize their own solutions for growth. For other learners, more assistance might be needed. Educators could recommend one or two ideas for learners to try or provide a menu of options from which learners select. It is of utmost importance to always provide feedback and strategies which position the learner as the thinker and owner of their choices.

YOUR TURN

LEARNING TARGET CHECK:	
I can	☐ reflect on my own feedback practices and plan next steps for growth.

Pause and reflect:

How might your practice change if you assessed learners using the same PDIs throughout each unit? What would be the benefits? What challenges would you need to overcome?

Feedback reflection guide:

Complete the guided self-assessment to evaluate your current feedback practices.

<table>
<tr><th colspan="2">GUIDED SELF-ASSESSMENT</th></tr>
<tr><td colspan="2">Write examples of teacher-designed feedback (opportunities in which the feedback is designed and provided by the teacher) that your provide to your language learners:</td></tr>
<tr><td>Option 1: If you provide learner-driven feedback (opportunities in which the learners take ownership and responsibility to self-assess, reflect, and plan next steps), write an example that you recently used with learners:</td><td>Option 2: If you do not provide learner-driven feedback, think of an example of feedback that you recently provided to a learner. How would you recast it to be learner-driven?</td></tr>
<tr><td colspan="2">How often do you provide feedback that is goal-referenced (feedback focuses on what learners can do in alignment with the overarching long-term performance goals of the course)?
☐ I do not yet provide goal-referenced feedback to my language learners.
☐ At times I provide goal-referenced feedback to my language learners.
☐ I provide goal-referenced feedback to my language learners multiple times throughout a course.</td></tr>
<tr><td>Option 1: If you provide goal-referenced feedback, write an example that you recently used with learners:</td><td>Option 2: If you do not provide goal-referenced feedback, think of an example of feedback that you recently provided to a learner. How would you recast it to be goal-referenced?</td></tr>
<tr><td colspan="2">How often do you provide feedback that is actionable, tangible, and transparent (feedback posed in the form of questions, inviting learners to consider how they might adjust their performance for language growth)?
☐ I do not yet provide feedback that is actionable, tangible, and transparent to my language learners.
☐ At times I provide feedback that is actionable, tangible, and transparent to my language learners.
☐ I provide feedback that is actionable, tangible, and transparent to my language learners multiple times throughout a course.</td></tr>
</table>

<table>
<tr><td>Option 1: If you provide feedback that is actionable, tangible, and transparent, write an example that you recently used with learners:</td><td>Option 2: If you do not provide feedback that is actionable, tangible, and transparent: think of an example of feedback that you recently provided to a learner. How would you recast it to be actionable, tangible, and transparent?</td></tr>
<tr><td colspan="2">How often do you provide feedback that is user-friendly (descriptive, specific, and developmentally appropriate feedback that highlights one skill the learner can do as well as one area for growth)?
☐ I do not yet provide user-friendly feedback to my language learners.
☐ At times I provide user-friendly feedback to my language learners.
☐ I provide user-friendly feedback to my language learners multiple times throughout a course.</td></tr>
<tr><td>Option 1: If you provide user-friendly feedback, write an example that you recently used with learners:</td><td>Option 2: If you do not provide user-friendly feedback, think of an example of feedback that you recently provided to a learner. How would you recast it to be user-friendly?</td></tr>
<tr><td colspan="2">How often do you provide feedback that is timely, ongoing, and consistent (feedback provided while learners are still working on the goal that includes opportunities for learners to self-assess)?
☐ I do not provide feedback that is timely, ongoing, and consistent to my language learners.
☐ At times I provide feedback that is timely, ongoing, and consistent to my language learners.
☐ I provide feedback that is timely, ongoing, and consistent to my language learners multiple times throughout a course.</td></tr>
<tr><td>Option 1: If you provide feedback that is timely, ongoing, and consistent, write an example that you recently used with learners:</td><td>Option 2: If you do not provide feedback that is timely, ongoing, and consistent: think of an example of feedback that you recently provided to a learner. How would you recast it to be timely, ongoing, and consistent?</td></tr>
<tr><td colspan="2">Evaluate your current feedback practices:
☐ I provide teacher-designed and teacher-driven feedback to language learners that does not include the key elements of effective feedback.
☐ I can provide teacher-designed and at times learner-driven feedback to language learners that uses the key elements of effective feedback.
☐ I can provide teacher-designed and learner-driven feedback to language learners that uses the key elements of effective feedback.
☐ I can provide a variety of teacher-designed and learner-driven feedback to language learners that uses the key elements of effective feedback.</td></tr>
<tr><td colspan="2">Think about your own experience and what you have done to improve in your feedback practices. What advice would you give other educators to help them develop more effective feedback practices?</td></tr>
</table>

Answer Key for Your Turn: Evaluating Feedback for Effectiveness (p. 50)

Feedback example	Is it goal-referenced?	Is it actionable, tangible, and transparent?	Is it user-friendly?	Is the feedback effective? Include evidence of your reasoning
You wrote a lot!	Yes / **No**	Yes / **No**	Yes / **No**	No. This statement provides praise about the learner's performance. It does not reference any communicative goals, indicate areas for growth, or promote learner thinking on how to achieve their goals.
You should include more complete sentences.	**Yes** / No	Yes / **No**	Yes / **No**	No. This statement provides advice. It references characteristics of the *Meeting* level and indicates next steps for learners. However, it does not provide an opportunity to promote learner thinking about how to achieve their goals.
You used memorized words and phrases most of the time to express your thoughts.	**Yes** / No	**Yes** / No	**Yes** / No	Yes. This statement is goal-referenced, transparent, user-friendly feedback that indicates the current level of performance and what the learner does well.
How might you combine some of your phrases to build complete sentences?	**Yes** / No	**Yes** / No	**Yes** / No	Yes. This statement is goal-referenced, transparent, user-friendly feedback that promotes learner thinking for language growth.
You are still at the developing stage. You didn't use many complete sentences.	**Yes** / No	Yes / **No**	Yes / **No**	No. This statement references the *Developing* level. It indicates what the learner did not do. It does not promote learner thinking about next steps for language growth.
You show evidence of using some simple sentences at times in your message.	**Yes** / No	**Yes** / No	**Yes** / No	Yes. This statement is goal-referenced, transparent, user-friendly feedback that indicates the current level of performance and what the learner does well.

References

ACTFL. (n.d.) *Provide effective feedback.* https://www.actfl.org/resources/guiding-principles-language-learning/effective-feedback

Biber, D., Nekrasova, T., & Horn, B. (2011). *The effectiveness of feedback for L-1 English and L2-writing development: A meta-analysis.* ETS TOEFL. https://files.eric.ed.gov/fulltext/EJ1111175.pdf

Brookhart, S. M. (2008). *How to give effective feedback to your students.* ASCD.

Erkens, C., Schimmer, T., & Vagle, N.D. (2017). *Essential assessment.* Solution Tree Press.

Fisher, D., Frey, N., & Almarode, J. (2021). *Student learning communities: A springboard for academic and social-emotional development.* ASCD.

Glisan, E. W., & Donato, R. (2017). *Enacting the work of language instruction: High leverage teaching practices* (Vol. 1). ACTFL.

Hammond, Z. (2015). *Culturally responsive teaching and the brain: Promoting authentic engagement and rigor among culturally and linguistically diverse students.* Corwin.

Moss, C. M., & Brookhart, S. M. (2012). *Learning targets: Helping students aim for understanding in today's lesson.* ASCD.

Reichelt, M. (2019). Contextual factors impacting feedback practices for non-English L2 writing. *Foreign Language Annals, 52*(4), 744-752.

Sánchez-Naranjo, J. (2019). Peer review and training: Pathways to quality and value in second language writing. *Foreign Language Annals, 52*(3), 612-643.

Sippel, L., & Jackson, C. N. (2015). Teacher vs. peer oral corrective feedback in the German language classroom. *Foreign Language Annals, 48*(4), 688-705.

Thorpe, R. G., & Gallimore, R. (1988). *Rousing minds to life: Teaching, learning, and schooling in social contexts.* Cambridge University Press.

Tunstall, P., & Gipps, C. (1996). Teacher feedback to young children in formative assessment: A typology. *British Educational Research Journal*, 22, 389-404.

Truscott, J. (2007). The effect of error correction on learners' ability to write accurately. *Journal of Second Language Writing*, 16, 255-272.

Wiggins, G. (2012). Seven keys to effective feedback. *Educational Leadership*, 70(1), 10-16.

CHAPTER 5 | LANGUAGE USE

Performance Domain

LEARNING TARGETS:	
I can	☐ describe the Language Use performance domain. ☐ describe how Language Use shows up in learners' performance at various levels. ☐ evaluate learner work using the Performance Domain Indicators (PDIs). ☐ give effective feedback using the Language Use PDIs. ☐ select learning experiences that support learners' growth with Language Use. ☐ provide learners with self-assessments to evaluate their work.

What do we mean by *Language Use*?

Language Use refers to the language a learner uses to best complete the language functions of a communicative task. This involves how a learner combines vocabulary and grammatical structures to make meaning. Learners differ in the variety and quantity of these linguistic resources, as well as their ability to effectively use them to complete a communicative task.

How does *Language Use* develop in learner performance?

Learners begin by using memorized and practiced vocabulary and formulaic structures (a set or patterned form) in everyday, familiar contexts. From there, they develop the ability to create with language by combining and/or recombining new and familiar vocabulary and grammatical structures in a growing variety of straight-forward contexts. As learners continue to progress, they use their growing linguistic resources to communicate in various time frames. They can eventually use a range, or wide variety, of vocabulary and grammatical forms/structures across various time frames. Their increased linguistic resources lead learners to make more decisions about the language. That is, learners develop the ability to purposefully select vocabulary and grammatical structures that most effectively and precisely carry out the language function (ACTFL, 2012).

What does *Language Use* look like in our learners' performance?

The sample learner performances in Table 5.1 show evidence of how learners differ in the language used to carry out the functions of each performance task. The learner performing within the Novice level uses memorized, practiced vocabulary (*volleyball, sport, team, practice*) and formulaic structures (*I like, to play*). Within the Intermediate level, the learner combines and recombines *to play* in different contexts (*played volleyball, played with my team*) and different verb forms (*I played, we winned*). This learner can attend to the present tense time frame (*it is*) as well as attempts working in the past time frame (*We winned*), although not all languages rely on verb tenses to indicate time frames or move to the Advanced level. The learner performing within the Advanced level uses language across various time frames. For example, they use the present perfect (*I have been*), which more precisely communicates the length of their experience that continues into their present day. They also use future tense (*I will*) in a conditional phrase to effectively communicate the real possibility of their dream. Additionally, this learner uses a greater variety of vocabulary (*tournament, commitment, selected, development, scouts*) that more precisely describes their experience with the sport.

Table 5.1
Sample Learner Performances

NOVICE	**Task:** Write a note to your new instructor telling about an activity you like to do.	Hello Mr. Yang. I like volleyball. Sport favorite. I to play 8 years. Team. Lots practice. We play?
INTERMEDIATE	**Task:** Email a friend to describe what you did this past weekend.	Hey Sierra. Well, this weekend I played volleyball. It is my favorite sport. I played with my team. We winned and it is really cool. I play volleyball for 8 years. How about you? What did you do?
ADVANCED	**Task:** Write a note to your coach reflecting on your journey and future goals of becoming a professional athlete.	Hey, coach! I am proud of how dedicated I have been! It hasn't always be easy and I sacrificed a lot to get here. There were times when I couldn't go out with friends because of practice or a weekend tournament, which sucked. In fact, the commitment was tough at times. You see, I love this sport so much, so much that I want to be on the Olympic team 8 years from now. But first, I need to get selected for their player development training series. This is why I will do everything to take our team to the state tournament. There, I know I can impress the scouts! Thanks for believing in us, for believing in me.

The Performance Domain Indicators and Descriptions

The following section presents the Performance Domain Indicators (PDIs) for Language Use by performance level: Novice (Table 5.2), Intermediate (Table 5.3), and Advanced (Table 5.4). The Language Use PDIs are primarily a combination of language from both the *NCSSFL-ACTFL Can-Do Statements: Performance Indicators for Language Learners* (NCSSFL-ACTFL, 2017) and the *ACTFL Proficiency Guidelines* (ACTFL, 2012), which are cited at each level. These PDIs focus on learner performance, or what a learner can do at one moment in time based on what they learned, versus proficiency, or what a learner can do within unrehearsed situations regardless of where, when, or how they learned the language. Learners can *perform* at or within a proficiency level, but they may not necessarily be *proficient* at that level.

The PDIs for this performance domain are applied to both interpersonal and presentational modes of communication. This is to promote ease and consistency among educators and learners. In order to illustrate Language Use, the PDIs are accompanied by a learner task and sample learner responses. In addition, the PDIs are accompanied by a description that is meant to deepen our understanding of how Language Use develops across the sublevels (Low, Mid, and High) in learner performance at each performance level (Novice, Intermediate, and Advanced).

Table 5.2
Language Use Performance Domain Indicators (PDIs) for Learners Performing Within the Novice Level

	NOVICE		
Sublevels	**LOW**	**MID**	**HIGH**
Context	familiar, informal, formal, predictable		
Content	very familiar	very familiar, everyday	familiar, everyday
Performance Domain Indicator	**I can** use *isolated*, **memorized** and **practiced** *vocabulary*.	**I can** use *isolated*, **memorized** and **practiced** *vocabulary* and *formulaic structures*.	**I can use practiced** *vocabulary* and *formulaic structures*, and at times *(re)combine vocabulary and structures to create with language*.

- The language in bold indicates the source is the *NCSSFL-ACTFL Can-Do Statements: Performance Indicators for Language Learners* (NCSSFL-ACTFL, 2017).
- The language in italics indicates that the source is the *ACTFL Proficiency Guidelines* (ACTFL, 2012).
- The underlined language indicates the source is Troyan et al. (2023).
- Some language may appear in additional levels to provide scaffolding, consistency and/or clarity.
- For classroom purposes, some language has been modified to be learner-friendly (i.e., *some attempts* to *at times*).

Novice Task: Send your friend a status update on social media describing your Saturday morning breakfast experience.

LEARNER SAMPLE RESPONSE

NOVICE LOW	NOVICE MID	NOVICE HIGH
Good morning! In restaurant. Food yummy!	Good morning! I am in restaurant. Is favorite. I like eggs and bread. Drink coffee. Yummy!	What's up, friend? I am in restaurant. My fav! I like to eat big breakfast. I like to eat eggs with bacon. So yummy! What you eat this morning?

Description of Learner Responses: Learners performing within the Novice levels are characterized by their use of memorized and formulaic, or a patterned set of, language. These learners tend to repeat what they hear, or have memorized or practiced. These learners rely on high-frequency vocabulary to communicate on very familiar and everyday topics (example: *breakfast, food*). Learners begin by using memorized and practiced vocabulary, primarily in isolation (*Good Morning. In restaurant. Food yummy!*). As they develop more language, they not only use isolated, memorized, and practiced vocabulary (*restaurant, favorite, drink coffee*) but also some formulaic structures (*I am, I like*) to express their ideas. As these learners progress, they can, at times use practiced vocabulary and structures in different ways. These learners begin to create with language by combining and/or recombining language (*big breakfast* and *eggs with bacon*). However, these attempts may or may not be successful and occur occasionally, rather than consistently, throughout their performance.

Table 5.3
Language Use Performance Domain Indicators (PDIs) for Learners Performing Within the Intermediate Level

	INTERMEDIATE		
Sublevels	LOW	MID	HIGH
Context	familiar, informal, formal, straight-forward		
Content	familiar	familiar, at times researched	familiar, concrete, at times researched
Performance Domain Indicator	**I can** *create with language by (re)combining vocabulary and structures.*	**I can** *create with language* by *(re)combining* a variety of *vocabulary* and *structures*, and at times use **various time frames**.	**I can** *create with language* by *(re)combining* a variety of *vocabulary* and *structures*, at times across **various time frames**.

- The language in bold indicates the source is the *NCSSFL-ACTFL Can-Do Statements: Performance Indicators for Language Learners* (NCSSFL-ACTFL, 2017).
- The language in italics indicates that the source is the *ACTFL Proficiency Guidelines* (ACTFL, 2012).
- Some language may appear in additional levels to provide scaffolding, consistency and/or clarity (ie. *use various time frames, across various time frames*).

Intermediate Task: Post a reply to your friend's breakfast photo message on social media and compare your breakfasts.

LEARNER SAMPLE RESPONSE

INTERMEDIATE LOW	INTERMEDIATE MID	INTERMEDIATE HIGH
Looks delicious! You like to eat eggs and bacon a lot. It is good for you. Is it your favorite meal? I like eggs also. I like to eat with rice and beans. This morning I eats cereals. It is not so yummy as you. Well, enjoy!	Lol. Again? I see that bacon and eggs is your favorite meal for breakfast! LOVE IT! I also eated eggs this morning, but I had with rice and beans. My dad says that eggs are good to us because they are very healthy. But, I prefer cereal like FruitySquares, because of all the sugar. YUM! Lol. Well, enjoy!	Lol! Are you having bacon and eggs for breakfast again today? Why am I not surprised? It is definitely your favorite meal. I also ate eggs this morning, but I had with rice and beans. My dad said that eggs are very healthy because they give protein. Do you always eat your eggs scrambled? Or have you had other eggs? Cereal is faster. I'm late! Ahhh! Ok well, enjoy!

Description of Learner Responses: Within the Intermediate level, learners are characterized by their ability to create with language; that is, to combine and recombine learned language. For example, they incorporate new vocabulary into learned language structures or, vice versa, apply new structures with learned vocabulary. Learners are first able to do this when primarily expressing themselves in one time frame (past, present, or future). Within a single time frame, these learners begin to use a variety of subject pronouns (*you like, I eats, it is*). As learners progress, they continue to create with language and, at times in various time frames. For example, in a performance assessment, these learners can, at times use more than one time frame, such as the present (*I see, my dad says*) and past time frames (*I also eated … this morning, I had*), or both present and future time frames, but are not able to move in and out of various time frames throughout the performance.

As they progress, learners performing within the Intermediate level can create with language (*bacon and eggs for breakfast, again?; give protein, eggs scrambled, other eggs*) at times across various time frames. That is, they can move in and out of different time frames, at times throughout their performance. For example, the learner moves from the present time frame (*It is…*) to the past time frame (*I also ate…, but I had…, My dad said…*) back to the present time frame (*Do you always eat…*). As they do, they do so with a variety of subject pronouns (the past: *I ate, my dad said*; and the present: *it is, you eat, I'm late*). Within a time frame (past, present or future), these learners may use grammatical aspects such as the progressive, imperfect, and perfect to convey duration, frequency, relation, and/or sequence. For example, the present progressive (*are you having*) refers to ongoing activities in the present time frame, while the present perfect (*have you had*) includes aspects of both the past and present time frames. In a performance assessment, learners performing within the Intermediate level can use verb form (example: verb tenses) and/or time markers (example: *today, this morning*) to communicate, at times across various time frames.

Table 5.4
Language Use Performance Domain Indicators (PDIs) for Learners Performing Within the Advanced Level

	ADVANCED		
Sublevels	**LOW**	**MID**	**HIGH**
Context	familiar, unfamiliar, informal, formal, complex		
Content	familiar, academic, social, concrete	academic, social, professional, concrete	academic, social, professional, concrete, abstract
Performance Domain Indicator	**I can** use a range of *vocabulary* and *structures* **across various time frames**.	**I can** use a *wide range* of *vocabulary* and *structures* that are, at times, *precise* **across various time frames**.	**I can** use *precise vocabulary, structures*, and *time frames.*

- The language in bold indicates the source is the *NCSSFL-ACTFL Can-Do Statements: Performance Indicators for Language Learners* (NCSSFL-ACTFL, 2017).
- The language in italics indicates that the source is the *ACTFL Proficiency Guidelines* (ACTFL, 2012).
- Some language may appear in additional levels to provide scaffolding, consistency and/or clarity (ie. *extensive* to *a wide range*).

Advanced Task: Create a podcast episode for your listeners that brings awareness to how nutrition impacts the human body.

LEARNER SAMPLE RESPONSE

ADVANCED LOW	ADVANCED MID	ADVANCED HIGH
Hello to all my listeners! This episode of The Body and Our Nutrition is about artificial sweeteners, like SweArtif and Azcufal. The artificial sweeteners taste like sugar but have zero calories, which is why they are super popular for peoples want to lose weight. The products that are popular is soda, cereals, chips, and cookies! However, did you know a health study finded that artificial sweeteners is linked to heart problems and also increase in weight? More research is needed in the future. So, the next time when you are in the grocery store, you can think twice about diet products. Is it worth it? Until then, thanks for listen and "Be well."	Hello to all my listeners! This is another episode of The Body and Our Nutrition. In today's episode I speak about health concerns that are linked to artificial sweeteners, such as SweArtif and Azcufal. If you know or not, the food industry is substituting sugar with artificial sweeteners. These are many products you see marketed as "diet" or "zero calorie", which are popular for soft drinks. But did you know that artificial sweeteners is used in more food products, such as salad dressings, soups? Bread has false sugars! However, recent health studies are questioning if they safe for the human body. The research has linked artificial sweeteners with maybe heart problems and also increases in weight. So, the next time you are in a grocery store, please read the label, because "zero" may not be better. Well, is everything for today. Thanks for listening and "Be well."	Many people think that "diet" or "zero calorie" products can help to lose weight. But is effective? Hello and welcome to another episode of The Body and Our Nutrition. In today's episode I address health concerns that are linked to artificial sweeteners. You may recognize artificial sweeteners by their names, like SweArtif and Azcufal. The popularity is due to they have zero calories but taste like sugar. So, same great taste without the calories. Well, according to recent health studies, fake sugars promote cravings, which can lead you to want to eat more. This is because the level of sweet is very high, which people then want more of. But if you eat more, you may gain weight, right? So, the next time you find yourself in a grocery store, be sure and read the label. As always, thank you for tuning in to today's episode of The Body and Our Nutrition. If you liked today, follow by clicking on the subscribe button. Until next week, "Be well" my friends.

Description of Learner Responses: A distinguishing feature of learners performing within the Advanced levels is their ability to use a range of vocabulary and structures *across* various time frames (past, present, and future). These learners can move through time frames with increased flexibility, in both quality and quantity. These learners incorporate vocabulary from specialized (academic, professional, etc.) topics (*nutrition, artificial sweeteners, calories, linked*) with vocabulary from previously learned content, or content that ranges from very familiar to everyday to researched topics (*body, sugar, weight, health, products*). In addition, these learners use a range of previously learned and new structures, such as the passive voice (*sweeteners is linked, research is needed*), and/or phrasal verbs/nouns, or verbs that are combined with an adverb or preposition (*taste like, think twice about*). Overall, these learners use their range of linguistic resources while communicating across various time frames (the past: *did you know, study finded*; the present: *episode is, sweeteners taste*; and the future: *when you are, Be well*).

As learners progress, they use a wide range (or a greater variety) of vocabulary and structures that are, at times, precise across various time frames, including grammatical aspects (the present progressive: *is substituting, are questioning*; the present perfect: *has linked*). Learners can, at times, use vocabulary that specifically matches the context and/or content (*substituting* instead of *using; marketed* instead of *sold; label* instead of *sticker*). This also applies to language structures (conditional phrase: *if you know*, gerund after a preposition: *for listening*) especially when communicating about concrete ideas and/or topics.

Eventually, learners performing within the Advanced levels can use precise vocabulary, structures, and time frames. For example, they can use terms like *address* instead of *speak about, recognize* instead of *know of, fake* instead of *false*; and *tuning in* instead of *listening to.* These learners can use specific structures like conditional phrases (*if you eat more, if you liked*) and modal verbs (*may, can*) to express uncertainty or probability. These learners can use precise language to communicate concrete and even abstract ideas.

YOUR TURN

LEARNING TARGETS CHECK:	
I can	☐ describe the Language Use performance domain. ☐ describe how Language Use shows up in learners' performance at various levels.

Pause and reflect:
How would you describe Language Use to your learners? Consider any explanations, examples, and/or visuals you might use to describe the performance domain:

Language Use in learner work:
The following exercise includes a sample task for each of the performance levels. Write a learner response that includes the characteristics of Language Use for learners performing within each level. Use the provided Intermediate sample to guide you.

NOVICE	**Task:** Write a note to a classmate describing your favorite class in school.	
INTERMEDIATE	**Task:** Write a note to the new student from [target language country] who just started attending your school. Summarize what is similar and different between your two schools.	Hey! Here is different about your school. Tell me is it true? In the school in [target language country], there are classes similar: math, English, science, physical education. There is no art class, but there is music class. School start at 7:30 in the morning. So early! But school end at 1:30 in the afternoon. Awesome! There is recess, but there is no lunch. Students go home at 1:30 and eat lunch with their families. It is a late lunch! Also, students wear uniforms at school. They cannot wear their clothing favorite or clothing colors different. It is different, but interesting school experience!
ADVANCED	**Task:** Write a letter to a middle school student providing advice on how to create a smooth transition to high school.	

The Performance Domain Indicators (PDIs) Assessment and Feedback Guide

The *Performance Domain Indicators (PDIs) Assessment and Feedback Guide* is a resource for both learners and educators to use when assessing learner performance. The information within each guide is based on PDIs of the following performance level targets: Novice High (Table 5.5), Intermediate Mid (Table 5.6), Intermediate High (Table 5.7), and Advanced Low (Table 5.8). However, these guides can serve as a template for other performance level targets. It is important to note that a performance assessment evaluates a learner's *performance*, and not *the learner*. Therefore, a learner is not *at* a level, but rather a learner's performance may be consistent *with* a level.

The purpose of the *Performance Domain Indicators (PDIs) Assessment and Feedback Guide* is to provide a visual pathway for evaluating the Language Use of a learner's performance. The left-hand column provides guiding questions that lead us to identify the Language Use consistent with a learner's performance. These guiding questions are based upon the performance levels' PDIs, which are presented lowest to highest. Starting at the *Beginning* level, evaluators progress through each question, responding "yes" or "no." If evaluators reply "yes" to all questions in the *Beginning* level, they continue to the next level (*Developing*), repeating the process, and continuing through the levels. If evaluators reply "no" to a question, they go back to the previous level, in which all their replies for the level's guiding questions are "yes." At the last level where all questions are answered "yes," evaluators continue across the chart. They can then refer to the second column labeled *Performance Domain Indicator* for the PDI that best aligns with the learner's performance. Based on this evaluation, the following two columns provide example GLOW and GROW comments. GLOW feedback states what the learner achieved and GROW feedback directs learners how to develop their language skills. This feedback is not unit specific, but rather supports overarching language performance goals that learners can work towards throughout a course. Including evidence from learner performance within the GLOW/GROW feedback is most effective.

Table 5.5
Performance Domain Indicators (PDIs) Assessment and Feedback Guide

Language Use Target performance level: **Novice High** Context: familiar, informal, formal, predictable Content: familiar, everyday			
Guiding questions	**Performance Domain Indicator**	**GLOW**	**GROW**
Novice Low **Beginning** Can the learner: • use memorized and practiced vocabulary in isolation?	I can use isolated, memorized and practiced vocabulary.	• You use memorized and practiced vocabulary in isolation to communicate your message.	• What additional vocabulary could you add to communicate more information to your partner/audience? • What formulaic, or patterned, structures could you use to communicate more information to your partner/audience?
Novice Mid **Developing** Can the learner: • use practiced vocabulary in isolation? • use formulaic, or patterned, structures?	I can use isolated, memorized and practiced vocabulary and formulaic structures.	• You use memorized and practiced vocabulary in isolation to communicate your message. • You use formulaic, or patterned, structures to communicate your message.	• How might you expand on what you say/write so you can move beyond using vocabulary in isolation? • How might you create with language by combining & recombining words in different ways?
Novice High **Meeting** Can the learner: • use memorized and practiced vocabulary? • use formulaic, or patterned, structures? • create with language, at times by combining and recombining vocabulary and structures in different ways?	I can use practiced vocabulary and formulaic structures, and at times (re)combine vocabulary and structures to create with language.	• You use practiced vocabulary to communicate your message. • You use formulaic, or patterned, structures to communicate your message. • You are beginning to create with language by combining and recombining vocabulary/structures in different ways.	• How might you create with language by combining and recombining vocabulary and structures throughout your performance?
Intermediate Low **Exceeding** Can the learner: • create with language by combining and recombining vocabulary and structures in different ways?	I can create with language by (re)combining vocabulary and structures.	• You create with language by combining & recombining vocabulary and structures.	• How might you combine and recombine a variety of vocabulary and structures? • How might you use various, or multiple, time frames to communicate your message?

Table 5.6

Performance Domain Indicators (PDIs) Assessment and Feedback Guide

Language Use Target performance level: **Intermediate Mid** Context: familiar, informal, formal, straight-forward Content: familiar, at times researched			
Guiding questions	**Performance Domain Indicator**	**GLOW**	**GROW**
Novice High **Beginning** Can the learner: • use practiced vocabulary? • use formulaic, or patterned, structures? • create with language, at times by combining and recombining vocabulary and structures in different ways?	I can use practiced vocabulary and formulaic structures, and at times (re)combine vocabulary and structures to create with language.	• You use practiced vocabulary to communicate your message. • You use formulaic, or patterned, structures to communicate your message. • You are beginning to create with language by combining and recombining vocabulary/structures in different ways.	• How might you create with language by combining and recombining vocabulary and structures throughout your performance?
Intermediate Low **Developing** Can the learner: • create with language by combining and recombining vocabulary and structures in different ways?	I can create with language by (re)combining vocabulary and structures.	• You create with language by combining & recombining vocabulary and structures.	• How might you combine and recombine a variety of vocabulary and structures? • How might you use various, or multiple, time frames to communicate your message?
Intermediate Mid **Meeting** Can the learner: • create with language by combining and recombining a variety of vocabulary and structures in different ways? • at times use various, or multiple, time frames?	I can create with language by (re)combining a variety of vocabulary and structures, and at times use various time frames.	• You create with language by combining & recombining a variety of vocabulary and structures. • At times you use various, or multiple, time frames to communicate your message.	• How might you use various, or multiple, time frames throughout your performance?
Intermediate High **Exceeding** Can the learner: • create with language by combining and recombining a variety of vocabulary and structures in different ways? • at times communicate across various, or multiple, time frames?	I can create with language by (re)combining a variety of vocabulary and structures, at times across various time frames.	• You create with language by combining & recombining a variety of vocabulary and structures. • At times you communicate your message across various, or multiple, time frames.	• How might you use a range, or a greater variety, of vocabulary and structures to communicate your message? • How might you communicate across various time frames (past, present, future) throughout your performance?

Table 5.7

Performance Domain Indicators (PDIs) Assessment and Feedback Guide

Language Use Target performance level: **Intermediate High** Context: familiar, informal, formal, straight-forward Content: familiar, concrete, at times researched			
Guiding questions	Performance Domain Indicator	GLOW	GROW
Intermediate Low **Beginning** Can the learner: • create with language by combining and recombining vocabulary and structures in different ways?	I can create with language by (re)combining vocabulary and structures.	• You create with language by combining & recombining vocabulary and structures.	• How might you combine and recombine a variety of vocabulary and structures? • How might you use various, or multiple, time frames to communicate your message?
Intermediate Mid **Developing** Can the learner: • create with language by combining and recombining a variety of vocabulary and structures in different ways? • at times use various, or multiple, time frames?	I can create with language by (re)combining a variety of vocabulary and structures, and at times use various time frames.	• You create with language by combining & recombining a variety of vocabulary and structures. • At times you use various, or multiple, time frames to communicate your message.	• How might you use various, or multiple, time frames throughout your performance?
Intermediate High **Meeting** Can the learner: • create with language by combining and recombining a variety of vocabulary and structures in different ways? • at times communicate across various, or multiple, time frames?	I can create with language by (re)combining a variety of vocabulary and structures, at times across various time frames.	• You create with language by combining & recombining a variety of vocabulary and structures. • At times you communicate your message across various, or multiple, time frames.	• How might you use a range, or a greater variety, of vocabulary and structures to communicate your message? • How might you communicate across various time frames (past, present, future) throughout your performance?
Advanced Low **Exceeding** Can the learner: • use a range, or variety, of vocabulary and structures? • communicate across various time frames (past, present, future)?	I can use a range of vocabulary and structures across various frames.	• You use a range of vocabulary and structures throughout your message. • You communicate across various time frames (past, present, future) throughout your message.	• How might you use more precise vocabulary to communicate your message? • What structures might help you communicate your message more precisely within a time frame?

Table 5.8

Performance Domain Indicators (PDIs) Assessment and Feedback Guide

Language Use Target performance level: **Advanced Low** Context: familiar, unfamiliar, informal, formal, complex Content: familiar, academic, social , concrete			
Guiding questions	**Performance Domain Indicator**	**GLOW**	**GROW**
Intermediate Mid **Beginning** Can the learner: • create with language by combining and recombining a variety of vocabulary and structures in different ways? • at times use various, or multiple, time frames?	I can create with language by (re)combining a variety of vocabulary and structures, and at times use various time frames.	• You create with language by combining & recombining a variety of vocabulary and structures. • At times you use various, or multiple, time frames to communicate your message.	• How might you use various, or multiple, time frames throughout your performance?
Intermediate High **Developing** Can the learner: • create with language by combining and recombining a variety of vocabulary and structures in different ways? • at times communicate across various, or multiple, time frames?	I can create with language by (re)combining a variety of vocabulary and structures, at times across various time frames.	• You create with language by combining & recombining a variety of vocabulary and structures. • At times you communicate your message across various, or multiple, time frames.	• How might you use a range, or a greater variety, of vocabulary and structures to communicate your message? • How might you communicate across various time frames (past, present, future) throughout your performance?
Advanced Low **Meeting** Can the learner: • use a range of vocabulary and structures? • communicate across various time frames (past, present, future)?	I can use a range of vocabulary and structures across various time frames.	• You use a range of vocabulary and structures throughout your message. • You communicate across various time frames (past, present, future) throughout your message.	• How might you use more precise vocabulary to communicate your message? • What structures might help you communicate your message more precisely within a time frame?
Advanced Mid **Exceeding** Can the learner: • use a wide range of vocabulary and structures? • at times use precise vocabulary and structures? • communicate across various time frames (past, present, future)?	I can use a wide range of vocabulary and structures that are, at times, precise across various time frames.	• You use a wide range of vocabulary and structures that are, at times, precise. • You communicate across various time frames (past, present, future).	• How might you use more precise vocabulary throughout your message? • What structures might help you communicate each part of your message more precisely within each time frame?

Performance Domain Indicators within a Rubric

In order to evaluate learners' performances, the PDIs are placed within a rubric with four performance level labels: *Beginning*, *Developing*, *Meeting*, and *Exceeding* (see Table 5.9). The *Meeting* level aligns with the target performance level for the learners. These labels communicate to learners how their performance compares to the standard; learners are *Beginning* to meet, *Developing* towards, *Meeting*, or *Exceeding* their target performance level. It is important to highlight that, similar to other ACTFL publications, when placed into a rubric, these four performance levels are arranged high to low, beginning with the highest on the left. This is so that learners read the highest level of performance first. Table 5.9 illustrates this rubric alignment and arrangement for the Language Use performance domain for both the presentational and Interpersonal mode of communication.

Table 5.9
Aligning the Language Use Performance Domain Indicators (PDIs) in a Rubric

Target performance level: **Novice High** Context: familiar, informal, formal, predictable Content: familiar, everyday				
	INTERMEDIATE LOW	NOVICE HIGH	NOVICE MID	NOVICE LOW
	EXCEEDING	MEETING	DEVELOPING	BEGINNING
Performance level description	I can create with language by (re)combining vocabulary and structures.	I can use practiced vocabulary and formulaic structures, and at times (re)combine vocabulary and structures to create with language.	I can use isolated, memorized and practiced vocabulary and formulaic structures.	I can use isolated, memorized and practiced vocabulary.

Target performance level: **Intermediate Mid** Context: familiar, informal, formal, straight-forward Content: familiar, at times researched				
	INTERMEDIATE HIGH	INTERMEDIATE MID	INTERMEDIATE LOW	NOVICE HIGH
	EXCEEDING	MEETING	DEVELOPING	BEGINNING
Performance level description	I can create with language by (re)combining a variety of vocabulary and structures, at times across various time frames.	I can create with language by (re)combining a variety of vocabulary and structures, and at times use various time frames.	I can create with language by (re)combining vocabulary and structures.	I can use practiced vocabulary and formulaic structures, and at times (re)combine vocabulary and structures to create with language.

Target performance level: **Advanced Low** Context: familiar, unfamiliar, informal, formal, complex Content: familiar, academic, social, concrete				
	ADVANCED MID	**ADVANCED LOW**	**INTERMEDIATE HIGH**	**INTERMEDIATE MID**
	EXCEEDING	**MEETING**	**DEVELOPING**	**BEGINNING**
Performance level description	I can use a wide range of vocabulary and structures that are, at times, precise across various time frames.	I can use a range of vocabulary and structures across various time frames.	I can create with language by (re)combining a variety of vocabulary and structures, at times across various time frames.	I can create with language by (re)combining a variety of vocabulary and structures, and at times use various time frames.

Performance Assessment in Action

As educators our understanding of the PDIs is critical to providing effective feedback that promotes language growth in our learners. Therefore, it is important to build our capacity to use the PDIs. Here, the goal is to model how to use the Language Use PDIs to evaluate learner work, which is the basis of the GLOW and GROW feedback that is provided. The focus of this section is to evaluate learner work and provide feedback, *not* to determine a learner's proficiency level. In other words, the evaluation indicates the learner's performance is consistent with a level and provides feedback to indicate next steps for language growth.

This section demonstrates how to use these rubrics to evaluate sample presentational and interpersonal learner performances within the Novice, Intermediate, and Advanced level. These learner samples exemplify products of a summative assessment. They show evidence from learners after exposure to and practice within a unit of study. That is, learners complete these tasks following classroom instruction and multiple opportunities for formative practice on these topics. After the evaluation of each learner sample there is a model of how to provide GLOW and GROW feedback using examples from the *Performance Domain Indicators (PDIs) Assessment and Feedback Guide.*

Each learner sample:

- indicates the PDI that best aligns with the performance in the rubric.
- uses the evaluation to explain what the learner can do in this performance sample.
- models how to provide GLOW and GROW feedback using examples from the *Performance Domain Indicators (PDIs) Assessment and Feedback Guide.*

LEARNERS PERFORMING WITHIN THE NOVICE LEVEL

Mode of communication: *Presentational*
Target performance level: **Novice High**
Context: familiar, formal, predictable
Content: familiar, everyday

Novice Task: For the hallway display, select one of the people we have studied in this unit. Create a descriptive writing in which you compare how you are similar in order to highlight what you have in common, and contrast how you are different in order to feature how you each make use of your attributes in our diverse world.

LEARNER SAMPLE RESPONSE

Hey! My name is Pari. I 12 years old. I am Persian.
Ingrid is sports. Ingrid like to dance. I am not to dance. I am to swim.
I is shy. Ingrid is shy. I is play sports
I am to read. Ingrid like to dance.
I am to draw. Ingrid like to dance. Well, see ya later!

Evaluation & Explanation

LANGUAGE USE			
EXCEEDING	**MEETING**	**DEVELOPING**	**BEGINNING**
I can create with language by (re)combining vocabulary and structures.	I can use practiced vocabulary and formulaic structures, and at times (re)combine vocabulary and structures to create with language.	I can use isolated, memorized and practiced vocabulary and formulaic structures.	I can use isolated, memorized and practiced vocabulary.

Evaluation: In this performance sample, the learner relies primarily on memorized vocabulary and formulaic structures to communicate their message. The learner relies heavily on the same vocabulary (*dance, shy, sports*) and formulaic structures (*I am, Ingrid like*) to give information about themselves and Ingrid. The learner attempts to combine vocabulary in a different way one time (*play sports*), but no other attempts to create with language are observed. Overall, the learner relies primarily on highly practiced vocabulary and structures to communicate this message.

Feedback

- GLOW: You use memorized and practiced vocabulary and formulaic structures to give information about yourself and Ingrid.
- GROW: How might you create with language by combining & recombining words in different ways?

LEARNERS PERFORMING WITHIN THE NOVICE LEVEL

Mode of communication: *Interpersonal*
Target performance level: **Novice High**
Context: familiar, informal, predictable
Content: familiar, everyday

Novice Task: Chat with your new classmate to find out how you both may be similar to and/or different from each other.

LEARNER SAMPLE RESPONSE

Learner 1: Hello.

Learner 2: Hey! How's it going?

Learner 1: Good. And you?

Learner 2: Very good. What do you like more, sports or ski?

Learner 1: Ski.

Learner 2: Me too (*points to self*)! I like to ski. A lot. Um, my favorite...my favorite sport...in the...in the winter. Um...do you like to sing?

Learner 1: I don't like to sing.

Learner 2: Do you like to do...soccer in it's hot or it's cold?

Learner 1: Um...repeat?

Learner 2: Do you like to do soccer in it's hot or it's cold?

Learner 1: ...

Learner 2: Do you like to do soccer... (*kicks leg*)...in it's hot or it's cold?

Learner 1: No...comprehend (*shrugs*).

Learner 2: Do you like...soccer (*kicks leg*)...in it's hot (*fans face*) or um... it's cold, brrr (*shivers and rubs arms*)?

Learner 1: Oh! Um, yes. I like...um, hot?

Learner 2: (*Nods*)

Learner 1: Yes. Hot.

Learner 2: Cool! Me...me too!

Learner 1: Ride bike?

Learner 2: Well, sometimes. Yes, I like to ride a bike. Sometimes. In the...in the summer?

Learner 1: Ok, bye.

Learner 2: See ya later!

Evaluation & Explanation

LANGUAGE USE | LEARNER 1			
EXCEEDING	MEETING	DEVELOPING	BEGINNING
I can create with language by (re)combining vocabulary and structures.	I can use practiced vocabulary and formulaic structures, and at times (re)combine vocabulary and structures to create with language.	I can use isolated, memorized and practiced vocabulary and formulaic structures.	I can use isolated, memorized and practiced vocabulary.

Evaluation: In this performance sample, Learner 1 uses isolated, memorized, and practiced vocabulary to communicate their message. Learner 1 responds with memorized and practiced vocabulary in isolation; that is, the responses consist of one word or phrase (*Ski, Yes. Hot.*). Learner 1 uses one formulaic structure (*I don't like...*) but provides no other evidence of formulaic structures in their performance.

Feedback

- GLOW: You use memorized and practiced vocabulary in isolation to communicate your message to your partner.
- GROW: How might you add the formulaic structure *I like* to your responses to communicate more information to your partner?

LANGUAGE USE | LEARNER 2			
EXCEEDING	MEETING	DEVELOPING	BEGINNING
I can create with language by (re)combining vocabulary and structures.	I can use practiced vocabulary and formulaic structures, and at times (re)combine vocabulary and structures to create with language.	I can use isolated, memorized, and practiced vocabulary and formulaic structures.	I can use isolated, memorized, and practiced vocabulary.

Evaluation: In this performance sample, Learner 2 uses practiced vocabulary and formulaic structures to communicate their message. Learner 2 uses practiced vocabulary such as activities (*sports, sing, soccer*), rejoinders (*Me too! Cool!*), weather (*it's hot or it's cold*), and seasons (*in the winter, in the summer*). At times Learner 2 combines vocabulary in different ways (*soccer in it's hot or it's cold, my favorite sport...in the... in the winter*). These attempts are not always successful in terms of accuracy (*soccer in it's hot or it's cold*). Additionally, the learner relies largely on combining separate memorized phrases together (*my favorite, in the winter*) rather than recombining vocabulary and structures in a novel way. Learner 2 uses formulaic structures (*What do you like more...? Do you like...? I like*) to craft their questions and responses.

Feedback

- GLOW: You are beginning to create with language by combining and recombining vocabulary/structures in different ways.
- GROW: How might you create with language by combining and recombining vocabulary and structures throughout your performance?

LEARNERS PERFORMING WITHIN THE INTERMEDIATE LEVEL

Mode of communication: *Presentational*
Target performance level: **Intermediate Mid**
Context: familiar, formal, straight-forward
Content: familiar, researched

Intermediate Task: As part of an Earth Day campaign in your community, write a formal letter to an influential leader advocating for change that would address an environmental issue that you have learned about.

LEARNER SAMPLE RESPONSE

Honorable Mayor Wilson,

Help! My name is Kai Meyer. I live in Elmdale now. I like to live in Elmdale We have strong engaged for community here. Since 3 years, Elmdale won the "Best city in the USA". We try to win that again and we could. We could to do more of to clean up and beautify our city. Maybe have like the BUGA garden show in Germany. Different cities host and make big gardens. And plant trees. Like big plant show at the fair.

A lot in Elmdale is full of garbage. When I run on hiking trails I see a lot of garbage. Nature reserves, like Forest Park, have more garbage. It is not pretty. I remember you to since 3 years. It would be great if mentality to our city. Run people need clean trails. They are impacted.

Here are things do. We could the volunteers clean up the parks. This would also help the people in the city do it. Other volunteers could the large places. The city could have event. The event would be "Consciousness about Garbage in Plymouth"

We could say, plant more trees in the neighborhoods. This would give back the trees we take for construction. Maybe be a tree hugger? Plants and gardens too but for now trees. When we plant more trees, this make our community a better place if we plant more trees. Plant now! Act now!

Sincerely,
Kai Meyer

Evaluation & Explanation

LANGUAGE USE			
EXCEEDING	**MEETING**	**DEVELOPING**	**BEGINNING**
I can create with language by (re)combining a variety of vocabulary and structures, at times across various time frames.	I can create with language by (re)combining a variety of vocabulary and structures, and at times use various time frames.	I can create with language by (re)combining vocabulary and structures.	I can use practiced vocabulary and formulaic structures, and at times (re)combine vocabulary and structures to create with language.

Evaluation: In this performance sample, the learner creates with language at times across various time frames to communicate their message. The learner combines and recombines a variety of vocabulary (*city, clean up, plants, trees*) in a variety of ways and contexts to communicate their message. The learner is also able to, at times, use structures across various time frames (present: *is, have, are, plant*; future: *we could, this would help, volunteers could, this would give back*). Overall, in this performance the learner creates with language and structures at times across various time frames.

Feedback

- GLOW: You create with language by combining & recombining a variety of vocabulary and structures.
- GROW: How might you communicate across various time frames (past, present, future) throughout your performance?

LEARNERS PERFORMING WITHIN THE INTERMEDIATE LEVEL

Mode of communication: *Interpersonal*
Target performance level: **Intermediate Mid**
Context: familiar, informal, straight-forward
Content: familiar, researched

Intermediate Task: After reading and viewing texts to learn about ways we can implement change, select an organization that works to better their community. Discuss your organization with a partner to learn more about the organizations you have each selected, why you selected yours, and how your organizations implement change for others.

LEARNER SAMPLE RESPONSE

Learner 1: Hi Paz!

Learner 2: Hi! How are you?

Learner 1: I'm alright. What is your organization called?

Learner 2: My organization is called the Family Stay House...But no place like home.

Learner 1: How interesting (*nods*)!

Learner 2: What is your organization called?

Learner 1: The organization...er, sorry...my organization favorite is called Renewing the Countryside.

Learner 2: Oh, how fantastic! What does it do? Renew, reuse, recycle (*laughs*)?

Learner 1: Renewing the Countryside gives money for the...for the farmers and help the children of poor families in rural communities.

Learner 2: Great! Great (*nods*)!

Learner 1: What does your organization try to do (*tilts head*)?

Learner 2: The Family Stay House tries to support and help families, families that need the help economically paying for pro-proced...when the children are sick. Where is the organization?

Learner 1: The organization...er, sorry...my organization favorite is called Renewing the Countryside.

Learner 2: My organization, um, is in the city.

Learner 1: Great! Did it do something in the past?

Learner 2: Every year, the Race for the Kids, um remember money for organization, um, to pay for the, um, pro-proced-procedures.

Learner 1: How cool (*smiles*)!

Learner 2: Um, yes, yes, yes (*nods*). Um, How many people serves the organization?

Learner 1: Many people serves the organization in the city because everyone wants to help the, the rural communities.

Learner 2: Yes, great!

Learner 1: I like your organization a lot. How can I help your organization? I pitch in?

Learner 2: Oh, how fantastic (*eyes widen*)! You can work as a volunteer – reading books to children, playing sports with the children, donating money and getting money for the organization.

Learner 1: How fun! Why should I help?

Learner 2: Um, because...because , in my opinion, it is important to help the people.

Learner 1: Great, great, yes (*nods*)!

Learner 2: What they do for your organization?

Learner 1: Um you can get money for the organization or you can donate. A little bit goes a long way!

Learner 2: I think so.

Learner 1: Bye (*waves*)!

Learner 2: Bye (*waves*)!

Learner 1: Thanks for talking with me.

Learner 2: I'll see you laters. Thanks for talking with me.

Evaluation & Explanation

LANGUAGE USE | LEARNER 1			
EXCEEDING	**MEETING**	**DEVELOPING**	**BEGINNING**
I can create with language by (re)combining a variety of vocabulary and structures, at times across various time frames.	I can create with language by (re)combining a variety of vocabulary and structures, and at times use various time frames.	I can create with language by (re)combining vocabulary and structures.	I can use practiced vocabulary and formulaic structures, and at times (re)combine vocabulary and structures to create with language.

Evaluation: In this performance sample, Learner 1 creates with language using a variety of (re)combined vocabulary. Vocabulary and structures such as *organization (my organization favorite, serves the organization, get money for the organization)* and *help (help the children, help the rural communities, help your organization)* are combined and recombined in a variety of different ways. The learner primarily uses one time frame – the present tense – and corresponding structures. The learner is only able to use another time frame – the past – once (*Did it do something in the past?*). However, Learner 1 is able to use an empty subject pronoun (*it*) and possessive pronouns (*my, your*) to demonstrate greater flexibility in how they use and apply grammatical structures when clarifying the word *organization*. Overall, Learner 1 is able to combine and recombine a variety of vocabulary and structures within one time frame to communicate their message.

Feedback

- GLOW: You create with language by combining and recombining a variety of vocabulary and structures.
- GROW: How might you use various, or multiple, time frames throughout your performance?

LANGUAGE USE | LEARNER 2			
EXCEEDING	**MEETING**	**DEVELOPING**	**BEGINNING**
I can create with language by (re)combining a variety of vocabulary and structures, at times across various time frames.	I can create with language by (re)combining a variety of vocabulary and structures, and at times use various time frames.	I can create with language by (re)combining vocabulary and structures.	I can use practiced vocabulary and formulaic structures, and at times (re)combine vocabulary and structures to create with language.

Evaluation: In this performance sample, Learner 2 creates with language using a variety of (re)combined vocabulary. Vocabulary and ideas such as *organization (my organization, your organization, money for the organization, serves the organization), money, (remember money, donating money and getting money)*, and *help (help families, help economically paying, to help the people)* are combined and recombined in a variety of ways. The learner primarily uses one time frame – the present tense – and corresponding structures. However, Learner 2 is able to use an empty subject pronoun (*it*) and possessive pronouns (*my, your*) to demonstrate greater flexibility in how they use and apply grammatical structures with the word *organization*. Overall, Learner 2 is able to combine and recombine vocabulary and structures within one time frame to communicate their message.

Feedback

- GLOW: You create with language by combining and recombining a variety of vocabulary and structures.
- GROW: How might you use various, or multiple, time frames throughout your performance?

LEARNERS PERFORMING WITHIN THE ADVANCED LEVEL

Mode of communication: *Presentational*
Target performance level: **Advanced Low**
Context: familiar, informal, complex
Content: familiar, academic, social, professional, concrete

Advanced Task: Based on the movie, write a diary entry from the perspective of one of the baseball players that includes their reflections of the recruitment practices of professional baseball leagues.

LEARNER SAMPLE RESPONSE

> Dear Diary,
>
> I cannot believe that this investigation about my age is still going on! It is just not fair! I am not a liar! How much analyses have I to do? Because of this, I did not get the chance to sign when I turned 16 years. In the Professional Baseball League they think that all us players are liars. There are some that lies, but there are a lot of us who tells the truth.
>
> But what are they suppose to do, if only one year older means you are worth $1 million less? Seriously, one year? The PBL uses us for our poverty. It's not fair that they treat us differently, pay us differently just because we live in poorer country. Why I don't make money because I am a great baseball player? Why am I the cheap export? If I am in power, I would talks with the representatives to work for changes in recruiting regulations, like age restrictions and equal pay.
>
> Yet I know that if I work hard, I will get a contract of any price which, for me, is the way out of poverty. It is also my family's way out of poverty because they are depending on me. The first thing I take on is buy my parents a house so they never have to worry about housing ever again! I just have to be patient. All I want to do is play baseball- it's what I love, it's what I borned to do, it's all I have ever done.
>
> Let's play ball!
> -Mike

Evaluation & Explanation

LANGUAGE USE			
EXCEEDING	**MEETING**	**DEVELOPING**	**BEGINNING**
I can use a wide range of vocabulary and structures that are, at times, precise across various time frames.	I can use a range of vocabulary and structures across various time frames.	I can create with language by (re)combining a variety of vocabulary and structures, at times across various time frames.	I can create with language by (re)combining a variety of vocabulary and structures, and at times use various time frames.

Evaluation: In this performance sample, the learner uses a range of vocabulary for this specialized topic of the politics of sports: *poverty, recruiting, regulations, league, restrictions, equal pay, contract* and *housing.* The learner also uses a range of structures such as phrasal verbs/nouns *(way out of, depending on, to worry about)*, "if" clauses *(if only one year older, if I am, if I work hard)*, and passive voice *(what are they suppose to do, what I borned to)*. In addition, this learner clearly demonstrates their ability to communicate across various time frames. Even though the majority of this letter is expressed in the present time frame, there are multiple uses the past *(I did not, I turned 16 years, it's what I borned to do...)* and future times frames *(If I am in power, I would talks, if I work hard, I will get a contract)* that are interwoven throughout the message.

Feedback

- GLOW: You use a range of vocabulary and structures to communicate your message.
- GROW: What structures might help you communicate your message more precisely when expressing hypothetical ideas within the future time frame?

LEARNERS PERFORMING WITHIN THE ADVANCED LEVEL

Mode of communication: *Interpersonal*
Target performance level: **Advanced Low**
Context: familiar, informal, complex
Content: familiar, academic, social, concrete

Advanced Task: After visiting a Monarch butterfly sanctuary, you and a friend discuss your reactions to learning about the monarch butterfly migrations and how it's being threatened.

LEARNER SAMPLE RESPONSE

Learner 1: So, what did ya think?... of the butterfly sanctuary?

Learner 2: I think that... um, the butterflies, the monarch butterflies are incredible. And these places, these sanctuaries, well, they are magical. I don´t know much things about the butterflies and their migrations before now.

Learner 1: Uhm... Same here. What fascinates me is how millions of butterflies, these tiny insects, come from all over the continent..., and to end up in these sanctuaries in Mexico, ya know?

Learner 2: Yeah, it is incredible. These places, they are so important to, to their migration process. They need these sanctuaries for, um.., this is where they sleep during the winter months.

Learner 1: Exactly. These sanctuaries are where the monarchs hibernate, so they are vital to this natural phenomenon. What's more, is the monarch's cultural influence on, like, the festival for Day of the Dead. For them, the butterflies represent the souls of their loved ones, like the butterflies (*air quotes*) are their loved ones coming back.

Learner 2: It's interesting how, how nature can influence cultural practices, like, what you said, about Day of the Dead. (...)

Learner 1: Right. This is why I am glad to have learned that they are taking measures to, um, conserve these spaces, um, these spaces that are their habitats. Right?

Learner 2: Yes. They are protecting against destruction because of people cutting down trees illegally. But, I understand why they have to do it.

Learner 1: How so? What do you mean by that?

Learner 2: Well, some peoples depends on cutting down the trees, because they need that money to buy food and clothes for their family.

Learner 1: Ah ha (*nods head*). Now I understand. Yeah, they are between a rock and a hard place. Ya know? I don't know what I would do if... if I was in that situation where, where my family depended on the income from illegal logging. What would you do?

Learner 2: It's difficult to say what I would do too, especially because there are no other good options for them, to have, to have different jobs.

Learner 1: And, on the other hand, it's not just about to conserve the sanctuaries. For example, the use of chemicals... or pesticides in fields kills butterflies along the migration routes. It's kind of gotten out of hand. I'm not sure what can be done.

Learner 2: Well, one thing we can do is plant more milkweed, which is a flower that the butterflies depend on for food.

Evaluation & Explanation

LANGUAGE USE | LEARNER 1			
EXCEEDING	**MEETING**	**DEVELOPING**	**BEGINNING**
I can use a wide range of vocabulary and structures that are, at times, precise across various time frames.	I can use a range of vocabulary and structures across various time frames.	I can create with language by (re)combining a variety of vocabulary and structures, at times across various time frames.	I can create with language by (re)combining a variety of vocabulary and structures, and at times use various time frames.

Evaluation: In this performance sample, Learner 1 uses a wide range of vocabulary *(sanctuary/sanctuaries, continent, hibernate, vital, natural phenomenon, cultural influence, souls, measures, conserve, habitats, income, pesticides, migration routes)*. This learner also uses a range of structures like phrasal verbs *(to end up, depended on)*, the subject pronoun "what" *(what fascinates me, what's more, what can be done)* and demonstrative pronouns *(what do you mean by that, this is why)*. Additionally, this learner uses various time frames. This includes the past *(What did ya think?, I am glad to have learned)*, the present *(what fascinates me, these sanctuaries are, the butterflies represent…)*, and the future time frames *(what I would do, What would you do?, what can be done)*. At times the learner is able to select structures that communicate a function more precisely within a time frame. For example, the learner uses the present progressive tense *(that they are taking measures)* to indicate work that is ongoing, as well as use the conditional within an *if* clause to create a hypothetical situation *(what would you do?)*.

Feedback

- GLOW: You use a wide range of vocabulary and structures that are, at times, precise.
- GROW: How might you use more precise vocabulary throughout your message?

LANGUAGE USE | LEARNER 2			
EXCEEDING	**MEETING**	**DEVELOPING**	**BEGINNING**
I can use a wide range of vocabulary and structures that are, at times, precise across various time frames.	I can use a range of vocabulary and structures across various time frames.	I can create with language by (re)combining a variety of vocabulary and structures, at times across various time frames.	I can create with language by (re)combining a variety of vocabulary and structures, and at times use various time frames.

Evaluation: In this performance sample, Learner 2 creates with language using a variety of (re)combined vocabulary, and, at times, uses various time frames. This learner combines and recombines vocabulary, such as *butterflies (butterflies, monarch butterflies)*, *migration (their migrations, migration process)*, and *depend (peoples depends on, butterflies depend on)*. The learner uses the present tense, but can do so using a variety of subject pronouns *(I think that, butterflies are, they are, it is)*. At times the learner uses language and structures to refer to other time frames, such as the past time frame *(what you said)* as well as the future *(what I would do)*. Overall, the learner is able to combine and recombine vocabulary and structures, and, at times, use various time frames.

Feedback

- GLOW: You create with language by combining & recombining a variety of vocabulary and structures.
- GROW: How might you use various, or multiple, time frames throughout your performance?

YOUR TURN

LEARNING TARGETS CHECK:	
I can	☐ evaluate learner work using the Performance Domain Indicators (PDIs). ☐ give effective feedback using the Language Use PDIs.

Now it is your turn to practice evaluating learner performances and providing feedback. Remember, learners complete these performance tasks following classroom instruction and multiple opportunities for formative practice on these topics. In this section, use the Language Use PDIs to indicate the level of performance that best corresponds with the following presentational and interpersonal learner performance samples. Then provide each learner GLOW and GROW feedback. You may want to use the *Performance Domain Indicators (PDIs) Assessment and Feedback Guide* to help guide your evaluation and feedback of the learner's performance in the Language Use performance domain.

Then, turn to APPENDIX A | Language Use (p.425-p.430) to compare your evaluation and feedback to one provided by the authors. Reflect on how your evaluation and feedback was similar and/or different and why. You can do this individually and/or with your colleagues (for example, with a Professional Learning Community (PLC)). This exercise can be an opportunity for rich discussion to help increase inter-rater reliability among educators.

LEARNERS PERFORMING WITHIN THE NOVICE LEVEL

Mode of communication: *Presentational*
Target performance level: **Novice High**
Context: familiar, formal, predictable
Content: familiar, everyday

Novice Task: For the hallway display, select one of the people we have studied in this unit. Create a descriptive writing in which you compare how you are similar in order to highlight what you have in common, and contrast how you are different in order to feature how you each make use of your attributes in our diverse world.

LEARNER SAMPLE RESPONSE

Greetings! My name is Leo. I am 12 years old.

Naiomi is 24 years old. She is Diné (Navajo).

Naiomi & I is similar. Naiomi is sports-minded because to skateboard. I do not like to skateboard. I like hockey but no skateboarding. I like hockey in the winter with my friends.

Naiomi is hard-working. Naiomi really likes to practice skateboarding. How interesting! I like hockey.

Naiomi not is lazy. She likes to work for more skate parks. How important! Many people to need more skate parks. Many people to need more hockey parks too. Is a problem. How important!

Naiomi and I is different but equal. Thank you for read!

Evaluation & Explanation

LANGUAGE USE			
EXCEEDING	**MEETING**	**DEVELOPING**	**BEGINNING**
I can create with language by (re)combining vocabulary and structures.	I can use practiced vocabulary and formulaic structures, and at times (re)combine vocabulary and structures to create with language.	I can use isolated, memorized and practiced vocabulary and formulaic structures.	I can use isolated, memorized and practiced vocabulary.

Evaluation:

Feedback:

- GLOW:
- GROW:

Turn to APPENDIX A | Language Use (p.425) to compare your evaluation and feedback to one provided by the authors.

LEARNERS PERFORMING WITHIN THE NOVICE LEVEL

Mode of communication: *Interpersonal*
Target performance level: **Novice High**
Context: familiar, informal, predictable
Content: familiar, everyday

Novice Task: Chat with your new classmate to find out how you both may be similar and/or different.

LEARNER SAMPLE RESPONSE

Learner 1: Um...Sports?

Learner 2: Yes (*nods*), I like sports a LOT (*smiles*). My favorite! And you?

Learner 1: Yes (*nods*).

Learner 2: What do you like more, baseball or football?

Learner 1: Baseball. I...mmm...baseball...yes. And you, sir?

Learner 2: I like baseball AND I like football! I like to play baseball in the summer. I like to watch football in the fall.

Learner 1: Ok. Um, television?

Learner 2: Yes, I like TV. I really like to watch sports on TV. And you?

Learner 1: Very good (*nods*).

Learner 2: Ok. Do you like to read?

Learner 1: Um...repeat?

Learner 2: Do you...do you like...to read?

Learner 1: ...

Learner 2: Do you like...to read?

Learner 1: Um... (*shrugs shoulders*)

Learner 2: Um, do you like to read? Um (*gestures with hands*) read...read. Um, books?

Learner 1: Oh! Yes (*nods*). I...I...yes.

Learner 2: Ok. I...um...I...too (*points to self, nods*)! I like read books. Um, do you like to swim?

Learner 1: Repeat?

Learner 2: Do you like to swim (*gestures swimming movements with arms*)?

Learner 1: Oh, yes (*nods*)! Yes, swim...yes! And you, sir?

Learner 2: Cool! I too. I like to swim in the summer. Sometimes I like to swim in the winter in the...um...in the...yeah.

Learner 1: ...

Learner 2: Ok, well, thanks! Bye (*waves*)!

Learner 1: Bye (*waves*)!

Evaluation & Explanation

LANGUAGE USE | LEARNER 1			
EXCEEDING	**MEETING**	**DEVELOPING**	**BEGINNING**
I can create with language by (re)combining vocabulary and structures.	I can use practiced vocabulary and formulaic structures, and at times (re)combine vocabulary and structures to create with language.	I can use isolated, memorized and practiced vocabulary and formulaic structures.	I can use isolated, memorized and practiced vocabulary.

Evaluation:

Feedback:

- GLOW:
- GROW:

LANGUAGE USE | LEARNER 2			
EXCEEDING	**MEETING**	**DEVELOPING**	**BEGINNING**
I can create with language by (re)combining vocabulary and structures.	I can use practiced vocabulary and formulaic structures, and at times (re)combine vocabulary and structures to create with language.	I can use isolated, memorized and practiced vocabulary and formulaic structures.	I can use isolated, memorized and practiced vocabulary.

Evaluation:

Feedback:

- GLOW:
- GROW:

Turn to APPENDIX A | Language Use (p.426) to compare your evaluation and feedback to one provided by the authors.

LEARNERS PERFORMING WITHIN THE INTERMEDIATE LEVEL

Mode of communication: *Presentational*
Target performance level: **Intermediate Mid**
Context: familiar, formal, straight-forward
Content: familiar, researched

Intermediate Task: As part of an Earth Day campaign in your community, write a formal letter to an influential leader advocating for change that would address an environmental issue that you have learned about.

LEARNER SAMPLE

Dear Mr. President,

Did you heared, one of the major problems environmental in the world is the increase of the ocean level as result of global warming. The increase of the ocean level is a problem Many Carribean countries are sinking and that is destroying the work or life of many people.

People are constructing sea barriers for flooding. One other thing Carribean countries are doing is transport help now, not help in the future. For the future, it's important that the world, specifically the United States, reduce the greenhouse gas emissions because a rise in greenhouse gases cause more global warming. As a result, the icebergs melt and the sea level rise. The problem is very important for you.

One example of this problem is of a little country in the Pacific Ocean. The country is Tuvalu. Tuvalu is home for 11,000 people and increase of sea level is a very big problem for this country. In the last decade, Tuvalu lost 2 islands a the ocean. This is very bad for that many people would have eliminate outside of their house and in 50 years, the whole country absent.

A protect millions of people and the health of our environments, I would think that is important you reduce the emissions greenhouse gas for the future of the world. Also, I would think that a good solution for now is <u>do</u> construct many sea barriers and raise to support for people and families close to the coast.

Thanks,
Avery

Evaluation & Explanation

LANGUAGE USE			
EXCEEDING	**MEETING**	**DEVELOPING**	**BEGINNING**
I can create with language by (re)combining a variety of vocabulary and structures, at times across various time frames.	I can create with language by (re)combining a variety of vocabulary and structures, and at times use various time frames.	I can create with language by (re)combining vocabulary and structures.	I can use practiced vocabulary and formulaic structures, and at times (re)combine vocabulary and structures to create with language.

Evaluation:

Feedback:

- GLOW:
- GROW:

Turn to APPENDIX A | Language Use (p.427) to compare your evaluation and feedback to one provided by the authors.

LEARNERS PERFORMING WITHIN THE INTERMEDIATE LEVEL

Mode of communication: *Interpersonal*
Target performance level: **Intermediate Mid**
Context: familiar, informal, straight-forward
Content: familiar, researched

Intermediate Task: After reading and viewing texts to learn about ways we can implement change, select an organization that works to better their community. Discuss your organization with a partner to learn more about the organizations you have each selected, why you selected yours, and how your organizations implement change for others.

LEARNER SAMPLE RESPONSE

Learner 1: Hi Kim (*waves*)!

Learner 2: Hi Hai (*waves*)!

Learner 1: What's up?

Learner 2: Um, not a lot (*shrugs shoulders*). And you?

Learner 1: Not a lot, not a lot. What is the name of your organization?

Learner 2: My organization is called Special Olympics.

Learner 1: Yes (*nods*) and what does that organization do?

Learner 2: Repeat please?

Learner 1: What does that organization do?

Learner 2: Me organization to try, um, to play sports with people with special you need...people with special needs.

Learner 1: How fantastic (*smiles*)!

Learner 2: What organization you work a volunteer?

Learner 1: My organization is called the Blizzard Foundation.

Learner 2: Very well (*nods*). Where is the organization?

Learner 1: My organization is in North Minneapolis. And...but it tries to work in all parts of Minnesota.

Learner 2: Very well (*nods*).

Learner 1: What did organization do in the past?

Learner 2: In the past, the Special Olympics to play sports...baseball, soccer, and basketball with a lot of people with special you need and...puts on the Polar Plunge.

Learner 1: Yes (*nods*).

Learner 2: What did your organization do in the past year?

Learner 1: My organization works as help people that want to play baseball but I can't buy. In the past, my organization worked with Miracle League. The children of Miracle League love baseball and it was very fun.

Learner 2: Very well. What is the priorities of the organization?

Learner 1: The first priority of my organization is donates money to children and families that can't buy baseball. And you, what is the priority?

Learner 2: Me priorities organization is helps people with special you need...did...no...has very fun.

Learner 1: And you volunteered with your organization in the past?

Learner 2: Ah no (*shakes head*), but I am going helps in the future.

Learner 1: Yes.

Learner 2: Bye (*waves*).

Learner 1: Ah, hold on.

Learner 2: Sorry.

Learner 1: How can I help your organization?

Learner 2: Repeat please?

Learner 1: How can I help your organization?

Learner 2: You work a volunteer to play sports with people with special you need and to donate money.

Learner 1: That's great! Thanks for talking with me!

Learner 2: Thanks, sir.

Evaluation & Explanation

LANGUAGE USE | LEARNER 1			
EXCEEDING	**MEETING**	**DEVELOPING**	**BEGINNING**
I can create with language by (re)combining a variety of vocabulary and structures, at times across various time frames.	I can create with language by (re)combining a variety of vocabulary and structures, and at times use various time frames.	I can create with language by (re)combining vocabulary and structures.	I can use practiced vocabulary and formulaic structures, and at times (re)combine vocabulary and structures to create with language.

Evaluation:

Feedback:

- GLOW:
- GROW:

LANGUAGE USE | LEARNER 2			
EXCEEDING	**MEETING**	**DEVELOPING**	**BEGINNING**
I can create with language by (re)combining a variety of vocabulary and structures, at times across various time frames.	I can create with language by (re)combining a variety of vocabulary and structures, and at times use various time frames.	I can create with language by (re)combining vocabulary and structures.	I can use practiced vocabulary and formulaic structures, and at times (re)combine vocabulary and structures to create with language.

Evaluation:

Feedback:

- GLOW:
- GROW:

Turn to APPENDIX A | Language Use (p.428) to compare your evaluation and feedback to one provided by the authors.

LEARNERS PERFORMING WITHIN THE ADVANCED LEVEL

Mode of communication: *Presentational*
Target performance level: **Advanced Low**
Context: familiar, informal, complex
Content: familiar, academic, social, professional, concrete

Advanced Task: Based on the movie, write a diary entry from the perspective of one of the baseball players that includes their reflections of the recruitment practices of professional baseball leagues.

LEARNER SAMPLE RESPONSE

Dear Diary,

I am angry! Even that my results are conclusive, I still have to do more tests. This means that I can lose my chance to sign with a professional baseball team. Out of all the 105 players, I have the best chance. It was to be a dream come true! However, because my tests are no decided, it is a controversy for teams to sign with me. I dreamed this my whole life. It's what I sacrificed so many years. What the Professional Baseball League has did to me, I think it an injustice. I did all those tests that show that I am 16 years and I did not lie. In fact my family gived the PBL all the documents that they needed. The PBL did no need the same documents or the same tests of the other baseball players. It's not fair that we give you more information. And because of this, no one wants to sign me.

If I were a different baseball player, I would no have to take the tests. I just want to be baseball player. I can help my family too. I wants to try to be as good as the other players, even better. I hope some team signs me. I won't accept that I've lost the opportunity. I will fight for my opportunity. I will not back down. Someday I will win the World Series.

Hugs, Mikey

Evaluation & Explanation

LANGUAGE USE			
EXCEEDING	**MEETING**	**DEVELOPING**	**BEGINNING**
I can use a wide range of vocabulary and structures that are, at times, precise across various time frames.	I can use a range of vocabulary and structures across various time frames.	I can create with language by (re)combining a variety of vocabulary and structures, at times across various time frames.	I can create with language by (re)combining a variety of vocabulary and structures, and at times use various time frames.

Evaluation:

Feedback:

- GLOW:
- GROW:

Turn to APPENDIX A | Language Use (p.429) to compare your evaluation and feedback to one provided by the authors.

LEARNERS PERFORMING WITHIN THE ADVANCED LEVEL

Mode of communication: *Interpersonal*
Target performance level: **Advanced Low**
Context: familiar, unfamiliar, informal, formal, complex
Content: familiar, academic, social, concrete

Advanced Task: After visiting a Monarch butterfly sanctuary, you and a friend discuss your reactions to learning about the monarch butterfly migrations and how it's being threatened.

LEARNER SAMPLE RESPONSE

Learner 1: Hey *(waves hand).*

Learner 2: Hey.

Learner 1: So, what do you think about what we learned, um, about the sanctuaries?

Learner 2: Well, to be honest, I didn't even know of them. I had no idea that there are places like these where millions of butterflies goes to, to hibernate, like clusters of them. It was incredible to see.

Learner 1: Agreed *(widens eyes).* It blew my mind to see them togethers on only a tree branch. And that there are too many that their weight may... may... break the tree branch! It's a place that I want to go..., to, like, to experience it.

Learner 2: Yeah, I wonder how it would be *(tilts head)*? I think that I might be scared, because of these tiny insects, ya know? I don't know how I could feel. You?

Learner 1: Huh. Yeah *(shrugs shoulders).* It makes me nervous, I guess... Um, well, the sanctuaries are importants to the lifecycle of these butterflies. With no reserves, there would no be butterflies.

Learner 2: Uh huh. It was interesting to learn that only here in this specific places does it have the perfect temperature, the perfect humidity and everything. Like everything is done only for the butterflies in this place and that is why they all come every year to spend the winter.

Learner 1: I know *(raises eyebrows)*! It's a perfect ecosystem, which me.., which makes me sad that peoples cut down the trees not legally in those areas, meaning they destroy their habitat.

Learner 2: I wonder if they do not knows about how these sanctuaries are important. Or, maybe they have no choice because they need to earn a living *(shrugs and raises hands).* But it's not just this. There is also climate change and the use of pesticides that, that contribute to the destruction of the habitats.

Learner 1: Oh, for sure *(nods head)*! For example, when the farmers there use pesticides in the fields for the migratory routes, the butterflies get, um... um..., sick *(looks at Learner 2)*?

Learner 2: Sick *(tilts head)*?

Learner 1: Yeah, they get sicks because the pesticides on their food.

Learner 2: Ah! You mean poison.

Learner 1: Yes, poison. They get poisons when they eat the flower, the, um... the milkweed.

Learner 2: Yes, there are many threats to this species. Well *(sighs)*, I only hope that they can protect it so one day in the future I can travel there and visit the sanctuaries.

Learner 1: Ha *(laughs)*! Yes, of course.

Evaluation & Explanation

LANGUAGE USE | LEARNER 1			
EXCEEDING	**MEETING**	**DEVELOPING**	**BEGINNING**
I can use a wide range of vocabulary and structures that are, at times, precise across various time frames.	I can use a range of vocabulary and structures across various time frames.	I can create with language by (re)combining a variety of vocabulary and structures, at times across various time frames.	I can create with language by (re)combining a variety of vocabulary and structures, and at times use various time frames.

Evaluation:

Feedback:

- GLOW:
- GROW:

LANGUAGE USE | LEARNER 2			
EXCEEDING	**MEETING**	**DEVELOPING**	**BEGINNING**
I can use a wide range of vocabulary and structures that are, at times, precise across various time frames.	I can use a range of vocabulary and structures across various time frames.	I can create with language by (re)combining a variety of vocabulary and structures, at times across various time frames.	I can create with language by (re)combining a variety of vocabulary and structures, and at times use various time frames.

Evaluation:

Feedback:

- GLOW:
- GROW:

Turn to APPENDIX A | Language Use (p.430) to compare your evaluation and feedback to one provided by the authors.

Learning Experiences to Facilitate Learner Growth

Once educators have clarified for learners the goals of performance and provided feedback, learners need learning experiences to help them *understand* the Language Use performance domain and PDIs as well as *develop* their language performance. Learning experiences to *understand* the performance domain are listed first, followed by learning experiences to *develop* learner performance. Each learning experience includes *Learner outcomes* (what learners can do upon successful completion of the experience) and an outline of logistical components *(time, preparation, materials, instructions). Alternatives* and *Differentiation* offer ways to personalize the experience for a variety of learners. Each learning experience includes short examples, often including learners' work, to help educators visualize each learning experience. The learning experiences can be used with an entire class of learners as a way to introduce and focus learner work on a particular performance domain. Learning experiences can also be assigned to learners by educators or self-selected by learners themselves for further practice within a performance domain. These examples can serve as a springboard for educators to develop their own learning experiences for each performance domain when working with their learners.

LEARNING EXPERIENCE: CLARIFYING EXPECTATIONS

Domain: Language Use **Focus:** Understanding how Language Use is evaluated *Note:* This learning experience can be replicated in multiple performance domains.			
Learner Outcomes	**Time**	**Materials**	**Prep**
I can identify how Language Use is evaluated by: • evaluating my own work using self-assessment questions. • determining the PDI that best aligns with my work. • using the GROW guiding questions to revise and/or add to my work.	• Prep time: 5 minutes • Implementation time: 30 minutes • Debrief time: 5 minutes	• The performance task • Learners' presentational or interpersonal performance such as a draft or a recording • The Language Use PDIs • Self-assessment questions • GROW guiding questions	• Prepare to display the PDIs, self-assessment questions, and the GROW guiding questions. • Be sure learners have access to their performance.

Instructions

1. (PURPOSE) Tell learners that they will learn how to self-assess their work and make changes to reach the next performance level.
2. (SET UP) Remind learners about the performance task for this interpersonal or presentational performance.
3. Display the PDIs and instruct learners to use the self-assessment questions to evaluate their work.
4. (GUIDANCE) Go through a few of the self-assessment questions with the learners, directing learners to reflect on their own performance to identify if it best aligns to the *Beginning*, *Developing*, *Meeting*, or *Exceeding* PDIs.
5. (ENGAGEMENT) Release the lesson to have learners continue reflecting on the self-assessment questions and have them mark which PDI best aligns to their work.
6. (GUIDANCE) When learners have identified the PDI that best aligns to their work, point them toward the GROW guiding questions for that level.
7. (ENGAGEMENT) Learners use the GROW guiding questions for that level to guide them to improve their work.
8. (DEBRIEF) Learners could share their reflections and improvements with a partner.
9. Ask learners to reflect on:
    a. What did you notice about your Language Use before and after you reflected on the self-assessment and used the GROW guiding questions?
    b. How might you apply what you learned to your future work when completing a summative task?

Alternatives

Learners could complete this learning experience multiple times with multiple interpersonal or presentational tasks throughout a unit.

As learners engage in this learning experience, it eventually can be done more independently and does not need to be guided by the educator.

Differentiation

Learners could work together to give and get feedback from each other. After exchanging drafts, each learner could complete the "self" assessment questions as feedback for their partner, turning it into a peer assessment. Learners could then discuss the assessment of each other's work and brainstorm changes to level up their work.

Learners could assess example work from an anonymous learner individually or in a group discussion.

EXAMPLE

Target performance level: **Novice High**
Context: familiar, formal, predictable
Content: familiar, everyday

Task: Write a note to your new teacher describing what you like to do.

Learner's draft:

I like games and I like music. I like to play games every day. I like to play gitarr.

Example of how a learner might fill out the sections of the guided self-assessment (Table 5.14) and identify their GROW guiding questions (from Table 5.5).

TARGET PERFORMANCE LEVEL	Novice High	**CONTEXT**	Familiar, informal, formal, predictable
PERFORMANCE DOMAIN	Language Use	**CONTENT**	Familiar, everyday

What description best matches your performance today?

- ☐ I used memorized and practiced vocabulary in isolation (example: speaking/writing with a one-word/phrase: *Yes. No. Sometimes. Sports.*).
- ☐ I used isolated, memorized, and practiced vocabulary (example: speaking/writing with one-word/phrase: *Yes. No. Sometimes. Sports with friends*) and formulaic, or patterned, structures (examples: *I like... I am...*).
- ☑ I used memorized and practiced vocabulary (example: *to play sports, to run, to dance, to swim*) and formulaic, or patterned, structures (examples: *I like... I am...*), but at times I attempted to create with language by combining and recombining vocabulary and structures in different ways (example: changing *to spend time with friends* to *to spend time with family*).
- ☐ I created with language by combining and recombining vocabulary and structures in different ways (example: changing *to spend time with friends* to *to spend time with family*).

Option 1: List examples of how you created with language by combining and recombining vocabulary and structures in different ways:

play games, play gitarr

Option 2: If you did not create with language today, how might you combine or recombine some of the vocabulary and structures you used in different ways?

Option 1: What words helped you combine and recombine vocabulary and structures in new and different ways?

- ☐ in
- ☐ of
- ☐ with
- ☐ without
- ☐ Other: ______________________

Option 2: What words helped you combine and recombine vocabulary and structures in new and different ways?

I used "play" with different activities

Evaluate how you think you performed in your use of Language Use today:

- ☐ **Beginning:** I can use isolated, memorized and practiced vocabulary.
- ☐ **Developing:** I can use isolated, memorized and practiced vocabulary and formulaic structures.
- ☑ **Meeting:** I can use practiced vocabulary and formulaic structures, and at times (re)combine vocabulary and structures to create with language.
- ☐ **Exceeding:** I can create with language by (re)combining vocabulary and structures.

Think about your own experience and what you have done to improve in Language Use. What advice would you give other learners to help them develop Language Use?

Put in when (at the weekend) or with somebody to add to it and combine. Use like with other people.

Learner directions: Use the GROW guiding questions for the level that best matches your performance. Reflect on the questions, then make changes to your work to reach the next level of performance.

GROW GUIDING QUESTIONS

EXCEEDING	MEETING	DEVELOPING	BEGINNING
• How might you combine and recombine a variety of vocabulary and structures? • How might you use various, or multiple, time frames to communicate your message?	• How might you create with language by combining and recombining vocabulary and structures throughout your performance?	• How might you expand on what you say/write so you can move beyond using vocabulary in isolation? • How might you create with language by combining & recombining words in different ways?	• What additional vocabulary could you add to communicate more information to your partner/audience? • What formulaic, or patterned, structures could you use to communicate more information to your partner/audience?

Example of what a learner engaged in this process might think and rewrite based on clarifying expectations. This example shows how the learner went from brainstorming ideas to writing them in a text.

Learner's thinking:

I could combine play with music. I could add to the structure by using with my friend. I could use like with other people.

Rewrite:

I like games and to play music. I like to play games every day. I like to play gitarr with my friend. My friend like to play flute. My friend and I like to play music.

LEARNING EXPERIENCE: CREATING COMBINATIONS

Domain: Language Use

Focus: Understanding Language Use by making new combinations

Note: Use with learners performing within the Novice and Intermediate level. The provided example targets the Novice level.

Learner outcomes	Time	Materials	Prep
I can identify how to create with language by combining and recombining vocabulary.	• Prep time: 5 minutes • Implementation time: 20 minutes • Debrief time: 5 minutes	• Colorful drawing materials or digital drawing tools for each student	• Come up with an idea, like salad, that allows for combinations and relates to the unit of study.

Instructions

1. (PURPOSE) Tell learners that they will experience how to create with language by combining and recombining vocabulary that is familiar to them.
2. (SET UP) Have learners take out colorful drawing supplies or use digital drawing tools.
3. Ask each learner to fold their paper into fourths, label the top left corner "salad" in the target language and draw a salad in the top left corner.
4. (ENGAGEMENT) Learners draw a salad.
5. Optional (GUIDANCE) Let them draw whatever comes to mind, but if they need more guidance, prompt them by saying a lettuce salad if necessary.
6. Next, ask learners to draw a fruit salad in the top right corner and label it in the target language.
7. (ENGAGEMENT) Learners each draw and label a fruit salad.
8. (GUIDANCE) Point out that the two pictures are both salads, but they look different and represent a different idea. They used the idea/word salad and the idea/word fruit and when combined, it made something entirely different, as evidenced in their drawings.
9. Next, have learners draw as many kinds of salad as they can think of by combining ideas/words in the target language (egg salad, chicken salad, pasta salad…). They can fill up their paper on one side and then use the back side if they have more ideas.
10. (DEBRIEF) Point out (in learners' base language if necessary) how the learners have created new things that are observably different from one another. Encourage learners to engage in this learning experience to verify they have combined language in new ways in their performances rather than just added descriptive details to their work.
11. Learners can share their drawings with each other.
12. Ask learners to reflect on:
    a. What did you notice when you combine and recombine ideas/vocabulary?
    b. How might you apply what you learned to your future work when completing a performance task?

Alternatives	Differentiation
If learners don't label their own creations, they could get other learners to guess what they combined to get their creation (example: egg and salad). Learners can apply their brainstormed creations in a presentational or interpersonal performance task. Learners could tally how many creations they used in a performance task.	Learners could brainstorm additional vocabulary (soup, juice, pie, smoothies, …) and make more (re)combinations. The educator could provide the pictures and ask learners to identify the differences to see something new and different in each picture. Learners could then generate the labels for each picture in the target language in order to create with language.

EXAMPLE

Below is how the learner's paper might look when they have finished drawing four different salads.

(first drawing) 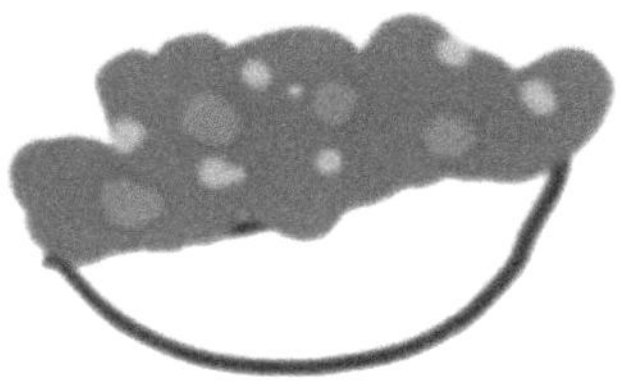 **SALAD**	(second drawing) 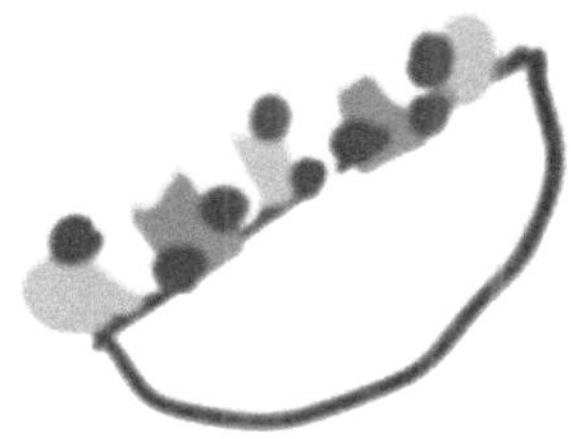 **FRUIT SALAD**
(continued drawing)  **EGG SALAD**	(continued drawing)  **CHICKEN SALAD**

Note: From Wayzata Public Schools, Minnesota (2018). Adapted with permission.

3-WAY MATCH: TASK, FUNCTION, STRUCTURE

Domain: Language Use

Focus: Understanding Language Use through structures that express functions & complete tasks

Note: Different performance levels may have more or less complex structures. The provided example targets the Intermediate Mid level.

Learner outcomes	Time	Materials	Prep
I can identify the relationship between tasks, functions, and structures by: • identifying specific structures that help express specific functions. • matching tasks to functions and structures.	• Prep time: 20 minutes • Implementation time: 10 minutes • Debrief time: 5 minutes	• Make 6 task cards and 6 function/structure cards for each group of learners (3-5 learners in a group) • Envelopes for each group	• Prepare six clearly different tasks. Label them with letters (A-F). Copy them onto one color of paper. Make enough copies for each group of learners. • Prepare six functions of what a learner would do to complete each of the six tasks. Add helpful structures (see example). Label them with numbers (1-6). Copy these onto a different color of paper. Make enough copies for each group of learners. • Cut each of the tasks sheet and each *functions/structures* sheet into six parts. Put one set of each into an envelope for each group.

Instructions

1. (PURPOSE) Tell learners that they will match tasks to the functions and grammatical structures needed to complete them. Give them an example:
    a. Task: *What did you do last summer?*
    b. Function: *Telling and retelling stories, sequencing, recounting events*
    c. Grammatical Structures: *I swam... I spent time with... I hiked...*
2. (SET UP) Divide learners into groups of about 3-5 learners each and explain that they will discuss the tasks in order to match them to the functions/structures.
3. Instruct learners to first take out only the *task* cards and discuss what functions/structures they think they might need to complete the tasks.
4. Optional (GUIDANCE) Discuss as a whole group one or more of the task cards and the anticipated functions/ structures that they will be matched with.
5. Instruct learners to take out the function/structure cards and match them to the task cards.
6. (ENGAGEMENT) Learners discuss and match the cards.
7. (DEBRIEF) Learners share one match with the whole group.
8. Ask learners to reflect on:
    a. What did you learn about how specific grammatical structures help you perform a function in order to complete a task?
    b. How might you apply what you learned to your future work when completing a performance task?

Alternatives	Differentiation
Learners could each get a task or a functions/structures card and walk around the room to find the learner with their match.	Learners could continue to come up with other tasks and the functions/structures to complete them. Learners could write sentences to complete the tasks using the function/structure suggestions. Learners could add to the structure suggestions on the cards. Learners could pick one task and see how multiple functions/structures could be used in completion of the task.

EXAMPLE

Task cards:

A: Convince your partner that your favorite band should headline at the environmental music festival this year.	**B:** Prepare a speech to use at a protest about a hopeful future and your role in it.	**C:** Describe how foods impact your moods.
D: Craft a story, capturing an experience or adventure you've had, for the *Personal Moments* contest put on by your favorite social media platform.	**E:** Prepare questions to interview a recent immigrant from a culture that you are studying. Where possible, include how you would respond to similar questions to later be able to compare your experiences.	**F:** Describe a role model or hero of yours.

Function/Structure cards:

1. Expressing hopes, dreams, possibilities (subjunctive) • If…then… • I might… • Could we… • …	**2. Describing people, places, things, how and how well** (adjective structures) • brown eyes • sparkling personality • Avery, who is 15, is the first… • …	**3. Telling & retelling stories, sequencing** (word order with adverbial time words) • first • then • after that • …
4. Asking and responding to questions (question structures) • What do you like…? • When do you…? • How do you… • Say more about that. • I agree. • …	**5. Expressing feelings and emotions** (structures the express emotions) • It makes me feel… • I'm happy when… • My emotions are impacted by… • …	**6. Supporting your opinions and preferences** (subordinating conjunctions) • because • For that reason… • That is why I think… • …

Answer Key: TASK A: 6, TASK B: 1, TASK C:5 , TASK D: 3, TASK E: 4, TASK F: 2

BRAINSTORM BUILDING

Domain: Language Use

Focus: Developing Language Use by creating with language

Note: This learning experience can be replicated in multiple performance domains.

Learner outcomes	Time	Materials	Prep
I can develop Language Use by brainstorming ways to (re)combine vocabulary and structures in order to create with language.	• Prep time: 5-15 minutes • Implementation time: 20 minutes • Debrief time: 5 minutes	• Lists of words that learners could (re)combine • Paper/pencil or digital writing tools for each learner	• Prepare word lists/ categories to (re)combine.

Instructions

1. (PURPOSE) Tell learners that they will brainstorm ways to (re)combining words to create language.
2. (SET UP) Give learners a few categories that include lists of vocabulary words/phrases that can be (re)combined. Show learners possible ways to (re)combine the words/phrases in order to create with language (see example).
3. (ENGAGEMENT) Brainstorm together as a class some additional details to further develop their ideas (see example).
4. Divide learners into groups of 3-5 learners each.
5. Display or hand out categories and lists of vocabulary words/phrases (see example).
6. (ENGAGEMENT) In groups, learners brainstorm how they might (re)combine words/phrases in order to create with language.
7. Learners write their ideas and add details.
8. (DEBRIEF) Learners could share their ideas with the class, between groups, and/or add to the previously brainstormed class chart of ideas.
9. Ask learners to reflect on:
   a. What did you notice about (re)combining in order to create with language?
   b. How might you apply what you learned to your future work when completing a performance task?

Alternatives	Differentiation
Learners could do this with structures instead of vocabulary words. Learners could do this individually instead of in groups, then share in small groups. Learners could apply their brainstormed ideas to a presentational/interpersonal task.	Learners could add more categories of ideas to (re)combine. Learners could use various/all time frames. Learners can work within different topics: abstract, academic, concrete, professional, social, and/or researched.

EXAMPLE

Learner Instructions: Brainstorm ways to (re)combine the vocabulary. Write your ideas and add details in order to further develop your examples.

Ideas displayed for learners:

VOCABULARY	IDEAS FOR COMBINATIONS	WAYS TO CONNECT IDEAS
to draw	book	in
to write	computer	of
to practice	family	with
to play	friends	without
to listen	Instruments	on
to watch	band	
to dance	i-Pad	
to talk	homework	
	sports	
	TV	
	games	

Learner work:

Learners brainstorm ways to (re)combine vocabulary.	→	*play games* *play instruments* *play sports*
Learners write their brainstormed ideas and add additional details to further develop their ideas.	→	*I play games with family.* *I play instruments with my friends in a band.* *I play sports in physical education.*

Note: Adapted from Wayzata Public Schools, Minnesota (2016). Adapted with permission.

LEVEL UP

Domain: Language Use

Focus: Developing Language Use by creating progressions

Note: This learning experience can be replicated in multiple performance domains.

Learner outcomes	Time	Materials	Prep
I can develop Language Use by building progressions of Language Use to "level up."	• Prep time: 5 minutes (longer if you prepare transcripts) • Implementation time: 30 minutes • Debrief time: 5 minutes	• PDIs for Language Use to display at the appropriate level (Novice, Intermediate, Advanced) • Interpersonal or presentational performance task • If working in the interpersonal mode: One set of transcriptions to use as a model • Paper/pencil or digital writing tools for each learner	• Prepare to display PDIs. • Have a performance task ready for learners to write or speak about. • If working in the interpersonal mode: Have all transcriptions available.

Instructions

1. (PURPOSE) Tell learners that they will develop their Language Use by working with a group to write/say an example performance at each level (*Beginning*, *Developing*, *Meeting*, and *Exceeding*).
2. (SET UP) Display and remind learners of the targeted PDIs for Language Use.
3. Divide learners into groups of 3-5 learners each and ask them to take out paper/pencil, digital writing tools, or digital recording tools.
4. Give learners an example presentational task or an interpersonal task with a transcript of one side of the interpersonal conversation.
5. Optional (GUIDANCE) Provide or do an example together as a whole class, writing one performance level together for presentational or write the other part of the interpersonal conversation for one performance level.
6. (ENGAGEMENT) Release the lesson to have learners work in groups to write one example of each level (*Beginning*, *Developing*, *Meeting*, and *Exceeding*) using the given task.
7. (GUIDANCE) Remind learners to look at the PDIs to be sure of what level they are aiming for with each example.
8. (DEBRIEF) Learners share their reflections and improvements with a partner, another group, or the class.
9. Ask learners to reflect on:
    a. What did you notice about each example as you progressed through the performance levels of Language Use?
    b. How might you apply what you learned to your future work when completing a performance task?

Alternatives	Differentiation
Learners could do this individually instead of in groups, then share in small groups. Learners could take turns writing an example for each level (Beginning, Developing, Meeting, Exceeding). Groups of students could write a presentational example or interpersonal script for each PDI, or groups could be assigned to write a presentational example or interpersonal script for one assigned PDI. One group could share their "leveled up" examples with another group to see if they can identify what level each example is meant to be.	After writing examples for each level about one task together as a class and another in groups, learners could each individually write an example for one level and then share it out with their group. The group can decide which performance level it best matches. Learners could evaluate example texts that have already been created as *Beginning, Developing, Meeting,* or *Exceeding.*

EXAMPLE

Target performance level: **Novice High**
Context: familiar, informal, predictable
Content: familiar, everyday

Task: Write a note to a friend describing your clothing choices for your favorite sport.

Learner instructions: Based on the PDIs, write an example of each level of performance.

PDIs displayed:

TARGET PERFORMANCE LEVEL: NOVICE HIGH				
	EXCEEDING	**MEETING**	**DEVELOPING**	**BEGINNING**
Performance Domain Indicators	I can create with language by (re)combining vocabulary and structures.	I can use practiced vocabulary and formulaic structures, and at times (re)combine vocabulary and structures to create with language.	I can use isolated, memorized and practiced vocabulary and formulaic structures.	I can use isolated, memorized and practiced vocabulary.

Learner work:

Learners were given the performance task. As a class, they brainstormed a written example for the *Beginning* level.

BEGINNING

My name Asher. I volleyball. Beach. T-shirt.

In small groups, learners then worked together to write "leveled up" examples for *Developing, Meeting,* and *Exceeding.*

EXCEEDING	**MEETING**	**DEVELOPING**
My name is Asher. I like volleyball. We plays volleyball in the Summer on the beach. It is Beach volleyball. Uniform is shorts and t-shirt. I am number is 20. The t-shirt is team name, Spiking Blockers.	*My name is Asher. I like volleyball in the summer on the beach. Uniform is shorts and t-shirt. I am 20. I am team Spiking Blockers.*	*My name is Asher. I like volleyball.* *On Beach.* *I shorts and t-shirt.*

DURING, BEFORE, AND AFTER

Domain: Language Use

Focus: Developing Language Use by telling/writing a story in all time frames

Note: Use with learners performing within the Intermediate or Advanced level who are familiar with multiple time frames.

Learner outcomes	Time	Materials	Prep
I can develop my Language Use by: • telling/writing what is happening right now. • telling/writing what happened before now. • telling/writing what will happen. • telling/writing a story in various time frames.	• Prep time: 20-30 minutes • Implementation time: 15-30 minutes (5-10 minutes a round) • Debrief time: 5 minutes	• A different photo for each learner: Choose intriguing photos that are connected to the themes being studied, are likely to elicit creative responses from learners, and include cultural products, practice, and perspectives • Paper/pencil or digital writing tools for each learner	• Find photos. • Optional: Prepare guidance, or scaffolds, especially for the time frame structures.

Instructions

1. (PURPOSE) Tell learners that they will be developing their Language Use by telling a story about a photo in various time frames.
2. (SET UP) Ask each learner to take out a pencil and a sheet of paper and fold the paper into thirds.
3. Divide learners into groups of 3 learners each, but explain that they will be writing individually.
4. Give each learner a different photo and have them think about what is happening in the photo.
5. Round 1: Instruct learners to write "during" in the target language at the top of the middle third of their paper.
6. Tell learners to look at their photo and imagine what is happening in the photo. Give them 5-10 minutes to write a few sentences about only what is currently happening in the photo.
7. (ENGAGEMENT) Learners look at their photos and write what is happening "during" the photo.
8. Optional (GUIDANCE) Review structures and vocabulary that learners could use to show that something is happening now.
9. (ENGAGEMENT) Have learners pass their papers to another one of their group members so everyone has one new paper (note – do not have learners pass their photos). Learners read what the other learner has written. Have them highlight what shows that the writing is in the "during" phase.
10. Optional (GUIDANCE) Ask the learners again to reflect on how a reader would know from their writing that this is happening right now. They can add to their highlighting.
11. (ENGAGEMENT) Have the learners pass their photo to match with each of the papers.
12. Round 2: Instruct learners to write "before" in the target language at the top of the first third of their paper.
13. Optional (GUIDANCE) Review structures and vocabulary that learners could use to show that something happened before now.
14. (ENGAGEMENT) Give learners 5-10 minutes to write a few sentences about what happened before the time of the photo.
15. Optional (GUIDANCE) Ask the learners again to reflect on how a reader would know from the writing that this happened before.
16. (ENGAGEMENT) Have learners pass each of their papers, but not each of their photos, to the next group member, so that learners can read what the other learner has written.
17. Optional (GUIDANCE) Ask the learners again to reflect on how a reader would know from their writing that this happened before. Have them highlight what shows that the writing is in the "before" phase.
18. (ENGAGEMENT) Have the learners pass each of their photos to match with their papers.
19. Round 3: Instruct learners to write "after" in the target language at the top of the last third of their paper.
20. Optional (GUIDANCE) Review structures and vocabulary that learners could use to show that something will happen.
21. (ENGAGEMENT) Give learners 5-10 minutes to write a few sentences about what will happen after the time of the photo.
22. Optional (GUIDANCE) Ask the learners again to reflect on how a reader would know from the writing that this will happen.
23. (ENGAGEMENT) Have learners pass each of their papers, but not their photos, to the next group member, so that learners can read what the other learner has written.
24. Optional (GUIDANCE) Ask the learners again to reflect on how a reader would know from the writing that this will happen. Have them highlight what shows that the writing is in the "after" phase.
25. (ENGAGEMENT) Have the learners pass each of their photos to match with their papers.
26. At the end, return each photo and its matching paper to the original learner and ask them to polish the story: correct structures, add in vocabulary and details, and connect the things that are happening, happened, or will happen in the three time frames. Advanced learners may even write a polished version of the story and appropriately mix the time frames throughout their text (see the example below).
27. (DEBRIEF) Learners can share their polished stories with their small group or with the class.
28. Ask learners to reflect on:
    a. What did you learn (or remember) about telling or writing in various frames?
    b. How might you apply what you learned to your future work when completing a performance task?

Alternatives	Differentiation
Learners could write all three rounds individually (during, before, and after) for their same photo instead of passing it to others. Learners could highlight the structures used for each time frame in their own work.	Learners could be given sentence starters, scaffolds, or examples of time frames. Learners performing within the Advanced level could add to the story to include other timeframes: What happened before that point in the past? In the future, what would have happened?

EXAMPLE

Learners fold their paper in thirds and add labels to create a graphic organizer.

Round 2 : BEFORE	Round 1 : DURING	Round 3 : AFTER

Learner work:

Example of how the finished product might look for one photo with highlights to show how a reader knows that the writing is in each phase. Each round was completed individually by a different learner.

Note: From *Person in Blue Denim Jeans and Blue Shoes Walking on Brown Dried Leaves During Daytime* [Photograph], by M. Spiske, 2020, Unsplash (https://unsplash.com/photos/h-CGKH94ols?utm_source=unsplash&utm_medium=referral&utm_content=creditShareLink).

Round 1: DURING
(completed by Learner 1)

Dani and Jules harvest sweet potatoes. The work is hard and the sun is hot. Their father owns land now.

Round 2: BEFORE
(completed by Learner 2)

Dani's father was migrant worker. He bought this land last year. He planted the potatoes last spring after the frost. He waited for his first harvest.

Round 3: AFTER
(completed by learner 3)

Jules will take the potatos to city farmers' market. Dani and Jules will eat potatos with their family. The potatos will last a long time, into the winter.

Example of how a learner, performing within the Advanced level, might rewrite a polished copy, interweaving various time frames.

The Land of Sweet Potatoes

Dani's father was a migrant worker. He bought this land last year. Now he owns land.

Dani's father planted sweet potatoes last spring after the last frost. Now Davi and Jules harvest them. The work is hard and the sun is hot.

Jules will take the sweet potatoes to farmers' market in the city. Now the family will get money from the market.

When Dani, Jules and their father eat sweet potatoes they will think about the hard migrant work and land they now own.

YOUR TURN

LEARNING TARGET CHECK:	
I can	☐ select learning experiences that support learners' growth with Language Use.

Complete the chart by identifying specific learning experiences from the *Learning Experiences to Facilitate Learner Growth* section (p. 98-114) that you could use in an upcoming unit to help learners *understand* or *develop* Language Use. Note any materials or prep needed to implement the learning experience in your upcoming unit. Consider any alternatives or differentiation that would better align the learning experience to your unit, the targeted level of performance, and/or your learners.

UNIT:			
PERFORMANCE DOMAIN: LANGUAGE USE			
Learning experience	**What type of learning experience is it?** (Circle one)	**Materials/Prep**	**Alternatives / Differentiation**
	Understanding/ Developing		
	Understanding/ Developing		
	Understanding/ Developing		

Learners' Self-Assessments

Self-assessment provides an opportunity for learners to reflect on their performance, set goals, and ultimately to own their learning. This section features three ways learners can self-assess their work: *Make It Visible, Glow and Grow Self-Assessment*, and *Guided Self-Assessments*. Each is educator-designed but learner-driven. That is, the self-assessment is designed by the educator around the PDIs but it is the learner who must reflect on their performance to complete it. The same self-assessments are used in each performance domain chapter to build consistency for learners. Each can be used for learner self-assessment after a formative or summative task. Educators might select self-assessments that have more scaffolding, such as the *Guided Self-Assessment* and *Make It Visible*, after formative tasks where learners may need more support to self-assess their performance, such as the beginning of a unit or a course. The *Glow and Grow Self-Assessment*, which is more open-ended, can be used when learners feel more comfortable reflecting on the PDIs and summarizing their work, such as after formative tasks that occur at the end of the unit or after a summative task. Overall, educators can make adjustments to any of these self-assessments and use them with intentionality based on their learners, their pacing within a unit or course, and the performance task.

Make It Visible

This self-assessment provides an opportunity for learners to visibly see their Language Use in a given formative or summative task. Learners might circle, highlight, color-code, or note the ways in which they used language in a given presentational or interpersonal performance (see Figures 5.1 and 5.2). Or learners can self-assess by marking yes/no and providing evidence (see Table 5.10 and Figure 5.3). Educators can provide opportunities for revisions and/or additions for learners who may find they are not yet *Meeting* expectations, so learners have opportunities for language growth.

The learner samples in this section demonstrate how each self-assessment can be used at one performance level. However, these self-assessments can be used at any level: Novice, Intermediate, or Advanced.

Figure 5.1
Presentational Self-Assessment Using the "Make It Visible" Approach

Directions: Read over your presentational work and circle examples of how you (re)combined language in different ways in order to create with language.
Example of how the learner, performing within the Novice level, completes this self-assessment:
Hey! My name is Pari. I 12 years old. I am Persian. *Ingrid is sports. Ingrid like to dance. I am not to dance. I am to swim.* *I is shy. Ingrid is shy. I is (play sports.)* *I am to read. Ingrid like to dance.* *I am to draw. Ingrid like to dance. Well, see ya later!*

Figure 5.2

Presentational Self-Assessment Using the "Make It Visible" Approach

Directions: Read over your presentational work and mark it accordingly:

- Highlight the language used to indicate the present time frame
- Underline the language used to indicate the past time frame
- **Bold** the language used to indicate the future time frame
- Use **(**parentheses**)** around the language used where you are uncertain of the time frame.

Example of how the learner, performing within the Advanced level, completes this self-assessment:

Dear diary,

I cannot believe that this investigation about my age is still going on! It is just not fair! I am not a liar! How much analyses **(**do I have to do**)**? Because of this, I did not even get the chance to sign when I turned 16 years. In the Professional Baseball League, they think that all us players are liars. There are some that lies, but there are a lot of us who tell the truth.

But what are they suppose to do, if only one year older means you are worth $1 million less? Seriously, one year? The PBL uses for our poverty. It's not fair that they treat us differently, pay us differently just because we live in a poorer country. Why I don't make money because I am a great baseball player? Why am I the cheap export?? If I am in power, I **would talks** with the representatives to work for changes in recruiting regulations, like age restrictions and equal pay.

Yet I know that if I **work** hard, I **will get** a contract of any price which, for me, is the way out of poverty. It is also my family's way out of poverty because they are depending on me. The first thing I **take** on **is** buy my parents a house so they never **(**have to worry**)** about housing ever again! I just have to be patient. All I want to do is play baseball – it's what I love, it's what I borned to do, it's all I have ever done.

Let's play ball!
-Mike

Table 5.10
Interpersonal Self-Assessment Using the "Make It Visible" Approach

Language Use Reflection Guide How do I use language to complete the task?			
	YES	**NO**	**EXAMPLES**
I can create with language by combining and recombining language in different ways			
I can use language to indicate the present time frame.			
I can use language to indicate the past time frame.			
I can use language to indicate the future time frame.			

Note: Not all languages rely on time frames to move to the Advanced level. Educators should adjust the reflection guide to best fit the target language.

Figure 5.3

Example of a Completed Interpersonal Self-Assessment Using the "Make It Visible" Approach

Directions: Listen to the recording of your interpersonal conversation. Complete the *Language Use Reflection Guide* and list examples of how you created with language and used various time frames (past, present, future).

LEARNER SAMPLE RESPONSE

Learner 1: Hi Paz!

Learner 2: Hi! How are you?

Learner 1: I'm alright. What is your organization called?

Learner 2: My organization is called the Family Stay House...But no place like home.

Learner 1: How interesting (*nods*)!

Learner 2: What is your organization called?

Learner 1: The organization...er, sorry...my organization favorite is called Renewing the Countryside.

Learner 2: Oh, how fantastic! What does it do? Renew, reuse, recycle (*laughs*)?

Learner 1: Renewing the Countryside gives money for the...for the farmers and help the children of poor families in rural communities.

Learner 2: Great! Great (*nods*)!

Learner 1: What does your organization try to do (*tilts head*)?

Learner 2: The Family Stay House tries to support and help families, families that need the help economically paying for pro-proced... when the children are sick. Where is the organization?

Learner 1: The organization...er, sorry...my organization favorite is called Renewing the Countryside.

Learner 2: My organization, um, is in the city.

Learner 1: Great! Did it do something in the past?

Learner 2: Every year, the Race for the Kids, um remember money for organization, um, to pay for the, um, pro-proced-procedures.

Learner 1: How cool (*smiles*)!

Learner 2: Um, yes, yes, yes (*nods*). Um, How many people serves the organization?

Learner 1: Many people serves the organization in the city because everyone wants to help the, the rural communities.

Learner 2: Yes, great!

Learner 1: I like your organization a lot. How can I help your organization? I pitch in?

Learner 2: Oh, how fantastic (*eyes widen*)! You can work as a volunteer – reading books to children, playing sports with the children, donating money and getting money for the organization.

Learner 1: How fun! Why should I help?

Learner 2: Um, because ...because in my opinion, it is important to help the people.

Learner 1: Great, great, yes (*nods*)!

Learner 2: What they do for your organization?

Learner 1: Um you can get money for the organization or you can donate. A little bit goes a long way!

Learner 2: I think so.

Learner 1: Bye (*waves*)!

Learner 2: Bye (*waves*)!

Learner 1: Thanks for talking with me.

Learner 2: I'll see you laters. Thanks for talking with me.

Example of how Learner 1, performing within the Intermediate level, completes this self-assessment:			
Language Use Reflection Guide How do I use language to complete the task?			
	YES	**NO**	**EXAMPLES**
I can create with language by combining and recombining language in different ways	X		• *your organization* • *my organization favorite* • *it (in place of organization)* • *serves the organization* • *get money for the organization* • *help the children* • *help the rural communities* • *help your organization*
I can use language to indicate the present time frame.	X		• *is called* • *help the children* • *many people serves* • *everyone wants* • *you can get money* • *you can donate*
I can use language to indicate the past time frame.	X		• *Did it do something in the past?*
I can use language to indicate the future time frame.		X	

GLOW and GROW Self Assessment

Using the *Meeting* Performance Domain Indicator for each level, learners can self-assess their work on a one-point rubric after a formative or summative task. In Tables 5.11, 5.12 and 5.13, learners would complete the *Where I GLOW (What are my strengths?)* and *How I can GROW (What can I do to improve?)* sections by citing evidence from their own interpersonal or presentational performance for each performance domain. The *GLOW/GROW* Ideas are given as prompts so that learners are reminded of what to look for or work toward.

Table 5.11
GLOW and GROW Self-Assessment

LANGUAGE USE Target performance level: **Novice High** Context: familiar, informal, formal, predictable Content: familiar, everyday		
Instructions: Complete the following reflection by writing where you GLOW and where you can GROW in each area. Make sure to include evidence from your work to support your reasoning.		
Where I GLOW: What are my strengths?	**Performance Domain Indicator**	**How can I GROW? What can I do to improve?**
	I can use practiced vocabulary and formulaic structures, and at times (re)combine vocabulary and structures to create with language.	

GLOW IDEAS	**GROW IDEAS**
• What practiced vocabulary did you use to communicate your message? • What formulaic, or patterned, structures did you use to communicate your message? • What combinations and recombinations of vocabulary/ structures did you use in order to create with language?	• How might you create with language by combining and recombining vocabulary and structures more consistently throughout your performance?

Table 5.12
GLOW and GROW Self-Assessment

LANGUAGE USE Target performance level: **Intermediate Mid** Context: familiar, informal, formal, straight-forward Content: familiar, at times researched		
Instructions: Complete the following reflection by writing where you GLOW and where you can GROW in each area. Make sure to include evidence from your work to support your reasoning.		
Where I GLOW: What are my strengths?	**Performance Domain Indicator**	**How can I GROW? What can I do to improve?**
	I can create with language by (re)combining a variety of vocabulary and structures, and at times use various time frames.	

GLOW IDEAS	**GROW IDEAS**
• What combinations and recombinations of a variety of vocabulary and structures did you use in order to create with language? • How did you use various, or multiple, time frames?	• How might you use various, or multiple, time frames throughout your performance?

Table 5.13
GLOW and GROW Self-Assessment

LANGUAGE USE Target performance level: **Advanced Low** Context: familiar, informal, formal, complex Content: familiar, academic, social, concrete		
Instructions: Complete the following reflection by writing where you GLOW and where you can GROW in each area. Make sure to include evidence from your work to support your reasoning.		
Where I GLOW: What are my strengths?	**Performance Domain Indicator**	**How can I GROW? What can I do to improve?**
	I can use a range of vocabulary and structures across various time frames.	

GLOW IDEAS	GROW IDEAS
• What range of vocabulary and structures did you use? • How did you communicate across various time frames (past, present, future)?	• How might you use more precise vocabulary to communicate your message? • What structures might help you communicate your message more precisely within a time frame?

Guided Self-Assessments

This self-assessment includes guiding questions to help learners evaluate their own performance after a formative or summative task (see Tables 5.14, 5.15 and 5.16). Options are included to help educators personalize the self-assessment for their learners, or learners can self-select which options to answer.

Table 5.14

Interpersonal/Presentational Guided Self-Assessment

TARGET PERFORMANCE LEVEL	Novice High	**CONTEXT**	Familiar, informal, formal, predictable
PERFORMANCE DOMAIN	Language Use	**CONTENT**	Familiar, everyday

What description best matches your performance today?

- ☐ I used memorized and practiced vocabulary in isolation (example: speaking/writing with a one-word/phrase: *Yes. No. Sometimes. Sports.*).
- ☐ I used isolated, memorized, and practiced vocabulary (example: speaking/writing with one-word/phrase: *Yes. No. Sometimes. Sports with friends*) and formulaic, or patterned, structures (examples: *I like…I am…*).
- ☐ I used memorized and practiced vocabulary (example: *to play sports, to run, to dance, to swim*) and formulaic, or patterned, structures (examples: *I like… I am…*), but at times I attempted to create with language by combining and recombining vocabulary and structures in different ways (example: changing *to spend time with friends* to *to spend time with family*).
- ☐ I created with language by combining and recombining vocabulary and structures in different ways (example: changing *to spend time with friends* to *to spend time with family*).

Option 1: List examples of how you created with language by combining and recombining vocabulary and structures in different ways:

Option 2: If you did not create with language today, how might you combine or recombine some of the vocabulary and structures you used in different ways?

Option 1: What words helped you combine and recombine vocabulary and structures in new and different ways?

- ☐ in
- ☐ of
- ☐ with
- ☐ without
- ☐ Other: ______________________

Option 2: What words helped you combine and recombine vocabulary and structures in new and different ways?

Evaluate how you think you performed in your use of Language Use today:

- ☐ **Beginning:** I can use isolated, memorized and practiced vocabulary.
- ☐ **Developing:** I can use isolated, memorized and practiced vocabulary and formulaic structures.
- ☐ **Meeting:** I can use practiced vocabulary and formulaic structures, and at times (re)combine vocabulary and structures to create with language.
- ☐ **Exceeding:** I can create with language by (re)combining vocabulary and structures.

Think about your own experience and what you have done to improve in Language Use. What advice would you give other learners to help them develop Language Use?

Table 5.15
Interpersonal/Presentational Guided Self-Assessment

TARGET PERFORMANCE LEVEL	Intermediate Mid	**CONTEXT**	familiar, informal, formal, straight-forward
PERFORMANCE DOMAIN	Language Use	**CONTENT**	familiar, at times researched

What description best matches your performance today?

- ☐ I used mostly memorized vocabulary and/or structures that we've practiced in class, but at times I attempted to create with language by combining and recombining vocabulary and structures in different ways.
- ☐ I created with language by combining and recombining vocabulary and structures in different ways.
- ☐ I created with language by combining and recombining a variety of vocabulary and structures in different ways.

List examples of how you created with language by combining and recombining vocabulary and structures in different ways:

Option 1: What words helped you combine and recombine vocabulary and structures in different ways?

☐ at ☐ by ☐ in ☐ for
☐ from ☐ of ☐ on ☐ when
☐ with ☐ without
☐ Other:________________________

Option 2: What words helped you combine and recombine vocabulary and structures in different ways?

Option 1: What time frames did you use in your performance today?

- ☐ Present time frame: *today, this year, an environmental problem is…*
- ☐ Past time frame: *yesterday, last year, an environmental problem was…*
- ☐ Future time frame: *tomorrow, next year, an environmental problem will be…*

Option 2: List examples of vocabulary and structures you used to indicate time frames in your performance today:

- ☐ Present time frame:
- ☐ Past time frame:
- ☐ Future time frame:

What description best matches your performance today?

- ☐ I used vocabulary and structures that indicated the present time frame throughout my performance.
- ☐ I used vocabulary and structures that indicated the present time frame throughout my performance, and at times one other time frame (past or future).
- ☐ I used vocabulary and structures that indicated the present time frame and one other time frame (past or present) throughout my performance.
- ☐ I used vocabulary and structures that indicated the present time frame throughout my performance, and at times multiple other time frames (past and present).

Evaluate how you think you performed in Language Use today:

- ☐ **Beginning:** I can use practiced vocabulary and formulaic structures, and at times (re)combine vocabulary and structures to create with language.
- ☐ **Developing:** I can create with language by (re)combining vocabulary and structures.
- ☐ **Meeting:** I can create with language by (re)combining a variety of vocabulary and structures, and at times use various time frames.
- ☐ **Exceeding:** I can create with language by (re)combining a variety of vocabulary and structures, at times across various time frames.

Think about your own experience and what you have done to improve in Language Use. What advice would you give other learners to help them develop Language Use?

Table 5.16
Interpersonal/Presentational Guided Self-Assessment

<table>
<tr><td>TARGET PERFORMANCE LEVEL</td><td>Advanced Low</td><td>CONTEXT</td><td>familiar, unfamiliar, informal, formal, complex</td></tr>
<tr><td>PERFORMANCE DOMAIN</td><td>Language Use</td><td>CONTENT</td><td>familiar, academic, social, concrete</td></tr>
<tr><td colspan="4">What description best matches your performance today?
☐ I created with language by combining and recombining a variety of vocabulary and structures in different ways.
☐ I used a range of vocabulary and structures.
☐ I used a wide range of vocabulary and structures that were, at times, precise.</td></tr>
<tr><td colspan="2">Option 1: Share examples of language you used today to demonstrate a range of vocabulary and structures:</td><td colspan="2">Option 2: What might you add or change to better demonstrate a range of vocabulary and structures?</td></tr>
<tr><td colspan="2">Option 1: What time frames did you use in your performance today?
☐ Present time frame: today, this year, is, ...
☐ Past time frame: yesterday, last year, was, ...
☐ Future time frame: tomorrow, next year, will be,...</td><td colspan="2">Option 2: List examples of vocabulary and structures you used to indicate time frames in your performance today:
☐ Present time frame:
☐ Past time frame:
☐ Future time frame:</td></tr>
<tr><td colspan="4">What description best matches your performance today?
☐ I used vocabulary and structures that indicated the present time frame and one other time frame (past or present) throughout my performance.
☐ I used vocabulary and structures that indicated the present time frame throughout my performance, and at times multiple other time frames (past and present).
☐ I used vocabulary and structures that indicated various time frames (past, present, future) throughout my performance.</td></tr>
<tr><td colspan="4">Evaluate how you think you performed in the your use of Language Use today:
☐ Beginning: I can create with language by (re)combining a variety of vocabulary and structures, and at times use various time frames.
☐ Developing: I can create with language by (re)combining a variety of vocabulary and structures, at times across various time frames.
☐ Meeting: I can use a range of vocabulary and structures across various time frames.
☐ Exceeding: I can use a wide range of vocabulary and structures that are, at times, precise across various time frames.</td></tr>
<tr><td colspan="4">Think about your own experience and what you have done to improve in Language Use. What advice would you give other learners to help them develop Language Use?</td></tr>
</table>

YOUR TURN

LEARNING TARGET CHECK:	
I can	☐ provide learners with self-assessments to evaluate their work.

Complete the chart by identifying specific self-assessments from the *Learners' Self-Assessments* section (p. 115-125) that could be used in an upcoming unit to help learners evaluate their own work. Next, describe a formative or summative performance task in your upcoming unit that learners could complete and then self-assess using the chosen self-assessment. Finally, list any additional materials or preparation that might be needed to implement this self-assessment in the *Notes* section of the chart.

UNIT:		
PERFORMANCE DOMAIN: LANGUAGE USE		
Learner self-assessments	**Performance task** Formative or summative	**Notes**

Advice From Learners

As a purposeful way for learners to become aware of their own learning, we asked learners to reflect on what worked for them to improve their performance in various performance domains. Sharing advice can build learner metacognitive skills, or awareness of one's own learning, which has been linked to improved learning outcomes (Hattie, 2017). Together learners build a bank of suggestions and advice that they can access when looking to improve in a specific performance domain. This is a way for learners to realize what they have learned about a performance domain, monitor their own understanding of the performance domain, suggest and choose which advice to employ, and evaluate whether particular choices are successful. Here is what some learners said, when asked to share their insights on Language Use and give advice.

Novice Interpersonal:

- *Be ready with sentence starters and vocabulary that you know you will need.*
- *Review all the words you think you will use.*
- *Think about what words you can put together to use.*

Novice Presentational:

- *Make a mind map with all the vocabulary you know and want to use. Then ask what words you still need and get help to fill those in.*
- *Connect words that go together. Think of new combinations.*
- *Say something new.*

Intermediate Interpersonal:

- *Connect what you say to what your partner says.*
- *Ask for more details from your partner.*
- *What words work together, what could work together?*
- *Ask/Tell what happened before or after.*

Intermediate Presentational:

- *Draw a picture of what you want to say, then describe it in detail. Then some more.*
- *Think about what led up to what you are writing about and what comes next.*
- *Use the new structures from class. Start simple, then put them together.*

Advanced Interpersonal:

- *Give each other time and opportunities to elaborate.*
- *Ask good questions so you can get deeper.*
- *Talk about other options, especially if you run out of what to say.*

Advanced Presentational:

- *Elaborate, elaborate, elaborate.*
- *Tell it from different perspectives and times.*
- *Say general things, but then get very specific too.*

References

ACTFL. (2012). *ACTFL proficiency guidelines – Speaking, writing, listening, and reading* (3rd ed.). https://www.actfl.org/educator-resources/actfl-proficiency-guidelines

Hattie, J. (2017). *250+ influences on student achievement.* Visible Learning Plus. https://visible-learning.org/wp-content/uploads/2018/03/VLPLUS-252-Influences-Hattie-ranking-DEC-2017.pdf

National Council of State Supervisors for Languages (NCSSFL) – ACTFL. (2017). *NCSSFL-ACTFL Can-Do Statements: Performance Indicators for Language Learners.* ACTFL. https://www.actfl.org/educator-resources/ncssfl-actfl-can-do-statements

Spiske, M. (2020, June 11). *Person in blue denim jeans and blue shoes walking on brown dried leaves during daytime* [Photograph]. Unsplash. https://unsplash.com/photos/h-CGKH94ols?utm_source=unsplash&utm_medium=referral&utm_content=creditShareLink

Troyan, F. J., Adair-Hauck, B., & Glisan, E. W. (2023). *The integrated performance assessment: Twenty years and counting.* ACTFL.

CHAPTER 6 | TEXT TYPE
Performance Domain

LEARNING TARGETS:	
I can	☐ describe the Text Type performance domain. ☐ describe how Text Type shows up in learners' performance at various levels. ☐ evaluate learner work using the Performance Domain Indicators (PDIs). ☐ give effective feedback using the Text Type PDIs. ☐ select learning experiences that support learners' growth with Text Type. ☐ provide learners with self-assessments to evaluate their work.

What do we mean by *Text Type*?

A *text* is "a stretch of understandable language" that can appear in various forms or *types*, be it a word, sentence, paragraph, or extended discourse (Nordquist, 2019). Differences in learners' performance can be seen in the types of text they can sustain and organize as understandable language.

How does *Text Type* develop in learners' performance?

Learners grow in their ability to express themselves first by using memorized words and phrases, then by forming sentences, next by connecting sentences and ideas together, that eventually create paragraphs, organized paragraphs, and connected paragraph-length discourse (ACTFL, 2012a). Additionally, learners develop ways to organize their language, and so as they continue towards creating extended discourse they can use a variety of sentence structures that include simple, compound, complex, and compound-complex.

What does *Text Type* look like in learners' performance?

The sample learner performances in Table 6.1 illustrate how learners differ in Text Type to communicate their message. The learner performing within the Novice level uses mostly words (*Hi. Bye!*) and phrases (*From Johnsville*) as their primary type of text to communicate their message. In contrast, the learner performing within the Intermediate level uses the sentence as their primary form of text. This learner uses a series of sentences, or multiple sentences on a related topic, as a way to communicate their message. In addition, this learner is able to connect sentences through the use of the coordinator *so*. Learners performing within the Advanced level use the paragraph as their text type. The simple paragraph is topic-related and includes complex sentences that show organization. For example, the use of the subordinating conjunction *for as long as*, *because*, and *when*.

Table 6.1
Sample Learner Performances

NOVICE	**Task:** Introduce yourself to the class on the discussion thread.	Hi. My name is Kathryn. I is 12. From Johnsville. Bye!
INTERMEDIATE	**Task:** Introduce yourself to the class on the discussion thread telling us what name you like and why.	Hey! My name is Kathryn. It is a long name. I like Kate. My grandma is Kathryn so I am Kate. I like to meet you too. What is your name and why?? I love to know. Thanks.
ADVANCED	**Task:** Describe to your class the history behind a name in your family by adding the description to the class board.	My name is Kathryn, but my friends and families call me Kate. It's my nickname for as long as I can remember. Kathryn is a family name because it was my grandma's name. I hope to continue the tradition of using this family name when I have own children someday.

The Performance Domain Indicators and Descriptions

The following section presents the Performance Domain Indicators (PDIs) for Text Type by performance level: Novice (Table 6.2), Intermediate (Table 6.3), and Advanced (Table 6.4). The Text Type PDIs are primarily a combination of language from both the *NCSSFL-ACTFL Can-Do Statements: Performance Indicators for Language Learners* (NCSSFL-ACTFL, 2017) and the *ACTFL Proficiency Guidelines* (ACTFL, 2012b), which are cited at each level. The PDIs for this performance domain are applied to both interpersonal and presentational modes of communication. This is to promote ease and consistency among educators and learners. In order to illustrate Text Type, the PDIs are accompanied by a learner task and sample learner responses. In addition, the PDIs are accompanied by a description that is meant to deepen our understanding of how Text Type develops across the sublevels (Low, Mid, and High) in learner performance at each performance level (Novice, Intermediate, and Advanced).

Table 6.2
Text Type Performance Domain Indicators (PDIs) for Learners Performing Within the Novice Level

	NOVICE		
Sublevels	LOW	MID	HIGH
Context	familiar, informal, formal, predictable		
Content	very familiar	very familiar, everyday	familiar, everyday
Performance Domain Indicator	**I can use practiced** and **memorized words and phrases**.	**I can use practiced** and **memorized words and phrases**, and at times **use simple sentences**.	**I can use simple sentences most of the time**.

- The language in bold indicates the source is the *NCSSFL-ACTFL Can-Do Statements: Performance Indicators for Language Learners* (NCSSFL-ACTFL, 2017).
- Some language may appear in additional levels to provide scaffolding, consistency and/or clarity (*at times*).

Novice Task: Send your friend a status update on social media describing your Saturday morning breakfast experience.

LEARNER SAMPLE RESPONSE

NOVICE LOW	NOVICE MID	NOVICE HIGH
Good morning! In restaurant. Food yummy!	Good morning! I am in restaurant. Is favorite. I like eggs and bread. Drink coffee. Yummy!	What's up, friend? I am in restaurant. My fav! I like to eat big breakfast. I like to eat eggs with bacon. So yummy! What you eat this morning?

Description of Learner Responses: Learners performing within the Novice levels are characterized by using *words and phrases* as their primary text type. These learners can use practiced and memorized words (*restaurant* and *food*) and phrases (*Good morning!* and *Drink coffee*). As learners progress, they bring together memorized phrases and chunks of language that, at times form simple sentences. A simple sentence is a subject and a verb that expresses a complete thought (*I am in restaurant* and *I like eggs and bread*). Eventually learners use simple sentences as their primary text type. They use simple sentences most of the time (*I am in restaurant, I like to eat big breakfast, I like to eat eggs with bacon*).

Table 6.3
Text Type Performance Domain Indicators (PDIs) for Learners Performing Within the Intermediate Level

	INTERMEDIATE		
Sublevels	LOW	MID	HIGH
Context	familiar, informal, formal, straight-forward		
Content	familiar	familiar, at times researched	familiar, concrete, at times researched
Performance Domain Indicator	**I can form simple sentences**, and at times **series of sentences**.	**I can form a series of connected sentences**, and at times complex sentences.	**I can form (a) series of connected** and complex **sentences that may combine to create a simple paragraph(s)** and/or paragraph-length *discourse*.

- The language in bold indicates the source is the *NCSSFL-ACTFL Can-Do Statements: Performance Indicators for Language Learners* (NCSSFL-ACTFL, 2017).
- The language in italics indicates that the source is the *ACTFL Proficiency Guidelines* (ACTFL, 2012b).
- Some language may appear in additional levels to provide scaffolding, consistency and/or clarity.

Intermediate Task: Post a reply to your friend's breakfast photo message on social media and compare your breakfasts.

LEARNER SAMPLE RESPONSE

INTERMEDIATE LOW	INTERMEDIATE MID	INTERMEDIATE HIGH
Looks delicious! You like to eat eggs and bacon a lot. It is good for you. Is it your favorite meal? I like eggs also. I like to eat with rice and beans. This morning I eats cereals. It is not so yummy as you. Well, enjoy!	Lol. Again? I see that bacon and eggs is your favorite meal for breakfast! LOVE IT! I also eated eggs this morning, but I had with rice and beans. My dad says that eggs are good to us because they are very healthy. But, I prefer cereal like FruitySquares, because of all the sugar. YUM! Lol. Well, enjoy!	Lol! Are you having bacon and eggs for breakfast again today? Why am I not surprised? It is definitely your favorite meal. I also ate eggs this morning, but I had with rice and beans. My dad said that eggs are very healthy because they give protein. Do you always eat your eggs scrambled? Or have you had other eggs? Cereal is faster. I'm late! Ahhh! Ok well, enjoy!

Description of Learner Responses: Learners performing within the Intermediate level use *sentences* as their primary text type for communicating. They begin by using simple sentences that, at times, form a series of sentences. A series of sentences are multiple sentences on a related topic (*You like to eat eggs and bacon a lot. It is good for you. Is it your favorite meal?*). As learners further combine language, they use coordinators (and, but, or, for, so) to form connected sentences (*I also eated eggs this morning, but I had with rice and beans*). These learners also use prepositional and/or noun phrases (*for breakfast* and *with rice and beans*) to add details within the sentence.

As learners progress, they form connected sentences with greater frequency to create a series of connected sentences. In addition, these learners can, at times, use complex sentences. A complex sentence uses subordinating conjunctions (that, where, when, etc.) to connect an idea that cannot not stand alone as a complete thought (a dependent clause) (*that bacon and eggs is your favorite meal for breakfast, that eggs are very healthy,* and *because they give protein*). These learners craft their message through sentence structures that show logic and organization. Eventually, learners form (a) series of connected and complex sentences that may even combine to create a simple paragraph(s) and/or paragraph-length discourse. These learners connect sentences in such a way that they cannot be rearranged without impacting the meaning of the text.

Table 6.4

Text Type Performance Domain Indicators (PDIs) for Learners Performing Within the Advanced Level

	ADVANCED		
Sublevels	**LOW**	**MID**	**HIGH**
Context	familiar, unfamiliar, informal, formal, complex		
Content	familiar, academic, social, concrete	academic, social, professional, concrete	academic, social, professional, concrete, abstract
Performance Domain Indicator	**I can** create **simple paragraphs** and/or *paragraph-length discourse.*	**I can** create **organized paragraphs** and/or *connected paragraph-length discourse.*	**I can create** organized paragraphs and/or *connected paragraph-length discourse,* and at times *cohesive extended discourse.*

- The language in bold indicates the source is the *NCSSFL-ACTFL Can-Do Statements: Performance Indicators for Language Learners* (NCSSFL-ACTFL, 2017).
- The language in italics indicates that the source is the *ACTFL Proficiency Guidelines* (ACTFL, 2012b).
- Some language may appear in additional levels to provide scaffolding, consistency and/or clarity.

Advanced Task: Create a podcast episode for your listeners that brings awareness to how nutrition impacts the human body.

LEARNER SAMPLE RESPONSE

ADVANCED LOW	ADVANCED MID	ADVANCED HIGH
Hello to all my listeners! This episode of The Body and Our Nutrition is about artificial sweeteners, like SweArtif and Azcufal. The artificial sweeteners taste like sugar but have zero calories, which is why they are super popular for peoples want to lose weight. The products that are popular is soda, cereals, chips, and cookies! However, did you know a health study finded that artificial sweeteners is linked to heart problems and also increase in weight? More research is needed in the future. So, the next time when you are in the grocery store, you can think twice about diet products. Is it worth it? Until then, thanks for listen and "Be well."	Hello to all my listeners! This is another episode of The Body and Our Nutrition. In today's episode I speak about health concerns that are linked to artificial sweeteners, such as SweArtif and Azcufal. If you know or not, the food industry is substituting sugar with artificial sweeteners. These are many products you see marketed as "diet" or "zero calories", which are popular for soft drinks. But did you know that artificial sweeteners is used in more food products, such as salad dressings, soups? Bread has false sugars! However, recent health studies are questioning if they safe for the human body. The research has linked artificial sweeteners with maybe heart problems and also increases in weight. So, the next time you are in a grocery store, please read the label, because "zero" may not be better. Well, is everything for today. Thanks for listening and "Be well."	Many people think that "diet" or "zero calorie" products can help to lose weight. But is effective? Hello and welcome to another episode of The Body and Our Nutrition. In today's episode I address health concerns that are linked to artificial sweeteners. You may recognize artificial sweeteners by their names, like SweArtif and Azcufal. The popularity is due to they have zero calories but taste like sugar. So, same great taste without the calories. Well, according to recent health studies, fake sugars promote cravings, which can lead you to want to eat more. This is because the level of sweet is very high, which people then want more of. But if you eat more, you may gain weight, right? So, the next time you find yourself in a grocery store, be sure and read the label. As always, thank you for tuning in to today's episode of The Body and Our Nutrition. If you liked today, follow by clicking on the subscribe button. Until next week, "Be well" my friends.

Description of Learner Responses: Learners performing within the Advanced level, use the *paragraph* as their length of understandable speech (or paragraph-length discourse when referring to the interpersonal mode). Again, a paragraph or paragraph-length discourse consists of a variety of sentence structures that cannot be rearranged without impacting the meaning of the text. Learners first create simple paragraph(s) and/or paragraph-length discourse. They use several sentences that support and develop a central topic (the health impact of artificial sweeteners). They may use discourse markers (*however, next time,* and *until then*), subordinate clauses (*which is why, that are*, and *that artificial sweeteners is linked*), and/or prepositional phrases to connect a series of connected and complex sentences.

From there, learners create organized paragraph(s) and/or connected paragraph-length discourse (interpersonal). In an organized paragraph, the grouping of sentences is unified around a central idea and the sentences are arranged in a clear order (Rosen & Behrens, 2003, p. 119).Learners may use organizational patterns like chronological, pros and cons, cause/effect (*sweeteners/health*), compare/contrast, biography/autobiography, storytelling, description, problem and solution, etc. (Troyan et al., 2023, Appendix D-3). Within their paragraphs, they can use sentence structures and cohesive devices to organize ideas; for example, conditional clauses (*if you know or not* and *if they safe*), subordinating clauses (*the next time you are in a grocery store*), and demonstrative pronouns (*this is* and *these are*).

From there, learners performing within the Advanced level can, at times, create cohesive extended discourse. These learners use the *text* as their length of understandable speech. They can, at times, apply the above patterns not only within their paragraphs, but to their overall text.

YOUR TURN

LEARNING TARGETS CHECK:	
I can	☐ describe the Text Type performance domain. ☐ describe how Text Type shows up in learners' performance at various levels.

Pause and reflect:

How would you describe Text Type to your learners? Consider any explanations, examples, and/or visuals you might use to describe the performance domain:

Text Type in learner work:

The following exercise includes a sample task for each of the performance levels. Write a learner response that includes the characteristics of Text Type for learners performing within each level. Use the provided Intermediate sample to guide you.

NOVICE	**Task:** Describe a person who is important to you and what makes them special for the *Special Person* classroom bulletin board display for the *Friends and Family Open House.*	
INTERMEDIATE	**Task:** A friend is coming to your house for dinner and to meet your family. Your friend has asked you to tell them a little bit about your family in order to have some topics of conversation when they meet. Call your friend and leave a voicemail describing your family.	Hey, here is about my family. I have a big family with 5 kids. Big happy family! I like my family big. Bigger is better! I am oldest. I have 2 brothers and I have 2 sisters. Everyone in my family is tall. One brother only is not tall. He is short. No short talking! We are very noisy, but we have fun. You will talk loud with us. In the summer we camp. In the winter we ski. We are nature lovers. If you talk about outdoor nature is good. We see my grandma sometimes. Grandma live in Florida. My cousins live at a lake. I prefer lake, because we have a boat there. Well, see ya soon!
ADVANCED	**Task:** Give a presentation to a small group of exchange students with examples of how culture influences the roles of family members.	

The Performance Domain Indicators (PDIs) Assessment and Feedback Guide

The *Performance Domain Indicators (PDIs) Assessment and Feedback Guide* is a resource for both learners and educators to use when assessing learner performance. The information within each guide is based on PDIs of the following performance level targets: Novice High (Table 6.5), Intermediate Mid (Table 6.6), Intermediate High (Table 6.7), and Advanced Low (Table 6.8). However, these guides can serve as a template for other performance level targets. It is important to note that a performance assessment evaluates a *learner's performance*, and not *the learner*. Therefore, a learner is not *at* a level, but rather a learner's performance may be consistent *with* a level.

The purpose of the *Performance Domain Indicators (PDIs) Assessment and Feedback Guide* is to provide a visual pathway for evaluating the Text Type of a learner's performance. The left-hand column provides guiding questions that lead us to identify the Text Type consistent with a learner's performance. These guiding questions are based upon the performance levels' PDIs, which are presented lowest to highest. Starting at the *Beginning* level, evaluators progress through each question, responding "yes" or "no." If evaluators reply "yes" to all questions in the *Beginning* level, they continue to the next level (*Developing*), repeating the process, and continuing through the levels. If evaluators reply "no" to a question, they go back to the previous level, in which all their replies for the level's guiding questions are "yes." At the last level where all questions are answered "yes," evaluators continue across the chart. They can then refer to the second column labeled *Performance Domain Indicator* for the PDI that best aligns with the learner's performance. Based on this evaluation, the following two columns provide example GLOW and GROW comments. GLOW feedback states what the learner achieved and GROW feedback directs learners how to develop their language skills. This feedback is not unit specific, but rather supports overarching language performance goals that learners can work towards throughout a course. Including evidence from learner performance within the GLOW/GROW feedback is most effective.

Table 6.5
Performance Domain Indicators (PDIs) Assessment and Feedback Guide

TEXT TYPE Target performance level: **Novice High** Context: familiar, informal, formal, predictable Content: familiar, everyday			
Guiding questions	**Performance Domain Indicator**	**GLOW**	**GROW**
Novice Low Beginning Can the learner • use words and/ or phrases to communicate their message?	I can use practiced and memorized words and phrases.	• You use words/ phrases to communicate your message.	• Which words/phrases might you combine to make a more complete thought? • What vocabulary could you add to express a more complete idea? • How might you use (*example sentence starter*) to create complete sentences?
Novice Mid Developing Can the learner: • use words and phrases to communicate their message? • at times use simple sentences?	I can use practiced and memorized words and phrases, and at times use simple sentences.	• You use words/ phrases to communicate your message. • You are beginning to use simple sentences to communicate your message.	• How might you combine some of your phrases to build complete sentences? • What vocabulary/structures might you add to create complete sentences? • How might you use (*example sentence starter*) to create complete sentences?
Novice High Meeting Can the learner: • use simple sentences most of the time throughout the performance?	I can use simple sentences most of the time.	• You use simple sentences most of the time throughout your performance.	• How might you group sentences on a related topic into a logical sequence to create a series of sentences? • How might you say/write multiple sentences on a related topic to create a series of sentences? • What coordinators (*and, but, or, for, so*) could you add to better connect your ideas?
Intermediate Low Exceeding Can the learner: • use simple sentences throughout the performance? • at times form multiple sentences on a related topic to create series of sentences?	I can form simple sentences, and at times series of sentences.	• You use simple sentences throughout your performance. • At times you say/ write multiple sentences on a related topic to create series of sentences.	• How might you group sentences on a related topic into a logical sequence to create series of sentences throughout your performance? • What coordinators (*and, but, or, for, so*) could you add to better connect your ideas? • How might you add complexity? Consider using subordinating conjunctions (*once, while, when, where, before, after…*).

Table 6.6
Performance Domain Indicators (PDIs) Assessment and Feedback Guide

TEXT TYPE Target performance level: **Intermediate Mid** Context: familiar, informal, formal, straight-forward Content: familiar, at times researched			
Guiding questions	**Performance Domain Indicator**	**GLOW**	**GROW**
Novice High Beginning Can the learner: • use simple sentences most of the time throughout the performance?	I can use simple sentences most of the time.	• You use simple sentences most of the time throughout your performance.	• How might you group sentences on a related topic into a logical sequence to create a series of sentences? • How might you say/write multiple sentences on a related topic to create a series of sentences? • What coordinators (*and, but, or, for, so*) could you add to better connect your ideas?
Intermediate Low Developing Can the learner: • use simple sentences throughout the performance? • at times form multiple sentences on a related topic to create series of sentences?	I can form simple sentences, and at times series of sentences.	• You use simple sentences throughout your performance. • At times you say/write multiple sentences on a related topic to create series of sentences.	• How might you group sentences on a related topic into a logical sequence to create series of sentences throughout your performance? • What coordinators (*and, but, or, for, so*) could you add to better connect your ideas? • How might you add complexity? Consider using subordinating conjunctions (*once, while, when, where, before, after…*).
Intermediate Mid Meeting Can the learner: • form multiple sentences on a related topic to create series of sentences? • use series of sentences throughout the performance? • use coordinators to connect ideas together? • at times use subordinating conjunctions to create complex sentences?	I can form a series of connected sentences, and at times complex sentences.	• You use series of connected sentences throughout your performance. • You connect your ideas with coordinators (*and, but, or, for, so…*). • At times you use subordinating conjunctions (*once, while, when, where, before, after…*) to create complex sentences.	• How might you add complexity? Consider using subordinating conjunctions (*once, while, when, where, before, after…*). • What might you add or change to your series of sentences to create a paragraph/paragraph-length response? • How might you organize your thoughts differently to create paragraphs/paragraph-length responses, where similar ideas are grouped together and elaborated on?

Intermediate High Exceeding Can the learner: • form multiple sentences on a related topic to create series of sentences? • form complex sentences by using coordinators, conjunctions, and/or discourse markers to connect ideas together? • at times combine connected and complex sentences to create simple paragraphs and/or paragraph-length responses?	I can form (a) series of connected and complex sentences that may combine to create a simple paragraph(s) and/or paragraph-length discourse.	• You use connected and complex sentences throughout your performance. • You connect your ideas together using coordinators (*and, but, or, for, so*...) and/or discourse markers (*also, next, however, for example*...). • You use subordinating conjunctions (*once, while, when, where, before, after*...) to organize your ideas within sentences. • You are beginning to organize and elaborate on your ideas to create paragraphs/paragraph-length discourse.	• How might you elaborate on an idea at length to create a paragraph and/or paragraph-length discourse? • How might you develop and support your ideas with more evidence and detail to create a simple paragraph/paragraph-length discourse? • How might you organize your thoughts differently to create a simple paragraph/paragraph-length discourse?

Table 6.7
Performance Domain Indicators (PDIs) Assessment and Feedback Guide

<table>
<tr><th colspan="4">TEXT TYPE
Target performance level: Intermediate High
Context: familiar, informal, formal, straight-forward
Content: familiar, concrete, at times researched</th></tr>
<tr><th>Guiding questions</th><th>Performance Domain Indicator</th><th>GLOW</th><th>GROW</th></tr>
<tr><td>Intermediate Low Beginning
Can the learner:
• use simple sentences throughout the performance?
• at times form multiple sentences on a related topic to create series of sentences?</td><td>I can form simple sentences, and at times series of sentences.</td><td>• You use simple sentences throughout your performance.
• At times you say/write multiple sentences on a related topic to create series of sentences.</td><td>• How might you group sentences on a related topic into a logical sequence to create series of sentences throughout your performance?
• What coordinators (and, but, or, for, so) could you add to better connect your ideas?
• How might you add complexity? Consider using subordinating conjunctions (once, while, when, where, before, after...).</td></tr>
<tr><td>Intermediate Mid Developing
Can the learner:
• form multiple sentences on a related topic to create series of sentences?
• use series of sentences throughout the performance?
• use coordinators to connect ideas together?
• at times use subordinating conjunctions to create complex sentences?</td><td>I can form a series of connected sentences, and at times complex sentences.</td><td>• You use series of connected sentences throughout your performance.
• You connect your ideas with coordinators (and, but, or, for, so...).
• At times you use subordinating conjunctions (once, while, when, where, before, after...) to create complex sentences.</td><td>• How might you add complexity? Consider using subordinating conjunctions (once, while, when, where, before, after...).
• What might you add or change to your series of sentences to create a paragraph/paragraph-length response?
• How might you organize your thoughts differently to create paragraphs/ paragraph-length responses, where similar ideas are grouped together and elaborated on?</td></tr>
</table>

Intermediate High Meeting Can the learner: • form multiple sentences on a related topic to create series of sentences? • form complex sentences by using coordinators, conjunctions, and/or discourse markers to connect ideas together? • at times combine connected and complex sentences to create simple paragraphs and/or paragraph-length responses?	I can form (a) series of connected and complex sentences that may combine to create a simple paragraph(s) and/or paragraph-length discourse.	• You use connected and complex sentences throughout your performance. • You connect your ideas together using coordinators (*and, but, or, for, so…*) and/or discourse markers (*also, next, however, for example…*). • You use subordinating conjunctions (*once, while, when, where, before, after…*) to create complex sentences. • You are beginning to organize and elaborate on your ideas to create paragraphs/paragraph-length discourse.	• How might you elaborate on an idea at length to create a paragraph and/or paragraph-length discourse? • How might you develop and support your ideas with more evidence and detail to create a simple paragraph/paragraph-length discourse? • How might you organize your thoughts differently to create a simple paragraph/paragraph-length discourse?
Advanced Low Exceeding Can the learner: • develop and support their ideas in detail? • use organizing language (discourse markers, coordinators, conjunctions) to link ideas together and create simple paragraphs/paragraph-like discourse? • create simple paragraphs/paragraph-like discourse throughout the performance?	I can create simple paragraphs and/or paragraph-length discourse.	• You create simple paragraphs and/or paragraph-length discourse throughout your performance. • You develop and support your ideas with evidence and details. • You use coordinators (*and, but, or, for, so…*) and/or discourse markers (*also, next, however, for example…*) and/or subordinating conjunctions (*once, while, when, where, before, after…*) to connect your ideas together into simple paragraphs and/or paragraph-length discourse. • You show logic and organization in how you express your ideas. This is seen by your use of…	• How might you use an organizational pattern (*chronological, general-to-specific, definition-example, problem-solution, compare-contrast, order of importance…*) to create organized paragraphs/paragraph-length discourse? • What organizing language (*discourse markers, coordinators, subordinating conjunctions*) might you use to transition between paragraphs? • How might you add more variety to the ways you connect your ideas together?

Table 6.8
Performance Domain Indicators (PDIs) Assessment and Feedback Guide

TEXT TYPE Target performance level: **Advanced Low** Context: familiar, unfamiliar, informal, formal, complex Content: familiar, academic, social , concrete			
Guiding questions	**Performance Domain Indicator**	**GLOW**	**GROW**
Intermediate Mid Beginning Can the learner: • form multiple sentences on a related topic to create series of sentences? • use series of sentences throughout the performance? • use coordinators to connect ideas together? • at times use subordinating conjunctions to form complex sentences?	I can form a series of connected sentences, and at times complex sentences.	• You use series of connected sentences throughout your performance. • You connect your ideas with coordinators (*and, but, or, for, so…*). • At times you use subordinating conjunctions (*once, while, when, where, before, after…*) to form complex sentences.	• How might you add complexity? Consider using subordinating conjunctions (*once, while, when, where, before, after…*). • What might you add or change to your series of sentences to create a paragraph/paragraph-length response? • How might you organize your thoughts differently to create paragraphs/paragraph-length responses, where similar ideas are grouped together and elaborated on?
Intermediate High Developing Can the learner: • form multiple sentences on a related topic to create series of sentences? • form complex sentences by using coordinators, conjunctions, and/or discourse markers to connect ideas together? • at times combine connected and complex sentences to create simple paragraphs and/or paragraph-length responses?	I can form (a) series of connected and complex sentences that may combine to create a simple paragraph(s) and/or paragraph-length discourse.	• You use connected and complex sentences throughout your performance. • You connect your ideas together using coordinators (*and, but, or, for, so…*) and/or discourse markers (*also, next, however, for example…*). • You use subordinating conjunctions (*once, while, when, where, before, after…*) to form complex sentences that organize your ideas within sentences. • You are beginning to organize and elaborate on your ideas to create paragraphs/paragraph-length discourse.	• How might you elaborate on an idea at length to create a paragraph and/or paragraph-length discourse? • How might you develop and support your ideas with more evidence and detail to create a simple paragraph/paragraph-length discourse? • How might you organize your thoughts differently to create a simple paragraph/paragraph-length discourse?

Advanced Low Meeting Can the learner: • develop and support their ideas in detail? • use organizing language (discourse markers, coordinators, subordinating conjunctions) to link ideas together and create simple paragraphs/paragraph-like discourse? • create simple paragraphs/paragraph-like discourse throughout the performance?	I can create simple paragraphs and/or paragraph-length discourse.	• You create simple paragraphs and/or paragraph-length discourse throughout your performance. • You develop and support your ideas with evidence and details. • You use coordinators (*and, but, or, for, so…*) and/or discourse markers (*also, next, however, for example…*) and/or subordinating conjunctions (*once, while, when, where, before, after…*) to connect your ideas together into simple paragraphs and/or paragraph-length discourse. • You show logic and organization in how you express your ideas. This is seen by your use of…	• How might you use an organizational pattern (*chronological, general-to-specific, definition-example, problem-solution, compare-contrast, order of importance…*) to create organized paragraphs/paragraph-length discourse? • What organizing language (*discourse markers, coordinators, subordinating conjunctions*) might you use to transition between paragraphs? • How might you add more variety to the ways you connect your ideas together?
Advanced Mid Exceeding Can the learner: • develop and support their ideas in detail? • use organizing language (discourse markers, coordinators, subordinating conjunctions) to link ideas together and create paragraphs/paragraph-like discourse? • use organizational patterns to create organized paragraphs/paragraph-length discourse?	I can create organized paragraphs and/or connected paragraph-length discourse.	• You show logic and organization in how you express your ideas. This is seen by your use of… • You use organizing language (*discourse markers, coordinators, subordinating conjunctions*) to connect your ideas within paragraphs/paragraph-length discourse. • You use an organizational pattern (*chronological, general-to-specific, definition-example, problem-solution, compare-contrast, order of importance…*) to create organized paragraphs/paragraph-length discourse.	• How might you apply an organizational pattern (*chronological, general-to-specific, definition-example, problem-solution, compare-contrast, order of importance…*) over a continuation of several paragraphs? • What organizing language (*discourse markers, coordinators, subordinating conjunctions*) might you use to transition between paragraphs? • How might you bring more variety to the ways you are connecting your ideas?

Performance Domain Indicators within a Rubric

In order to evaluate learners' performances, the PDIs are placed within a rubric with four performance level labels: *Beginning, Developing, Meeting,* and *Exceeding* (see Table 6.9). The *Meeting* level aligns with the target performance level for the learners. These labels communicate to learners how their performance compares to the standard; learners are *Beginning* to meet, *Developing* towards, *Meeting,* or *Exceeding* their target performance level. It is important to highlight that, similar to other ACTFL publications, when placed within a rubric, these four performance levels are arranged high to low, beginning with the highest on the left. This is so that learners read the highest level of performance first. Table 6.9 illustrates this rubric alignment and arrangement for the Text Text performance domain for both the presentational and interpersonal mode of communication.

Table 6.9
Aligning the Text Type Performance Domain Indicators (PDIs) in a Rubric:

Target performance level: **Novice High** Context: familiar, informal, formal, predictable Content: familiar, everyday				
	INTERMEDIATE LOW	NOVICE HIGH	NOVICE MID	NOVICE LOW
	EXCEEDING	MEETING	DEVELOPING	BEGINNING
Performance level description	I can form simple sentences, and at times series of sentences.	I can use simple sentences most of the time.	I can use practiced and memorized words and phrases, and at times use simple sentences.	I can use practiced and memorized words and phrases.

Target performance level: **Intermediate Mid** Context: familiar, informal, formal, straight-forward Content: familiar, at times researched				
	INTERMEDIATE HIGH	INTERMEDIATE MID	INTERMEDIATE LOW	NOVICE HIGH
	EXCEEDING	MEETING	DEVELOPING	BEGINNING
Performance level description	I can form (a) series of connected and complex sentences that may combine to create a simple paragraph(s) and/or paragraph-length discourse.	I can form a series of connected sentences, and at times complex sentences.	I can form simple sentences, and at times series of sentences.	I can use simple sentences most of the time.

Target performance level: **Advanced Low** Context: familiar, unfamiliar, informal, formal, complex Content: familiar, academic, social, concrete				
	ADVANCED MID	ADVANCED LOW	INTERMEDIATE HIGH	INTERMEDIATE MID
	EXCEEDING	MEETING	DEVELOPING	BEGINNING
Performance level description	I can create organized paragraphs and/ or connected paragraph-length discourse.	I can create simple paragraphs and/or paragraph-length discourse.	I can form (a) series of connected and complex sentences that may combine to create a simple paragraph(s) and/ or paragraph-length discourse.	I can form a series of connected sentences, and at times complex sentences.

Performance Assessment in Action

As educators our understanding of the PDIs is critical to providing effective feedback that promotes language growth in our learners. Therefore, it is important to build our capacity to use the PDIs. Here, the goal is to model how to use the Text Type PDIs to evaluate learner work, which is the basis of the GLOW and GROW feedback that is provided. The focus of this section is to evaluate learner work and provide feedback, *not* to determine a learner's proficiency level. In other words, the evaluation indicates the learner's performance is consistent with a level and provides feedback to indicate next steps for language growth.

This section demonstrates how to use these rubrics to evaluate sample presentational and interpersonal learner performances within the Novice, Intermediate, and Advanced level. These learner samples exemplify products of a summative assessment. They show evidence from learners after exposure to and practice within a unit of study. That is, learners complete these tasks following classroom instruction and multiple opportunities for formative practice on these topics. After the evaluation of each learner sample there is a model of how to provide GLOW and GROW feedback using examples from the *Performance Domain Indicators (PDIs) Assessment and Feedback Guide.*

Each learner sample:

- indicates the PDI that best aligns with the performance in the rubric.
- uses the evaluation to explain what the learner can do in this performance sample.
- models how to provide GLOW and GROW feedback using examples from the *Performance Domain Indicators* (PDIs) *Assessment and Feedback Guide.*

LEARNERS PERFORMING WITHIN THE NOVICE LEVEL

Mode of communication: *Presentational*
Target performance level: **Novice High**
Context: familiar, formal, predictable
Content: familiar, everyday

Novice Task: For the hallway display, select one of the people we have studied in this unit. Create a descriptive writing in which you compare how you are similar in order to highlight what you have in common, and contrast how you are different in order to feature how you each make use of your attributes in our diverse world.

LEARNER SAMPLE RESPONSE

Hey! My name is Pari. I 12 years old. I am Persian.
Ingrid is sports. Ingrid like to dance. I am not to dance. I am to swim.
I is shy. Ingrid is shy. I is play sports.
I am to read. Ingrid like to dance.
I am to draw. Ingrid like to dance. Well, see ya later!

Evaluation & Explanation

TEXT TYPE			
EXCEEDING	**MEETING**	**DEVELOPING**	**BEGINNING**
I can form simple sentences, and at times series of sentences.	I can use simple sentences most of the time.	I can use practiced and memorized words and phrases, and at times use simple sentences.	I can use practiced and memorized words and phrases.

Evaluation: The learner is able to combine memorized words and phrases (*I am, Ingrid is, Ingrid like*) to communicate their message. At times an occasional simple sentence appears (*My name is Pari, I am Persian, Ingrid is shy*). However, the learner is not able to sustain, or consistently use, simple sentences most of the time throughout the performance.

Feedback

- GLOW: You use memorized words and phrases, and at times simple sentences to communicate your message.
- GROW: You are beginning to show evidence of creating a simple sentence using structures like *Ingrid is...* How might you use the structure *I like* to create simple sentences throughout your performance?

LEARNERS PERFORMING WITHIN THE NOVICE LEVEL

Mode of communication: *Interpersonal*
Target performance level: **Novice High**
Context: familiar, informal, predictable
Content: familiar, everyday

Novice Task: Chat with your new classmate to find out how you both may be similar to and/or different from each other.

LEARNER SAMPLE RESPONSE

Learner 1: Hello.

Learner 2: Hey! How's it going?

Learner 1: Good. And you?

Learner 2: Very good. What do you like more, sports or ski?

Learner 1: Ski.

Learner 2: Me too (*points to self*)! I like to ski. A lot. Um, my favorite...my favorite sport...in the...in the winter. Um...do you like to sing?

Learner 1: I don't like to sing.

Learner 2: Do you like to do...soccer in it's hot or it's cold?

Learner 1: Um...repeat?

Learner 2: Do you like to do soccer in it's hot or it's cold?

Learner 1: ...

Learner 2: Do you like to do soccer... (*kicks leg*)...in it's hot or it's cold?

Learner 1: No...comprehend (*shrugs*).

Learner 2: Do you like...soccer (*kicks leg*)...in it's hot (*fans face*) or um... it's cold, brrr (*shivers and rubs arms*)?

Learner 1: Oh! Um, yes. I like...um, hot?

Learner 2: (*Nods*)

Learner 1: Yes. Hot.

Learner 2: Cool! Me...me too!

Learner 1: Ride bike?

Learner 2: Well, sometimes. Yes, I like to ride a bike. Sometimes. In the...in the summer?

Learner 1: Ok, bye.

Learner 2: See ya later!

Evaluation & Explanation

TEXT TYPE | LEARNER 1			
EXCEEDING	**MEETING**	**DEVELOPING**	**BEGINNING**
I can form simple sentences, and at times series of sentences.	I can use simple sentences most of the time.	I can use practiced and memorized words and phrases, and at times use simple sentences.	I can use practiced and memorized words and phrases.

Evaluation: In this performance sample, Learner 1 relies on a mixture of memorized words (*Good, repeat?, Yes, Hot*) and phrases (*And you?, No...comprehend, I like...um, hot? Ride bike?*) as their primary type of text to communicate their message. The learner uses one simple sentence (*I don't like to sing*) but provides no other evidence of simple sentences in their performance.

Feedback:

- GLOW: You use practiced words and phrases to communicate your message.
- GROW: How might you use "*I like...*" to create simple sentences when you respond to your partner's questions?

TEXT TYPE | LEARNER 2			
EXCEEDING	**MEETING**	**DEVELOPING**	**BEGINNING**
I can form simple sentences, and at times series of sentences.	I can use simple sentences most of the time.	I can use practiced and memorized words and phrases, and at times use simple sentences.	I can use practiced and memorized words and phrases.

Evaluation: In this performance sample, Learner 2 uses simple sentences most of the time as their primary type of text when communicating with their partner. This is evident in both the learner's responses and questions. At times the learner tries to extend their response with more detail to create a series of sentences (*Me too! I like to ski. A lot. Um, my favorite...my favorite sport...in the...in the winter*). However, the learner tends to fall back to practiced words and phrases in each of their attempts to do so.

Feedback:

- GLOW: You use simple sentences most of the time throughout your performance.
- GROW: How might you use words like *because* or *and* to better connect your ideas and create a series of sentences?

LEARNERS PERFORMING WITHIN THE INTERMEDIATE LEVEL

Mode of communication: *Presentational*
Target performance level: **Intermediate Mid**
Context: familiar, formal, straight-forward
Content: familiar, researched

Intermediate Task: As part of an Earth Day campaign in your community, write a formal letter to an influential leader advocating for change that would address an environmental issue that you have learned about.

LEARNER SAMPLE RESPONSE

Honorable Mayor Wilson,

Help! My name is Kai Meyer. I live in Elmdale now. I like to live in Elmdale We have strong engaged for community here. Since 3 years, Elmdale won the "Best city in the USA". We try to win that again and we could. We could to do more of to clean up and beautify our city. Maybe have like the BUGA garden show in Germany. Different cities host and make big gardens. And plant trees. Like big plant show at the fair.

A lot in Elmdale is full of garbage. When I run on hiking trails I see a lot of garbage. Nature reserves, like Forest Park, have more garbage. It is not pretty. I remember you to since 3 years. It would be great if mentality to our city. Run people need clean trails. They are impacted.

Here are things do. We could the volunteers clean up the parks. This would also help the people in the city do it. Other volunteers could the large places. The city could have event. The event would be "Consciousness about Garbage in Elmdale"

We could say, plant more trees in the niehgborhoods. This would give back the trees we take for construction. Maybe be a tree hugger? Plants and gardens too but for now trees. When we plant more trees, this make our community a better place, if we plant more trees. Plant now! Act now!

Sincerely,
Kai Meyer

Evaluation & Explanation

TEXT TYPE			
EXCEEDING	**MEETING**	**DEVELOPING**	**BEGINNING**
I can form (a) series of connected and complex sentences that may combine to create a simple paragraph(s) and/or paragraph-length discourse.	I can form a series of connected sentences, and at times complex sentences.	I can form simple sentences, and at times series of sentences.	I can use simple sentences most of the time.

Evaluation: In this performance sample, the learner writes using a series of sentences as their primary type of text to communicate their message. That is, the learner is able to write multiple sentences on a related topic (*A lot in Elmdale is full of garbage. When I run on hiking trails I see a lot of garbage. Nature reserves, like Forest Park, have more garbage*). The sentences are connected through the use of discourse markers (*also*), coordinators (*and, but*), and prepositional phrases (*at the fair, like Forest Park, in the city*). At times the learner uses subordinating conjunctions to form complex sentences (*When I run on hiking trails…, When we plant more trees…*), but does not yet show evidence of paragraphs, in which ideas are organized and developed at length. Rather, the learner largely relies on a series of sentences, moving from one topic to the next, as their text type to communicate their ideas.

Feedback:

- GLOW: You use series of sentences throughout your performance. You connect your ideas with coordinators such as *and, also*, and *but*.
- GROW: How might you add complexity? Consider using subordinating conjunctions such as *once, while, where, unless*, and *rather than*.

LEARNERS PERFORMING WITHIN THE INTERMEDIATE LEVEL

Mode of communication: *Interpersonal*
Target performance level: **Intermediate Mid**
Context: familiar, informal, straight-forward
Content: familiar, researched

Intermediate Task: After reading and viewing texts to learn about ways we can implement change, select an organization that works to better their community. Discuss your organization with a partner to learn more about the organizations you have each selected, why you selected yours, and how your organizations implement change for others.

LEARNER SAMPLE RESPONSE

Learner 1: Hi Paz!

Learner 2: Hi! How are you?

Learner 1: I'm alright. What is your organization called?

Learner 2: My organization is called the Family Stay House...But no place like home.

Learner 1: How interesting (*nods*)!

Learner 2: What is your organization called?

Learner 1: The organization...er, sorry...my organization favorite is called Renewing the Countryside.

Learner 2: Oh, how fantastic! What does it do? Renew, reuse, recycle (*laughs*)?

Learner 1: Renewing the Countryside gives money for the...for the farmers and help the children of poor families in rural communities.

Learner 2: Great! Great (*nods*)!

Learner 1: What does your organization try to do (*tilts head*)?

Learner 2: The Family Stay House tries to support and help families, families that need the help economically paying for pro-proced... when the children are sick. Where is the organization?

Learner 1: The organization...er, sorry...my organization favorite is called Renewing the Countryside.

Learner 2: My organization, um, is in the city.

Learner 1: Great! Did it do something in the past?

Learner 2: Every year, the Race for the Kids, um remember money for organization, um, to pay for the, um, pro-proced-procedures.

Learner 1: How cool (*smiles*)!

Learner 2: Um, yes, yes, yes (*nods*). Um, How many people serves the organization?

Learner 1: Many people serves the organization in the city because everyone wants to help the, the rural communities.

Learner 2: Yes, great!

Learner 1: I like your organization a lot. How can I help your organization? I pitch in?

Learner 2: Oh, how fantastic (*eyes widen*)! You can work as a volunteer – reading books to children, playing sports with the children, donating money and getting money for the organization.

Learner 1: How fun! Why should I help?

Learner 2: Um, because ...because, in my opinion, it is important to help the people.

Learner 1: Great, great, yes (*nods*)!

Learner 2: What they do for your organization?

Learner 1: Um you can get money for the organization or you can donate. A little bit goes a long way!

Learner 2: I think so.

Learner 1: Bye (*waves*)!

Learner 2: Bye (*waves*)!

Learner 1: Thanks for talking with me.

Learner 2: I'll see you laters. Thanks for talking with me

Evaluation & Explanation

TEXT TYPE | LEARNER 1			
EXCEEDING	**MEETING**	**DEVELOPING**	**BEGINNING**
I can form (a) series of connected and complex sentences that may combine to create a simple paragraph(s) and/or paragraph-length discourse.	I can form a series of connected sentences, and at times complex sentences.	I can form simple sentences, and at times series of sentences.	I can use simple sentences most of the time.

Evaluation: In this performance sample, Learner 1 uses simple sentences and at times a series of sentences as their primary type of text to communicate their message. The learner is able to respond to their partner's questions using simple sentences. At times the learner uses multiple sentences on a related topic (*Renewing the Countryside gives money for the...for the farmers and help the children of poor families in rural communities, Many people serves the organization in the city because everyone wants to help the, the rural communities*). These sentences are connected through coordinators (*and, or*) and a subordinating conjunction (*because*).

Feedback:

- GLOW: You use series of sentences throughout your performance and connect your ideas with coordinators (*and, or*) and a subordinating conjunction (*because*).
- GROW: How might you add complexity? Consider using subordinating conjunctions such as *while, when, where*, and *that*.

TEXT TYPE | LEARNER 2			
EXCEEDING	**MEETING**	**DEVELOPING**	**BEGINNING**
I can form (a) series of connected and complex sentences that may combine to create a simple paragraph(s) and/or paragraph-length discourse.	I can form a series of connected sentences, and at times complex sentences.	I can form simple sentences, and at times series of sentences.	I can use simple sentences most of the time.

Evaluation: In this performance sample, Learner 2 communicates using series of connected sentences as their primary type of text to communicate their message. They use coordinators (*but, and*) and prepositional phrases (*to pay for the procedures, as a volunteer, in my opinion*) to connect their ideas. The learner, at times, uses embedded/subordinate clauses (*that need the help economically, when the children are sick*) to form complex sentences. However, the learner is not yet able to demonstrate paragraph-length discourse.

Feedback:

- GLOW: You use series of connected sentences throughout your performance. You connect your ideas using coordinators (*and*), subordinating conjunctions (*because, that, when*) and prepositional phrases (*in my opinion, as a volunteer...*).
- GROW: How might you elaborate on your ideas at length to create paragraph-length responses?

LEARNERS PERFORMING WITHIN THE ADVANCED LEVEL

Mode of communication: *Presentational*
Target performance level: **Advanced Low**
Context: familiar, informal, complex
Content: familiar, academic, social, professional, concrete

Advanced Task: Based on the movie, write a diary entry from the perspective of one of the baseball players that includes their reflections of the recruitment practices of professional baseball leagues.

LEARNER SAMPLE RESPONSE

Dear diary,

I cannot believe that this investigation about my age is still going on! It is just not fair! I am not a liar! How much analyses have I to do? Because of this, I did not get the chance to sign when I turned 16 years. In the Professional Baseball League they think that all us players are liars. There are some that lies, but there are a lot of us who tells the truth.

But what are they suppose to do, if only one year older means you are worth $1 million less? Seriously, one year? The PBL uses us for our poverty. It's not fair that they treat us differently, pay us differently just because we live in poorer country. Why I don't make money because I am a great baseball player? Why am I the cheap export? If I am in power, I would talks with the representatives to work for changes in recruiting regulations, like age restrictions and equal pay.

Yet I know that if I work hard, I will get a contract of any price which, for me, is the way out of poverty. It is also my family's way out of poverty because they are depending on me. The first thing I take on is buy my parents a house so they never have to worry about housing ever again! I just have to be patient. All I want to do is play baseball- it's what I love, it's what I borned to do, it's all I have ever done.

Let's play ball!
-Mike

Evaluation & Explanation

TEXT TYPE			
EXCEEDING	**MEETING**	**DEVELOPING**	**BEGINNING**
I can create organized paragraphs and/or connected paragraph-length discourse.	I can create simple paragraphs and/ or paragraph-length discourse.	I can form (a) series of connected and complex sentences that may combine to create a simple paragraph(s) and/ or paragraph-length discourse.	I can form a series of connected sentences, and at times complex sentences.

Evaluation: In this performance sample, this learner is able to create simple paragraphs as their primary text type. These simple paragraphs are made up of a series of connected sentences (*there are some that lies, but...*) and complex sentences that include subordinating conjunctions (*I cannot believe that..., It's not fair that..., If I ...*). Each paragraph is developed around a main topic: the first paragraph is about age discrimination; the second paragraph is about fair pay; and the third paragraph is about future hopes. The learner does not yet show evidence of organized paragraphs.

Feedback:

- GLOW: You create simple paragraphs throughout your performance.
- GROW: How might you use an organizational pattern such as (*chronological, general-to-specific, definition-example, problem-solution, compare-contrast, order of importance...*) to create organized paragraphs?

LEARNERS PERFORMING WITHIN THE ADVANCED LEVEL

Mode of communication: *Presentational*
Target performance level: **Advanced Low**
Context: familiar, informal, complex
Content: familiar, academic, social, concrete

Advanced Task: After visiting a Monarch butterfly sanctuary, you and a friend discuss your reactions to learning about the monarch butterfly migrations and how it's being threatened.

LEARNER SAMPLE:

Learner 1: So, what did ya think?... of the butterfly sanctuary?

Learner 2: I think that... um, the butterflies, the monarch butterflies are incredible. And these places, these sanctuaries, well, they are magical. I don´t know much things about the butterflies and their migrations before now.

Learner 1: Uhm... Same here. What fascinates me is how millions of butterflies, these tiny insects, come from all over the continent..., and to end up in these sanctuaries in Mexico, ya know?

Learner 2: Yeah, it is incredible. These places, they are so important to, to their migration process. They need these sanctuaries for, um.., this is where they sleep during the winter months.

Learner 1: Exactly. These sanctuaries are where the monarchs hibernate, so they are vital to this natural phenomenon. What's more, is the monarch's cultural influence on, like, the festival for Day of the Dead. For them, the butterflies represent the souls of their loved ones, like the butterflies (*air quotes*) are their loved ones coming back.

Learner 2: It's interesting how, how nature can influence cultural practices, like, what you said, about Day of the Dead. (...)

Learner 1: RIght. This is why I am glad to have learned that they are taking measures to, um, conserve these spaces, um, these spaces that are their habitats. Right?

Learner 2: Yes. They are protecting against destruction because of people cutting down trees illegally. But, I understand why they have to do it.

Learner 1: How so? What do you mean by that?

Learner 2: Well, some peoples depends on cutting down the trees, because they need that money to buy food and clothes for their family.

Learner 1: Ah ha (*nods head*). Now I understand. Yeah, they are between a rock and a hard place. Ya know? I don't know what I would do if... if I was in that situation where, where my family depended on the income from illegal logging. What would you do?

Learner 2: It's difficult to say what I would do too, especially because there are no other good options for them, to have, to have different jobs.

Learner 1: And, on the other hand, it's not just about conserve the sanctuaries. For example, the use of chemicals... or pesticides in fields kills butterflies along the migration routes. It's kind of gotten out of hand. I'm not sure what can be done.

Learner 2: Well, one thing we can do is plant more milkweed, which is a flower that the butterflies depend on for food.

Evaluation & Explanation

TEXT TYPE | LEARNER 1			
EXCEEDING	**MEETING**	**DEVELOPING**	**BEGINNING**
I can create organized paragraphs and/or connected paragraph-length discourse.	I can create simple paragraphs and/or paragraph-length discourse.	I can form (a) series of connected and complex sentences that may combine to create a simple paragraph(s) and/or paragraph-length discourse.	I can form a series of connected sentences, and at times complex sentences.

Evaluation: In this performance sample, Learner 1 uses connected paragraph-length discourse as their primary text type. Within the paragraph-length discourse, they use a variety of sentences that are related to the same topic. They use the phrases *exactly* and *on the other hand* to link or connect their ideas to their interlocutor. They use a variety of complex sentences (*so they are vital to this natural phenomenon, that are their habitats,* and *if I was*) to make connections with their ideas. Learner 1 also uses discourse markers (*what's more, on the other hand* and *for example*) to create connected paragraph-length discourse.

Feedback:

- GLOW: You use discourse markers (*what's more, for example*) and complex sentences (*that are their habitats, if...*) to connect your ideas together into paragraph-length discourse.
- GROW: How might you use an organizational pattern such as (*chronological, general-to-specific, definition-example, problem-solution, compare-contrast, order of importance...*) to create organized paragraph-length discourse?

TEXT TYPE | LEARNER 2			
EXCEEDING	**MEETING**	**DEVELOPING**	**BEGINNING**
I can create organized paragraphs and/or connected paragraph-length discourse.	I can create simple paragraphs and/or paragraph-length discourse.	I can form (a) series of connected and complex sentences that may combine to create a simple paragraph(s) and/or paragraph-length discourse.	I can form a series of connected sentences, and at times complex sentences.

Evaluation: In this performance sample, Learner 2 uses the sentence as their primary type of text. They are able to use both connected and complex sentences within their responses. For example, Learner 2 frequently uses the coordinators *and* and *but* to make connected sentences. Learner 2 is also able to use subordinating conjunctions to create complex sentences (*that...the monarch butterflies are incredible, where they sleep during the winter months, which is a flower...*). They are able to form these sentences in isolation, but they do not elaborate or support their ideas with enough evidence or detail to create paragraph-length discourse.

Feedback:

- GLOW: You use a variety of connected and complex sentences throughout your performance.
- GROW: How might you elaborate on your ideas at length to create paragraph-length discourse?

YOUR TURN

LEARNING TARGETS CHECK:	
I can	☐ evaluate learner work using the Performance Domain Indicators (PDIs). ☐ give effective feedback using the Text Type PDIs.

Now it is your turn to practice evaluating learner performances and providing feedback. Remember, learners complete these performance tasks following classroom instruction and multiple opportunities for formative practice on these topics. In this section, use the Text Type PDIs to indicate the level of performance that best corresponds with the following presentational and interpersonal learner performance samples. Then provide each learner GLOW and GROW feedback. You may want to use the *Performance Domain Indicators (PDIs) Assessment and Feedback Guide* to help guide your evaluation and feedback of the learner's performance in the Text Type performance domain.

Then, turn to APPENDIX B | Text Type (p.431-p.436) to compare your evaluation and feedback to one provided by the authors. Reflect on how your evaluation and feedback was similar and/or different, and why. You can do this individually and/or with your colleagues (for example, with a Professional Learning Community (PLC)). This exercise can be an opportunity for rich discussion to help increase inter-rater reliability among educators.

LEARNERS PERFORMING WITHIN THE NOVICE LEVEL

Mode of communication: *Presentational*
Target performance level: **Novice High**
Context: familiar, formal, predictable
Content: familiar, everyday

Novice Task: For the hallway display, select one of the people we have studied in this unit. Create a descriptive writing in which you compare how you are similar in order to highlight what you have in common, and contrast how you are different in order to feature how you each make use of your attributes in our diverse world.

LEARNER SAMPLE RESPONSE

Greetings! My name is Leo. I am 12 years old.

Naiomi is 24 years old. She is Diné (Navajo).

Naiomi & I is similar. Naiomi is sports-minded because to skateboard. I do not like to skateboard. I like hockey but no skateboarding. I like hockey in the winter with my friends.

Naiomi is hard-working. Naiomi really likes to practice skateboarding. How interesting! I like hockey.

Naiomi not is lazy. She likes to work for more skate parks. How important! Many people to need more skate parks. Many people to need more hockey parks too. Is a problem. How important!

Naiomi and I is different but equal. Thank you for read!

Evaluation & Explanation

TEXT TYPE			
EXCEEDING	**MEETING**	**DEVELOPING**	**BEGINNING**
I can form simple sentences, and at times series of sentences.	I can use simple sentences most of the time.	I can use practiced and memorized words and phrases, and at times use simple sentences.	I can use practiced and memorized words and phrases.

Evaluation:

Feedback:
- GLOW:

- GROW:

Turn to APPENDIX B | Text Type (p.431) to compare your evaluation and explanation to one provided by the authors.

LEARNERS PERFORMING WITHIN THE NOVICE LEVEL

Mode of communication: *Interpersonal*
Target performance level: **Novice High**
Context: familiar, formal, predictable
Content: familiar, everyday

Novice Task: Chat with your new classmate to find out how you both may be similar and/or different.

LEARNER SAMPLE RESPONSE

Learner 1: Um...Sports?

Learner 2: Yes (*nods*), I like sports a LOT (*smiles*). My favorite! And you?

Learner 1: Yes (*nods*).

Learner 2: What do you like more, baseball or football?

Learner 1: Baseball. I...mmm...baseball...yes. And you, sir?

Learner 2: I like baseball AND I like football! I like to play baseball in the summer. I like to watch football in the fall.

Learner 1: Ok. Um, television?

Learner 2: Yes, I like TV. I really like to watch sports on TV. And you?

Learner 1: Very good (*nods*).

Learner 2: Ok. Do you like to read?

Learner 1: Um...repeat?

Learner 2: Do you...do you like...to read?

Learner 1: ...

Learner 2: Do you like...to read?

Learner 1: Um... (*shrugs shoulders*)

Learner 2: Um, do you like to read? Um (*gestures with hands*) read...read. Um, books?

Learner 1: Oh! Yes (*nods*). I...I...yes.

Learner 2: Ok. I...um...I...too (*points to self, nods*)! I like read books. Um, do you like to swim?

Learner 1: Repeat?

Learner 2: Do you like to swim (*gestures swimming movements with arms*)?

Learner 1: Oh, yes (*nods*)! Yes, swim...yes! And you, sir?

Learner 2: Cool! I too. I like to swim in the summer. Sometimes I like to swim in the winter in the...um...in the...yeah.

Learner 1: ...

Learner 2: Ok, well, thanks! Bye (*waves*)!

Learner 1: Bye (*waves*)!

Evaluation & Explanation

TEXT TYPE | LEARNER 1			
EXCEEDING	**MEETING**	**DEVELOPING**	**BEGINNING**
I can form simple sentences, and at times series of sentences.	I can use simple sentences most of the time.	I can use practiced and memorized words and phrases, and at times use simple sentences.	I can use practiced and memorized words and phrases.

Evaluation:

Feedback:

- GLOW:
- GROW:

TEXT TYPE | LEARNER 2			
EXCEEDING	**MEETING**	**DEVELOPING**	**BEGINNING**
I can form simple sentences, and at times series of sentences.	I can use simple sentences most of the time.	I can use practiced and memorized words and phrases, and at times use simple sentences.	I can use practiced and memorized words and phrases.

Evaluation:

Feedback:

- GLOW:
- GROW:

Turn to APPENDIX B | Text Type (p.432) to compare your evaluation and explanation to one provided by the authors.

LEARNERS PERFORMING WITHIN THE INTERMEDIATE LEVEL

Mode of communication: *Presentational*
Target performance level: **Intermediate Mid**
Context: familiar, formal, straight-forward
Content: familiar, researched

Intermediate Task: As part of an Earth Day campaign in your community, write a formal letter to an influential leader advocating for change that would address an environmental issue that you have learned about.

LEARNER SAMPLE RESPONSE

Dear Mr. President,

Did you heared, one of the major problems environmental in the world is the increase of the ocean level as result of global warming. The increase of the ocean level is a problem Many Carribean countries are sinking and that is destroying the work or life of many people.

People are constructing sea barriers for flooding. One other thing Carribean countries are doing is transport help now, not help in the future. For the future, it's important that the world, specifically the United States, reduce the greenhouse gas emissions because a rise in greenhouse gases cause more global warming. As a result, the icebergs melt and the sea level rise. The problem is very important for you.

One example of this problem is of a little country in the Pacific Ocean. The country is Tuvalu. Tuvalu is home for 11,000 people and increase of sea level is a very big problem for this country. In the last decade, Tuvalu lost 2 islands a the ocean. This is very bad for that many people would have eliminate outside of their house and in 50 years, the whole country absent.

A protect millions of people and the health of our environments, I would think that is important you reduce the emissions greenhouse gas for the future of the world. Also, I would think that a good solution for now is do construct many sea barriers and raise to support for people and families close to the coast.

Thanks,
Avery

Evaluation & Explanation

TEXT TYPE			
EXCEEDING	**MEETING**	**DEVELOPING**	**BEGINNING**
I can form (a) series of connected and complex sentences that may combine to create a simple paragraph(s) and/or paragraph-length discourse.	I can form a series of connected sentences, and at times complex sentences.	I can form simple sentences, and at times series of sentences.	I can use simple sentences most of the time.

Evaluation:

Feedback:

- GLOW:
- GROW:

Turn to APPENDIX B | Text Type (p.433) to compare your evaluation and explanation to one provided by the authors.

LEARNERS PERFORMING WITHIN THE INTERMEDIATE LEVEL

Mode of communication: *Interpersonal*
Target performance level: **Intermediate Mid**
Context: familiar, informal, straight-forward
Content: familiar, researched

Intermediate Task: After reading and viewing texts to learn about ways we can implement change, select an organization that works to better their community. Discuss your organization with a partner to learn more about the organizations you have each selected, why you selected yours, and how your organizations implement change for others.

LEARNER SAMPLE RESPONSE

Learner 1: Hi Kim (*waves*)!

Learner 2: Hi Hai (*waves*)!

Learner 1: What's up?

Learner 2: Um, not a lot (*shrugs shoulders*). And you?

Learner 1: Not a lot, not a lot. What is the name of your organization?

Learner 2: My organization is called Special Olympics.

Learner 1: Yes (*nods*) and what does that organization do?

Learner 2: Repeat please?

Learner 1: What does that organization do?

Learner 2: Me organization to try, um, to play sports with people with special you need...people with special needs.

Learner 1: How fantastic (*smiles*)!

Learner 2: What organization you work a volunteer?

Learner 1: My organization is called the Blizzard Foundation.

Learner 2: Very well (*nods*). Where is the organization?

Learner 1: My organization is in North Minneapolis. And...but it tries to work in all parts of Minnesota.

Learner 2: Very well (*nods*).

Learner 1: What did organization do in the past?

Learner 2: In the past, the Special Olympics to play sports...baseball, soccer, and basketball with a lot of people with special you need and...puts on the Polar Plunge.

Learner 1: Yes (*nods*).

Learner 2: What did your organization do in the past year?

Learner 1: My organization works as help people that want to play baseball but I can't buy. In the past, my organization worked with Miracle League. The children of Miracle League love baseball and it was very fun.

Learner 2: Very well. What is the priorities of the organization?

Learner 1: The first priority of my organization is donates money to children and families that can't buy baseball. And you, what is the priority?

Learner 2: Me priorities organization is helps people with special you need...did...no...has very fun.

Learner 1: And you volunteered with your organization in the past?

Learner 2: Ah no (*shakes head*), but I am going helps in the future.

Learner 1: Yes.

Learner 2: Bye (*waves*).

Learner 1: Ah, hold on.

Learner 2: Sorry.

Learner 1: How can I help your organization?

Learner 2: Repeat please?

Learner 1: How can I help your organization?

Learner 2: You work a volunteer to play sports with people with special you need and to donate money.

Learner 1: That's great! Thanks for talking with me!

Learner 2: Thanks, sir.

Evaluation & Explanation

TEXT TYPE | LEARNER 1			
EXCEEDING	**MEETING**	**DEVELOPING**	**BEGINNING**
I can form (a) series of connected and complex sentences that may combine to create a simple paragraph(s) and/or paragraph-length discourse.	I can form a series of connected sentences, and at times complex sentences.	I can form simple sentences, and at times series of sentences.	I can use simple sentences most of the time.

Evaluation:

Feedback:

- GLOW:
- GROW:

TEXT TYPE | LEARNER 2			
EXCEEDING	**MEETING**	**DEVELOPING**	**BEGINNING**
I can form (a) series of connected and complex sentences that may combine to create a simple paragraph(s) and/or paragraph-length discourse.	I can form a series of connected sentences, and at times complex sentences.	I can form simple sentences, and at times series of sentences.	I can use simple sentences most of the time.

Evaluation:

Feedback:

- GLOW:
- GROW:

Turn to APPENDIX B | Text Type (p.434) to compare your evaluation and explanation to one provided by the authors.

LEARNERS PERFORMING WITHIN THE ADVANCED LEVEL

Mode of communication: *Presentational*
Target performance level: **Advanced Low**
Context: familiar, informal, complex
Content: familiar, academic, social, professional, concrete

Advanced Task: Based on the movie, write a diary entry from the perspective of one of the baseball players that includes their reflections of the recruitment practices of professional baseball leagues.

LEARNER SAMPLE RESPONSE

Dear Diary,

I am angry! Even that my results are conclusive, I still have to do more tests. This means that I can lose my chance to sign with a professional baseball team. Out of all the 105 players, I have the best chance. It was to be a dream come true! However, because my tests are no decided, it is a controversy for teams to sign with me. I dreamed this my whole life. It's what I sacrificed so many years. What the Professional Baseball League has did to me, I think it an injustice. I did all those tests that show that I am 16 years and I did not lie. In fact my family gived the PBL all the documents that they needed. The PBL did no need the same documents or the same tests of the other baseball players. It's not fair that we give you more information. And because of this, no one wants to sign me.

If I were a different baseball player, I would no have to take the tests. I just want to be baseball player. I can help my family too. I wants to try to be as good as the other players, even better. I hope some team signs me. I won't accept that I've lost the opportunity. I will fight for my opportunity. I will not back down. Someday I will win the World Series.

Hugs,
Mikey

Evaluation & Explanation

TEXT TYPE			
EXCEEDING	**MEETING**	**DEVELOPING**	**BEGINNING**
I can create organized paragraphs and/or connected paragraph-length discourse.	I can create simple paragraphs and/ or paragraph-length discourse.	I can form (a) series of connected and complex sentences that may combine to create a simple paragraph(s) and/ or paragraph-length discourse.	I can form a series of connected sentences, and at times complex sentences.

Evaluation:

Feedback:

- GLOW:
- GROW:

Turn to APPENDIX B | Text Type (p.435) to compare your evaluation and explanation to one provided by the authors.

LEARNERS PERFORMING WITHIN THE ADVANCED LEVEL

Mode of communication: *Presentational*
Target performance level: **Advanced Low**
Context: familiar, informal, complex
Content: familiar, academic, social, concrete

Advanced Task: After visiting a Monarch butterfly sanctuary, you and a friend discuss your reactions to learning about the monarch butterfly migrations and how it's being threatened.

LEARNER SAMPLE RESPONSE

Learner 1: Hey *(waves hand)*.

Learner 2: Hey.

Learner 1: So, what do you think about what we learned, um, about the sanctuaries?

Learner 2: Well, to be honest, I didn't even know of them. I had no idea that there are places like these where millions of butterflies goes to, to hibernate, like clusters of them. It was incredible to see.

Learner 1: Agreed *(widens eyes)*. It blew my mind to see them togethers on only a tree branch. And that there are too many that their weight may... may... break the tree branch! It's a place that I want to go..., to, like, to experience it.

Learner 2: Yeah, I wonder how it would be *(tilts head)*? I think that I might be scared, because of these tiny insects, ya know? I don't know how I could feel. You?

Learner 1: Huh. Yeah *(shrugs shoulders)*. It makes me nervous, I guess... Um, well, the sanctuaries are importants to the lifecycle of these butterflies. With no reserves, there would no be butterflies.

Learner 2: Uh huh. It was interesting to learn that only here in this specific places does it have the perfect temperature, the perfect humidity and everything. Like everything is done only for the butterflies in this place and that is why they all come every year to spend the winter.

Learner 1: I know *(raises eyebrows)*! It's a perfect ecosystem, which me.., which makes me sad that peoples cut down the trees not legally in those areas, meaning they destroy their habitat.

Learner 2: I wonder if they do not knows about how these sanctuaries are important. Or, maybe they have no choice because they need to earn a living *(shrugs and raises hands)*. But it's not just this. There is also climate change and the use of pesticides that, that contribute to the destruction of the habitats.

Learner 1: Oh, for sure *(nods head)*! For example, when the farmers there use pesticides in the fields for the migratory routes, the butterflies get, um...um..., sick *(looks at Learner 2)*?

Learner 2: Sick *(tilts head)*?

Learner 1: Yeah, they get sicks because the pesticides on their food.

Learner 2: Ah! You mean poison.

Learner 1: Yes, poison. They get poisons when they eat the flower, the, um... the milkweed.

Learner 2: Yes, there are many threats to this species. Well *(sighs)*, I only hope that they can protect it so one day in the future I can travel there and visit the sanctuaries.

Learner 1: Ha *(laughs)*! Yes, of course.

Evaluation & Explanation

TEXT TYPE | LEARNER 1			
EXCEEDING	**MEETING**	**DEVELOPING**	**BEGINNING**
I can create organized paragraphs and/or connected paragraph-length discourse.	I can create simple paragraphs and/or paragraph-length discourse.	I can form (a) series of connected and complex sentences that may combine to create a simple paragraph(s) and/or paragraph-length discourse.	I can form a series of connected sentences, and at times complex sentences.

Evaluation:

Feedback:

- GLOW:
- GROW:

TEXT TYPE | LEARNER 2			
EXCEEDING	**MEETING**	**DEVELOPING**	**BEGINNING**
I can create organized paragraphs and/or connected paragraph-length discourse.	I can create simple paragraphs and/or paragraph-length discourse.	I can form (a) series of connected and complex sentences that may combine to create a simple paragraph(s) and/or paragraph-length discourse.	I can form a series of connected sentences, and at times complex sentences.

Evaluation:

Feedback:

- GLOW:
- GROW:

Turn to APPENDIX B | Text Type (p.436) to compare your evaluation and explanation to one provided by the authors.

Learning Experiences to Facilitate Learner Growth

Once educators have clarified for learners the goals of performance and provided feedback, learners need learning experiences to help them *understand* the Text Type performance domain and PDIs as well as *develop* their language performance. Learning experiences to *understand* the performance domain are listed first, followed by learning experiences to *develop* learner performance. Each learning experience includes *Learner outcomes* (what learners can do upon successful completion of the experience) and an outline of logistical components (*time, preparation, materials, instructions*). *Alternatives* and *Differentiation* offer ways to personalize the experience for a variety of learners. Each learning experience includes short examples, often including learners' work, to help educators visualize each learning experience. The learning experiences can be used with an entire class of learners as a way to introduce and focus learner work on a particular performance domain. Learning experiences can also be assigned to learners by educators or self-selected by learners themselves for further practice within a performance domain. These examples can serve as a springboard for educators to develop their own learning experiences for each performance domain when working with their learners.

CLARIFYING EXPECTATIONS

Domain: Text Type

Focus: Understanding how Text Type is evaluated

Note: This learning experience can be replicated in multiple performance domains.

Learner outcomes

I can identify how Text Type is evaluated by:

- evaluating my own work using self-assessment questions.
- determining the PDI that best aligns with my work.
- using the GROW guiding questions to revise and/or add to my work.

Time

- Prep time: 5 minutes
- Implementation time: 30 minutes
- Debrief time: 5 minutes

Materials

- The performance task
- Learners' presentational or interpersonal performance such as a draft or a recording
- The Text Type PDIs
- Self-assessment questions
- GROW guiding questions

Prep

- Prepare to display the PDIs, self-assessment questions, and the GROW guiding questions.
- Be sure learners have access to their performance.

Instructions

1. (PURPOSE) Tell learners that they will learn how to self-assess their work and make changes in order to reach the next performance level.
2. (SET UP) Remind learners about the performance task for this interpersonal or presentational performance.
3. Display the PDIs and instruct learners to use the self-assessment questions to evaluate their work.
4. (GUIDANCE) Go through a few of the self-assessment questions with the learners, directing learners to reflect on their own performance to identify if it best aligns to the *Beginning, Developing, Meeting,* or *Exceeding* PDIs.
5. (ENGAGEMENT) Release the lesson to have learners continue reflecting on the self-assessment questions and have them mark which PDI best aligns to their work.
6. (GUIDANCE) When learners have identified the PDI that best aligns to their work, point them toward the GROW guiding questions for that level.
7. (ENGAGEMENT) Learners use the GROW guiding questions for that level to guide them to improve their work.
8. (DEBRIEF) Learners could share their reflections and improvements with a partner.
9. Ask learners to reflect on:
    a. What did you notice about your Text Type before and after you reflected on the self-assessment and used the GROW guiding questions?
    b. How might you apply what you learned to your future work when completing a summative task?

Alternatives

Learners could complete this learning experience multiple times with multiple interpersonal or presentational tasks throughout a unit.

As learners engage in this learning experience, it eventually can be done more independently and does not need to be guided by the educator.

Differentiation

Learners could work together to give and get feedback from each other. After exchanging drafts, each learner could complete the "self" assessment questions as feedback for their partner, turning it into a peer assessment. Learners could then discuss the assessment of each other's work and brainstorm changes to level up their work.

Learners could assess example work from an anonymous learner individually or in a group discussion.

EXAMPLE

Target performance level: **Novice High**
Context: familiar, informal, predictable
Content: familiar, everyday

Task: *Flip the Stereotype:* Create a flipchart that describes things that are easily seen by other people on the outside. Under each description, in parentheses, write what people might think based on what stereotypes they may think or see (*I am*. . .). Then, on the inside of the paper, write things that others might not easily see or know about you (personality, likes/dislikes. . .) to "flip" the stereotype.

LEARNER'S DRAFT:

OUTSIDE

I red hair.
(I am different.)

I not smile.
(I am unfriendly.)

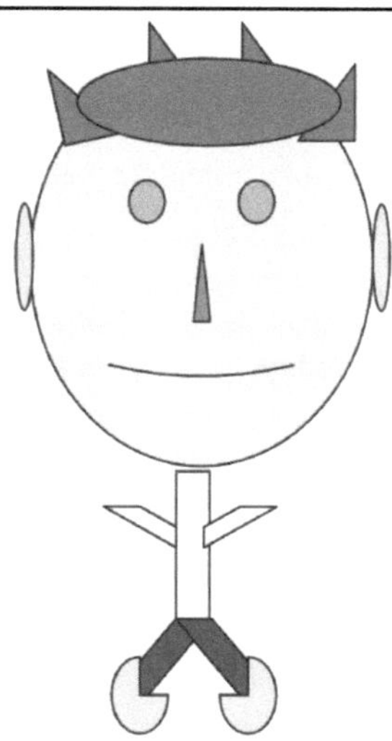

I small short.
(I am weak.)

I have shoes nice
(I am rich.)

INSIDE

I athlete.

I am strong.

I am friend.

I am some worry.

I like my hair.

I student good.

I helps brothers.

Note: Adapted from Sherrow (2018).

Example of how a learner might fill out the sections of the guided self-assessment (Table 6.14) and identify their GROW guiding questions (from Table 6.5).

TARGET PERFORMANCE LEVEL	Novice High	**CONTEXT**	Familiar, informal, formal, predictable
PERFORMANCE DOMAIN	Text Type	**CONTENT**	Familiar, everyday

What description best matches your performance today?

☐ Practiced or memorized words and phrases
☑ A mixture of practiced or memorized words, phrases, and simple sentences
☐ Simple sentences most of the time
☐ Simple sentences, and at times a series of sentences

Write or record an example of a complete sentence that you used today:

Option 1: Select vocabulary/structures that helped you create complete sentences today:

☑ I like... ☐ I do not like...
☑ I am... ☐ I am not...

Option 2: What vocabulary/structures did you use to create complete sentences today?

How often did you use a series of sentences (*multiple sentences on a related topic*)?

☑ I did not use a series of sentences today.
☐ I used a series of sentences once today.
☐ I used a series of sentences multiple times today.

Option 1: If you used a series of sentences, write an example of a series of sentences that you used today:

Option 2: If you did not use a series of sentences today, think of one sentence you used today. How would you add or extend the sentence to create multiple sentences on a related topic?

People think I am weak. Not good on team. I am athlete. I am strong.

Option 1: What coordinators did you use today to connect your ideas?

☐ also ☐ because
☐ but ☐ when
☐ Other: ______________________

Option 2: What coordinators could you add to better connect your ideas?

I red hair but I like my red hair.

Evaluate how you think you performed in your use of Text Type today:

☐ **Beginning:** I can use practiced and memorized words and phrases.
☐ **Developing:** I can use practiced and memorized words and phrases, and at times use simple sentences.
☑ **Meeting:** I can use simple sentences most of the time.
☐ **Exceeding:** I can form simple sentences, and at times series of sentences

Think about your own experience and what you have done to improve in Text Type. What advice would you give other learners to help them develop text type?

Write sentences. Then see if they go together. Maybe with coordinators.

Learner instructions: Use the GROW guiding questions for the level that best matches your performance. Reflect on the questions, then make changes to your work in order to reach the next level of performance.

GROW GUIDING QUESTIONS:

EXCEEDING	MEETING	DEVELOPING	BEGINNING
• How might you group sentences on a related topic into a logical sequence to create series of sentences throughout your performance? • What coordinators (*and, but, or, for, so*) could you add to better connect your ideas? • How might you add complexity? Consider using subordinating conjunctions (*once, while, when, where, before, after…*).	• How might you group sentences on a related topic into a logical sequence to create a series of sentences? • How might you say/write multiple sentences on a related topic to create a series of sentences? • What coordinators (*and, but, or, for, so*) could you add to better connect your ideas?	• How might you combine some of your phrases to build complete sentences? • What vocabulary/structures might you add to create complete sentences? • How might you use (*example sentence starter*) to create complete sentences?	• Which words/phrases might you combine to make a more complete thought? • What vocabulary could you add to express a more complete idea? • How might you use (*example sentence starter*) to create complete sentences?

Example of what a learner engaged in this process might think and rewrite based on clarifying expectations. This example shows how the learner went from brainstorming ideas around the picture to writing them in a text.

Learner's thinking:

I can use "I am not." I could put together physical traits like hair and size and make series of sentences.

I could add "People think" and "Really."

Rewrite:

I red hair, but I like my red hair.

I small short. People think I am weak. Not good on team. I am athlete. I am strong.

I not always smile. I am sometimes worry. Really I am friend. I helps brothers.

...

RUNNING DICTATION

Domain: Text Type

Focus: Understanding language chunks (words – phrases – sentences)

Learner outcomes	Time	Materials	Prep
I can chunk language by: • reading and remembering chunks of a text. • reciting chunks of text to my partner. • listening and writing chunks of text that my partner tells me.	• Prep time: 20-30 minutes • Implementation time: 15-20 minutes • Debrief time: 5 minutes	• An authentic text, or two texts if they are very short, in the target language on the topic of study. The text should be accessible to the level of the learners (100-200 words with two paragraphs is a good length). • Paper/pencil or digital writing tools for each learner	• Mark a halfway point on the text (or use two short texts). • Make 3-4 copies of the text and hang them at one end of the room. • Do not let learners see the text(s) until they begin. • Make a few extra copies for learners who finish early, so they can check their work.

Instructions

1. (PURPOSE) Tell learners that they will be dictating a text to a partner in order to practice chunking language. Explain that using chunks of language helps us move beyond the word level; we can communicate an idea with a phrase or short sentence.
2. (SET UP) Divide learners into groups of two. One partner takes out paper and a pencil.
3. The paired learners should be next to each other at one end of the room (the opposite end from where the texts are taped).
4. One learner (Learner 1) sits at a desk with paper and pencil. The other learner (Learner 2) stands next to the desk, ready to "run."
5. Instruct learners that Learner 2 will run to look at the text hanging at the other end of the room. All the texts are the same, and there are more than one, so learners don't get bunched up or run into each other. They will read the text, remember what they can (in chunks) and run back to their partner.
6. They will recite what they remember reading to Learner 1, who will write down what Learner 2 says.
7. Learner 2 will run back and continue the process until Learner 2 gets to the halfway mark.
8. At the halfway mark, the partners switch roles. Learner 1 will run and dictate and Learner 2 will write.
9. (ENGAGEMENT) Learners begin "running" back and forth from the text to their partners, dictating the text. Their partners write what they say.
10. (GUIDANCE) Educators can stimulate thinking by asking the learners who are the writers to ask themselves the following questions as they wait at their desks for their partners to return.
    a. Is your partner chunking language to remember it well? Can you hear it in chunks?
    b. Which parts are they able to chunk in bigger chunks, and where might they come back with only one or two words?
11. (DEBRIEF) As groups finish, have them compare their texts to a copy of the original.
12. When all learners are done, display the text on a screen. Have groups discuss how they were able to chunk the text.
13. Ask learners to reflect on:
    a. What did you notice about chunking language and how it impacted the writing process?
    b. How might you apply what you learned to your future work when completing a performance task?

Alternatives	Differentiation
Learners could do this individually, just reading, remembering, (possibly reciting) and writing the text. This could be done with an audio text, if learners can access it without their partner hearing it, and keep their spot in the audio text.	The text could be shortened, or partners could switch off more often. The text could be read by Learner 2, and flipped over or hidden, before dictating to Learner 1. This would involve no running. When completed, learners could come up with the best title for the text, or for a longer text they could add subheadings for various sections of the text.

EXAMPLE

Text 1:	Learner 2 says:		Learner 1 writes:
Rainbow Run 5K presented by UnitedHealth Group 5K Your Way. Dress your Rainbow and join the Fun! Join the live Run in Minneapolis, or plan your own run where you're at. Because of COVID-19, the Rainbow Run 5K Presented by UnitedHealth Group will look different again this year because social distancing cannot stop Pride Celebrations! The Run is going HYBRID! That [...] (Twin Cities Pride, 2021b)	*...Dress your Rainbow ...and join in the Fun!* *Dress your Rainbow... and... join in the Fun!*	↘	*Rainbow Run 5K Presented by United Health Group* *5K your way.* *Dress your rainbow and join in the fun.*

Text 2:	Learner 1 says:		Learner 2 writes:
Pride Movie Night @ MOA – Moonlight As a proud supporter for the LGBT community, B&B Theatres and the Mall of America are presenting a repertoire of 4 special films weekly, every Wednesday in June at 7pm, starting June 9th, which includes: June 9 – Wizard of Oz June 16 – Milk June 23 [...] (Twin Cities Pride, 2021a)	*...* *As a proud supporter for the...*	↘	*Pride Movie Night at MOA -Moonlight* *As a proud supporter for the...*

Note: Text 1 and text 2 reprinted with permission.

REASSEMBLING TEXT

Domain: Text Type

Focus: Understanding text organization

Note: Use primarily with learners performing within the Intermediate and/or Advanced level.

Learner outcomes	Time	Materials	Prep
I can identify how a text is organized by: • grouping sentences by topic. • identifying connections between sentences. • identifying connections between paragraphs. • reassembling a written text.	• Prep time: 30 minutes, depending on how many cut-up copies of the text you need • Implementation time: 20 minutes • Debrief time: 5 minutes	• An authentic text on the topic of study that has clear paragraph topics and connecting words, which help to clarify the order of the sentences in the text	• Separate and number the sentences in the text. • Make copies of the text. One for each group of 3-5 learners. • Cut the text into sentences and put them into envelopes. Have one envelope for each group of 3-5 learners.

Instructions

1. (PURPOSE) Tell learners that they will group sentences by topic as well as identify connections between sentences and paragraphs in order to reassemble a written text.
2. Divide the learners into groups of 3-5 learners each.
3. (SET UP) Pass out an envelope with the cut up text to each group.
4. Instruct learners to discuss the sentences as a group to put them in the order.
5. (ENGAGEMENT) Learners begin looking through, reading aloud, and discussing sentences.
6. (GUIDANCE) Educators can provide the following guiding questions to help facilitate learner discussion (these guiding questions can be adapted to best match the level of the text):
   a. Which sentences are about the same topic? Could you group those together into a paragraph?
   b. Which sentences start an idea? Which sentences continue an idea? Which sentences conclude an idea?
   c. Are there clues to where a paragraph might begin with a new idea?
   d. Are there clues to where an idea/paragraph ends?
   e. Are there clues to the order of the sentences/paragraphs?
   f. Have you thought about the organization of the ideas within each topic and throughout the entire text?
7. (DEBRIEF) Have groups share their version of the final text with the whole class and discuss the clues they used to reassemble it.
8. Ask learners to reflect on:
   a. What did you notice about how a text is organized?
   b. How might you apply what you learned to your future work when completing a performance task?

Alternatives	Differentiation
Assign sentences from each of the different paragraphs of the same text to different groups. Learners could reassemble their assigned paragraph from the same text in their small group. Learners could then work together as a class to put their assembled paragraphs in order. Learners could be given paragraphs instead of sentences and reassemble the text focusing on how the paragraphs fit together.	Learners could be given a template to place the sentences into a specific type of structure (topic sentence, supporting details, closing sentence). Learners could add discourse markers (*first, last, earlier, later...*) to the reassembled text to better sequence or connect ideas.

EXAMPLE

Reassemble this text by moving the sentences into a logical order to create a paragraph.

Learner work:

Example of sentences laid out according to one learner:

4. My cousin is a lot like Megan Rapinoe.
1. First she grew up in a small town in California.
2. There she started playing soccer when she was very young.
5. Her parents influenced her all through her childhood to appreciate life and stand up for what she feels is right.
7. When she got older she began working for other people's rights.
3. Rapinio impacts others and my cousin does too.
6. They are both advocates for positive change, but my cousin is not as famous.

BRAINSTORM BUILDING

Domain: Text Type

Focus: Developing Text Type by brainstorming series of sentences

Note: This learning experience can be replicated in multiple performance domains.

Learner outcomes	Time	Materials	Prep
I can develop Text Type by brainstorming sentences on a related topic in order to create a series of sentences.	• Prep time: 5-15 minutes • Implementation time: 20 minutes • Debrief time: 5 minutes	• Performance tasks • Example sentences to begin (each) series of sentences • Paper/pencil or digital writing tools for each learner	• Prepare performance tasks and sentences from which learners can build a series of sentences.

Instructions

1. (PURPOSE) Tell learners that they will brainstorm multiple sentences on a related topic to create a series of sentences.
2. (SET UP) Give learners a performance task and an example sentence that could begin a series of sentences.
3. (ENGAGEMENT) Brainstorm ideas of how learners might add to the sentence (see example).
4. (ENGAGEMENT) Brainstorm together as a class some additional sentences that could be added to develop the idea and create a series of sentences (see example).
5. Divide learners into groups of 3-5 learners each.
6. Display or hand out additional performance tasks and example sentences from which learners create their own series of sentences (see example).
7. (ENGAGEMENT) Learners brainstorm additional sentences on a related topic to create a series of sentences.
8. In groups, learners add to the example sentence by writing their brainstormed sentences.
9. (DEBRIEF) Learners could share their ideas with the class or between groups.
10. Ask learners to reflect on:
    a. What did you notice when you added more sentences about the topic?
    b. How might you apply what you learned to your future work when completing a performance task?

Alternatives	Differentiation
Learners could complete this learning experience multiple times with multiple presentational/interpersonal performance tasks throughout a unit. As learners engage in this learning experience, it eventually can be done more independently and does not need to be guided by the educator. Learners could do this individually instead of in groups, then share in small groups.	Learners could begin by brainstorming related ideas (who, what, when, where, why), then write the additional sentences to create a series of sentences. Learners could extend their ideas from creating a series of sentences to making paragraphs.

EXAMPLE

Target performance level: **Intermediate Low**
Context: familiar, informal, straight-forward
Content: familiar

Task: Write a note describing your favorite sport to a friend.

Brainstorm Building as a class

Sample sentence: **My favorite sport is skiing.**

Ideas brainstormed by learners in the class:		As a whole class, brainstorm more sentences to make a series of sentences that connect with the sample sentence:
Tell why it is favorite. *Tell how it make me feel?* *What makes it fun?* ...	→	*I like skiing because all my friends ski.* *When I ski I feel free.* *I love the challenge and getting better.* ...

Brainstorm Building as a small group

Sample sentence: **To become a good skier takes a lot of practice**

Learners' conversation that illustrates their brainstorming as a small group:		Brainstorm in a small group and write more sentences to make a series of sentences that connect with the sample sentence:
Learner 1: We could say when or how often we have practice. **Learner 2:** Yeah, and what we do. Not just ski to practice. **Learner 3:** Okay, so... *I ski 3 times a week.* **Learner 2:** Yeah, and *I run and lift weights to keep shape.* **Learner 1:** Okay, write that. **Learner 3:** And talk about my instructor too. ...	→	*I ski 3 times a week.* *I run and lift weights to keep in shape.* *My ski instructor is strict.*

LEVEL UP

Domain: Text Type

Focus: Developing Text Type by creating progressions

Note: This learning experience can be replicated in multiple performance domains.

Learner outcomes	Time	Materials	Prep
I can develop Text Type by building progressions of Text Type to "level up."	• Prep time: 5 minutes (longer if you prepare transcripts) • Implementation time: 30 minutes • Debrief time: 5 minutes	• PDIs for Text Type to display at the appropriate level (Novice, Intermediate, Advanced) • Interpersonal or presentational performance task • If working in the interpersonal mode: One set of transcriptions to use as a model • Paper/pencil or digital writing tools for each learner	• Prepare to display PDIs. • Have a performance task ready for learners to write or speak about. • If working in the interpersonal mode: Have all transcriptions available.

Instructions

1. (PURPOSE) Tell learners that they will develop their Text Type by working with a group to write/say an example performance at each level (*Beginning, Developing, Meeting,* and *Exceeding*).
2. (SET UP) Display and remind learners of the targeted PDIs for Text Type.
3. Divide learners into groups of 3-5 learners each and ask them to take out paper/pencil, digital writing tools, or digital recording tools.
4. Give learners an example presentational task or an interpersonal task with a transcript of one side of the interpersonal conversation.
5. Optional (GUIDANCE) Provide or do an example together as a whole class, writing one performance level together for presentational or write the other part of the interpersonal conversation for one performance level.
6. (ENGAGEMENT) Release the lesson to have learners work in groups to write one example of each level (*Beginning, Developing, Meeting,* and *Exceeding*) using the given task.
7. (GUIDANCE) Remind learners to look at the PDIs to be sure of what level they are aiming for with each example.
8. (DEBRIEF) Learners share their reflections and improvements with a partner, another group, or the class.
9. Ask learners to reflect on:
    a. What did you notice about each example as you progressed through the performance levels of Text Type?
    b. How might you apply what you learned to your future work when completing a performance task?

Alternatives	Differentiation
Learners could do this individually instead of in groups, then share in small groups. Learners could take turns writing an example for each level (*Beginning, Developing, Meeting, Exceeding*). Groups of students could write a presentational example or interpersonal script for each PDI, or groups could be assigned to write a presentational example or interpersonal script for one assigned PDI. One group could share their "leveled up" examples with another group to see if they can identify what level each example is meant to be.	After writing examples for each level about one task together as a class and another in groups, learners could each individually write an example for one level and then share it out with their group. The group can decide which performance level it best matches. Learners could evaluate example texts that have already been created as *Beginning, Developing, Meeting,* or *Exceeding.*

EXAMPLE

Target performance level: **Novice High**
Context: familiar, formal, predictable
Content: familiar, everyday

Task: Create a public service announcement that describes food banks and meal programs.

Learner instructions: Based on the PDIs, write an example of each level of performance.

PDIs displayed:

TARGET PERFORMANCE LEVEL: NOVICE HIGH				
	EXCEEDING	**MEETING**	**DEVELOPING**	**BEGINNING**
Performance Domain Indicators	I can form simple sentences, and at times series of sentences.	I can use simple sentences most of the time.	I can use practiced and memorized words and phrases, and at times use simple sentences.	I can use practiced and memorized words and phrases.

Learner work:

Learners were given the performance task. As a class, they brainstormed a written example for the *Beginning* level.

BEGINNING

> Food free store.
>
> No money
>
> Eat
>
> And Meal Program

In small groups, learners then worked together to write "leveled up" examples for *Developing*, *Meeting*, and *Exceeding*.

EXCEEDING

> Have no money? It is okay. A Food Bank is free food store, so come to the Food Bank.
>
> Or a Meal Program is like restaurant. Go to Meal Program or eat at home from the Bank.

MEETING

> Free food at a store. Have no money? It is okay. Come to the Food Bank. Come to the Meal Program. It is a Restaurant. Store and eat at home. Meal Program and eat.

DEVELOPING

> Food free store.
>
> No money
>
> Eat
>
> Meal Program Restaurant No money? Is okay.
>
> It is a restaurant.

BANK OF CONNECTORS

Domain: Text Type **Focus:** Developing complexity			
Learner outcomes	**Time**	**Materials**	**Prep**
I can develop complexity in my Text Type by using coordinators, discourse markers, and/or subordinating conjunctions to connect ideas.	• Prep time: 30 minutes • Implementation time: 20 minutes, or throughout the lesson or learning • Debrief time: 5 minutes	• A list of some coordinators, discourse markers, and/or subordinating conjunctions • Paper/pencil or digital writing tools for each learner • A way to keep the *Bank of Connectors* available to be used throughout the learning experience • A display of the *Bank of Connectors* that can be amended with additions • Multiple sets of simple sentences to be connected	• Depending on the level and content of the task, create a few categories of connecting words/phrases with examples that learners can use and add to. • Prepare sentences that could be connected using coordinators, discourse markers, and/or subordinating conjunctions.

Instructions

1. (PURPOSE) Tell learners that they will improve their Text Type by using coordinators, discourse markers, and/or subordinating conjunctions to connect ideas.
2. (SET UP) Show the learners two simple sentences and ask them how the sentences might relate to one another and what words could be used to connect the two sentences.
3. Show the learners the *Bank of Connectors* chart with a few examples already on it. If needed, add the connector(s) that the learners shared in step 2.
4. (GUIDANCE) Model the process of pulling a connector from the *Bank of Connectors* and using it to combine the simple sentences.
5. (ENGAGEMENT) Learners work to add connectors to combine the two simple sentences into new combinations. Examples: I go to the park, *but* I don't play softball. *Although* I go to the park, I don't play softball. I go to the park, *despite that* I don't play softball.
6. Learners continue by using the additional sets of simple sentences (provided by the educator) and creating combinations using various connectors for each set to make multiple combinations.
7. As the learners engage, some new connectors may surface. If so, have them add them to the *Bank of Connectors*.
8. (DEBRIEF) Have learners share their new sentences and any additions they made to the *Bank of Connectors* charts.
9. Ask learners to reflect on:
    a. What did you notice about how many different connectors there are for the same function/purpose?
    b. How might you apply what you learned to your future work when completing a performance task?

Alternatives

Learners could list connectors by functions. (*in addition, furthermore*, and *besides* would be ways too add on to a thought or *instead, nevertheless*, and *still* would be ways to contrast two things)

Learners identify connectors (coordinators, discourse markers, and subordinating conjunctions) from a text (written or audio) provided by the educator. Learners could add these to the given categories in the *Bank of Connectors*, or they could create additional categories.

Learners could work in groups or individually.

Differentiation

Learners could be given a list of more coordinators, discourse markers, and/or subordinating conjunctions to connect ideas together. Learners could add these to the given categories in the *Bank of Connectors*, or they could create additional categories.

Learners brainstorm a wider variety of coordinators, discourse markers, and subordinating conjunctions and categorize them according to their function/purpose.

EXAMPLE

This is how a *Bank of Connectors* might look, once several words are added to each category.

also	then	however	although	for example	because	of course	in summary	in other words
as well furthermore in addition besides what's more	next after that so	but nevertheless nonetheless still In contrast	even though even if while despite that	for instance to illustrate in other words	therefore due to accordingly as	naturally certainly needless to say	basically to sum up to recap	especially expressly that is to say

Example of sentences that could be combined using connectors.

1. There are food programs at schools.
2. There are students who are hungry.

Learner work:

Learners identify these two statements as incongruous, before they write the examples below. The connectors they chose are underlined.

There are food programs at schools, but nevertheless there are students who are hungry.

There are students who are hungry, despite the food programs at schools.

YOUR TURN

LEARNING TARGET CHECK:	
I can	☐ select learning experiences that support learners' growth with Text Type.

Complete the chart by identifying specific learning experiences from the *Learning Experiences to Facilitate Learner Growth* section (p. 167-181) that you could use in an upcoming unit to help learners *understand* or *develop* Text Type. Note any materials or prep needed to implement the learning experience in your upcoming unit. Consider any alternatives or differentiation that would better align the learning experience to your unit, the targeted level of performance, and/or your learners.

UNIT:			
PERFORMANCE DOMAIN: TEXT TYPE			
Learning experience	**What type of learning experience is it?** (Circle one)	**Materials/Prep**	**Alternatives / Differentiation**
	Understanding/ Developing		
	Understanding/ Developing		
	Understanding/ Developing		

Learners' Self-Assessment

Self-assessment provides an opportunity for learners to reflect on their performance, set goals, and ultimately to own their learning. This section features three ways learners can self-assess their work: *Make It Visible, Glow and Grow Self-Assessment*, and *Guided Self-Assessments*. Each is educator-designed but learner-driven. That is, the self-assessment is designed by the educator around the PDIs but it is the learner who must reflect on their performance to complete it. The same self-assessments are used in each performance domain chapter to build consistency for learners. Each can be used for learner self-assessment after a formative or summative task. Educators might select self-assessments that have more scaffolding, such as the *Guided Self-Assessment* and *Make It Visible*, after formative tasks where learners may need more support to self-assess their performance, such as the beginning of a unit or a course. The *Glow and Grow Self-Assessment*, which is more open-ended, can be used when learners feel more comfortable reflecting on the PDIs and summarizing their work, such as after formative tasks that occur at the end of the unit or after a summative task. Overall, educators can make adjustments to any of these self-assessments and use them with intentionality based on their learners, their pacing within a unit or course, and the performance task.

Make It Visible

This self-assessment provides an opportunity for learners to visibly see their Text Type in a given formative or summative task. Learners might circle, highlight, color-code, or note the ways in which they used language in a given presentational or interpersonal performance (see Figure 6.1). Or learners can self-assess by marking yes/no and providing evidence (see Table 6.10 and Figure 6.2). Educators can provide opportunities for revisions and/or additions for learners who may find they are not yet *Meeting* expectations, so learners have opportunities for language growth.

The learner samples in this section demonstrate how each self-assessment can be used at one performance level. However, these self-assessments can be used at any level: Novice, Intermediate, or Advanced.

Figure 6.1

Presentational Self-Assessment Using the "Make It Visible" Approach

Directions: Read over your presentational work and mark it accordingly:

- highlight series of sentences
- **bold** coordinators that created connected sentences
- put **(**parenthesis**)** around complex sentences

Example of how the learner, performing within the Intermediate level, completes this self-assessment:

Honorable Mayor Wilson,

Help! My name is Kai Meyer. I live in Elmdale now. I like to live in Elmdale We have strong engaged for community here. Since 3 years, Elmdale won the "Best city in the USA". We try to win that again **and** we could. We could to do more of to clean up **and** beautify our city. Maybe have like the BUGA garden show in Germany. Different cities host **and** make big gardens. And plant trees. Like big plant show at the fair.

A lot in Elmdale is full of garbage **(**When I run on hiking trails I see a lot of garbage.**)** Nature reserves, like Forest Park, have more garbage. It is not pretty. I remember you to since 3 years. **(**It would be great if mentality to our city.**)** Run people need clean trails. They are impacted.

Here are things do. We could the volunteers clean up the parks. This would also help the people in the city do it. Other volunteers could the large places. The city could have event. The event would be "Consciousness about Garbage in Elmdale."

We could say, plant more trees in the niehgborhoods. This would give back the trees we take for construction. Maybe be a tree hugger? **(**Plants and gardens too **but** for now trees.**)** **(**When we plant more trees, this make our community a better place, if we plant more trees.**)** Plant now! Act now!

Sincerely,
Kai Meyer

Table 6.10
Interpersonal Self-Assessment Using the "Make It Visible" Approach

Text Type Reflection Guide What type of text do I use and how do I organize it?			
	YES	**NO**	**EXAMPLES**
words			
phrases			
sentences			
series of sentences			

Figure 6.2
Example of a Completed Interpersonal Self-Assessment Using the "Make It Visible" Approach

Directions: Listen to the recording of your interpersonal conversation. Complete the *Text Type Reflection Guide* and list examples of how you used words, phrases, sentences, and/or series of sentences to communicate your message.

LEARNER SAMPLE

Learner 1: Hello.

Learner 2: Hey! How's it going?

Learner 1: Good. And you?

Learner 2: Very good. What do you like more, sports or ski?

Learner 1: Ski.

Learner 2: Me too (*points to self*)! I like to ski. A lot. Um, my favorite...my favorite sport...in the...in the winter. Um...do you like to sing?

Learner 1: I don't like to sing.

Learner 2: Do you like to do...soccer in it's hot or it's cold?

Learner 1: Um...repeat?

Learner 2: Do you like to do soccer in it's hot or it's cold?

Learner 1: ...

Learner 2: Do you like to do soccer... (*kicks leg*)...in it's hot or it's cold?

Learner 1: No...comprehend (*shrugs*).

Learner 2: Do you like...soccer (*kicks leg*)...in it's hot (*fans face*) or um... it's cold, brrr (*shivers and rubs arms*)?

Learner 1: Oh! Um, yes. I like...um, hot?

Learner 2: (*Nods*)

Learner 1: Yes. Hot.

Learner 2: Cool! Me...me too!

Learner 1: Ride bike?

Learner 2: Well, sometimes. Yes, I like to ride a bike. Sometimes. In the...in the summer?

Learner 1: Ok, bye.

Learner 2: See ya later!

Example of how Learner 1, performing within the Novice level, completes this self-assessment:

Text Type Reflection Guide
What type of text do I use and how do I organize it?

	YES	NO	EXAMPLES
words	X		• *Hello* • *Good* • *Ski* • *Repeat* • *Hot* • *Yes. Hot*
phrases	X		• *And you?* • *No...comprehend* • *I like* • *Ride bike?* • *Ok, bye*
sentences	X		• *I don't like to sing.*
series of sentences		X	

GLOW and GROW Self Assessment

Using the *Meeting* Performance Domain Indicator for each level, learners can self-assess their work on a one-point rubric after a formative or summative task. In Tables 6.11, 6.12, and 6.13, learners would complete the *Where I GLOW (What are my strengths?)* and *How I can GROW (What can I do to improve?)* sections by citing evidence from their own interpersonal or presentational performance for each domain. The *GLOW/GROW Ideas* are given as prompts so that learners are reminded of what to look for or work toward.

Table 6.11
GLOW and GROW Self-Assessment

TEXT TYPE Target performance level: **Novice High** Context: familiar, informal, formal, predictable Content: familiar, everyday		
Instructions: Complete the following reflection by writing where you GLOW and where you can GROW in each area. Make sure to include evidence from your work to support your reasoning.		
Where I GLOW: What are my strengths?	**Performance Domain Indicator**	**How can I GROW? What can I do to improve?**
	I can use simple sentences most of the time.	

GLOW IDEAS	GROW IDEAS
• Did you use simple sentences most of the time throughout your performance?	• How might you group sentences on a related topic into a logical sequence to create a series of sentences? • How might you say/write multiple sentences on a related topic to create a series of sentences? • What coordinators (*and, but, or, for, so*) could you add to better connect your ideas?

Table 6.12
GLOW and GROW Self-Assessment

TEXT TYPE Target performance level: **Intermediate Mid** Context: familiar, informal, formal, straight-forward Content: familiar, at times researched		
Instructions: Complete the following reflection by writing where you GLOW and where you can GROW in each area. Make sure to include evidence from your work to support your reasoning.		
Where I GLOW: What are my strengths?	Performance Domain Indicator	How can I GROW? What can I do to improve?
	I can form a series of connected sentences, and at times complex sentences.	

GLOW IDEAS	**GROW IDEAS**
• Did you use series of connected sentences throughout your performance? • Did you connect your ideas with coordinators (*and, but, or, for, so...*)? • Did you form complex sentences using subordinating conjunctions (*once, while, when, where, before, after...*)?	• How might you add complexity? Consider using subordinating conjunctions (*once, while, when, where, before, after...*) • What might you add or change to your series of sentences to create a paragraph/paragraph-length response? • How might you organize your thoughts differently to create paragraphs/paragraph-length responses, where similar ideas are grouped together and elaborated on?

Table 6.13
GLOW and GROW Self-Assessment

TEXT TYPE Target performance level: **Advanced Low** Context: familiar, informal, formal, complex Content: familiar, academic, social, concrete		
Instructions: Complete the following reflection by writing where you GLOW and where you can GROW in each area. Make sure to include evidence from your work to support your reasoning.		
Where I GLOW: What are my strengths?	**Performance Domain Indicator**	**How can I GROW? What can I do to improve?**
	I can create simple paragraphs and/or paragraph-length discourse.	

GLOW IDEAS	GROW IDEAS
• Did you create simple paragraphs and/or paragraph-length discourse throughout your performance? • Did you develop and support your ideas with evidence and details? • Did you use coordinators (*and, but, or, for, so…*) and/or discourse markers (*also, next, however, for example…*) and/or subordinating conjunctions to connect your ideas together into simple paragraphs and/or paragraph-length discourse? • How did you show logic and organization in how you express your ideas?	• How might you use an organizational pattern (*chronological, general-to-specific, definition-example, problem-solution, compare-contrast, order of importance…*) to create organized paragraphs/paragraph-length discourse? • What organizing language (*discourse markers, coordinators, subordinating conjunctions*) might you use to transition between paragraphs? • How might you add more variety to the ways you connect your ideas together?

Guided Self-Assessments

This self-assessment includes guiding questions to help learners evaluate their own performance after a formative or summative task (see Tables 6.14, 6.15, 6.16). Options are included to help educators personalize the self-assessment for their learners, or learners can self-select which options to answer.

Table 6.14

Interpersonal/Presentational Guided Self-Assessment

<table>
<tr><td>TARGET PERFORMANCE LEVEL</td><td>Novice High</td><td>CONTEXT</td><td>Familiar, informal, formal, predictable</td></tr>
<tr><td>PERFORMANCE DOMAIN</td><td>Text Type</td><td>CONTENT</td><td>Familiar, everyday</td></tr>
<tr><td colspan="4">What description best matches your performance today?
☐ Practiced or memorized words and phrases
☐ A mixture of practiced or memorized words, phrases, and simple sentences
☐ Simple sentences most of the time
☐ Simple sentences, and at times a series of sentences</td></tr>
<tr><td colspan="4">Write or record an example of a complete sentence that you used today:</td></tr>
<tr><td colspan="2">Option 1: Select vocabulary/structures that helped you create complete sentences today:
☐ I like... ☐ I do not like...
☐ I am... ☐ I am not...</td><td colspan="2">Option 2: What vocabulary/structures did you use to create complete sentences today?</td></tr>
<tr><td colspan="4">How often did you use a series of sentences (multiple sentences on a related topic)?
☐ I did not use a series of sentences today.
☐ I used a series of sentences once today.
☐ I used a series of sentences multiple times today.</td></tr>
<tr><td colspan="2">Option 1: If you used a series of sentences, write an example of a series of sentences that you used today:</td><td colspan="2">Option 2: If you did not use a series of sentences today, think of one sentence you used today. How would you add or extend the sentence to create multiple sentences on a related topic?</td></tr>
<tr><td colspan="2">Option 1: What coordinators did you use today to connect your ideas?
☐ also ☐ because
☐ but ☐ when
☐ Other: ____________________</td><td colspan="2">Option 2: What coordinators could you add to better connect your ideas?</td></tr>
<tr><td colspan="4">Evaluate how you think you performed in your use of Text Type today:
☐ Beginning: I can use practiced and memorized words and phrases.
☐ Developing: I can use practiced and memorized words and phrases, and at times use simple sentences.
☐ Meeting: I can use simple sentences most of the time.
☐ Exceeding: I can form simple sentences, and at times series of sentences.</td></tr>
<tr><td colspan="4">Think about your own experience and what you have done to improve in Text Type. What advice would you give other learners to help them develop text type?</td></tr>
</table>

Table 6.15
Interpersonal/Presentational Guided Self-Assessment

<table>
<tr><td>TARGET PERFORMANCE LEVEL</td><td>Intermediate Mid</td><td>CONTEXT</td><td>familiar, informal, formal, straight-forward</td></tr>
<tr><td>PERFORMANCE DOMAIN</td><td>Text Type</td><td>CONTENT</td><td>familiar, at times researched</td></tr>
<tr><td colspan="4">What description best matches your performance today?
☐ Sentences ☐ Series of sentences
☐ Connected series of sentences ☐ Complex sentences</td></tr>
<tr><td colspan="4">Write or record an example of a connected series of sentences that you used today:</td></tr>
<tr><td colspan="2">Option 1: What helped you create a connected series of sentences today? Mark all that apply:
☐ Multiple sentences on a related topic
☐ Coordinators (and, but, or, for, so...)
☐ Discourse markers (also, too,...) or sequencing words (first, second,..)</td><td colspan="2">Option 2: What coordinators or discourse markers helped you create a connected series of sentences today?</td></tr>
<tr><td colspan="4">How often did you use complex sentences?
☐ I did not use any complex sentences today.
☐ I used a complex sentence once today.
☐ I used complex sentences multiple times today.</td></tr>
<tr><td colspan="2">Option 1: If you used a complex sentence, write an example of a complex sentence that you used today:</td><td colspan="2">Option 2: If you did not use a complex sentence today, how might you use a clause that has a subject and a verb but cannot stand alone in order to create a complex sentence?</td></tr>
<tr><td colspan="2">Option 1: What subordinating conjunctions did you use today to create complex sentences?
☐ as long as ☐ although ☐ if
☐ despite ☐ even though ☐ who
☐ while ☐ now that ☐ where
☐ rather than ☐ so that ☐ unless
☐ Other ______________________</td><td colspan="2">Option 2: What subordinating conjunctions could you add to create complex sentences:</td></tr>
<tr><td colspan="4">Evaluate how you think you performed in your use of Text Type today:
☐ Beginning: I can use simple sentences most of the time.
☐ Developing: I can form simple sentences, and at times series of sentences.
☐ Meeting: I can form a series of connected sentences, and at times complex sentences.
☐ Exceeding: I can form (a) series of connected and complex sentences that may combine to create a simple paragraph(s) and/or paragraph-length discourse.</td></tr>
<tr><td colspan="4">Think about your own experience and what you have done to improve in Text Type. What advice would you give other learners to help them develop Text Type?</td></tr>
</table>

Table 6.16
Interpersonal/Presentational Guided Self-Assessment

<table>
<tr><td>TARGET PERFORMANCE LEVEL</td><td>Advanced Low</td><td>CONTEXT</td><td>familiar, unfamiliar, informal, formal, complex</td></tr>
<tr><td>PERFORMANCE DOMAIN</td><td>Text Type</td><td>CONTENT</td><td>familiar, academic, social , concrete</td></tr>
<tr><td colspan="4">What description best matches your performance today?
☐ Series of connected sentences, and at times complex sentences
☐ Series of connected and complex sentences that may combine to create a simple paragraph(s) and/or paragraph-length discourse
☐ Simple paragraphs and/or paragraph-length discourse
☐ Organized paragraphs and/or connected paragraph-length discourse</td></tr>
<tr><td colspan="4">Write or record an example of a simple paragraph/paragraph-length discourse that you used today:</td></tr>
<tr><td colspan="4">Think of a simple paragraph/paragraph-length response that you used today. How was it organized and connected? Check all that apply:
☐ I developed and supported my ideas with evidence and details.
☐ I used discourse markers (also, however, in other words, in conclusion…) to connect/organize my ideas.
☐ I used subordinating conjunctions (once, while, when, where, before, after…) to connect/organize my ideas.</td></tr>
<tr><td colspan="4">How often did you communicate using simple paragraphs/paragraph-length discourse?
☐ I did not yet communicate with simple paragraphs/paragraph-length discourse.
☐ I used simple paragraphs/paragraph-length discourse once today.
☐ I used simple paragraphs/paragraph-length discourse multiple times today.</td></tr>
<tr><td colspan="2">Option 1: If you communicated using simple paragraphs/paragraph-length discourse, what made it a paragraph? How did you connect the ideas together?</td><td colspan="2">Option 2: If you did not yet communicate using simple paragraphs/paragraph-length discourse, what are your next steps to level up your responses?</td></tr>
<tr><td colspan="2">Option 1: What discourse markers did you use today to connect your ideas?
☐ Adding: additionally, besides, furthermore…
☐ Comparing: similarly, likewise…
☐ Contrasting: although, however, on the other hand…
☐ Emphasizing: in conclusion, finally…
☐ Giving examples: for example, such as…
☐ Indicating time: in the past, presently…
☐ Sequencing: first, second, third…
☐ Showing cause and effect: therefore, thus, consequently…
☐ Other:____________________</td><td colspan="2">Option 2: What discourse markers could you add to better connect your ideas?</td></tr>
<tr><td colspan="4">Evaluate how you think you performed in your use of Text Type today:
☐ Beginning: I can form a series of connected sentences, and at times complex sentences.
☐ Developing: I can form (a) series of connected and complex sentences that may combine to create a simple paragraph(s) and/or paragraph-length discourse.
☐ Meeting: I can create simple paragraphs and/or paragraph-length discourse.
☐ Exceeding: I can create organized paragraphs and/or connected paragraph-length discourse.</td></tr>
<tr><td colspan="4">Think about your own experience and what you have done to improve in Text Type. What advice would you give other learners to help them develop Text Type?</td></tr>
</table>

YOUR TURN

LEARNING TARGET CHECK:	
I can	☐ provide learners with self-assessments to evaluate their work.

Complete the chart by identifying specific self-assessments from the *Learners' Self-Assessments* section (p. 182-191) that could be used in an upcoming unit to help learners evaluate their own work. Next, describe a formative or summative performance task in your upcoming unit that learners could complete and then self-assess using the chosen-self-assessment. Finally, list any additional materials or preparation that might be needed to implement this self-assessment in the *Notes* section of the chart.

UNIT:		
PERFORMANCE DOMAIN: TEXT TYPE		
Learner self-assessments	**Performance task** Formative or summative	**Notes**

Advice From Learners

As a purposeful way for learners to become aware of their own learning, we asked learners to reflect on what worked for them to improve their performance in various performance domains. Sharing advice can build learner metacognitive skills, or awareness of one's own learning, which has been linked to improved learning outcomes (Hattie, 2017). Together learners build a bank of suggestions and advice that they can access when looking to improve in a specific performance domain. This is a way for learners to realize what they have learned about a performance domain, monitor their own understanding of the performance domain, suggest and choose which advice to employ, and evaluate whether particular choices are successful. Here is what some learners said, when asked to share their insights and give advice on Text Type.

Novice Presentational:

- *Use the sentence structure you practiced in class.*
- *You don't have to get fancy to still say what you want to say and be understood.*
- *Start with words and phrases and then finish your thought into a complete sentence.*

Novice Interpersonal:

- *Memorize words and phrases, then practice sentence starters.*
- *Practice the phrases you want to use. These are your "go tos."*
- *Start with a framework, then add your own stuff on the fly.*
- *Even if you can answer with just one word, say more to show that you can.*

Intermediate Presentational:

- *Start with words in a brainstorm map. Write simple sentences. Look for ways they connect (or look for connectors you have learned to see if they work).*
- *Use different sentence lengths.*
- *Try writing some ideas and check to see that you have complete thoughts. Those usually make complete sentences. Then add transitions between sets of sentences.*
- *When you write complex sentences, go back and check your patterns and word order.*

Intermediate Interpersonal

- *Be aware of not just reacting, but say complete sentences and expand on your ideas. Give the other person a chance to keep talking and don't cut them off.*
- *Use different sentence lengths. Short ones where you are less sure, longer ones when you are confident. Write out some ideas of what you might want to say so you can see the Text Type.*
- *String together the sentences and add all the details that you can.*
- *Be kind to your partner and go in a logical order. Don't jump around.*

Advanced Presentational:

- *Highlight your presentational showing where you use more simple sentences, more complex sentences and where you connect all of the ideas into the entire text. That way you make sure you have developed text type.*

Advanced Interpersonal:

- *You don't need to always talk in complex sentences, but if you give each other time to talk that will happen. Take time to describe things and go deeper.*

References

ACTFL. (2012a). *ACTFL performance descriptors for language learners.* https://www.actfl.org/educator-resources/actfl-performance-descriptors

ACTFL. (2012b). *ACTFL proficiency guidelines – Speaking, writing, listening, and reading* (3rd ed.). https://www.actfl.org/educator-resources/actfl-proficiency-guidelines

Hattie, J. (2017). *250+ influences on student achievement.* Visible Learning Plus. https://visible-learning.org/wp-content/uploads/2018/03/VLPLUS-252-Influences-Hattie-ranking-DEC-2017.pdf

National Council of State Supervisors for Languages (NCSSFL) – ACTFL. (2017). *NCSSFL-ACTFL Can-Do Statements: Performance Indicators for Language Learners.* ACTFL. https://www.actfl.org/educator-resources/ncssfl-actfl-can-do-statements

Nordquist, R. (2019, July 3). *Definition and examples of text in language studies.* ThoughtCo. https://www.thoughtco.com/text-language-studies-1692537

Rosen, L. J., & Behrens, L. (2003). *The Allyn & Bacon handbook* (5th ed.). Longman.

Sherrow, H. (2018). *Soy yo: Bringing life, purpose, and meaning to your Novice descriptions unit* [Conference session]. ACTFL Convention, New Orleans, LA.

Troyan, F. J., Adair-Hauck, B., & Glisan, E. W. (2023). *The integrated performance assessment: Twenty years and counting.* ACTFL.

Twin Cities Pride. (2021a). *Pride movie night @ MOA – Moonlight.* https://tcpride.org/event/pride-movie-night-moa-moonlight/

Twin Cities Pride. (2021b). *Rainbow run 5K presented by UnitedHealth Group.* https://tcpride.org/event/rainbow-run-5k-presented-by-unitedhealth-group/

CHAPTER 7 | INTERCULTURAL COMMUNICATION
Performance Domain

LEARNING TARGETS:	
I can	☐ describe the Intercultural Communication performance domain. ☐ describe how Intercultural Communication shows up in learners' performance at various levels. ☐ evaluate learner work using the Performance Domain Indicators (PDIs). ☐ give effective feedback based on the Intercultural Communication PDIs. ☐ select learning experiences that support learners' growth with Intercultural Communication. ☐ provide learners with self-assessments to evaluate their work.

What do we mean by *Intercultural Communication*?

The Intercultural Communication performance domain focuses on the "Interact" portion of the *NCSSFL-ACTFL Can-Do Statements: Performance Indicators for Language Learners* (NCSSFL-ACTFL, 2017). That is, the performance domain refers to the ways learners appropriately interact within a sociocultural (social and cultural) context in the interpersonal and presentational modes. Intercultural Communication skills are both linguistic and cultural. According to the *NCSSFL-ACTFL Can-Do Statements: Performance Indicators for Language Learners* (NCSSFL-ACTFL, 2017), "Intercultural communication is a complex activity that combines cross-cultural knowledge and language skills. It involves initiating, understanding and responding to what is communicated, using culturally appropriate language and behavior in a given context" (p. 6). In a performance task, learners can use language (speech acts, idiomatic expressions, slang) and behaviors (body language, turn-taking, writing mechanics) to communicate appropriately within the sociocultural context.

Why incorporate the *Intercultural Communication* domain?

All communication occurs within a social and cultural context. There is just as much of a social and cultural context when interacting with friends as there is when writing a letter to a public official in another country. Therefore, the inclusion of the Intercultural Communication performance domain is an important step towards building understanding and awareness of the sociocultural context when communicating with individuals across diverse communities. We cannot assume that our audience or interlocutor(s) operate within a shared sociocultural context. The Intercultural Communication performance domain challenges learners to consider *both* the social and cultural context, therefore avoiding stereotypes and/or broad generalizations.

Just as learning another language often teaches us more about our own language's grammatical structures, so too can Intercultural Communication teach us how we intentionally and unintentionally use language and behaviors. The Intercultural Communication performance domain encourages both educators and learners to explore the social and cultural influences of communication. This awareness oftentimes requires reflection and identification of one's own communicative practices. Liddicoat (2004) asserts that "problems of cultural mismatch often create significant problems for communication and for social relationships, largely because people are much less aware of their cultural rules for interaction than they are of other aspects of language" (p. 17). Therefore, it is not enough to just know the language, but learners must also know *how* and *when* to appropriately use language and behaviors. In other words, effective communication is conditioned upon the appropriate ways learners interact within a sociocultural context.

How does *Intercultural Communication* develop in learner performance?

Learner growth within the Intercultural Communication performance domain is relative to a learner's base language, culture, and awareness of social and cultural contexts. However, all learners can learn to use language and behaviors to interact appropriately in their specific performance task. At the *Beginning* level, learners use language and/or behaviors that communicate a message but show no awareness of or are not appropriate to the social/cultural context. For example, a learner may transfer behaviors that are appropriate in their culture, such as refusal rituals or a formal "you," but which are not appropriate to the sociocultural context of the performance. At the *Developing* level, learners begin to interact using language and/or behaviors that are, at times appropriate to the social/cultural context. For example, learners may use formal speech acts, honorifics, and slang in an informal social context. With each new context practiced and performed in the classroom, learners add more language and behaviors to their repertoire. Learners are *Meeting* expectations when they are able to use language and/or behaviors that are appropriate to the social/cultural context. Learners are *Exceeding* expectations when they use a variety of language and/or behaviors to communicate appropriately within the social/cultural context. The ways learners interact within the performance tasks will differ according to their language resources, as well as their cultural knowledge and awareness. However, all learners can use a range of language and behaviors to show their sociocultural awareness of that specific task.

What are the characteristics of *Intercultural Communication* in learner performance?

The sample learner performances in Table 7.1 show how learners can appropriately interact within a similar performance task but different social and cultural contexts. All learners can greet others, but each learner uses language and behaviors appropriate to their performance level that match the sociocultural context. The learners performing within the Novice level can perform a greeting ritual with a friend and use the appropriate informal language (*It's good to see you*) and gestures (*waves hand, thumbs up*). Additionally, the use of slang (*Hey*) is appropriate for this highly informal context. The learners performing within the Intermediate level can make use of the same language and behavior, but now within an unfamiliar, informal context. They use informal language (*It's nice to meet you* and *I'll see you around*), gestures (*waves hand*), slang (*Cool, For sure!*), as well as a colloquial expression (*I'm into*) which means interested/involved). In addition to the previous sociocultural contexts, the learners performing within the Advanced level use language and behaviors appropriately within a more formal context. These learners use formal language (*It's a pleasure to meet you* and *I look forward to*), gestures (*shakes hands*), learned expressions (*It's a pleasure to meet you, a fish out of water, feel right at home*) as well as an honorific (the title *Professor* in front of the last name *Scheider*).

Table 7.1
Sample Learner Performances

Note: The setting for these tasks is the Midwest region of the United States of America.

Novice	Intermediate	Advanced
Task: You are going back to school and are excited to see your friends. When you get to your classroom, you greet a friend and share about your summer vacation.	**Task:** A family with a person your age just moved in next door. When you are outside, you happen to see each other, and so you greet them and get to know more about who they are.	**Task:** You just started your first semester of classes. After class, you decide to stay behind so you can greet your instructor to make a good impression and begin a good working relationship.
Learner 1: Elena! Hi (*waves hand*)! **Learner 2:** Hey (*waves hand*)! **Learner 1:** It's good to see you! **Learner 2:** Yeah! You too! **Learner 1:** How are you? **Learner 2:** Good (*thumbs up*). And you? **Learner 1:** Yes. Good. **Learner 2:** Fun summer? **Learner 1:** Yeah, at my cabin on... lake. And you? **Learner 2:** At the pool. But, ready for school!	**Learner 1:** Hello (*waves hand*). I'm Peter, your new neighbor. **Learner 2:** Hi, Peter (*waves hand*). I'm Jack. **Learner 1:** It's nice to meet you, Jack. **Learner 2:** Nice to meet you too. **Learner 1:** So, what do you like to do, ya know, in your freetime? **Learner 2:** I like to play video games. **Learner 1:** Oh, yeah. Me too! What's your favorite game? **Learner 2:** I'm really into Chomp'ems Master right now. **Learner 1:** Cool, me too. Maybe we can play together sometime? **Learner 2:** For sure! Sounds fun. **Learner 1:** Well, I gotta run. But it was nice to meet you (*waves hand*). **Learner 2:** You too. I'll see you around (*nods head upward*).	**Learner 1:** Professor Schneider? **Learner 2:** Yes? **Learner 1:** I'm Ling (*extends and shakes hand with professor*). **Learner 2:** Hello, Ling (*shakes hands with Ling*). It's a pleasure to meet you. **Learner 1:** The pleasure is all mine. **Learner 2:** What can I do for you? **Learner 1:** Oh, nothing. I just wanted to introduce myself to you. I know you have a lot of students. **Learner 2:** I do. So I appreciate that you came up to greet me. Is this your first semester at college? **Learner 1:** Yes. I feel a bit like a fish out of water. **Learner 2:** I understand. Although, you'll feel right at home in no time. We have a strong community here. **Learner 1:** Yes, I'm excited. **Learner 2:** Good. Well, Ling, feel free to reach out if you need anything. **Learner 1:** Thanks, Professor Schneider. I look forward to your class this semester. Bye (*waves hand*)! **Learner 2:** Bye (*smiles*)!

Intercultural Communication: Language and Behaviors Reference Guide

Culture lives in the linguistic and pragmatic use of language, as well as in the mental models used to communicate: "cultures shape the ways language is structured and the ways in which language is used" (Liddicoat, 2004, p. 18). Learners demonstrate Intercultural Communication when they use language and behaviors that are appropriate to the social and cultural context of the performance task. Next is a reference guide for the ways that learners can interact appropriately. The following are examples of the ways in which a learner can use language and behaviors that contribute towards Intercultural Communication. It is important to note that Intercultural Communication is not limited to the following examples, nor is their use universal. It is meant as a reference guide.

LANGUAGE

Speech Acts: Speech acts are the words used to carry out a language function; they are performative sentences/utterances "in which to *say* something is to *do* something" (Austin, 2018, p. 12). They are apologies, complaints, disagreements, expressions of gratitude, greetings, leave-takings, advice, invitations, refusals, requests, etc. For example, uttering the expression *That's nice* is the language used to give a compliment. Speech acts are multi-dimensional because layered into the language of speech acts are politeness, formality, directness, as well as intensifiers (Ishihara & Cohen, 2014). Speech acts reflect the sociocultural context of communication: for example, greeting your friend versus greeting your boss requires different speech acts (see Table 7.2). These examples can be present in both interpersonal and presentational modes of communication. The University of Minnesota's Center for Advanced Research on Language Acquisition (CARLA) has a collection of speech act research and pedagogical tools for further study (2021a).

Table 7.2
Layers Within Speech Acts: Greetings

	INFORMAL	FORMAL
Direct	*Hey there, Ted!*	*Hello, Mr. Smith.*
Indirect	*What brings you here?*	*How can I help you, Mr. Smith?*
Polite	*It's nice to see you.*	*It's a pleasure to meet you.*
Intensifier	*It's really nice to see you.*	*It's certainly a pleasure to meet you.*

Honorifics/Kinship terms: Honorifics is the title of honor that conveys position, esteem, and courtesy. In English, a common prefix is the title *Mister* and/or its abbreviation *Mr.*, which can be used before a surname, for example *Mr. Davila*. Within religious, academic, and political communities, honorifics distinguish rank and/or duty, like *captain* and *lieutenant*. In addition, multiple languages differentiate between the informal and formal forms of *you*, which are communicated through different pronouns and/or verb-endings. Kinship terms are the notations that communicate distance and proximity of family members. For example, in English *great grandmother* refers to the grandmother of a parent. The observed language may appear only as a prefix or a suffix, but can also require additional attention to specific language forms and structures.

Expressions: This refers to the figurative language used to communicate ideas such as idioms or sayings (fixed phrases), proverbs (moral teachings), metaphors, and colloquialisms. An example of an idiomatic expression or proverb in English is *The early bird gets the worm.* This teaches the value of *getting up early* in order to have the best chance of success and productivity. Another English example is the saying *to be under the weather*, which is commonly used in the U.S. when referring to someone who is feeling unwell or sick. Researcher John I. Liantos (2008, 2017) asserts that idioms are a prominent feature in everyday communication, and therefore, idiomatic usage contributes to more authentic, native-like conversations. Learners develop and use such expressions just as they do vocabulary.

Slang/Jargon: Slang refers to the ever changing colloquial words and phrases used to establish or reinforce social identities and connectedness (Eble, 1996). Eble notes its use is characteristic of informal social settings: "Slang words always diminish the formality of a conversation in which they occur" (p. 25). An example in American English is *My bad!* which is slang for saying *It was my mistake.* Jargon, on the other hand, is the specialized language particular to an academic/professional setting. It is the discipline speak of teammates who share the same work or interest. For example, those in the sports industry commonly refer to a game won by a last-second score as *a buzzer beater.* The main difference between slang (not profanity) and jargon is the register, or the formal or informal context.

Abbreviations: Abbreviations refer to the use of language in shortened forms or acronyms. An example is the acronym ASAP which is short for *as soon as possible.* Abbreviations can appear in the interpersonal mode, and are most prevalent in written communication. For example, in an informal text exchange a learner shortens *To be honest, I don't know* by using the abbreviations *tbh, idk.* Social media and technology have greatly impacted this mode of communication. Hwang and Matsumoto (2012) suggest that in computer-mediated communication, abbreviations and emoticons function as nonverbal behaviors and provide emotional context; such as the abbreviation *lol* (laughing out loud) and the frown face emoticon :(or frowning face emoji 🙁. However, they caution that the uses of these abbreviations and emoticons are not universal and must reflect the social and cultural context of communication.

Systems of Measurement: This refers to the cultural representations and notations of mass, distance, area, as well as time, dates and currency. This not only includes the appropriate units, but also how those units are expressed in the target language, which may differ by word order, punctuation, and/or fractions. For example, some cultures use the 12-hour clock or the 24-hour clock (which is also similar to 'military time') when communicating about time. Therefore, a learner could say *Let's meet up at 4 p.m.* or *Let's meet up at 16:00 hours.* Another example is the notation of currency, specifically order and punctuation. In American English, the US dollar symbol precedes total amount and the decimal point is the separator of dollars and cents. When written it appears as $2.30, however, when spoken, both word order and punctuation change to 2 dollars and 30 cents.

BEHAVIORS

Body Language: Specific to the interpersonal communication mode, nonverbal behaviors include eye contact, posture, facial expressions, gestures, and distance. For example, the act of greeting others may be performed with a handshake, a bow, a kiss (or two), a hug, a head nod, or a smile. Facial expressions are another example of nonverbal behaviors, and are important to communicating emotions. The widening of eyes may signal surprise, or a smile might convey happiness or mask fear. While facial expressions are universal, their use is culturally conditioned; there are *cultural display rules* that govern the use of facial expressions (Ekman & Friesen, 1969). Likewise, the use of gestures can positively contribute to or cause misunderstandings and breakdowns. For example, a circle with your thumb and your index finger (*OK*) or a closed fist held with the thumb extended upward (*thumbs up*) have a variety of meanings: approval, agreement, offensive, and/or obscene. The appropriate use of either depends on the social and cultural context of communication.

Paralinguistics: Considered as a nonverbal behavior, a learner can use their voice, or not, as a communication tool. These vocal features and cues include "the tone of voice, intonation, pitch, speech rate, use of silence, and volume" (Hwang & Matsumoto, 2012, p. 120). For example, the raising of one's tone at the end of a sentence could signal a question, invite a response, or convey less direct behavior. In addition, the use of silence, or rather, the length of pauses, in some cultures is used to show deference to a social hierarchy or a politeness system. For example, in Chinese culture one can infer that someone who keeps silent is subordinate or of lower hierarchy (Yuan Quan, 2015).

Turn-taking/Rituals: "The principles [of turn-taking] have to do with how the right to speak is distributed – who speaks with whom, for how long, about what, when, and in which way." (Allwood, 1985, p. 11). Examples of patterns include alternating turns, overlapping talk, interrupting, and/or deferring to silent pauses. In some cultures turn-taking is determined by social status, so *speaking out of turn* may be interpreted negatively and impede successful communication. Turn-taking may also be evident through a patterned speech act ritual. For example, a learner may knowingly reject the first (and possibly subsequent) invitations, thus demonstrating the practice of *ritual refusal* through both speech acts and this observable pattern of behavior (CARLA, 2021b).

Writing Mechanics: Particular to written communication, writing mechanics refer to the use of punctuation, capitalization and/or directionality (i.e. writing left to right). For example, in English the subject pronoun *I* is always capitalized whereas in other languages this subject pronoun is not. Another example is the use of inverted punctuation, like in Spanish for questions (¿) and exclamations (¡). For languages that can be written in script, learners can attend to directionality (left-to-right or right-to-left). Moreover, for those written right-to-left, learners can use mirrored punctuation, like the question mark (؟).

Format: Format refers to the pattern and/or template that corresponds to a particular speech genre and genre of writing. For example, the conversational format of a job interview includes a stage where the interviewer asks the candidate questions particular to their professional skills and experiences. It then also includes an opportunity for the candidate to ask the interviewer questions about the culture and climate of the company. This format is generic, and so will depend on the culture and industry of the job. Likewise, in the presentational mode, a letter of admission to an academic program is formatted differently than a journal entry in a personal diary.

Style: Style is the manner in which an individual expresses themselves and/or communicates ideas. In his book *Writing around the World: A Guide to Writing Across Cultures*, author Matthew McCool (2009) describes the complexities with intercultural writing because "[C]ultures do not write using the same assumptions, strategies, and goals" (p. 2). The author describes the difference between "reader responsible cultures" and "writer responsible cultures." In reader responsible cultures, the writing style is a sequential progression with loosely connected sentences. In this way, the reader shares the responsibility of making inferences and meaning, and drawing conclusions of the text. On the other hand, in writer responsible cultures, the style is thesis-driven and linear and emphasizes clarity and concision. In this way, the writer assumes the communicative burden of the message. American writing is considered a writer responsible culture, for example. Another example of style is in the cultural approaches to persuasion. The rhetorical style of an argument may include anecdotes and metaphors, or it may include facts and counter-arguments.

The Performance Domain Indicators

The following section presents the Performance Domain Indicators (PDIs) for Intercultural Communication. The Intercultural Communication PDIs were developed from the *NCSSFL-ACTFL Can-Do Statements: Performance Indicators for Language Learners* (NCSSFL-ACTFL, 2017), specifically the "Intercultural Communication: Interact" Can-Do Statements (see Table 7.3).

Table 7.3

Intercultural Communication: Interact Can-Do Statements (NCSSFL-ACTFL, 2017)

NOVICE	I can interact at a survival level in some familiar everyday contexts.
INTERMEDIATE	I can interact at a functional level in some familiar contexts.
ADVANCED	I can interact at a competent level in familiar and some unfamiliar contexts.

The Intercultural Communication PDIs are used with both the interpersonal and presentational mode of communication. The same four levels (*Beginning, Developing, Meeting, Exceeding*) are applied to all three of the performance levels (Novice, Intermediate, Advanced) (see Table 7.4).

Table 7.4

Intercultural Communication Performance Domain Indicators (PDIs)

BEGINNING	DEVELOPING	MEETING	EXCEEDING
I use language and/or behaviors that are not appropriate to the social/cultural context.	**I can,** at times, **use language and/or behaviors that are appropriate** to the social/cultural context.	**I can use language and/or behaviors that are appropriate** to the social/cultural context.	**I can use** a variety of **language and/or behaviors that are appropriate** to the social/cultural context.

- The language in bold indicates the source is the *NCSSFL-ACTFL Can-Do Statements: Performance Indicators for Language Learners* (NCSSFL-ACTFL, 2017).
- For classroom purposes, some language has been modified to be learner-friendly (ie: *sociocultural context* to *social/cultural context*).

The Performance Domain Descriptions

In order to illustrate Intercultural Communication, the PDIs are accompanied by a learner task and sample learner responses for each performance level: Novice (Table 7.5), Intermediate (Table 7.6), and Advanced (Table 7.7). In addition, the PDIs are accompanied by a description that is meant to deepen our understanding of how Intercultural Communication develops across the levels (*Beginning, Developing, Meeting, Exceeding*) in learner performance at each performance level (Novice, Intermediate, and Advanced).

Table 7.5
Intercultural Communication Performance Domain Indicators (PDIs) for Learners Performing Within the Novice Level

	NOVICE			
Sublevels	BEGINNING	DEVELOPING	MEETING	EXCEEDING
Context	familiar, informal, formal, predictable			
Content	very familiar, familiar, everyday			
Performance Domain Indicator	I use language and/or behaviors that are not appropriate to the social/cultural context.	I can, at times, use language and/or behaviors that are appropriate to the social/cultural context.	I can use language and/or behaviors that are appropriate to the social/cultural context.	I can use a variety of language and/or behaviors that are appropriate to the social/cultural context.

Novice Task: Discuss and compare what you and your friend prefer to eat for lunch at school.

Sample Learner Responses: All four sample responses exhibit **Novice High** characteristics and therefore are similar, if not almost exact responses. This is intentional so as to highlight how learners incorporate language and behaviors as they progress through the levels (*Beginning* to *Exceeding*). As you read, **Learner 2** demonstrates the PDIs.

NOVICE			
BEGINNING	**DEVELOPING**	**MEETING**	**EXCEEDING**
Learner 1: Hi! **Learner 2:** Good afternoon! I'm thirsty. I eat! **Learner 1:** Sure! What do you like to eat? **Learner 2:** I don't understand (*smiles*). **Learner 1:** What do you like to eat (*mimics eating food with hands*)? **Learner 2:** No, I don't agree (*frowns*). I like pizza. **Learner 1:** Cool! I like pizza too! What do you prefer, cheese or sausage? **Learner 2:** I prefer cheese. How interesting (*no intonation*). What do you prefer, sir? **Learner 1:** I like cheese sometimes too. **Learner 2:** Do you like sausage? **Learner 1:** ... **Learner 2:** Do you like sausage? **Learner 1:** Um, I don't know (*shrugs*). **Learner 2:** Do you like, um, do you like... meat? **Learner 1:** Oh! No way! Gross! **Learner 2:** I'm sorry! I love sausage! Is my meat favorite.	**Learner 1:** Hi! **Learner 2:** Good afternoon! I'm hungry. I eat! **Learner 1:** Sure! What do you like to eat? **Learner 2:** I don't understand (*shrugs*). **Learner 1:** What do you like to eat (*mimics eating food with hands*)? **Learner 2:** Yes. I like pizza. **Learner 1:** Cool! I like pizza too! What do you prefer, cheese or sausage? **Learner 2:** I prefer cheese (*rubs stomach*). How interesting! What do you prefer? **Learner 1:** I like cheese sometimes too. **Learner 2:** Do you like sausage? **Learner 1:** :... **Learner 2 :** Do you like sausage? **Learner 1:** Um, I don't know (*shrugs*). **Learner 2:** Do you like, um, do you like... meat? **Learner 1:** Oh! No way! Gross! **Learner 2:** I'm sorry! I love sausage! Is my meat favorite. So yummy!	**Learner 1:** Hi! **Learner 2:** Hey! I'm hungry. Let's eat! **Learner 1:** Sure! What do you like to eat? **Learner 2:** I don't understand (*shrugs*). **Learner 1:** What do you like to eat (*mimics eating food with hands*)? **Learner 2:** Ah (*nods*). I like pizza. **Learner 1:** Cool! I like pizza too! What do you prefer, cheese or sausage? **Learner 2:** I prefer cheese. So yummy! (*rubs stomach*) What do you prefer? **Learner 1:** I like cheese sometimes too. **Learner 2:** So yummy! Do you like sausage? **Learner 1:**... **Learner 2:** Do you like sausage? **Learner 1:** Um, I don't know (*shrugs*). **Learner 2:** Do you like, um, do you like... meat? **Learner 1:** Oh! No way! Gross! **Learner 2:** Really? I love sausage! Is my meat favorite. So yummy!	**Learner 1:** Hi! **Learner 2:** Hey! I'm starving. Let's eat! **Learner 1:** Sure! What do you like to eat? **Learner 2:** I don't understand (*shrugs*). **Learner 1:** What do you like to eat (*mimics eating food with hands*)? **Learner 2:** Ah, gotcha (*nods*). I like pizza. **Learner 1:** Cool! I like pizza too! What do you prefer, cheese or sausage? **Learner 2:** I prefer cheese. So yummy! (*rubs stomach*) What do you prefer? **Learner 1:** I like cheese sometimes too. **Learner 2:** How delish! Do you like sausage? **Learner 1:**... **Learner 2:** Do you like sausage? **Learner 1:** Um, I don't know (*shrugs*). **Learner 2:** Do you like, um, do you like (*thumbs up*), you know...meat? **Learner 1:** Oh! No way! Gross! **Learner 2:** Wow, seriously (*raises eyebrows*)? I love sausage! Is my meat favorite.

Description of Learner Responses: In this Novice task, the sociocultural context is an informal conversation with a friend. At the *Beginning* level, learners performing within the Novice level use language (*Good afternoon, I'm thirsty, I don't agree, How interesting, sir, I'm sorry!*) and/or behaviors (*smiles, no intonation*) that are not appropriate to the social/cultural context. At the *Developing* level, the learners are, at times, able to use language (*I'm hungry*) and/or behaviors (*shrugs*) that are appropriate to the social/cultural context. Learners are *Meeting* expectations when they are able to use language (*Hey! Let's eat! Ah, So yummy!, Really?*) and/or behaviors (*nods, rubs stomach*) that are appropriate to the social/cultural context. Learners are *Exceeding* expectations when they use a variety of language (*I'm starving! Ah, gotcha, How delish! Wow, seriously?*) and behaviors (*thumbs up, raises eyebrows*) to interact appropriately within the sociocultural context.

Table 7.6
Intercultural Communication Performance Domain Indicators (PDIs) for Learners Performing Within the Intermediate Level

	INTERMEDIATE			
Sublevels	BEGINNING	DEVELOPING	MEETING	EXCEEDING
Context	familiar, informal, formal, straight-forward			
Content	familiar, concrete, at times researched			
Performance Domain Indicator	I use language and/or behaviors that are not appropriate to the social/cultural context.	I can, at times, use language and/or behaviors that are appropriate to the social/cultural context.	I can use language and/or behaviors that are appropriate to the social/cultural context.	I can use a variety of language and/or behaviors that are appropriate to the social/cultural context.

Intermediate Task: You and your friend discuss and decide where to eat lunch together.

Sample Learner Responses: All four sample responses exhibit **Intermediate Mid** characteristics and therefore are similar, if not almost exact responses. This is intentional so as to highlight how learners incorporate language and behaviors as they progress through the levels (*Beginning* to *Exceeding*). As you read, **Learner 2** demonstrates the indicators.

INTERMEDIATE			
BEGINNING	**DEVELOPING**	**MEETING**	**EXCEEDING**
Learner 1: Hey you! Are you hungry? **Learner 2:** Yes, I'm hungry. **Learner 1:** Good! May we eat lunch now? **Learner 2:** We may (*laughs*). Where would you like to go (*no intonation*). **Learner 1:** I like the restaurant over there (*points in that direction*). **Learner 2:** The restaurant over there… which restaurant (*no intonation*). **Learner 1:** Um, the one at the corner (*points in that direction*). **Learner 2:** What kind of food. I like BTL. **Learner 1:** The pizza restaurant. At the end. They have a lot of different pizzas. **Learner 2:** The pizza restaurant on the corner. Do you like pizza. **Learner 1:** I love pizza! Yummy! **Learner 2:** Ok. It's my favorite. What kind of pizza do you like.	**Learner 1:** Hey you! Are you hungry? **Learner 2:** Yes, I'm very hungry. **Learner 1:** Good! May we eat lunch now? **Learner 2:** Yes, please! Where would you like to go? **Learner 1:** I like the restaurant over there (*points in that direction*). **Learner 2:** The restaurant over there… which restaurant (*no intonation*). **Learner 1:** Um, the one at the corner (*points in that direction*). **Learner 2:** The one at the end. What kind of food do they have? I like BTLs. **Learner 1:** The pizza restaurant. At the end. They have a lot of different pizzas. **Learner 2:** Ok? The pizza restaurant on the corner. Do you like pizza? **Learner 1:** I love pizza! Yummy! **Learner 2:** Me too. It's my favorite. What kind of pizza do you like?	**Learner 1:** Hey you! Are you hungry? **Learner 2:** OMG, I'm SO (*said with emphasis*) hungry! **Learner 1:** Good! May we eat lunch now? **Learner 2:** Yes, please (*laughs*)! Where do you want to go? **Learner 1:** I like the restaurant over there (*points in that direction*). **Learner 2:** The restaurant over there… which restaurant? **Learner 1:** Um, the one at the corner (*points in that direction*). **Learner 2:** The one at the end? What kind of food do they have? I like BLTs. **Learner 1:** The pizza restaurant. At the end. They have a lot of different pizzas. **Learner 2:** Ok, the pizza restaurant on the corner. Do you like pizza? **Learner 1:** I love pizza! Yummy! **Learner 2:** Me too (*smiles*)! It's my favorite. What kind of pizza do you like?	**Learner 1:** Hey you! Are you hungry? **Learner 2:** OMG, I'm SO (*said with emphasis*) hungry (*rubs stomach*). I could eat a horse (*laughs*)! **Learner 1:** Good! May we eat lunch now? **Learner 2:** Of course! Yes, please (*laughs*)! Where do you want to go? **Learner 1:** I like the restaurant over there (*points in that direction*). **Learner 2:** The restaurant over there… which restaurant? **Learner 1:** Um, the one at the end (*points in that direction*). **Learner 2:** The one at the end? What kind of food do they have? I like BLTs. **Learner 1:** The pizza restaurant. At the end. They have a lot of different pizzas. **Learner 2:** Ah, I see. The pizza restaurant on the corner. Do you like pizza? **Learner 1:** I love pizza! Yummy! **Learner 2:** Awesome (*smiles*)! Me too! It's my fav. What kind of pizza do you like?

Learner 1: I prefer pepperoni. **Learner 2:** Really. Do they have, um, the pizza from Chicago... **Learner 1:** What do you mean? **Learner 2:** The one with very thick crust. **Learner 1:** Oh yeah (*nods*). It's ok (*shrugs*). **Learner 2:** Yes! Do they have that. **Learner 1:** I'm not sure. May we go and see? **Learner 2:** We may!	**Learner 1:** I prefer pepperoni. **Learner 2:** Really? Do they have, um, the pizza from Chicago... **Learner 1:** What do you mean? **Learner 2:** The one with very thick crust? **Learner 1:** Oh yeah (*nods*). It's ok (*shrugs*). **Learner 2:** Yeah! Do they have that? **Learner 1:** I'm not sure. May we go and see? **Learner 2:** Sure! Let's go!	**Learner 1:** I prefer pepperoni. **Learner 2:** Yum! Do they have, um, the pizza from Chicago... **Learner 1:** What do you mean? **Learner 2:** The one with the very thick crust? **Learner 1:** Oh yeah (*nods*). It's ok (*shrugs*). **Learner 2:** Yeah! Do they have that? **Learner 1:** I'm not sure. May we go and see? **Learner 2:** Sure! Let's go (*waves Learner 2 toward themselves and starts walking*)!	**Learner 1:** I prefer pepperoni pizza. **Learner 2:** No kidding?! Do they have, um, the pizza from Chicago... **Learner 1:** What do you mean? **Learner 2:** You know, with very thick crust? **Learner 1:** Oh yeah (*nods*). It's ok (*shrugs*). **Learner 2:** Yeah! Do they have that? **Learner 1:** I'm not sure. May we go and see? **Learner 2:** Of course! Come on, let's go (*waves Learner 2 toward themselves and starts walking*)!

Description of Learner Responses: In this Intermediate task, the sociocultural context is an informal conversation with a friend. At the *Beginning* level, learners performing within the Intermediate level use language (*We may, Where would you like to go, BTL* instead of BLT) and/or behaviors (*laughs* in response to other learner's use of formal language, lack of intonation with questions) that are not appropriate to the social/cultural context. At the *Developing* level, the learners are, at times, able to use language (*Really? Yeah! Sure! Let's go!*) and/or behaviors (intonation when asking questions) more appropriately within the social/cultural context. Learners are *Meeting* expectations when they are able to use language (*OMG, Yes, please! Where do you want to go? BLTs, Let's go!*) and/or behaviors (*laughs, waves Learner 2 toward themselves and starts walking*) that are appropriate to the social/cultural context. Learners are *Exceeding* expectations when they use a variety of language (*I could eat a horse! Of course! Ah, I see. No kidding?! You know, Come on*) and/or behaviors (*rubs stomach, laughs*) to interact appropriately within the sociocultural context.

Table 7.7

Intercultural Communication Performance Domain Indicators (PDIs) for Learners Performing Within the Advanced Level

	ADVANCED			
Sublevels	**BEGINNING**	**DEVELOPING**	**MEETING**	**EXCEEDING**
Context	familiar, unfamiliar, informal, formal, complex			
Content	familiar, academic, social, professional, concrete, abstract			
Performance Domain Indicator	I use language and/or behaviors that are not appropriate to the social/cultural context.	I can, at times, use language and/or behaviors that are appropriate to the social/cultural context.	I can use language and/or behaviors that are appropriate to the social/cultural context.	I can use a variety of language and/or behaviors that are appropriate to the social/cultural context.

Advanced Task: After watching a news report about locally grown food, discuss with a friend if you think it is a sustainable option.

Sample Learner Responses: Notice that all four sample responses exhibit **Advanced Low** characteristics and therefore are similar, if not almost exact responses. This is intentional so as to highlight how learners incorporate language and behaviors as they progress through the levels (*Beginning* to *Exceeding*). As you read, **Learner 2** demonstrates the indicators.

ADVANCED			
BEGINNING	**DEVELOPING**	**MEETING**	**EXCEEDING**
Learner 1: Well, that was interesting. I doesn't know that we have these local farms in our community. **Learner 2:** I disagree (*nods*). It's sad that I have not hear of them until now. **Learner 1:** After watch that, I feel I am more motivated to help and buy from these farms. **Learner 2:** What a shame (*frowns*). I think to eat locally grown food is healthier, especially since the produce does no travel long distances. Therefore, it tastes better. **Learner 1:** Yeah (*head nods*). I appreciate the freshness of the food when I buy from the farmer's market…, which I think it has more nutrients, meaning that is healthier too. **Learner 2:** Is that odd (*no intonation*). We know that eating locally grown is better, but we don't do it so often. Why is that? **Learner 1:** Well, I think it's because it cost more than to buy at the grocery store. **Learner 2:** Certainly (*crosses arms*). The reporter said that… that the high cost of groceries is impacting many families.	**Learner 1:** Well, that was interesting. I doesn't know that we have these local farms in our community. **Learner 2:** Me too. It's sad that I have not hear of them until now. **Learner 1:** After watch that, I feel I am more motivated to help and buy from these farms. **Learner 2:** For sure (*nods head*)! I think to eat locally grown food is healthier, especially since the produce does no travel long distances. Therefore, it tastes better. **Learner 1:** Yeah (*head nods*). I appreciate the freshness of the food when I buy from the farmer's market…, which I think it has more nutrients, meaning that is healthier too. **Learner 2:** Is that odd? Like, we know that eating locally grown is better, but we don't do it so often. Why is that? **Learner 1:** Well, I think because it cost more than to buy at the grocery store. **Learner 2:** Yeah (*head nods*). The reporter said, eh, that… that the high cost of groceries is impacting many families.	**Learner 1:** Well, that was interesting. I doesn't know that we have these local farms in our community. **Learner 2:** Same here. It's kind of sad that I have not hear of them until now. **Learner 1:** After watch that, I feel I am more motivated to help and buy from these farms. **Learner 2:** For sure (*nods head*)! I think to eat locally grown food is healthier, especially since the produce does no travel long distances. Therefore, it tastes better. **Learner 1:** Yeah (*nods head*). I appreciate the freshness of the food when I buy from the farmer's market…, which I think it has more nutrients, meaning that is healthier too. **Learner 2:** Is that weird (*tilts head*)? Like, we know that eating locally grown is better, but we don't do it so often. Why is that? **Learner 1:** Well, I think because it cost more than to buy at the grocery store. **Learner 2:** Yeah (*nods head*), like the reporter said, um, that… that the high cost of groceries is impacting many families.	**Learner 1:** Well, that was interesting. I doesn't know that we have these local farms in our community. **Learner 2:** Same here. It's kinda sad that I have not hear of them until now. **Learner 1:** After watch that, I feel I am more motivated to help and buy from these farms. **Learner 2:** For sure (*nods head*)! I think to eat locally grown food is healthier, especially since the produce does no travel long distances. Therefore, it tastes better. **Learner 1:** Yeah (*nods head*). I appreciate the freshness of the food when I buy from the farmer's market…, which I think it has more nutrients, meaning that is healthier too. **Learner 2:** Is that weird (*tilts head*)? Like, we know that eating locally grown is better, but we don't do it so often. Why is that? **Learner 1:** Well, I think because it cost more than to buy at the grocery store. **Learner 2:** Yeah (*nods head*), like the reporter said, um, that… that the steep cost of groceries is impacting many families.

Learner 1: Right. I mean, for a family that does no have a lot of money, there's no question why they shop at wholesale market. Because they buy in bulk, they offer much low prices. **Learner 2:** Yes. For example, there's a cooperative near my house, but I think we have only shopped there a few times. I will ask my mother…, but probably it's the cost, especially since we are a large family. What do your family? **Learner 1:** Like I said, sometimes we go to the farmer's market, which is really fun. **Learner 2:** I forgot about that. This year I might plant a vegetable garden this spring. **Learner 1:** I like your idea. Maybe I do it too.	**Learner 1:** Right. I mean, for a family that does no have a lot of money, there's no question why they shop at wholesale market. Because they buy in bulk, they offer much low prices. **Learner 2:** Yeah. For example, there's a cooperative near my house, but I think we have only shopped there a few times. I will ask my mom…, but probably it's the cost, especially since we are a large family. What do your family? **Learner 1:** Like I said, sometimes we go to the farmer's market, which is really fun! **Learner 2:** I forgot about that. This year I might plant a vegetable garden this spring. **Learner 1:** I like your idea. Maybe I do it too.	**Learner 1:** Right. I mean, for a family that does no have a lot of money, there's no question why they shop at wholesale market. Because they buy in bulk, they offer much low prices. **Learner 2:** That makes sense. For example, there's a co-op near to my house, but I think we shopped there a few times. I will ask my mom…, but probably it's the cost, especially since we are a large family. What do your family? **Learner 1:** Like I said, sometimes we go to the farmer's market, which is really fun! **Learner 2:** I totally forgot about that! You know what (*tilts head*)? Maybe I will plant a vegetable garden this spring. **Learner 1:** I like your idea. Maybe I do it too.	**Learner 1:** Right. I mean, for a family that can no make ends meet, there's no question why they shop at wholesale market. Because they buy in bulk, they offer much low prices. **Learner 2:** That makes perfect sense (*leans back*). For example, there's a co-op near to my house, but I think we shopped there a handful of times. I will ask my mom…, but probably it's the cost, especially since we are a large family. What do your family? **Learner 1:** Like I said, sometimes we go to the farmer's market, which is pretty fun! **Learner 2:** I totally forgot about that (*leans forward*)! Ya know what (*tilts head*)? Maybe I will plant a vegetable garden this spring. **Learner 1:** I like your idea. Maybe I do it too.

Description of Learner Responses: In this Advanced task, the sociocultural context is an informal conversation with a friend. At the *Beginning* level, learners performing within the Advanced level may either use inappropriate language (*I disagree, What a shame*) and/or behaviors (*no intonation, crosses arm*) or use language (formal language such as *Certainly, mother*) and/or behaviors that show no awareness of the sociocultural context. At the *Developing* level, learners can, at times, use language (*For sure, Like, Yeah, eh, mom*) and/or behaviors (*nods head*) appropriate to the social/cultural context. Learners are *Meeting* expectations when they are able to use appropriate language (*Same here, Is that weird?, like the reporter said, um, totally, You know what?*) and/or behaviors (*nods head* and *tilts head*) throughout the task. Learners are *Exceeding* expectations when they use a variety of language (*yeah, kinda, steep, That makes perfect sense, Ya know what?*) and behaviors (*nods head, tilts head*, and *leans back*) to interact appropriately within the social and cultural context.

YOUR TURN

LEARNING TARGETS CHECK:	
I can	☐ describe the Intercultural Communication performance domain. ☐ describe how Intercultural Communication shows up in learners' performance at various levels.

Pause and reflect:
How would you describe Intercultural Communication to your learners? Consider any explanations, examples, and/or visuals you might use to describe the performance domain:

Intercultural Communication in learner work:
The following exercise includes a sample task for the Intermediate performance level. Write a learner response that includes the characteristics of Intercultural Communication for learners performing within each level. Use the provided *Developing* sample to guide you.

Intermediate task:
Complete an interview with an educator from the target culture about what school is like for you.

Learner sample responses exhibiting Intermediate Mid characteristics:
(the **Learner** demonstrates the PDIs)

INTERMEDIATE			
BEGINNING	**DEVELOPING**	**MEETING**	**EXCEEDING**
Educator: Hello. Thanks for taking time to talk with me about your school. **Learner:**	**Educator:** Hello. Thanks for taking time to talk with me about your school. **Learner:** Hey, what's up? (*shakes hands with educator*). Questions for me?	**Educator:** Hello. Thanks for taking time to talk with me about your school. **Learner:**	**Educator:** Hello. Thanks for taking time to talk with me about your school. **Learner:**
Educator: What would you like to tell me about your school? **Learner:**	**Educator:** What would you like to tell me about your school? **Learner:** My school is big and is many classes. We must have math, English and social studies.	**Educator:** What would you like to tell me about your school? **Learner:**	**Educator:** What would you like to tell me about your school? **Learner:**
Educator: Do you have other things you can choose too? **Learner:**	**Educator:** Do you have other things you can choose too? **Learner:** Yes, I also have languages, music, art and physical education.	**Educator:** Do you have other things you can choose too? **Learner:**	**Educator:** Do you have other things you can choose too? **Learner:**

Educator: How many classes do you have each day?	**Educator:** How many classes do you have each day?	**Educator:** How many classes do you have each day?	**Educator:** How many classes do you have each day?
Learner:	**Learner:** We have many 4 each day. Many days are the same, but sometimes we have a class not every day. Like music. I have music on Monday, Wednesday and Friday, and the next week on Tuesday and Thursday.	**Learner:**	**Learner:**
Educator: Every other day, I see.	**Educator:** Every other day, I see.	**Educator:** Every other day, I see.	**Educator:** Every other day, I see.
Learner:	**Learner:** Wanna hear about lunch (*tilts head*)? I think it is different from your lunch.	**Learner:**	**Learner:**
Educator: Sure, That would be great.	**Educator:** Sure, That would be great.	**Educator:** Sure, That would be great.	**Educator:** Sure, That would be great.
Learner:	**Learner:** Yummy (*laughs*)! Before lunch was from home. We have 2 choices. Usually rice or pasta for one and meat food the other one. Always there is salad.	**Learner:**	**Learner:**
Educator: That sounds good. Thanks for talking with me.	**Educator:** That sounds good. Thanks for talking with me.	**Educator:** That sounds good. Thanks for talking with me.	**Educator:** That sounds good. Thanks for talking with me.
Learner:	**Learner:** Sure! See ya (*waves*)!	**Learner:**	**Learner:**

The Performance Domain Indicators (PDIs) Assessment and Feedback Guide

The *Performance Domain Indicators (PDIs) Assessment and Feedback Guide* is a resource for both learners and educators to use when assessing learner performance. The information within this guide is based on the PDIs of Intercultural Communication: *Beginning, Developing, Meeting, Exceeding.* This guide can be used at each proficiency level: Novice, Intermediate, and Advanced (see Table 7.8). It is important to note that a performance assessment evaluates a learner's *performance*, and not *the learner*. Therefore, a learner is not *at* a level, but rather a learner's performance may be consistent *with* a level.

The purpose of the *Performance Domain Indicators (PDIs) Assessment and Feedback Guide* is to provide a visual pathway for evaluating the Intercultural Communication of a learner's performance. The left-hand column provides guiding questions that lead us to identify the Intercultural Communication consistent with a learner's performance. These guiding questions are based upon the performance levels' PDIs, which are presented lowest to highest. Starting at the *Beginning* level, evaluators progress through each question, responding "yes" or "no." If evaluators reply "yes" to all questions in the *Beginning* level, they continue to the next level (*Developing*), repeating the process, and continuing through the levels. If evaluators reply "no" to a question, they go back to the previous level, in which all their replies for the level's guiding questions are "yes." At the last level where all questions are answered "yes," evaluators continue across the chart. They can then refer to the second column labeled *Performance Domain Indicator* for the PDI that best aligns with the learner's performance. Based on this evaluation, the following two columns provide example GLOW and GROW comments. GLOW feedback states what the learner achieved and GROW feedback directs learners how to develop their language skills. This feedback is not unit specific, but rather supports overarching language performance goals that learners can work towards throughout a course. Including evidence from learner performance within the GLOW/GROW feedback is most effective.

Table 7.8

Performance Domain Indicators (PDIs) Assessment and Feedback Guide

<table>
<tr><th colspan="4">Intercultural Communication
Target performance level: Meeting</th></tr>
<tr><td rowspan="3">The context and content corresponds to the proficiency level a learner is working within.</td><td>NOVICE</td><td colspan="2">Context: familiar, informal, formal, predictable
Content: very familiar, familiar, everyday</td></tr>
<tr><td>INTERMEDIATE</td><td colspan="2">Context: familiar, informal, formal, straight-forward
Content: familiar, concrete, at times researched</td></tr>
<tr><td>ADVANCED</td><td colspan="2">Context: familiar, unfamiliar, informal, formal, complex
Content: familiar, academic, social, professional, concrete, abstract</td></tr>
<tr><th>Guiding questions</th><th>Performance Domain Indicator</th><th>GLOW</th><th>GROW</th></tr>
<tr><td>Beginning
Does the learner:
• use language and/or behaviors to communicate their essage, but they are not appropriate to the social/cultural context?</td><td>I use language and/or behaviors that are not appropriate to the social/cultural context.</td><td>• You use language (speech acts, honorifics, expressions, slang/jargon, abbreviations, systems of measurement), to communicate your message, but it is (not appropriate to the/appropriate in your culture and not the) social/cultural context of the task.
• You use behaviors (body language, paralinguistics, turn-taking rituals, writing mechanics, format, style), to communicate your message, but it is (not appropriate to the/appropriate in your culture and not the) social/cultural context of the task.</td><td>• Your use of (language and/or behavior) does not match the social/cultural context. How might you adjust this to be more appropriate to the social/cultural context?
• What language (speech act, honorifics, expressions, slang/jargon, abbreviations, systems of measurement) might you add to communicate your message appropriately within the social/cultural context?
• What behaviors (body language, paralinguistics, turn-taking rituals, writing mechanics, format, style) might you add to communicate your message appropriately to the social/cultural context?</td></tr>
</table>

Developing Can the learner: • at times use language and/or behaviors to communicate their message appropriately within the social/cultural context?	I can, at times, use language and/ or behaviors that are appropriate to the social/cultural context.	• You use language (*speech acts, honorifics, expressions, slang/jargon, abbreviations, systems of measurement*), to communicate your message appropriately within the social/cultural context. • You use behaviors (*body language, paralinguistics, turn-taking rituals, writing mechanics, format, style*), to communicate your message appropriately within the social/cultural context.	• Your use of (language/behavior) does not match the social/cultural context. How might you adjust this in a future performance with a similar social/cultural context? • What language and behaviors could you add to be more appropriate to the social/cultural context? • What (language and/or behavior) might you use to enhance the communication of your message?
Meeting Can the learner: • use language and/or behaviors to communicate their message appropriately within the social/cultural context?	I can use language and/or behaviors that are appropriate to the social/cultural context.	• You use language (*speech acts, honorifics, expressions, slang/jargon, abbreviations, systems of measurement*), to communicate your message appropriately within the social/cultural context. • You use behaviors (*body language, paralinguistics, turn-taking rituals, writing mechanics, format, style*), to communicate your message appropriately within the social/cultural context.	• In this performance, you do not use any ____. How might you incorporate it in a future performance with a similar social/ cultural context? • How might you add ____ appropriately in a future performance with a similar social/ cultural context? • How might you incorporate a variety of language and/or behaviors to communicate your message appropriately within the social/cultural context? • How might you use language and/ or behaviors to resolve a social/ cultural misunderstanding?
Exceeding Can the learner: • use a variety of language and/or behaviors to communicate their message appropriately within the social/cultural context?	I can use a variety of language and/ or behaviors that are appropriate to the social/cultural context.	• You use a variety of language (*speech acts, honorifics, expressions, slang/jargon, abbreviations, systems of measurement*) to communicate your message appropriately within the social/cultural context. • You use a variety of behaviors (*body language, paralinguistics, turn-taking rituals, writing mechanics, format, style*), to communicate your message appropriately within the social/cultural context.	• In this performance, you do not use any ____. How might you incorporate it in a future performance with a similar social/ cultural context? • How might you add ____ appropriately in a future performance with a similar social/ cultural context? • How might you use language and/ or behaviors to resolve a social/ cultural misunderstanding? • How might you adjust your use of (language and/or behavior) to demonstrate sensitivity to the social/cultural context? • In what ways could you suspend judgment to communicate a message appropriately within the social/cultural context? • How might you verify the appropriateness of your language and/or behaviors within an unfamiliar social/cultural context?

Performance Domain Indicators within a Rubric

In order to evaluate learners' performances, the PDIs are placed within a rubric with four performance level labels: *Beginning, Developing, Meeting,* and *Exceeding* (see Table 7.9). The *Meeting* level aligns with the target performance level for the learners. These labels communicate to learners how their performance compares to the standard; learners are *Beginning* to meet, *Developing* towards, *Meeting*, or *Exceeding* their target performance level. It is important to highlight that, similar to other ACTFL publications, when placed within a rubric, these four performance levels are arranged high to low, beginning with the highest on the left. This is so that learners read the highest level of performance first. Table 7.9 illustrates the rubric alignment and arrangement for the Intercultural Communication performance domain for both the presentational and interpersonal modes of communication.

Table 7.9
Aligning the Intercultural Communication Performance Domain Indicators (PDIs) in a Rubric

Target performance level: **Meeting** Context: familiar, informal, formal, predictable Content: very familiar, familiar, everyday				
NOVICE				
	EXCEEDING	**MEETING**	**DEVELOPING**	**BEGINNING**
Performance level description	I can use a variety of language and/or behaviors that are appropriate to the social/cultural context.	I can use language and/or behaviors that are appropriate to the social/cultural context.	I can, at times, use language and/or behaviors that are appropriate to the social/cultural context.	I use language and/or behaviors that are not appropriate to the social/cultural context.

Target performance level: **Meeting** Context: familiar, informal, formal, straight-forward Content: familiar, concrete, at times researched				
INTERMEDIATE				
	EXCEEDING	**MEETING**	**DEVELOPING**	**BEGINNING**
Performance level description	I can use a variety of language and/or behaviors that are appropriate to the social/cultural context.	I can use language and/or behaviors that are appropriate to the social/cultural context.	I can, at times, use language and/or behaviors that are appropriate to the social/cultural context.	I use language and/or behaviors that are not appropriate to the social/cultural context.

Target performance level: **Meeting** Context: familiar, unfamiliar, informal, formal, complex Content: familiar, academic, social, professional, concrete, abstract				
	ADVANCED			
	EXCEEDING	**MEETING**	**DEVELOPING**	**BEGINNING**
Performance level description	I can use a variety of language and/or behaviors that are appropriate to the social/cultural context.	I can use language and/or behaviors that are appropriate to the social/cultural context.	I can, at times, use language and/or behaviors that are appropriate to the social/cultural context.	I use language and/or behaviors that are not appropriate to the social/cultural context.

Performance Assessment in Action

As educators our understanding of the PDIs is critical to providing effective feedback that promotes language growth in our learners. Therefore, it is important to build our capacity to use the PDIs. Here, the goal is to model how to use the Intercultural Communication PDIs to evaluate learner work, which is the basis of the GLOW and GROW feedback is provided. The focus of this section is to evaluate learner work and provide feedback, *not* to determine a learner's proficiency level. In other words, the evaluation indicates the learner's performance is consistent with a level and provides feedback to indicate next steps for language growth.

This section demonstrates how to use these rubrics to evaluate sample presentational and interpersonal learner performances within the Novice, Intermediate, and Advanced level. These learner samples exemplify products of a summative assessment. They show evidence from learners after exposure to and practice within a unit of study. That is, learners complete these tasks following classroom instruction and multiple opportunities for formative practice on these topics. After the evaluation of each learner sample there is a model of how to provide GLOW and GROW feedback using examples from the *Performance Domain Indicators (PDIs) Assessment and Feedback Guide*

Each learner sample:

- indicates the PDI that best aligns with the performance in the rubric.
- uses the evaluation to explain what the learner can do in this performance sample.
- models how to provide GLOW and GROW feedback using examples from the *Performance Domain Indicators (PDIs) Assessment and Feedback Guide.*

LEARNERS PERFORMING WITHIN THE NOVICE LEVEL

Mode of communication: *Presentational*
Target performance level: **Meeting**
Context: familiar, formal, predictable
Content: familiar, everyday

Novice Task: For the hallway display, select one of the people we have studied in this unit. Create a descriptive writing in which you compare how you are similar in order to highlight what you have in common, and contrast how you are different in order to feature how you each make use of your attributes in our diverse world.

LEARNER SAMPLE RESPONSE

Hey! My name is Pari. I 12 years old. I am Persian.
Ingrid is sports. Ingrid like to dance. I am not to dance. I am to swim.
I is shy. Ingrid is shy. I is play sports.
I am to read. Ingrid like to dance.
I am to draw. Ingrid like to dance. Well, see ya later!

Evaluation & Explanation

INTERCULTURAL COMMUNICATION			
NOVICE			
EXCEEDING	**MEETING**	**DEVELOPING**	**BEGINNING**
I can use a variety of language and/ or behaviors that are appropriate to the social/ cultural context.	I can use language and/ or behaviors that are appropriate to the social/ cultural context.	I can, at times, use language and/or behaviors that are appropriate to the social/ cultural context.	I use language and/or behaviors that are not appropriate to the social/ cultural context.

Evaluation: In this performance sample, the learner can, at times, use language and behaviors that are appropriate to the social and cultural context (formal writing for a hallway display). This includes English writing conventions, such as capitalization (*I, Ingrid,* at the beginning of a sentence) and punctuation (ending sentences with a period or exclamation mark).

Feedback:

- GLOW: You use behaviors, such as writing mechanics (capitalization and punctuation), to communicate your message appropriately within the social/cultural context of a hallway display.
- GROW: Your use of language (*Hey, see ya later*) does not always match the formal social/cultural context needed for a hallway display. How might you adjust this to use more formal language in another performance with a similar social/cultural context (formal writing for a display)?

LEARNERS PERFORMING WITHIN THE NOVICE LEVEL

Mode of communication: *Interpersonal*
Target performance level: **Meeting**
Context: familiar, informal, predictable
Content: familiar, everyday

Novice Task: Chat with your new classmate to find out how you both may be similar to and/or different from each other.

LEARNER SAMPLE RESPONSE

Learner 1: Hello.

Learner 2: Hey! How's it going?

Learner 1: Good. And you?

Learner 2: Very good. What do you like more, sports or ski?

Learner 1: Ski.

Learner 2: Me too (*points to self*)! I like to ski. A lot. Um, my favorite...my favorite sport...in the...in the winter. Um...do you like to sing?

Learner 1: I don't like to sing.

Learner 2: Do you like to do...soccer in it's hot or it's cold?

Learner 1: Um...repeat?

Learner 2: Do you like to do soccer in it's hot or it's cold?

Learner 1: ...

Learner 2: Do you like to do soccer... (*kicks leg*)...in it's hot or it's cold?

Learner 1: No...comprehend (*shrugs*).

Learner 2: Do you like...soccer (*kicks leg*)...in it's hot (*fans face*) or um... it's cold, brrr (*shivers and rubs arms*)?

Learner 1: Oh! Um, yes. I like...um, hot?

Learner 2: (*Nods*)

Learner 1: Yes. Hot.

Learner 2: Cool! Me...me too!

Learner 1: Ride bike?

Learner 2: Well, sometimes. Yes, I like to ride a bike. Sometimes. In the...in the summer?

Learner 1: Ok, bye.

Learner 2: See ya later!

Evaluation & Explanation

INTERCULTURAL COMMUNICATION | LEARNER 1			
NOVICE			
EXCEEDING	**MEETING**	**DEVELOPING**	**BEGINNING**
I can use a variety of language and/ or behaviors that are appropriate to the social/ cultural context.	I can use language and/ or behaviors that are appropriate to the social/ cultural context.	I can, at times, use language and/or behaviors that are appropriate to the social/ cultural context.	I use language and/or behaviors that are not appropriate to the social/ cultural context.

Evaluation: In this performance sample, Learner 1 uses language and behaviors that are appropriate to the social and cultural context (informal conversation with a classmate). This includes speech acts (*Hello, bye*), slang (*bye* for *good-bye*), and body language (*shrugs*).

Feedback:

- GLOW: You use language, such as speech acts (*Hello, bye*), and behaviors, such as body language (*shrugs*), to communicate your message appropriately within the social/cultural context.
- GROW: How might you incorporate a variety of language and/or behaviors to communicate your message appropriately within the social/cultural context?

INTERCULTURAL COMMUNICATION | LEARNER 2			
NOVICE			
EXCEEDING	**MEETING**	**DEVELOPING**	**BEGINNING**
I can use a variety of language and/ or behaviors that are appropriate to the social/ cultural context.	I can use language and/ or behaviors that are appropriate to the social/ cultural context.	I can, at times, use language and/or behaviors that are appropriate to the social/ cultural context.	I use language and/or behaviors that are not appropriate to the social/ cultural context.

Evaluation: In this performance, Learner 2 uses a variety of language and behaviors that are appropriate to the social and cultural context. This includes speech acts (*Hey! See ya later!*), slang (*Hey! How's it going? Cool! See ya later!*), and body language (*points to self, kicks leg, fans face, shivers and rubs arms*).

Feedback:

- GLOW: You use a variety of language and behaviors to communicate your message appropriately within the social/cultural context.
- GROW: How might you add the learned slang, for example *No way!*, appropriately in a future performance with a similar social/cultural context (informal conversation with a friend)?

LEARNERS PERFORMING WITHIN THE INTERMEDIATE LEVEL

Mode of communication: *Presentational*
Target performance level: **Meeting**
Context: familiar, formal, straight-forward
Content: familiar, researched

Intermediate Task: As part of an Earth Day campaign in your community, write a formal letter to an influential leader advocating for change that would address an environmental issue that you have learned about.

LEARNER SAMPLE RESPONSE

Honorable Mayor Wilson,

Help! My name is Kai Meyer. I live in Elmdale now. I like to live in Elmdale We have strong engaged for community here. Since 3 years, Elmdale won the "Best city in the USA". We try to win that again and we could. We could to do more of to clean up and beautify our city. Maybe have like the BUGA garden show in Germany. Different cities host and make big gardens. And plant trees. Like big plant show at the fair.

A lot in Elmdale is full of garbage. When I run on hiking trails I see a lot of garbage. Nature reserves, like Forest Park, have more garbage. It is not pretty. I remember you to since 3 years. It would be great if mentality to our city. Run people need clean trails. They are impacted.

Here are things do. We could the volunteers clean up the parks. This would also help the people in the city do it. Other volunteers could the large places. The city could have event. The event would be "Consciousness about Garbage in Elmdale"

We could say, plant more trees in the niehgborhoods. This would give back the trees we take for construction. Maybe be a tree hugger? Plants and gardens too but for now trees. When we plant more trees, this make our community a better place, if we plant more trees. Plant now! Act now!

Sincerely,
Kai Meyer

Evaluation & Explanation

INTERCULTURAL COMMUNICATION			
INTERMEDIATE			
EXCEEDING	**MEETING**	**DEVELOPING**	**BEGINNING**
I can use a variety of language and/or behaviors that are appropriate to the social/cultural context.	I can use language and/or behaviors that are appropriate to the social/cultural context.	I can, at times, use language and/or behaviors that are appropriate to the social/cultural context.	I use language and/or behaviors that are not appropriate to the social/cultural context.

Evaluation: In this performance sample, the learner can, at times, use language and behaviors that are appropriate to the social and cultural context (formal letter to an influential leader). This includes an honorific (*Honorable*), polite, indirect language (*could, would*), format (beginning with *Honorable Mayor Wilson*, ending with *Sincerely, Kai Meyer*), and style (introducing oneself and providing background information before making a request).

Feedback:

- GLOW: You use formal language, such as honorifics (*Honorable*), speech acts (*Sincerely*), and polite, indirect language (*could, would*) to communicate your message appropriately within the social/cultural context.
- GROW: Your use of direct language (*Help! Here are things do, Plant now! Act now!*) and slang (*tree hugger*) does not match the social/cultural context. How might you adjust this to polite, indirect language in a future performance with similar social/cultural context (formal letter to an authority figure)?

LEARNERS PERFORMING WITHIN THE INTERMEDIATE LEVEL

Mode of communication: *Interpersonal*
Target performance level: **Meeting**
Context: familiar, informal, straight-forward
Content: familiar, researched

Intermediate Task: After reading and viewing texts to learn about ways we can implement change, select an organization that works to better their community. Discuss your organization with a partner to learn more about the organizations you have each selected, why you selected yours, and how your organizations implement change for others.

LEARNER SAMPLE RESPONSE

Learner 1: Hi Paz!

Learner 2: Hi! How are you?

Learner 1: I'm alright. What is your organization called?

Learner 2: My organization is called the Family Stay House...But no place like home.

Learner 1: How interesting (*nods*)!

Learner 2: What is your organization called?

Learner 1: The organization...er, sorry...my organization favorite is called Renewing the Countryside.

Learner 2: Oh, how fantastic! What does it do? Renew, reuse, recycle (*laughs*)?

Learner 1: Renewing the Countryside gives money for the...for the farmers and help the children of poor families in rural communities.

Learner 2: Great! Great (*nods*)!

Learner 1: What does your organization try to do (*tilts head*)?

Learner 2: The Family Stay House tries to support and help families, families that need the help economically paying for pro-proced... when the children are sick. Where is the organization?

Learner 1: The organization...er, sorry...my organization favorite is called Renewing the Countryside.

Learner 2: My organization, um, is in the city.

Learner 1: Great! Did it do something in the past?

Learner 2: Every year, the Race for the Kids, um remember money for organization, um, to pay for the, um, pro-proced-procedures.

Learner 1: How cool (*smiles*)!

Learner 2: Um, yes, yes, yes (*nods*). Um, How many people serves the organization?

Learner 1: Many people serves the organization in the city because everyone wants to help the, the rural communities.

Learner 2: Yes, great!

Learner 1: I like your organization a lot. How can I help your organization? I pitch in?

Learner 2: Oh, how fantastic (*eyes widen*)! You can work as a volunteer – reading books to children, playing sports with the children, donating money and getting money for the organization.

Learner 1: How fun! Why should I help?

Learner 2: Um, because ...because, in my opinion, it is important to help the people-.

Learner 1: Great, great, yes (*nods*)!

Learner 2: What they do for your organization?

Learner 1: Um you can get money for the organization or you can donate. A little bit goes a long way!

Learner 2: I think so.

Learner 1: Bye (*waves*)!

Learner 2: Bye (*waves*)!

Learner 1: Thanks for talking with me.

Learner 2: I'll see you laters. Thanks for talking with me.

Evaluation & Explanation

INTERCULTURAL COMMUNICATION | LEARNER 1			
INTERMEDIATE			
EXCEEDING	MEETING	DEVELOPING	BEGINNING
I can use a variety of language and/ or behaviors that are appropriate to the social/ cultural context.	I can use language and/ or behaviors that are appropriate to the social/ cultural context.	I can, at times, use language and/or behaviors that are appropriate to the social/ cultural context.	I use language and/or behaviors that are not appropriate to the social/ cultural context.

Evaluation: In this performance sample, Learner 1 uses a variety of language and behaviors that are appropriate to the social/cultural context (informal conversation with a friend). This includes speech acts, such as a greeting (*Hi*), apologizing (*sorry*), thanking (*Thanks*), leave-taking (*Bye*), expressions (*A little bit goes a long way!* and *I pitch in?*), and slang (*Hi, alright, cool, Thanks, Bye*). Additionally, Learner 1 uses body language (*nods, tilts head, smiles, waves*) and direct, informal behaviors, such as proceeding directly to asking a question after a short greeting and being very direct in asking *Why should I help?* This directness and informality are appropriate to the learner's role as a peer in this social context.

Feedback:

- GLOW: You use language, such as speech acts, expressions, informal and direct language, that are appropriate to the social/cultural context.
- GROW: How might you add a variety of slang that would be appropriate in a future performance with a similar social/cultural context (informal conversation with a friend)?

INTERCULTURAL COMMUNICATION | LEARNER 2			
INTERMEDIATE			
EXCEEDING	MEETING	DEVELOPING	BEGINNING
I can use a variety of language and/ or behaviors that are appropriate to the social/ cultural context.	I can use language and/ or behaviors that are appropriate to the social/ cultural context.	I can, at times, use language and/or behaviors that are appropriate to the social/ cultural context.	I use language and/or behaviors that are not appropriate to the social/ cultural context.

Evaluation: In this performance sample, Learner 2 uses language and behaviors appropriate to this social/cultural context (informal conversation with a friend). This includes language such as speech acts, such as a greeting (*Hi! How are you?*), farewell (*Bye! I'll see you laters*), and thanking (*Thanks for...*), an expression (*Renew, reuse, recycle*), and slang (*Bye! I'll see you laters*). Additionally, Learner 2 uses behaviors such as body language (*laughs, nods, eyes widen, waves*) to appropriately communicate their message.

Feedback:

- GLOW: You use language, such as speech acts, an expression, and slang, as well as behaviors, such as body language, to appropriately communicate your message within the social/cultural context.
- GROW: How might you incorporate a variety of language and/or behaviors to communicate your message appropriately within the social/cultural context?

LEARNERS PERFORMING WITHIN THE ADVANCED LEVEL

Mode of communication: *Presentational*
Target performance level: **Meeting**
Context: familiar, informal, complex
Content: familiar, academic, social, professional, concrete

Advanced Task: Based on the movie, write a diary entry from the perspective of one of the baseball players that includes their reflections of the recruitment practices of professional baseball leagues.

LEARNER SAMPLE RESPONSE

> Dear diary,
>
> I cannot believe that this investigation about my age is still going on! It is just not fair! I am not a liar! How much analyses have I to do? Because of this, I did not get the chance to sign when I turned 16 years. In the Professional Baseball League they think that all us players are liars. There are some that lies, but there are a lot of us who tells the truth.
>
> But what are they suppose to do, if only one year older means you are worth $1 million less? Seriously, one year? The PBL uses us for our poverty. It's not fair that they treat us differently, pay us differently just because we live in poorer country. Why I don't make money because I am a great baseball player? Why am I the cheap export? If I am in power, I would talks with the representatives to work for changes in recruiting regulations, like age restrictions and equal pay.
>
> Yet I know that if I work hard, I will get a contract of any price which, for me, is the way out of poverty. It is also my family's way out of poverty because they are depending on me. The first thing I take on is buy my parents a house so they never have to worry about housing ever again! I just have to be patient. All I want to do is play baseball- it's what I love, it's what I borned to do, it's all I have ever done.
>
> Let's play ball!
> -Mike

Evaluation & Explanation

INTERCULTURAL COMMUNICATION			
ADVANCED			
EXCEEDING	MEETING	DEVELOPING	BEGINNING
I can use a variety of language and/ or behaviors that are appropriate to the social/ cultural context.	I can use language and/ or behaviors that are appropriate to the social/ cultural context.	I can, at times, use language and/or behaviors that are appropriate to the social/ cultural context.	I use language and/or behaviors that are not appropriate to the social/ cultural context.

Evaluation: The learner is able to use a variety of language and behaviors that are appropriate to the social context of writing a diary entry. The learner uses the appropriate format as observed with the familiar greeting *Dear diary,* which is also an affectionate speech act. To close the diary entry, the learner uses a personal signature at the end. Throughout their writing, the learner consistently writes in first person. The learner uses intensifiers such as *still, only, just because* to enhance the emotional context. The learner also includes two different idiomatic expressions, such as to *take on* and *Let's play ball!,* the latter being very specific to American baseball culture.

Feedback:

- GLOW: You use a variety of language and behaviors, including speech acts, writing conventions, and idiomatic expressions, that are appropriate to the social/cultural context of a diary entry.
- GROW: How might you add learned expressions like *no matter what* appropriately in a future performance with a similar social/cultural context (diary)?

LEARNERS PERFORMING WITHIN THE ADVANCED LEVEL

Mode of communication: *Interpersonal*
Target performance level: **Meeting**
Context: familiar, informal, complex
Content: familiar, academic, social, concrete

Advanced Task: After visiting a Monarch butterfly sanctuary, you and a friend discuss your reactions to learning about the monarch butterfly migrations and how it's being threatened.

LEARNER SAMPLE RESPONSE

Learner 1: So, what did ya think?... of the butterfly sanctuary?

Learner 2: I think that... um, the butterflies, the monarch butterflies are incredible. And these places, these sanctuaries, well, they are magical. I don´t know much things about the butterflies and their migrations before now.

Learner 1: Uhm... Same here. What fascinates me is how millions of butterflies, these tiny insects, come from all over the continent..., and to end up in these sanctuaries in Mexico, ya know?

Learner 2: Yeah, it is incredible. These places, they are so important to, to their migration process. They need these sanctuaries for, um.., this is where they sleep during the winter months.

Learner 1: Exactly. These sanctuaries are where the monarchs hibernate, so they are vital to this natural phenomenon. What's more, is the monarch's cultural influence on, like, the festival for Day of the Dead. For them, the butterflies represent the souls of their loved ones, like the butterflies (*air quotes*) are their loved ones coming back.

Learner 2: It's interesting how, how nature can influence cultural practices, like, what you said, about Day of the Dead. (...)

Learner 1: RIght. This is why I am glad to have learned that they are taking measures to, um, conserve these spaces, um, these spaces that are their habitats. Right?

Learner 2: Yes. They are protecting against destruction because of people cutting down trees illegally. But, I understand why they have to do it.

Learner 1: How so? What do you mean by that?

Learner 2: Well, some peoples depends on cutting down the trees, because they need that money to buy food and clothes for their family.

Learner 1: Ah ha (*nods head*). Now I understand. Yeah, they are between a rock and a hard place. Ya know? I don't know what I would do if... if I was in that situation where, where my family depended on the income from illegal logging. What would you do?

Learner 2: It's difficult to say what I would do too, especially because there are no other good options for them, to have, to have different jobs.

Learner 1: And, on the other hand, it's not just about to conserve the sanctuaries. For example, the use of chemicals... or pesticides in fields kills butterflies along the migration routes. It's kind of gotten out of hand. I'm not sure what can be done.

Learner 2: Well, one thing we can do is plant more milkweed, which is a flower that the butterflies depend on for food.

Evaluation & Explanation

INTERCULTURAL COMMUNICATION | LEARNER 1			
ADVANCED			
EXCEEDING	**MEETING**	**DEVELOPING**	**BEGINNING**
I can use a variety of language and/ or behaviors that are appropriate to the social/ cultural context.	I can use language and/ or behaviors that are appropriate to the social/ cultural context.	I can, at times, use language and/or behaviors that are appropriate to the social/ cultural context.	I use language and/or behaviors that are not appropriate to the social/ cultural context.

Evaluation: In this performance sample, Learner 1 uses a variety of language and behaviors that are appropriate to the social/cultural context, which is an informal discussion with a classmate. Learner 1 uses an informal, colloquial subject pronoun (*Ya* and *Ya know?*). The learner appropriately uses behaviors, such as using air quotes at the beginning of the quotation. Additionally, Learner 1 uses informal expressions (*same here*) and idiomatic expressions (*gotten out of hand* and *between a rock in a hard place*), as well as intensifiers (*so, just,* and *kind of*), which are appropriate to the social/cultural context.

Feedback:

- GLOW: You use a variety of language, such as the colloquial form of *you* – *ya* – when addressing your classmate in this informal discussion and two different idiomatic expressions, to interact appropriately within the social/cultural context.
- GROW: How might you add an informal speech act to greet your classmate in a future performance with a similar social/cultural context (informal discussion with a friend)?

INTERCULTURAL COMMUNICATION | LEARNER 2			
ADVANCED			
EXCEEDING	**MEETING**	**DEVELOPING**	**BEGINNING**
I can use a variety of language and/ or behaviors that are appropriate to the social/ cultural context.	I can use language and/ or behaviors that are appropriate to the social/ cultural context.	I can, at times, use language and/or behaviors that are appropriate to the social/ cultural context.	I use language and/or behaviors that are not appropriate to the social/ cultural context.

Evaluation: In this performance sample, Learner 2 can, at times, use language and behaviors that are appropriate to the social/cultural context, which is an informal discussion with a classmate. Learner 2 appropriately uses the informal register with their classmate (*you*), slang (*Yeah*), as well as a couple intensifiers (*so* and *especially*).

Feedback:

- GLOW: You use language, such as the informal register *you*, to communicate your message appropriately within the social/cultural context.
- GROW: What language and behaviors could you add to be more appropriate to the social/cultural context?

YOUR TURN

LEARNING TARGETS CHECK:	
I can	☐ evaluate learner work using the Performance Domain Indicators (PDIs). ☐ give effective feedback using the Intercultural Communication PDIs.

Now it is your turn to practice evaluating learner performances and providing feedback. Remember, learners complete these performance tasks following classroom instruction and multiple opportunities for formative practice on these topics. In this section, use the Intercultural Communication PDIs to indicate the level of performance that best corresponds with the following presentational and interpersonal learner performance samples. Then provide each learner GLOW and GROW feedback. You may want to use the *Performance Domain Indicators (PDIs) Assessment and Feedback Guide* to help guide your evaluation and feedback of the learner's performance in the Intercultural Communication performance domain.

Then, turn to APPENDIX C | Intercultural Communication (p.437-442) to compare your evaluation and feedback to one provided by the authors. Reflect on how your evaluation and feedback was similar and/or different, and why. You can do this individually and/or with your colleagues (for example, with a Professional Learning Community (PLC)). This exercise can be an opportunity for rich discussion to help increase inter-rater reliability among educators.

LEARNERS PERFORMING WITHIN THE NOVICE LEVEL

Mode of communication: *Presentational*
Target performance level: **Meeting**
Context: familiar, formal, predictable
Content: familiar, everyday

Novice Task: For the hallway display, select one of the people we have studied in this unit. Create a descriptive writing in which you compare how you are similar in order to highlight what you have in common, and contrast how you are different in order to feature how you each make use of your attributes in our diverse world.

LEARNER SAMPLE RESPONSE:

> Greetings! My name is Leo. I am 12 years old.
>
> Naiomi is 24 years old. She is Diné (Navajo).
>
> Naiomi & I is similar. Naiomi is sports-minded because to skateboard. How interesting! I do not like to skateboard. I like hockey but no skateboarding. I like hockey in the winter with my friends.
>
> Naiomi is hard-working. Naiomi really likes to practice skateboarding. How interesting! I like hockey.
>
> Naiomi not is lazy. She likes to work for more skate parks. How important! Many people to need more skate parks. Many people to need more hockey parks too. Is a problem. How important!
>
> Naiomi and I is different but equal. Thank you for read!

Evaluation & Explanation

INTERCULTURAL COMMUNICATION			
NOVICE			
EXCEEDING	MEETING	DEVELOPING	BEGINNING
I can use a variety of language and/or behaviors that are appropriate to the social/cultural context.	I can use language and/or behaviors that are appropriate to the social/cultural context.	I can, at times, use language and/or behaviors that are appropriate to the social/cultural context.	I use language and/or behaviors that are not appropriate to the social/cultural context.

Evaluation:

Feedback:

- GLOW:
- GROW:

Turn to APPENDIX C | Intercultural Communication (p.437) to compare your evaluation and explanation to one provided by the authors.

LEARNERS PERFORMING WITHIN THE NOVICE LEVEL

Mode of communication: *Interpersonal*
Target performance level: **Meeting**
Context: familiar, informal, predictable
Content: familiar, everyday

Novice Task: Chat with your new classmate to find out how you both may be similar and/or different.

LEARNER SAMPLE RESPONSE

Learner 1: Um...Sports?

Learner 2: Yes (*nods*), I like sports a LOT (*smiles*). My favorite! And you?

Learner 1: Yes (*nods*).

Learner 2: What do you like more, baseball or football?

Learner 1: Baseball. I...mmm...baseball...yes. And you, sir?

Learner 2: I like baseball AND I like football! I like to play baseball in the summer. I like to watch football in the fall.

Learner 1: Ok. Um, television?

Learner 2: Yes, I like TV. I really like to watch sports on TV. And you?

Learner 1: Very good (*nods*).

Learner 2: Ok. Do you like to read?

Learner 1: Um...repeat?

Learner 2: Do you...do you like...to read?

Learner 1: ...

Learner 2: Do you like...to read?

Learner 1: Um... (*shrugs shoulders*)

Learner 2: Um, do you like to read? Um (*gestures with hands*) read...read. Um, books?

Learner 1: Oh! Yes (*nods*). I...I...yes.

Learner 2: Ok. I...um...I...too (*points to self, nods*)! I like read books. Um, do you like to swim?

Learner 1: Repeat?

Learner 2: Do you like to swim (*gestures swimming movements with arms*)?

Learner 1: Oh, yes (*nods*)! Yes, swim...yes! And you, sir?

Learner 2: Cool! I too. I like to swim in the summer. Sometimes I like to swim in the winter in the...um...in the...yeah.

Learner 1: ...

Learner 2: Ok, well, thanks! Bye (*waves*)!

Learner 1: Bye (*waves*)!

Evaluation & Explanation

INTERCULTURAL COMMUNICATION | LEARNER 1			
NOVICE			
EXCEEDING	**MEETING**	**DEVELOPING**	**BEGINNING**
I can use a variety of language and/ or behaviors that are appropriate to the social/ cultural context.	I can use language and/ or behaviors that are appropriate to the social/ cultural context.	I can, at times, use language and/or behaviors that are appropriate to the social/ cultural context.	I use language and/or behaviors that are not appropriate to the social/ cultural context.

Evaluation:

Feedback:

- GLOW:
- GROW:

INTERCULTURAL COMMUNICATION | LEARNER 2			
NOVICE			
EXCEEDING	**MEETING**	**DEVELOPING**	**BEGINNING**
I can use a variety of language and/ or behaviors that are appropriate to the social/ cultural context.	I can use language and/ or behaviors that are appropriate to the social/ cultural context.	I can, at times, use language and/or behaviors that are appropriate to the social/ cultural context.	I use language and/or behaviors that are not appropriate to the social/ cultural context.

Evaluation:

Feedback:

- GLOW:
- GROW:

Turn to APPENDIX C | Intercultural Communication (p.438) to compare your evaluation and explanation to one provided by the authors.

LEARNERS PERFORMING WITHIN THE INTERMEDIATE LEVEL

Mode of communication: *Presentational*
Target performance level: **Meeting**
Context: familiar, formal, straight-forward
Content: familiar, researched

Intermediate Task: As part of an Earth Day campaign in your community, write a formal letter to an influential leader advocating for change that would address an environmental issue that you have learned about.

LEARNER SAMPLE RESPONSE

Dear Mr. President,

Did you heared, one of the major problems environmental in the world is the increase of the ocean level as result of global warming. The increase of the ocean level is a problem Many Carribean countries are sinking and that is destroying the work or life of many people.

People are constructing sea barriers for flooding. One other thing Carribean countries are doing is transport help now, not help in the future. For the future, it's important that the world, specifically the United States, reduce the greenhouse gas emissions because a rise in greenhouse gases cause more global warming. As a result, the icebergs melt and the sea level rise. The problem is very important for you.

One example of this problem is of a little country in the Pacific Ocean. The country is Tuvalu. Tuvalu is home for 11,000 people and increase of sea level is a very big problem for this country. In the last decade, Tuvalu lost 2 islands a the ocean. This is very bad for that many people would have eliminate outside of their house and in 50 years, the whole country absent.

A protect millions of people and the health of our environments, I would think that is important you reduce the emissions greenhouse gas for the future of the world. Also, I would think that a good solution for now is do construct many sea barriers and raise to support for people and families close to the coast.

Thanks,
Avery

Evaluation & Explanation

INTERCULTURAL COMMUNICATION			
INTERMEDIATE			
EXCEEDING	**MEETING**	**DEVELOPING**	**BEGINNING**
I can use a variety of language and/or behaviors that are appropriate to the social/cultural context.	I can use language and/or behaviors that are appropriate to the social/cultural context.	I can, at times, use language and/or behaviors that are appropriate to the social/cultural context.	I use language and/or behaviors that are not appropriate to the social/cultural context.

Evaluation:

Feedback:

- GLOW:
- GROW:

Turn to APPENDIX C | Intercultural Communication (p.439) to compare your evaluation and explanation to one provided by the authors.

LEARNERS PERFORMING WITHIN THE INTERMEDIATE LEVEL

Mode of communication: *Interpersonal*
Target performance level: **Meeting**
Context: familiar, informal, straight-forward
Content: familiar, researched

Intermediate Task: After reading and viewing texts to learn about ways we can implement change, select an organization that works to better their community. Discuss your organization with a partner to learn more about the organizations you have each selected, why you selected yours, and how your organizations implement change for others.

LEARNER SAMPLE RESPONSE

Learner 1: Hi Kim (*waves*)!

Learner 2: Hi Hai (*waves*)!

Learner 1: What's up?

Learner 2: Um, not a lot (*shrugs shoulders*). And you?

Learner 1: Not a lot, not a lot. What is the name of your organization?

Learner 2: My organization is called Special Olympics.

Learner 1: Yes (*nods*) and what does that organization do?

Learner 2: Repeat please?

Learner 1: What does that organization do?

Learner 2: Me organization to try, um, to play sports with people with special you need...people with special needs.

Learner 1: How fantastic (*smiles*)!

Learner 2: What organization you work a volunteer?

Learner 1: My organization is called the Blizzard Foundation.

Learner 2: Very well (*nods*). Where is the organization?

Learner 1: My organization is in North Minneapolis. And...but it tries to work in all parts of Minnesota.

Learner 2: Very well (*nods*).

Learner 1: What did organization do in the past?

Learner 2: In the past, the Special Olympics to play sports...baseball, soccer, and basketball with a lot of people with special you need and...puts on the Polar Plunge.

Learner 1: Yes (*nods*).

Learner 2: What did your organization do in the past year?

Learner 1: My organization works as help people that want to play baseball but I can't buy. In the past, my organization worked with Miracle League. The children of Miracle League love baseball and it was very fun.

Learner 2: Very well. What is the priorities of the organization?

Learner 1: The first priority of my organization is donates money to children and families that can't buy baseball. And you, what is the priority?

Learner 2: Me priorities organization is helps people with special you need...did...no...has very fun.

Learner 1: And you volunteered with your organization in the past?

Learner 2: Ah no (*shakes head*), but I am going helps in the future.

Learner 1: Yes.

Learner 2: Bye (*waves*).

Learner 1: Ah, hold on.

Learner 2: Sorry.

Learner 1: How can I help your organization?

Learner 2: Repeat please?

Learner 1: How can I help your organization?

Learner 2: You work a volunteer to play sports with people with special you need and to donate money.

Learner 1: That's great! Thanks for talking with me!

Learner 2: Thanks, sir.

Evaluation & Explanation

INTERCULTURAL COMMUNICATION | LEARNER 1			
INTERMEDIATE			
EXCEEDING	MEETING	DEVELOPING	BEGINNING
I can use a variety of language and/ or behaviors that are appropriate to the social/ cultural context.	I can use language and/ or behaviors that are appropriate to the social/ cultural context.	I can, at times, use language and/or behaviors that are appropriate to the social/ cultural context.	I use language and/or behaviors that are not appropriate to the social/ cultural context.

Evaluation:

Feedback:
- GLOW:
- GROW:

INTERCULTURAL COMMUNICATION | LEARNER 2			
INTERMEDIATE			
EXCEEDING	MEETING	DEVELOPING	BEGINNING
I can use a variety of language and/ or behaviors that are appropriate to the social/ cultural context.	I can use language and/ or behaviors that are appropriate to the social/ cultural context.	I can, at times, use language and/or behaviors that are appropriate to the social/ cultural context.	I use language and/or behaviors that are not appropriate to the social/ cultural context.

Evaluation:

Feedback:
- GLOW:
- GROW:

Turn to APPENDIX C | Intercultural Communication (p.440) to compare your evaluation and explanation to one provided by the authors.

LEARNERS PERFORMING WITHIN THE INTERMEDIATE LEVEL

Mode of communication: *Presentational*
Target performance level: **Meeting**
Context: familiar, informal, complex
Content: familiar, academic, social, professional, concrete

Advanced Task: Based on the movie, write a diary entry from the perspective of one of the baseball players that includes their reflections of the recruitment practices of professional baseball leagues.

LEARNER SAMPLE RESPONSE

Dear Diary

I am angry! Even that my results are conclusive, I still have to do more tests. This means that I can lose my chance to sign with a professional baseball team. Out of all the 105 players, I have the best chance. It was to be a dream come true! However, because my tests are no decided, it is a controversy for teams to sign with me. I dreamed this my whole life. It's what I sacrificed so many years. What the Professional Baseball League has did to me, I think it an injustice. I did all those tests that show that I am 16 years and I did not lie. In fact my family gived the PBL all the documents that they needed. The PBL did no need the same documents or the same tests of the other baseball players. It's not fair that we give you more information. And because of this, no one wants to sign me.

If I were a different baseball player, I would no have to take the tests. I just want to be baseball player. I can help my family too. I wants to try to be as good as the other players, even better. I hope some team signs me. I won't accept that I've lost the opportunity. I will fight for my opportunity. I will not back down. Someday I will win the World Series.

Hugs,
Mikey

Evaluation & Explanation

INTERCULTURAL COMMUNICATION			
ADVANCED			
EXCEEDING	MEETING	DEVELOPING	BEGINNING
I can use a variety of language and/or behaviors that are appropriate to the social/cultural context.	I can use language and/or behaviors that are appropriate to the social/cultural context.	I can, at times, use language and/or behaviors that are appropriate to the social/cultural context.	I use language and/or behaviors that are not appropriate to the social/cultural context.

Evaluation:

Feedback:

- GLOW:
- GROW:

Turn to APPENDIX C | Intercultural Communication (p.441) to compare your evaluation and explanation to one provided by the authors.

LEARNERS PERFORMING WITHIN THE ADVANCED LEVEL

Mode of communication: *Interpersonal*
Target performance level: **Meeting**
Context: familiar, informal, complex
Content: familiar, academic, social, concrete

Advanced Task: After visiting a Monarch butterfly sanctuary, you and a friend discuss your reactions to learning about the monarch butterfly migrations and how it's being threatened.

LEARNER SAMPLE RESPONSE

Learner 1: Hey (*waves hand*).

Learner 2: Hey.

Learner 1: So, what do you think about what we learned, um, about the sanctuaries?

Learner 2: Well, to be honest, I didn't even know of them. I had no idea that there are places like these where millions of butterflies goes to, to hibernate, like clusters of them. It was incredible to see.

Learner 1: Agreed (*widens eyes*). It blew my mind to see them togethers on only a tree branch. And that there are too many that their weight may... may... break the tree branch! It's a place that I want to go..., to, like, to experience it.

Learner 2: Yeah, I wonder how it would be (*tilts head*)? I think that I might be scared, because of these tiny insects, ya know? I don't know how I could feel. You?

Learner 1: Huh. Yeah (*shrugs shoulders*). It makes me nervous, I guess... Um, well, the sanctuaries are importants to the lifecycle of these butterflies. With no reserves, there would no be butterflies.

Learner 2: Uh huh. It was interesting to learn that only here in this specific places does it have the perfect temperature, the perfect humidity and everything. Like everything is done only for the butterflies in this place and that is why they all come every year to spend the winter.

Learner 1: I know (*raises eyebrows*)! It's a perfect ecosystem, which me.., which makes me sad that peoples cut down the trees not legally in those areas, meaning they destroy their habitat.

Learner 2: I wonder if they do not knows about how these sanctuaries are important. Or, maybe they have no choice because they need to earn a living (*shrugs and raises hands*). But it's not just this. There is also climate change and the use of pesticides that, that contribute to the destruction of the habitats.

Learner 1: Oh, for sure (*nods head*)! For example, when the farmers there use pesticides in the fields for the migratory routes, the butterflies get, um...um..., sick (*looks at Learner 2*)?

Learner 2: Sick (*tilts head*)?

Learner 1: Yeah, they get sicks because the pesticides on their food.

Learner 2: Ah! You mean poison.

Learner 1: Yes, poison. They get poisons when they eat the flower, the, um... the milkweed.

Learner 2: Yes, there are many threats to this species. Well (*sighs*), I only hope that they can protect it so one day in the future I can travel there and visit the sanctuaries.

Learner 1: Ha (*laughs*)! Yes, of course.

Evaluation & Explanation

INTERCULTURAL COMMUNICATION | LEARNER 1			
ADVANCED			
EXCEEDING	MEETING	DEVELOPING	BEGINNING
I can use a variety of language and/ or behaviors that are appropriate to the social/ cultural context.	I can use language and/ or behaviors that are appropriate to the social/ cultural context.	I can, at times, use language and/or behaviors that are appropriate to the social/ cultural context.	I use language and/or behaviors that are not appropriate to the social/ cultural context.

Evaluation:

Feedback:

- GLOW:
- GROW:

INTERCULTURAL COMMUNICATION | LEARNER 2			
ADVANCED			
EXCEEDING	MEETING	DEVELOPING	BEGINNING
I can use a variety of language and/ or behaviors that are appropriate to the social/ cultural context.	I can use language and/ or behaviors that are appropriate to the social/ cultural context.	I can, at times, use language and/or behaviors that are appropriate to the social/ cultural context.	I use language and/or behaviors that are not appropriate to the social/ cultural context.

Evaluation:

Feedback:

- GLOW:
- GROW:

Turn to APPENDIX C | Intercultural Communication (p.442) to compare your evaluation and explanation to one provided by the authors.

Learning Experiences to Facilitate Learner Growth

Once educators have clarified for learners the goals of performance and provided feedback, learners need learning experiences to help them *understand* the Intercultural Communication performance domain and PDIs as well as *develop* their language performance. Learning experiences to *understand* the performance domain are listed first, followed by learning experiences to *develop* learner performance. Each learning experience includes *Learner outcomes* (what learners can do upon successful completion of the experience) and an outline of logistical components (*time, preparation, materials, instructions*). *Alternatives* and *Differentiation* offer ways to personalize the experience for a variety of learners. Each learning experience includes short examples, often including learners' work, to help educators visualize each learning experience. The learning experiences can be used with an entire class of learners as a way to introduce and focus learner work on a particular performance domain. Learning experiences can also be assigned to learners by educators or self-selected by learners themselves for further practice within a performance domain. These examples can serve as a springboard for educators to develop their own learning experiences for each performance domain when working with their learners.

CLARIFYING EXPECTATIONS

Domain: Intercultural Communication

Focus: Understanding how Intercultural Communication is evaluated

Note: This learning experience can be replicated in multiple performance domains.

Learner outcomes	Time	Materials	Prep
I can identify how Intercultural Communication is evaluated by: • evaluating my own work using self-assessment questions. • determining the PDI that best aligns with my work. • using the GROW guiding questions to revise and/or add to my work.	• Prep time: 5 minutes • Implementation time: 30 minutes • Debrief time: 5 minutes	• The performance task • Learners' presentational or interpersonal performance such as a draft or a recording • The Intercultural Communication PDIs • Self-assessment questions • GROW guiding questions	• Prepare to display the PDIs, self-assessment questions, and the GROW guiding questions. • Be sure learners have access to their performance.

Instructions

1. (PURPOSE) Tell learners that they will learn how to self-assess their work and make changes in order to reach the next performance level.
2. (SET UP) Remind learners about the performance task for this interpersonal or presentational performance.
3. Display the PDIs and instruct learners to use the self-assessment questions to evaluate their work.
4. (GUIDANCE) Go through a few of the self-assessment questions with the learners, directing learners to reflect on their own performance to identify if it best aligns to the *Beginning*, *Developing*, *Meeting*, or *Exceeding* PDIs.
5. (ENGAGEMENT) Release the lesson to have learners continue reflecting on the self-assessment questions and have them mark which PDI best aligns to their work.
6. (GUIDANCE) When learners have identified the PDI, point them toward the GROW guiding questions for that level.
7. (ENGAGEMENT) Learners use the GROW guiding questions for that level to guide them to improve their work.
8. (DEBRIEF) Learners could share their reflections and improvements with a partner.
9. Ask learners to reflect on:
    a. What did you notice about your Intercultural Communication before and after you reflected on the self-assessment and used the GROW guiding questions?
    b. How might you apply what you learned to your future work when completing a summative task?

Alternatives	Differentiation
Learners could complete this learning experience multiple times with multiple interpersonal or presentational tasks throughout a unit. As learners engage in this learning experience, it eventually can be done more independently and does not need to be guided by the educator.	Learners could work together to give and get feedback from each other. After exchanging drafts, each learner could complete the "self" assessment questions as feedback for their partner, turning it into a peer assessment. Learners could then discuss the assessment of each other's work and brainstorm changes to level up their work. Learners could assess an example of work from an anonymous learner individually or in a group discussion.

EXAMPLE

Target performance level: **Meeting**
Context: familiar, formal, predictable
Content: familiar, everyday

Task: Write a response to the invitation indicating that you do or do not want to accept. Think about the social/cultural context and how you might use language and/or behaviors to show you are aware of the social/cultural context.

Learner's draft:

Situation in the target language given to the learner:

Your boss/educator offers you a job that you would like to have.

↘

What the learner thinks while deciding how to respond:

I want the job. I need to be formal. (behavior/language)
I need to thank them. (speech act)
How can I sound enthusiastic? (expression)

↗

The first draft of what the learner writes:

Thank you for offers. (smiles) I would like the job. I apprecite. Cool!

<table>
<tr><td colspan="4">Example of how a learner might fill out the sections of the guided self-assessment (Table 7.13) and identify their GROW guiding questions (from Table 7.8).</td></tr>
<tr><td>TARGET PERFORMANCE LEVEL</td><td>Meeting</td><td>CONTEXT</td><td>Corresponds to the proficiency level a learner is working with</td></tr>
<tr><td>PERFORMANCE DOMAIN</td><td>Intercultural Communication</td><td>CONTENT</td><td>Corresponds to the proficiency level a learner is working with</td></tr>
<tr><td colspan="4">Describe your role in the social/cultural context of the situation:
I am an employee talking to my boss.</td></tr>
<tr><td colspan="4">Did you use language that was appropriate to the social/cultural context?
☐ Yes ☑ Sometimes ☐ Not yet</td></tr>
<tr><td colspan="4">What language did you use appropriately to demonstrate Intercultural Communication?
☑ Speech acts (apologies, complaints, disagreements, expressions of gratitude, greetings, leave-takings, advice, invitations, refusals, requests, etc.)
☐ Honorifics/Kinship terms (Mr., captain, informal and formal you, grandma, etc.)
☐ Expressions (idioms, proverbs, metaphors, colloquialisms)
☐ Slang/jargon (My bad!, Cool!, ect.)
☐ Abbreviations (ASAP, LOL, ect.)
☐ Systems of measurement (cultural representations of mass, distance, area, time, dates, currency)</td></tr>
<tr><td colspan="2">Option 1: Give examples of what language you used that was appropriate to your role in the social/cultural context of the situation:
Thank you. I apprecite.</td><td colspan="2">Option 2: Select which language you included in your performance that was appropriate to your role in the social/cultural context of the situation:
☐ Speech acts:
☐ Honorifics:
☐ Expressions:
☐ Slang/jargon:
☐ Abbreviation:
☐ Systems of measurement:</td></tr>
<tr><td colspan="4">Did you use behavior that was appropriate to the social/cultural context?
☑ Yes ☐ Sometimes ☐ Not yet</td></tr>
<tr><td colspan="4">What behavior did you use appropriately to demonstrate Intercultural Communication?
☑ Body language (eye contact, posture, facial expressions, gestures, distance)
☐ Paralinguistics (nonverbal behavior such as tone of voice, intonation, pitch, speech rate, use of silence, volume)
☐ Turn-taking/rituals (alternating turns, overlapping talk, interrupting, deferring to silent pauses)
☑ Writing mechanics (punctuation, capitalization, directionality)
☐ Format (how the template of the text corresponds appropriately to the genre)
☑ Style (the manner in which an individual expresses themselves and/or communicates ideas)</td></tr>
</table>

<table>
<tr><td>Option 1: Give examples of behaviors you used that was appropriate to your role in the social/cultural context of the situation:</td><td>Option 2: Select which behaviors you included in your performance that were appropriate to your role in the social/cultural context of the situation:
☑ Body language: smiled
☐ Paralinguistics:
☐ Rituals:
☑ Writing mechanics: periods at the end and capitalizations at the beginning of sentences
☐ Format:
☑ Style: I would like the job.</td></tr>
<tr><td colspan="2">Evaluate how you think you performed in your use of Intercultural Communication today:
☐ Beginning: I use language and/or behaviors that are not appropriate to the social/cultural context.
☑ Developing: I can, at times, use language and/or behaviors that are appropriate to the social/cultural context.
☐ Meeting: I can use language and/or behaviors that are appropriate to the social/cultural context.
☐ Exceeding: I can use a variety of language and/or behaviors that are appropriate to the social/cultural context.</td></tr>
<tr><td colspan="2">Think about your own experience and what you have done to improve in Intercultural Communication. What advice would you give other learners to help them develop Intercultural Communication?
Do this self-assessment! You will find things to change or add.</td></tr>
</table>

Learner directions: Use the GROW guiding questions for the level that best matches your performance. Reflect on the questions, then make changes to your work in order to reach the next level of performance.

GROW GUIDING QUESTIONS:

EXCEEDING	MEETING	DEVELOPING	BEGINNING
• In this performance, you do not use any ____. How might you incorporate it in a future performance with a similar social/ cultural context? • How might you add ____ appropriately in a future performance with a similar social/ cultural context? • How might you use language and/or behaviors to resolve a social/cultural misunderstanding? • How might you adjust your use of (language and/or behavior) to demonstrate sensitivity to the social/cultural context? • In what ways could you suspend judgment to communicate a message appropriately within the social/ cultural context? • How might you verify the appropriateness of your language and/ or behaviors within an unfamiliar social/ cultural context?	• In this performance, you do not use any ____. How might you incorporate it in a future performance with a similar social/ cultural context? • How might you add ____ appropriately in a future performance with a similar social/ cultural context? • How might you incorporate a variety of language and/ or behaviors to communicate your message appropriately within the social/ cultural context? • How might you use language and/or behaviors to resolve a social/cultural misunderstanding?	• Your use of (language/ behavior) does not match the social/ cultural context. How might you adjust this in a future performance with a similar social/ cultural context? • What language and behaviors could you add to be more appropriate to the social/cultural context? • What (language and/ or behavior) might you use to enhance the communication of your message?	• Your use of (language and/or behavior) does not match the social/ cultural context. How might you adjust this to be more appropriate to the social/cultural context? • What language (*speech act, honorifics, expressions, slang/ jargon, abbreviations, systems of measurement*) might you add to communicate your message appropriately within the social/ cultural context? • What behaviors (*body language, paralinguistics, turn-taking rituals, writing mechanics, format, style*) might you add to communicate your message appropriately to the social/cultural context?

Example of what a learner engaged in this process might think and rewrite based on clarifying expectations. This example shows how the learner went from brainstorming ideas to writing them in a text.

Learner's thinking:		Rewrite:
I can say Mr. Lee. (honorific) *Is there a behavior I could add that would show my gratitude? (behavior)* *What expression could I add and still be formal? How can I sound enthusiastic, but still be formal? (expression)*	→	*Thank you Mr Lee for offers. (smiles, put hand to my heart) I would like the job. I apprecite. ~~Cool!~~ I go the extra mile!*

WHAT'S THAT EXPRESSION?

<table>
<tr><td colspan="4">Domain: Intercultural Communication
Focus: Understanding Intercultural Communication through expressions</td></tr>
<tr><td>Learner outcomes
I can use language that is appropriate to the social/cultural context by incorporating expressions into my messages.</td><td>Time
• Prep time: 20 minutes
• Implementation time: 10 minutes
• Debrief time: 5 minutes</td><td>Materials
• Cards with a variety of expressions, each with an explanation and an example in which it is used. One for each learner.
• Drawing/writing materials or digital tools for each learner</td><td>Prep
• Create cards with expressions, explanations, and an example in which it is used in context.</td></tr>
<tr><td colspan="4">Instructions
1. (PURPOSE) Tell learners that they will learn about and use expressions, which carry nonliteral, figurative meanings. Sometimes they provide insight into cultural norms or values and are often used by people accustomed to speaking the target language.
2. (SET UP) Ask each learner to take out drawing/writing materials and hand each learner a card. Each card includes an expression, an explanation of what the expression means, and an example of the expression used in context.
3. Instruct each learner to read their text to identify their expression, its explanation, and to see how the expression is used in context.
4. (ENGAGEMENT) Learners read their card to see what their expression means, literally and figuratively.
5. Instruct all learners to draw a representation that illustrates the meaning of their expression.
6. Instruct learners also write an example using their expression in another context.
7. (ENGAGEMENT) Learners draw and write their expressions (see example).
8. (DEBRIEF) One-by-one, each learner reads their learner-created example aloud together, stopping to have their classmates "guess" the meaning of each expression. Then, have each learner reveal the meaning to the whole group by using their drawing.
9. Ask learners to reflect on:
a. What did you notice about using expressions?
b. How might you apply what you learned to your future work when completing a performance task?</td></tr>
<tr><td colspan="2">Alternatives
Learners could act out a scenario and the learner audience can guess the expression that best fits.
Learners could work in groups to discuss ideas and then each illustrate their own expression.</td><td colspan="2">Differentiation
The educator could provide pictures of the literal translations of the expressions and have learners add the figurative layer by drawing a new picture and writing an example using the expression in context.</td></tr>
</table>

EXAMPLE

Example of a card that is provided to a learner:

Expression: to cost an arm and a leg

Explanation: to be very expensive

Example: My mom said I can't get a new car because it costs an arm and a leg and we can't afford it.

Learner drawing and an example of the expression written in a new context:

BRAINSTORM BUILDING

Domain: Intercultural Communication

Focus: Developing Intercultural Communication by brainstorming possibilities

Note: This learning experience can be replicated in multiple performance domains.

Learner outcomes	Time	Materials	Prep
I can develop Intercultural Communication by brainstorming language and/or behaviors that are appropriate to the social/cultural context.	• Prep time: 5-15 minutes • Implementation time: 20 minutes • Debrief time: 5 minutes	• Situations with various social/cultural contexts • An example to do together as a class (see example below) • Paper/pencil or digital writing tools for each learner	• Prepare situations and an example to do together as a class.

Instructions

1. (PURPOSE) Tell learners that they will brainstorm appropriate language and/or behaviors based on specific social/cultural situations.
2. (SET UP) Model the process by doing an example together as a class (see example).
3. Divide learners into groups of 3-5 learners each.
4. Instruct learners to consider various situations and what different language and/or behaviors they might use in each situation.
5. (ENGAGEMENT) Learners brainstorm in their groups, making lists of things they could say/do that are appropriate to social/cultural context.
6. (GUIDANCE) Learners may benefit from more concrete situations. Example – You are interviewing a friend in order to write their profile.
7. (DEBRIEF) Learners could share their ideas with the class or between groups.
8. Ask learners to reflect on:
    a. What did you notice about adding appropriate language and/or behaviors for each social/cultural context?
    b. How might you apply what you learned to your future work when completing a performance task?

Alternatives	Differentiation
Learners could do this individually instead of in groups, then share in small groups. Learners could make chat mats with some of their brainstorming ideas (see the chat mat learning experience in the Communication Strategies chapter).	Instead of brainstorming, learners could be given a variety of language and/or behaviors and they could categorize them. Example: functions (apologizing, refusing..) or contexts (formal/informal) Learners could create situations in which specific language and/or behaviors demonstrate their awareness of the social/cultural context.

EXAMPLE

Learner Instructions: Brainstorm language and/or behaviors that are appropriate to the social/cultural context of each situation.

Situation: You run into someone you know on the street. What might you consider about how to greet them?

Learner work:

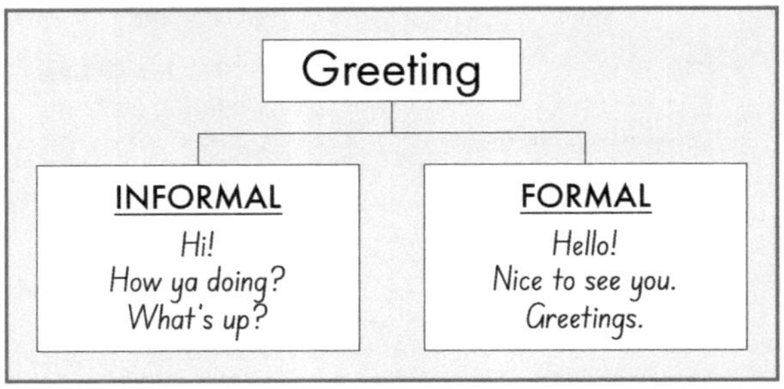

Situation: Prepare interview questions for a teenager and interview questions for an adult. If interviewing a teenager, the language can be informal and direct. If interviewing an adult, the language might be more formal and indirect.

Learner work:

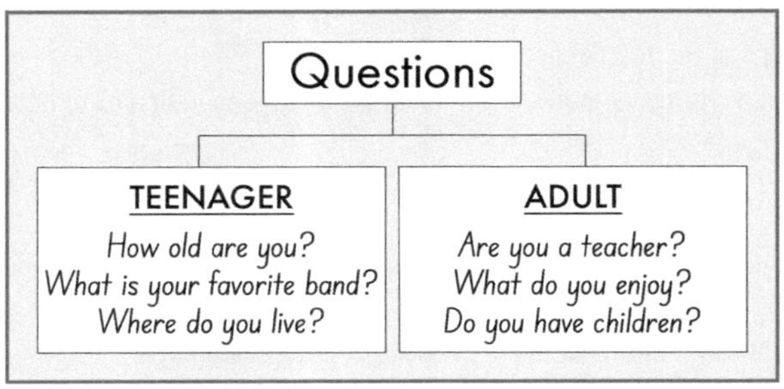

Situation: What behaviors might you exhibit if you are interacting with someone you know well or with someone who you do not know well?

Learner work:

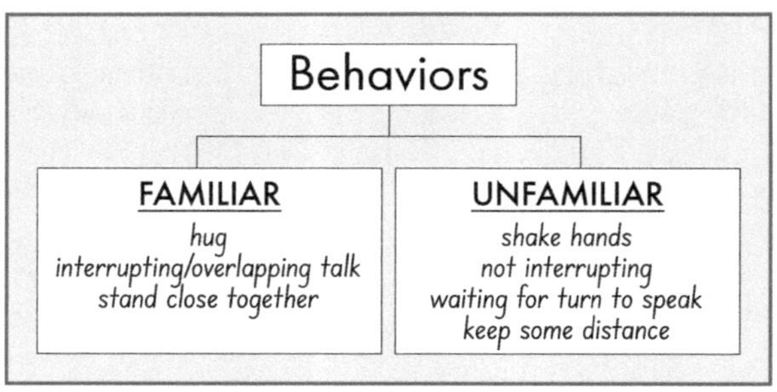

LEVEL UP

Domain: Intercultural Communication

Focus: Developing Intercultural Communication by creating progressions

Note: This learning experience can be replicated in multiple performance domains.

Learner outcomes	Time	Materials	Prep
I can develop Intercultural Communication by building progressions of Intercultural Communication to "level up."	• Prep time: 5 minutes (longer if you prepare transcripts) • Implementation time: 30 minutes • Debrief time: 5 minutes	• PDIs for Intercultural Communication to display at the appropriate level (Novice, Intermediate, Advanced) • Interpersonal or presentational performance task • If working in the interpersonal mode: One set of transcriptions to use as a model • Paper/pencil or digital writing tools for each learner	• Prepare to display PDIs. • Have a performance task for learners to write or speak about. • If working in the interpersonal mode: Have all transcriptions available.

Instructions

1. (PURPOSE) Tell learners that they will develop their Intercultural Communication by working with a group to write/say an example performance at each level (*Beginning*, *Developing*, *Meeting*, and *Exceeding*).
2. (SET UP) Display and remind learners of the targeted PDIs for Intercultural Communication.
3. Divide learners into groups of 3-5 learners each and ask them to take out paper/pencil, digital writing tools, or digital recording tools.
4. Give learners an example presentational task or an interpersonal task with a transcript of one side of the interpersonal conversation.
5. Optional (GUIDANCE) Provide or do an example together as a whole class, writing one performance level together for presentational or write the other part of the interpersonal conversation for one performance level.
6. (ENGAGEMENT) Release the lesson to have learners work in groups to write one example of each level (*Beginning*, *Developing*, *Meeting*, and *Exceeding*) using the given task.
7. (GUIDANCE) Remind learners to look at the PDIs to be sure of what level they are aiming for with each example.
8. (DEBRIEF) Learners share their reflections and improvements with a partner, another group, or the class.
9. Ask learners to reflect on:
    a. What did you notice about each example as you progressed through the performance levels of Intercultural Communication?
    b. How might you apply what you learned to your future work when completing a performance task?

Alternatives	Differentiation
Learners could do this individually instead of in groups, then share in small groups. Learners could take turns writing an example for each level (*Beginning, Developing, Meeting, Exceeding*). Groups of students could write a presentational example or interpersonal script for each PDI, or groups could be assigned to write a presentational example or interpersonal script for one assigned PDI. One group could share their "leveled up" examples with another group to see if they can identify what level each example is meant to be.	After creating samples for each level about one task together as a class and another in groups, learners could each individually create an example for one level and then share it out with their group. The group can decide which performance level it best matches. Learners could evaluate example texts that have already been created as *Beginning, Developing, Meeting,* or *Exceeding.*

EXAMPLE

Target performance level: **Meeting**
Context: familiar, formal, straight-forward
Content: familiar, concrete, researched

Task: Discuss different clothing requirements for men's and women's sports with an athletic director.

Learner instructions: Based on the PDIs, write an example of each level of performance.

PDIs displayed:

TARGET PERFORMANCE LEVEL: MEETING				
	EXCEEDING	**MEETING**	**DEVELOPING**	**BEGINNING**
Performance Domain Indicators	I can use a variety of language and/or behaviors that are appropriate to the social/cultural context.	I can use language and/or behaviors that are appropriate to the social/cultural context.	I can, at times, use language and/or behaviors that are appropriate to the social/cultural context.	I use language and/or behaviors that are not appropriate to the social/cultural context.

Learner work:

Learners were given the performance task. As a class, they brainstormed sample questions and statements on the *Conversation* card for the *Beginning* level. Learners also wrote evidence to support their reasoning on the *Learner Evaluation* card.

Note: The sample questions and statements on the *Conversation* card would be written in the target language. The *Learner Evaluation* could be written in the base language or target language, depending on the performance level of the learners.

CONVERSATION - BEGINNING

Do you have minute?

What must athletics to wear at the school when they compete and different for boys and girls and why?

Do you know recent changes in national and olympic women's teams clothing? What do you think?

I think girls shorts is shorter.

I think girls should wear unitards or leggings. If girls want. If boys too. Or anyone.

LEARNER EVALUATION – BEGINNING

Evidence to support reasoning

- *Informal*
  - *Do you have a minute?*
- *Direct*
  - *Do you know...*
  - *What do you think? (Ask for opinion, no time to think)*
  - *I think... (Give own opinion)*

Ideas to level up: more formal, give an intro, not as direct with opinions in this culture.

In small groups, learners then worked together to write "leveled up" sample questions and statements for *Developing, Meeting,* and *Exceeding*. Learners also wrote evidence to support their reasoning.

CONVERSATION - DEVELOPING

Do you have minute?

What recent changes in national and olympic women's teams clothing?

What must athletics to wear at the school when they compete and different for boys and girls?

Are girls shorts is shorter?

Are unitards or leggings much better? If girls want. If boys too. Or anyone.

LEARNER EVALUATION – DEVELOPING

Evidence to support reasoning

- *Informal*
  - *Do you have a minute?*
- *Direct*
  - *What must athletics to wear..? Are girls shorts is shorter? (Asking, but really hidden answers/suggestions/kinda telling)*

Ideas to level up: more formal, add a greeting, and thank you, ask open-ended questions.

CONVERSATION - MEETING

Excuse me.

We are learning about recent changes in clothing/unifrom requirements for national and olympic wormen. It made me wonder.

Can you tell us what our athletes have to when competing wear?

Sports, like gymnastics, that have both a girls and boys team, but have different uniforms require.

Is there explaining for this?

Thank you for time.

LEARNER EVALUATION – MEETING

Evidence to support reasoning

- *Formal, but too direct/telling*
  - *Excuse me,*
  - *gymnasitcs...different uniforms require*
- *Indirect:*
  - *We are learning about...*
  - *Can you tell us...*
- *Get attention and thank*
  - *Excuse me*
  - *Thank you*

To improve: Be more indirect (Could you tell us...) to be more polite. Don't tell, ask.

CONVERSATION - EXCEEDING

Excuse me, do you have time now for talk or can I make the appointment?

We are learning about recent changes in clothing/unifrom requirements for national and olympic wormen. It made me wonder.

Can you tell us what our athletes have to when competing wear?

Do we sports, like gymnastics, that have both a girls and boys team, but have different uniforms?

Would you mind explaining for this?

LEARNER EVALUATION – EXCEEDING

Evidence to support reasoning

- *Polite/formal (Speech Acts)*
  - *Excuse me, appointment (Get attention)*
  - *We are learning... (Give context)*
  - *Can you tell us... (Not assuming)*
  - *It made me wonder (Asking questions, not telling)*
  - *Would you mind..? (Ask for help)*

To improve: Give questions in advance, then meet to interview the director.

WHO'S WHO? WHAT DO WE DO?

Domain: Intercultural Communication

Focus: Understanding Intercultural Communication through social/cultural cues

Additional focus: Developing Intercultural Communication through language and/or behaviors

Learner outcomes	Time	Materials	Prep
I can understand and demonstrate my awareness of the social/cultural context by: • interpreting non-verbal behaviors. • using language and/or behaviors that are appropriate to the social/cultural context to communicate my message	• Prep time: Find a video • Implementation time: 30 minutes • Debrief time: 5 minutes	• A video clip (related to the topic of the unit) showing interaction among people in various roles (see example) • Paper/pencil or digital writing tools for each learner	• Find the video clip. • Consider what ideas learners will brainstorm.

Instructions

1. (PURPOSE) Tell learners that they will be viewing a video clip, without listening to the sound, from the target culture. Ask them to watch carefully and notice the various behaviors people use to interact. They will be asked to make guesses about the social/cultural context as well as the relationships between the people in the video clip. Then they will watch the video again, still with no sound, and write a script of what the people might say to each other.
2. (SET UP) Have learners take out their writing materials and make a chart with four columns with the following headings: Roles, Context, Clues, and Behaviors.
3. (GUIDANCE) Instruct learners to pay close attention to the video as it is played and fill in the chart after the video.
4. (ENGAGEMENT) Learners watch the video (once or multiple times, but all without the sound) and fill in the charts for each person and action seen in the video.
5. (DEBRIEF) Learners share their discoveries, with evidence from the video to back up their ideas.
6. Discuss the behaviors seen and brainstorm what language might be heard. Be sure to address any stereotypes that come up.
7. (GUIDANCE) Instruct learners to watch the video again, and then each write a possible script for what some of the characters say to each other. The script should use language and behaviors that are appropriate to the social/cultural context displayed in the video clip. Learners can indicate behaviors as stage directions in the script.
8. Ask learners to highlight their script: learners should use one color to highlight *language* that is appropriate to the social/cultural context and a different color to highlight appropriate *behaviors* (see example).
9. Ask learners to reflect on:
   a. What did you notice about your first impressions? Were you tempted to stereotype?
   b. What did you notice about roles in this social and cultural context?
   c. How might you apply what you learned to your future work when completing a performance task?

Alternatives	Differentiation
Learners could use photos instead of videos. Learners could work in groups instead of individually to discuss the video, fill out the chart, and write the script.	Learners could add to the script, writing not only what the characters say to each other, but also what they are thinking. Learners could further discuss how they might address stereotypes and how roles and norms may differ in various social and cultural contexts.

EXAMPLE

Description of the video that learners watch without sound:

A woman is waiting at the corner with some children. She says something to one of the children and the child answers back. When the bus arrives, the woman kisses one of the children. As the children get on the bus, the woman waves goodbye. Several children, including the one she kissed, wave back to her.

Learner work:

Learners filled in the chart for each person and action as they watched the video.

ROLES	CONTEXT	CLUES	BEHAVIORS
kid his mom other kids	wait and get the bus to school say goodbye	kid gets kiss mom kiss one kid waves	moms kiss her kid not others wave to all kids wave to mom

Learner's script with underline showing language and (parenthesis showing behaviors) appropriate to the social/cultural context. *Note:* Learners used learned idioms to complete this script.

MOM: Do you have everything sugar?

KID: Yes mom. My friends. Do not embarrass me. (smiles)

MOM: Here is the bus.

Be careful. Make good choices. Have a good day! (kiss kid)

KID (get on bus) Bye! (waves)

OTHER KIDS (wave)

MOM (wave)

YOUR TURN

LEARNING TARGET CHECK:	
I can	☐ select learning experiences that support learners' growth with Intercultural Communication.

Complete the chart by identifying specific learning experiences from the *Learning Experiences to Facilitate Learner Growth* section (p. 237-252) that you could use in an upcoming unit to help learners *understand* or *develop* Intercultural Communication. Note any materials or prep needed to implement the learning experience in your upcoming unit. Consider any alternatives or differentiation that would better align the learning experience to your unit, the targeted level of performance, and/or your learners.

UNIT:			
PERFORMANCE DOMAIN: INTERCULTURAL COMMUNICATION			
Learning experience	**What type of learning experience is it?** (Circle one)	**Materials/Prep**	**Alternatives / Differentiation**
	Understanding/ Developing		
	Understanding/ Developing		
	Understanding/ Developing		

Learners' Self-Assessment

Self-assessment provides an opportunity for learners to reflect on their performance, set goals, and ultimately to own their learning. This section features three ways learners can self-assess their work: *Make It Visible, Glow and Grow Self-Assessment*, and *Guided Self-Assessments*. Each is educator-designed but learner-driven. That is, the self-assessment is designed by the educator around the PDIs but it is the learner who must reflect on their performance to complete it. The same self-assessments are used in each performance domain chapter to build consistency for learners. Each can be used for learner self-assessment after a formative or summative task. Educators might select self-assessments that have more scaffolding, such as the *Guided Self-Assessment* and *Make It Visible*, after formative tasks where learners may need more support to self-assess their performance, such as the beginning of a unit or a course. The *Glow and Grow Self-Assessment,* which is more open-ended, can be used when learners feel more comfortable reflecting on the PDIs and summarizing their work, such as after formative tasks that occur at the end of the unit or after a summative task. Overall, educators can make adjustments to any of these self-assessments and use them with intentionality based on their learners, their pacing within a unit or course, and the performance task.

Make It Visible

This self-assessment provides an opportunity for learners to visibly see their Intercultural Communication in a given formative or summative task. Learners might circle, highlight, color-code, or note the ways in which they used language or behaviors in a given presentational or interpersonal performance (see Figure 7.1). Or learners can self-assess by marking yes/no and providing evidence (see Table 7.10, Figure 7.2, Table 7.11, and Figure 7.3). Educators can provide opportunities for revisions and/or additions for learners who may find they are not yet *Meeting* expectations, so learners have opportunities for language growth.

The learner samples in this section demonstrate how each self-assessment can be used at one performance level. However, these self-assessments can be used at any level: Novice, Intermediate, or Advanced.

Figure 7.1
Presentational Self-Assessment Using the "Make It Visible" Approach

Directions: Read over your presentational work and mark each use of language appropriate to the social/cultural context accordingly:

- highlight speech acts
- (circle) honorifics/kinship terms
- **bold** expressions
- put **(**parentheses**)** around slang/jargon
- put **[**brackets**]** around abbreviations
- underline systems of measurement

Example of how the learner, performing within the Advanced level, completes this self-assessment:

Dear diary,

I cannot believe that this investigation about my age is still going on! It is just not fair! I am not a liar! How much analyses have I to do? Because of this, I did not get the chance to sign when I turned 16 years. In the Professional Baseball League they think that all us players are liars. There are some that lies, but there are a lot of us who tells the truth.

But what are they suppose to do, if only one year older means you are worth $1 million less? Seriously, one year? The **[**PBL**]** uses us for our poverty. It's not fair that they treat us differently, pay us differently just because we live in poorer country. Why I don't make money because I am a great baseball player? Why am I the cheap export? If I am in power, I would talks with the representatives to work for changes in recruiting regulations, like age restrictions and equal pay.

Yet I know that if I work hard, I will get a contract of any price which, for me, is the way out of poverty. It is also my family's way out of poverty because they are depending on me. The first thing I **take on** is buy my parents a house so they never have to worry about housing ever again! I just have to be patient. All I want to do is play baseball- it's what I love, it's **what I borned to do**, it's all I have ever done.

Let's play ball!
-Mike

Table 7.10
Interpersonal Self-Assessment Using the "Make It Visible" Approach

Intercultural Communication Reflection Guide: How do I use language and behaviors that are appropriate to the social/cultural context?			
LANGUAGE I USED:	**YES**	**NO**	**COMMENTS/EXAMPLES**
Speech acts (apologies, complaints, disagreements, expressions of gratitude, greetings, leave-takings, advice, invitations, refusals, requests, etc.)			
Honorifics/kinship terms (*Mr.*, *captain*, informal and formal *you*, *grandma*, etc.)			
Expressions (idioms, proverbs, metaphors, colloquialisms)			
Slang/jargon (*My bad!*, *Cool!*, etc.)			
Abbreviations (*ASAP*, *LOL*, etc.)			
Systems of measurement (cultural representations of mass, distance, area, time, dates, currency)			
BEHAVIORS I USED:	**YES**	**NO**	**COMMENTS/EXAMPLES**
Body language (eye contact, posture, facial expressions, gestures, distance)			
Paralinguistics (nonverbal behavior such as tone of voice, intonation, pitch, speech rate, use of silence, volume)			
Turn-taking/rituals (alternating turns, overlapping talk, interrupting, deferring to silent pauses)			

Figure 7.2

Example of a Completed Interpersonal Self-Assessment Using the "Make It Visible" Approach

Directions: Listen to the recording of your interpersonal conversation. Complete the *Intercultural Communication Reflection Guide* and list examples of how you used language and/or behaviors to interact appropriately within the social/cultural context.

LEARNER SAMPLE

Learner 1: Hello.

Learner 2: Hey! How's it going?

Learner 1: Good. And you?

Learner 2: Very good. What do you like more, sports or ski?

Learner 1: Ski.

Learner 2: Me too (*points to self*)! I like to ski. A lot. Um, my favorite...my favorite sport...in the...in the winter. Um...do you like to sing?

Learner 1: I don't like to sing.

Learner 2: Do you like to do...soccer in it's hot or it's cold?

Learner 1: Um...repeat?

Learner 2: Do you like to do soccer in it's hot or it's cold?

Learner 1: ...

Learner 2: Do you like to do soccer... (*kicks leg*)...in it's hot or it's cold?

Learner 1: No...comprehend (*shrugs*).

Learner 2: Do you like...soccer (*kicks leg*)... in it's hot (*fans face*) or um... it's cold, brrr (*shivers and rubs arms*)?

Learner 1: Oh! Um, yes. I like...um, hot?

Learner 2: (*Nods*)

Learner 1: Yes. Hot.

Learner 2: Cool! Me...me too!

Learner 1: Ride bike?

Learner 2: Well, sometimes. Yes, I like to ride a bike. Sometimes. In the...in the summer?

Learner 1: Ok, bye.

Learner 2: See ya later!

Example of how Learner 2, performing within the Novice level, completes this self-assessment:

Intercultural Communication Reflection Guide:
How do I use language and behaviors that are appropriate to the social/cultural context?

LANGUAGE I USED:	YES	NO	COMMENTS/EXAMPLES
Speech acts (apologies, complaints, disagreements, expressions of gratitude, greetings, leave-takings, advice, invitations, refusals, requests, etc.)	X		• *Greetings: Hey! How's it going?* • *Leave taking: See ya later!*
Honorifics/kinship terms (*Mr., captain,* informal and formal *you, grandma,* etc.)		X	
Expressions (idioms, proverbs, metaphors, colloquialisms)		X	
Slang/jargon (*My bad!, Cool!,* etc.)	X		• *Hey* • *Brr* • *Cool!* • *ya*
Abbreviations (*ASAP, LOL,* etc.)		X	
Systems of measurement (cultural representations of mass, distance, area, time, dates, currency)		X	
BEHAVIORS I USED:	**YES**	**NO**	**COMMENTS/EXAMPLES**
Body language (eye contact, posture, facial expressions, gestures, distance)	X		• *points to self* • *kicks leg* • *fans face* • *shivers* • *rubs arms* • *nods*
Paralinguistics (nonverbal behavior such as tone of voice, intonation, pitch, speech rate, use of silence, volume)		X	
Turn-taking/rituals (alternating turns, overlapping talk, interrupting, deferring to silent pauses)	X		• *Do you like...*

Table 7.11
Presentational Self-Assessment Using the "Make It Visible" Approach

Intercultural Communication Reflection Guide: How do I use language and behaviors that are appropriate to the social/cultural context?			
LANGUAGE I USED:	**YES**	**NO**	**COMMENTS/EXAMPLES**
Speech acts (apologies, complaints, disagreements, expressions of gratitude, greetings, leave-takings, advice, invitations, refusals, requests, etc.)			
Honorifics/kinship terms (*Mr.*, *captain*, informal and formal *you*, *grandma*, etc.)			
Expressions (idioms, proverbs, metaphors, colloquialisms)			
Slang/jargon (*My bad!*, *Cool!*, etc.)			
Abbreviations (*ASAP*, *LOL*, etc.)			
Systems of measurement (cultural representations of mass, distance, area, time, dates, currency)			
BEHAVIORS I USED:	**YES**	**NO**	**COMMENTS/EXAMPLES**
Writing mechanics (punctuation, capitalization, directionality)			
Format (how the template of the text corresponds appropriately to the genre)			
Style (the manner in which an individual expresses themselves and/or communicates ideas)			

Figure 7.3

Example of a Completed Presentational Self-Assessment Using the "Make It Visible" Approach

Directions: Read over your presentational work. Complete the *Intercultural Communication Reflection Guide* and list examples of how you used language and/or behaviors to communicate your message appropriately within the social/cultural context.

Honorable Mayor Wilson,

Help! My name is Kai Meyer. I live in Elmdale now. I like to live in Elmdale We have strong engaged for community here. Since 3 years, Elmdale won the "Best city in the USA". We try to win that again and we could. We could to do more of to clean up and beautify our city. Maybe have like the BUGA garden show in Germany. Different cities host and make big gardens. And plant trees. Like big plant show at the fair.

A lot in Elmdale is full of garbage. When I run on hiking trailsI see a lot of garbage. Nature reserves, like Forest Park, have more garbage. It is not pretty. I remember you to since 3 years. It would be great if mentality to our city. Run people need clean trails. They are impacted.

Here are things do. We could the volunteers clean up the parks.This would also help the people in the city do it. Other volunteers could the large places. The city could have event. The event would be "Consciousness about Garbage in Elmdale"

We could say, plant more trees in the niehgborhoods. This would give back the trees we take for construction. Maybe be a tree hugger? Plants and gardens too but for now trees. When we plant more trees, this make our community a better place, if we plant more trees. Plant now! Act now!

Sincerely,
Kai Meyer

Example of how the learner, performing within the Intermediate level, completes this self-assessment:			
Intercultural Communication Reflection Guide: How do I use language and behaviors that are appropriate to the social/cultural context?			
LANGUAGE I USED:	**YES**	**NO**	**COMMENTS/EXAMPLES**
Speech acts (apologies, complaints, disagreements, expressions of gratitude, greetings, leave-takings, advice, invitations, refusals, requests, etc.)	X		• Sincerely
Honorifics/kinship terms (*Mr., captain*, informal and formal *you, grandma*, etc.)	X		• Honorable Mayor Wilson
Expressions (idioms, proverbs, metaphors, colloquialisms)	X		• tree hugger
Slang/jargon (*My bad!, Cool!*, etc.)		X	
Abbreviations (*ASAP, LOL*, etc.)	X		• BUGA • USA
Systems of measurement (cultural representations of mass, distance, area, time, dates, currency)		X	
BEHAVIORS I USED:	**YES**	**NO**	**COMMENTS/EXAMPLES**
Writing mechanics (punctuation, capitalization, directionality)	X		• Use of commas: Honorable Mayor Wilson, • Use of quotation marks: "Consciousness about Garbage in Elmdale" "Best City in the USA" • Use of exclamation marks: Help! Plant now! Act now!
Format (how the template of the text corresponds appropriately to the genre)	X		• Formal letter: • salutation Honorable Mayor Willson • Sign-off: Sincerely + signature
Style (the manner in which an individual expresses themselves and/or communicates ideas)	X		• Formal, indirect language: • We could... • It would be great... • This would...

GLOW and GROW Self Assessment

Using the *Meeting* Performance Domain Indicator, learners can self-assess their work on a one-point rubric after a formative or summative task. In Table 7.12, learners would complete the *Where I GLOW (What are my strengths?)* and *How I can GROW (What can I do to improve?)* sections by citing evidence from their own interpersonal or presentational performance for each performance domain. The *GLOW/GROW Ideas* are given as prompts so that learners are reminded of what to look for or work toward.

Table 7.12
GLOW and GROW Self-Assessment

Intercultural Communication Target performance level: **Meeting**		
The context and content corresponds to the proficiency level a learner is working within.	**NOVICE**	Context: familiar, informal, formal, predictable Content: very familiar, everyday
	INTERMEDIATE	Context: familiar, informal, formal, straight-forward Content: familiar, concrete, at times researched
	ADVANCED	Context: familiar, unfamiliar, informal, formal, complex Content: familiar, academic, social, professional, concrete, abstract

Instructions: Complete the following reflection by writing where you GLOW and where you can GROW in each area. Make sure to include evidence from your work to support your reasoning.		
Where I GLOW: What are my strengths?	**Performance Domain Indicator**	**How can I GROW What can I do to improve?**
	I can use language and/or behaviors that are appropriate to the social/cultural context.	

GLOW IDEAS	**GROW IDEAS**
• What language did you use (*speech acts, honorifics, expressions, slang/jargon, abbreviations, systems of measurement*), to communicate your message appropriately within the social/cultural context? • What behaviors did you use (*body language, paralinguistics, turn-taking rituals, writing mechanics, format, style*), to communicate your message appropriately within the social/cultural context?	• How might you add (*speech acts, honorifics, expressions, slang/jargon, abbreviations, systems of measurement*) appropriately in a future performance with a similar social/cultural context? • How might you add (*body language, paralinguistics, turn-taking rituals, writing mechanics, format, style*) appropriately in a future performance with a similar social/cultural context? • How might you incorporate a variety of language and/or behaviors to communicate your message appropriately within the social/cultural context? • How might you use language and/or behaviors to resolve a social/cultural misunderstanding?

Guided Self-Assessments

This self-assessment includes guiding questions to help learners evaluate their own performance after a formative or summative task (see Table 7.13). Options are included to help educators personalize the self-assessment for their learners, or learners can self-select which options to answer.

Table 7.13

Interpersonal/Presentational Guided Self-Assessment

<table>
<tr><td>TARGET PERFORMANCE LEVEL</td><td>Meeting</td><td>CONTEXT</td><td>Corresponds to the proficiency level a learner is working with</td></tr>
<tr><td>PERFORMANCE DOMAIN</td><td>Intercultural Communication</td><td>CONTENT</td><td>Corresponds to the proficiency level a learner is working with</td></tr>
<tr><td colspan="4">Describe your role in the social/cultural context of the situation:</td></tr>
<tr><td colspan="4">Did you use language that was appropriate to the social/cultural context?
☐ Yes ☐ Sometimes ☐ Not yet</td></tr>
<tr><td colspan="4">What language did you use appropriately to demonstrate Intercultural Communication?
☐ Speech acts (apologies, complaints, disagreements, expressions of gratitude, greetings, leave-takings, advice, invitations, refusals, requests, etc.)
☐ Honorifics/Kinship terms (Mr., captain, informal and formal you, grandma, etc.)
☐ Expressions (idioms, proverbs, metaphors, colloquialisms)
☐ Slang/jargon (My bad!, Cool!, etc.)
☐ Abbreviations (ASAP, LOL, etc.)
☐ Systems of measurement (cultural representations of mass, distance, area, time, dates, currency)</td></tr>
<tr><td colspan="2">Option 1: Give examples of what language you used that was appropriate to your role in the social/cultural context of the situation:</td><td colspan="2">Option 2: Select which language you included in your performance that was appropriate to your role in the social/cultural context of the situation (example: ordering a meal in a restaurant):
Speech acts:
☐ Used formal greeting (How are you?)
☐ Made formal requests (I would like... May I have...?)
☐ Made a formal, polite complaint (Excuse me...I'm so sorry...)
☐ Used a formal expression of gratitude (Thank you, Thank you for your service.)
☐ Honorifics (used sir or ma'am)
Expressions:
☐ Grab a bite to eat.
☐ My stomach is growling!
☐ I could eat a horse!
☐ I'm dying of thirst!
☐ Let's dig in!
☐ Until next time!</td></tr>
<tr><td colspan="4">Did you use behavior that was appropriate to the social/cultural context?
☐ Yes ☐ Sometimes ☐ Not yet</td></tr>
</table>

What behavior did you use appropriately to demonstrate Intercultural Communication?

- ☐ **Body language** (eye contact, posture, facial expressions, gestures, distance)
- ☐ **Paralinguistics** (nonverbal behavior such as tone of voice, intonation, pitch, speech rate, use of silence, volume)
- ☐ **Turn-taking/rituals** (alternating turns, overlapping talk, interrupting, deferring to silent pauses)
- ☐ **Writing mechanics** (punctuation, capitalization, directionality)
- ☐ **Format** (how the template of the text corresponds appropriately to the genre)
- ☐ **Style** (the manner in which an individual expresses themselves and/or communicates ideas)

Option 1: Give examples of behaviors you used that was appropriate to your role in the social/cultural context of the situation:

Option 2: Select which behaviors you included in your performance that were appropriate to your role in the social/cultural context of the situation (example: ordering a meal in a restaurant):

Body language:

- ☐ Used eye contact, raised hand, or index finger to get the waiter's attention
- ☐ Rubbed stomach to indicate hunger or that something was delicious

Paralinguistics:

- ☐ Used intonation when asking a question
- ☐ Used volume appropriate for a restaurant

Rituals:

- ☐ Placed napkin on your lap
- ☐ Waited until everyone's food arrived to begin eating
- ☐ Placed silverware on the plate when you were done eating
- ☐ Asked for the bill
- ☐ Asked for a to-go box for left-overs
- ☐ Left a tip

Evaluate how you think you performed in the your use of Intercultural Communication today:

- ☐ **Beginning:** I use language and/or behaviors that are not appropriate to the social/cultural context.
- ☐ **Developing:** I can, at times, use language and/or behaviors that are appropriate to the social/cultural context.
- ☐ **Meeting:** I can use language and/or behaviors that are appropriate to the social/cultural context.
- ☐ **Exceeding:** I can use a variety of language and/or behaviors that are appropriate to the social/cultural context.

Think about your own experience and what you have done to improve in Intercultural Communication. What advice would you give other learners to help them develop Intercultural Communication?

YOUR TURN

LEARNING TARGET CHECK:	
I can	☐ provide learners with self assessments to evaluate their work.

Complete the chart by identifying specific self-assessments from the *Learners' Self-Assessments* section (p. 253-263) that could be used in an upcoming unit to help learners evaluate their own work. Next, describe a formative or summative performance task in your upcoming unit that learners could complete and then self-assess using the chosen-self-assessment. Finally, list any additional materials or preparation that might be needed to implement this self-assessment in the *Notes* section of the chart.

UNIT:		
PERFORMANCE DOMAIN: INTERCULTURAL COMMUNICATION		
Learner self-assessments	**Performance task** Formative or summative	**Notes**

Advice From Learners

As a purposeful way for learners to become aware of their own learning, we asked learners to reflect on what worked for them to improve their performance in various performance domains. Sharing advice can build learner metacognitive skills, or awareness of one's own learning, which has been linked to improved learning outcomes (Hattie, 2017). Together learners build a bank of suggestions and advice that they can access when looking to improve in a specific performance domain. This is a way for learners to realize what they have learned about a performance domain, monitor their own understanding of the performance domain, suggest and choose which advice to employ, and evaluate whether particular choices are successful. Here is what some learners said, when asked to share their insights on Intercultural Communication and give advice.

Novice Presentational:

- *Remember to use some phrases that you practiced, especially for things that might be different.*
- *Think about who you are and who the other person is in the situation.*

Novice Interpersonal:

- *If you learn an idiom, try using it a lot to see how it works.*
- *Play your role, but be you too.*

Intermediate Presentational:

- *Think about who you are and who you are communicating with.*
- *Do you need any special format or ritual words to do this task?*

Intermediate Interpersonal:

- *Think about who you are and who your partner is.*
- *What expressions work with this topic? Use language to show what you know about culture.*
- *React with an expression and be positive (That's incredible, but I believe you!).*
- *Practice ways to apologize, disagree, interrupt, so you have them ready.*

Advanced Presentational:

- *Show that you know something about your audience's culture by the way you behave and what you say.*
- *Use idioms and cultural references we learned, but be careful that you know what you are doing.*

Advanced Interpersonal:

- *Take cues from your partner and switch up your language to match, but help them too, but not in a condescending way.*
- *Show you know your place in the world. We're all in it.*

References

Allwood, J. (1985). Tvärkulturell kommunikation [Intercultural communication]. In J. Allwood (Ed.). *Papers in Anthropological Linguistics 12.* (pp. 1-29). Göteborg University: Department of Linguistics. https://www.academia.edu/3956907/Intercultural_communication

Austin, J. L. (2018). *How to do things with words.* (J.O. Urmson, Ed). Martino Fine Books. (Original work published 1962)

Center for Advanced Research on Language Acquisition (CARLA). (2021a, March 3). *Pragmatics and speech acts.* Regents of the University of Minnesota. https://carla.umn.edu/speechacts/index.html

Center for Advanced Research on Language Acquisition (CARLA). (2021b, March 4). *Chinese refusals.* Regents of the University of Minnesota. https://carla.umn.edu/speechacts/refusals/chinese.html

Eble, C. (1996). *Slang and sociability: In-group language among college students.* The University of North Carolina Press.

Ekman, P., & Friesen, W. V. (1969). The repertoire of nonverbal behavior: Categories, origins, usage, and coding. *Semiotica, 1*(1), 49 – 98. https://doi.org/10.1515/semi.1969.1.1.49

Hattie, J. (2017). *250+ influences on student achievement.* Visible Learning Plus. https://visible-learning.org/wp-content/uploads/2018/03/VLPLUS-252-Influences-Hattie-ranking-DEC-2017.pdf

Hwang, H., & Matsumoto, D. (2012). Nonverbal behaviors and cross-cultural communication in the new era. In Sharifian, F., & Jamarani, M. (Eds.). *Language and intercultural communication in the new era* (pp. 116-137). Taylor & Francis Group.

Ishihara, N., & Cohen, A. D. (2014). *Teaching and learning pragmatics: Where language and culture meet.* Routledge.

Liontas, J. I. (2008). Toward a critical pedagogy of idiomaticity. *Indian Journal of Applied Linguistics, 34*(1-2), 11-30. https://link.gale.com/apps/doc/A258816621/AONE?u=googlescholar &sid=bookmark-AONE&xid=48a2feca

Liontas, J. I. (2017) Why teach idioms? A challenge to the profession. *Iranian Journal of Language Teaching Research, 5*(3), 5-25. https://files.eric.ed.gov/fulltext/EJ1156198.pdf

Liddicoat, A. J. (2004). Intercultural language teaching: Principles for practice. *New Zealand Language Teacher, 30,* 17-24. https://www.researchgate.net/publication/281571069_ Intercultural_language_teaching_principles_for_practice

McCool, M. (2009). *Writing around the world: A guide to writing across cultures.* Continuum.

National Council of State Supervisors for Languages (NCSSFL) – ACTFL. (2017). *NCSSFL-ACTFL Can-Do Statements: Performance Indicators for Language Learners.* ACTFL. https://www.actfl.org/educator-resources/ncssfl-actfl-can-do-statements

Yuan Quan, Y. (August 2015). Analysis of silence in intercultural communication. *Proceeding of the International Conference on Economy, Management and Education Technology,* 155-159. Atlantis Press. https://doi.org/10.2991/icemet-15.2015.35

CHAPTER 8 | IMPACT
Performance Domain

LEARNING TARGETS:	
I can	☐ describe the Impact domain. ☐ describe how Impact shows up in learners' performance at various levels. ☐ evaluate learner work using the Performance Domain Indicators (PDIs). ☐ give effective feedback using the Impact PDIs. ☐ select learning experiences that support learners' growth with Impact. ☐ provide learners with self-assessments to evaluate their work.

What do we mean by *Impact*?
Impact refers to the ways a learner's performance engages and maintains the attention of their audience. The focus of this performance domain is for presentational performance assessments. When learners communicate for an audience, they communicate for a purpose: "The point in any performance is to cause the appropriate effects in a performance, i.e. achieve the purpose of the performance" (Wiggins, 2012). The purpose of performance in a presentational task might be to describe, persuade, compare, etc. Within the Impact performance domain, learners can use organization, details, and originality to achieve the purpose of their performance.

How does *Impact* develop in learners' performance?
All learners can make creative and strategic decisions to capture and maintain their audience's attention. At the *Beginning* level, learners present their ideas, but are not able to maintain the attention of their audience. At the *Developing* level, they can, at times, maintain their audience's attention through the use of organization, descriptive details, and/or originality. With each performance, learners grow in their ability to present their ideas in a way that captures and maintains the attention of their audience, eliciting the intended effects. Learners are *Meeting* expectations when they present their ideas in a way that captures and maintains the attention of their audience. They might do this by organizing their ideas so their audience can follow along, adding descriptive details to better illustrate their ideas, and/or presenting their ideas in novel and imaginative ways. Learners are *Exceeding* expectations when they capture and maintain the attention of their audience by using all three elements: organization, details, and originality. The ways in which learners attend to Impact in their performance will differ according to their language resources, the performance task, and their audience. However, all learners, regardless of performance level (Novice, Intermediate, Advanced), can use organization, details, and originality to produce work that is original, personalized, and tailored to impact their audience and produce the desired effects.

What does *Impact* look like in learners' performance?
The sample learner performances in Table 8.1 show how learners can maintain the attention of their audience within a similar task, but each learner uses organization, descriptive details, and originality appropriate to their performance level. The learner performing within the Novice level organizes their performance by starting with the why (*school destruction*), then who can help (*Our School*), what is needed (*school supplies, tables, chairs*), and how to help (*donations*). The learner provides descriptive details using adjectives (*very important and practical,*) and explanations (*Our School to help!, Need school supplies, tables, chairs, Donations for students and*

teachers). Questions (*How to help?*) and strategically placed memorized phrases (*Very important and practical! To donate today! Students thank you!*) add interest, originality, and maintain the attention of the reader.

Within the Intermediate level, the learner organizes their writing by beginning with a topic sentence (*Schools are important to communities*), followed by supporting details (*After the hurricane…How can we help… Please donate to…*), and a closing statement (*Donate today and support communities everywhere!*). Ideas within the supporting details are further organized by sequencing (*they can help in three ways*). The learner's increased linguistic resources support lengthier descriptive details (*Schools are important to communities, After the hurricane…They can help in three ways…Please donate to Our School. Your donation helps…*). The learner shows originality by featuring the theme of community throughout the text, adding details of interest (*Kitchens can't provide meals without ovens and refrigerators! When school starts, these supplies will be important!*) to maintain the audience's attention.

Within the Advanced level, the learner uses organizational structures such as cause and effect (*natural disasters can wreak havoc…media reports have show broken walls…*), sequencing (*first, second, third*), and problem-solution (*Yet @OurSchool can't do it alone, YOU can make a difference to organizations like @OurSchool!*). The strategic repetition of the word *thrive* creates cohesion among the three different paragraph structures. Descriptive details first paint a picture of the scene (*severely damaged…broken walls, damaged appliances, students without supplies*), then later provide explanations (*@OurSchool supports schools in three ways. First…, Yet @OurSchool can't do it alone. They need…*). The learner adds originality by incorporating creative social media tags (*@[target language country], #[hurricane's name], @OurSchool*) and using emphasis (*YOU can make a difference…*) to engage the audience and maintain their attention.

Table 8.1
Sample Learner Performances

NOVICE	**Task:** Create a podcast that persuades students in our school to donate to an organization that supports education in (target language country).	Oh no, school destruction! How to help? *Our School* to help! *Our School* organization to help schools. Need school supplies, tables, chairs. Very important and practical! *Our School* need your help. Please to donate to *Our School*. Donations for students and teachers. To donate today! Students thank you!
INTERMEDIATE	**Task:** Create a podcast that persuades community members to donate to an organization that supports education in (target language country).	Schools are important to communities. After the hurricane, there was a lot of destruction in the [target language country]. There was school destruction. How can we help this community? Support *Our School*! *Our School* is an organization that help schools. They can help in three ways: reconstruct schools, offer meals, and provide school supplies. To reconstruct schools, they need construction supplies. To offer meals, they need ovens and refrigerators. Kitchens can't provide meals without ovens and refrigerators! To provide schools supplies, they need notebooks, pencils, and markers. When school starts, these supplies will be important! *Our School* needs your help to support schools in their community. Please donate to *Our School*. Your donation helps build strong communities. Donate today and support communities everywhere!
ADVANCED	**Task:** Create a podcast that persuades social media users to support an educational organization in (target language country).	Schools help communities thrive. However, natural disasters can wreak havoc on schools and communities. Schools in #[target language country] were severely damaged by #[hurricane's name]. Media reports have show broken walls, damaged appliances, and students without supplies. Fortunately, *@OurSchool* is an organization that can help schools thrive. *@OurSchool* supports schools in three ways. First, they reconstruct schools who have experienced damage. Second, they provide nutritious meals for students. Third, they provide school supplies such as notebooks, pencils, and markers. Yet *@OurSchool* can't do it alone. They need construction supplies, ovens, refrigerators, and school supplies so they can continue to support schools. YOU can make a difference to organizations like *@OurSchool*! Click [link] now to donate $5. Your donation will help schools in [target language country] thrive. Donate today!

Impact Reference Guide

"All real performance is ultimately about impact, intended or otherwise" (Wiggins, 1998, p. 39). Learners demonstrate Impact through their use of organization, details, and/or originality to capture and maintain their attendance's attention. Next is a reference guide for the ways learners can use these elements in a presentational task. It is important to note that all learners can use the language resources they currently have to demonstrate these elements and that Impact includes skills that are not necessarily nor solely determined by linguistic ability.

Organization

Organization is a key component of effective communication that directly affects the experience of the audience. How a learner chooses to organize their performance is influenced by the type of writing (fiction, nonfiction, poetry…) and audience. Learners can choose to organize their message using an organizational structure such as cause/effect, chronological, compare/contrast, description, problem and solution, pros/cons, sequential, or storytelling (Troyan et al., 2023). Within any organizational structure, learners can further organize their ideas by grouping similar ideas together. Additionally, learners can sequence ideas by arranging them in a particular order. As learners' language skills grow, text options increase and organization may be evidenced in multiple ways. For example, learners performing within the Advanced level can organize their message within extended writings, such as essays, using paragraph-level structures (for example: topic sentence, supporting details, closing statement). All learners, regardless of performance level, can organize their message in ways that demonstrate their understanding of how structure impacts delivery, and how organizational features impact an audience. Overall, organization is a way to show originality in how the learner decides to structure the message.

Details

Details are information that further explains and describes an idea. The descriptive details that a learner chooses to include should serve a purpose. That is, learners must select *which* details to include (or not) that best support their ideas. Purposeful details enhance and clarify the learner's intended message for the audience. To craft a message that maintains the audience's attention, learners need a sufficient amount of detail to help their audience visualize their intended message, they need to vary the types of details they include so their work is not repetitive, and they need to select details that are relevant to the purpose of the message (Serravallo, 2017). Learners can accomplish this by including sensory details, or those that use the five senses (taste, touch, hear, smell, see), to create vivid, concrete images that engage readers (Myers, 2023). Adding details to a message by using adjectives and adverbs can help an audience form more vivid visual images. Giving examples, explanations, or reasons is a way learners can use details to further explain their ideas. Metaphors, analogies, similes, and imagery are all ways a learner can creatively use details to paint a visual picture for the audience.

It is important to understand that as learners' language resources increase, so too do the expectations of descriptive details. For example, *the yellow sun hot* may be considered descriptive when performing within the Novice level, however, when performing within the Advanced level, this may not. One might expect a learner performing within the Advanced level to say *the heat from the sun's golden rays*. All learners, regardless of performance level, have the capacity to use descriptive details using the language available to them, within the range in which they are performing, to communicate their ideas with purpose and maintain the attention of their audience.

Originality

Originality is how the learner presents ideas in a novel and imaginative manner. There are multiple ways learners at every performance level can attend to originality. For example, this may be done by including an "unexpected feature" which is an unusual and/or surprising element that truly engages the audience (Elisondo et al., 2013). Learners may also demonstrate originality by presenting their ideas in an imaginative way. For example, a learner may repeat a word or idea for effect or to develop a theme throughout the performance. Learners may offer a novel perspective or approach towards an idea, such as presenting ideas from an unexpected point of view. Or, they may use a rhetorical question to make an assertion. Originality may also be the addition of information that the learner researched independently of the learned content and then included in their performance. It may be the inclusion of an anecdote or dialogue or learners may craft a message in a way that deeply resonates with the intended audience. There are multiple ways that learners can add originality or an unexpected feature to the message in order to capture and maintain the audience's attention, and none of the above examples are exclusive to a performance level. Of utmost importance is to consider how a learner uses language to show an imaginative way of presenting information to capture and maintain their audience's attention.

The Performance Domain Indicators

The following section presents the Performance Domain Indicators (PDIs) for Impact. The Impact PDIs were developed from *Implementing Integrated Performance Assessments* (Adair-Hauck et al., 2013) and *The Integrated Performance Assessment: Twenty Years and Counting* (Troyan et al., 2023). The Impact PDIs are used with the presentational mode of communication. The same four levels (*Beginning, Developing, Meeting, Exceeding*) are applied to all three of the performance levels (Novice, Intermediate, and Advanced) (see Table 8.2). This is because Impact includes skills that are not necessarily nor solely determined by linguistic ability.

Table 8.2
Impact Performance Domain Indicators (PDIs)

BEGINNING	DEVELOPING	MEETING	EXCEEDING
I can present my ideas, but do not <u>maintain my audience's attention</u>.	**I can present** my ideas in a way that, at times, captures <u>and maintains the attention of my audience by using organization, descriptive details, and/or originality</u>.	**I can present** my ideas in a way that <u>captures and maintains the attention of my audience by using organization, descriptive details, and/or originality</u>.	**I can present** my ideas in a way that <u>captures and maintains the attention of my audience by using organization, descriptive details, and originality</u>.

- The language in bold indicates the source is the *NCSSFL-ACTFL Can-Do Statements: Performance Indicators for Language Learners* (NCSSFL-ACTFL, 2017).
- The underlined language indicates the source is Adair-Hauck et al. (2013) and Troyan et. al. (2023).
- Some language has been modified to provide scaffolding, consistency and/or clarity.
- For classroom purposes some language has been modified to be learner-friendly (ie. *rich details* to *descriptive details, unexpected feature* to *originality*).

The Performance Domain Descriptions

In order to illustrate Impact, the PDIs are accompanied by a learner task and sample learner responses. In addition, the PDIs are accompanied by a description that is meant to deepen our understanding of how Impact develops across the levels (*Beginning, Developing, Meeting, Exceeding*) in learner performance at each performance level: Novice (Table 8.3), Intermediate (Table 8.4), and Advanced (Table 8.5).

Table 8.3

Impact Performance Domain Indicators (PDIs) for Learners Performing Within the Novice Level

	NOVICE			
Sublevels	**BEGINNING**	**DEVELOPING**	**MEETING**	**EXCEEDING**
Context	familiar, informal, formal, predictable			
Content	very familiar, familiar, everyday			
Performance Domain Indicator	I can present my ideas, but do not maintain my audience's attention.	I can present my ideas in a way that, at times, captures and maintains the attention of my audience by using organization, descriptive details, and/or originality.	I can present my ideas in a way that captures and maintains the attention of my audience by using organization, descriptive details, and/or originality.	I can present my ideas in a way that captures and maintains the attention of my audience by using organization, descriptive details, and originality.

Novice Task: Send your friend a status update on social media describing your Saturday morning breakfast experience.

Sample Learner Responses: All four sample responses exhibit **Novice High** characteristics and therefore are similar, if not almost exact responses. This is intentional so as to highlight how learners use organization, descriptive details, and/or originality as they progress through the levels (*Beginning* to *Exceeding*).

NOVICE			
BEGINNING	**DEVELOPING**	**MEETING**	**EXCEEDING**
I like breakfast. I am in restaurant. I like eggs. What's up, friend?	What's up, friend? I am in restaurant. So yummy! I like to eat eggs. I like to eat breakfast.	What's up, friend? I am in restaurant. My fav! I like to eat breakfast. I like to eat eggs. So yummy!	What's up, friend? I am in restaurant. My fav! I like to eat big breakfast. I like to eat eggs with bacon. So yummy! What you eat this morning?

Description of Learner Responses: At the *Beginning* level, the learner performing within the Novice level presents their ideas, but in a way that does not maintain their audience's attention. At the *Developing* level, they are able to capture, and at times maintain their audience's attention by using organization, descriptive details, and/or originality. In this sample performance, the learner is able to capture (*What's up, friend?*) and at times maintain the audience's attention by organizing their ideas in a logical manner and adding some additional details (*So yummy!* and *to eat*). Learners are *Meeting* expectations when they are able to capture and maintain the audience's attention by using some, but not all, elements of Impact (organization, details, and/or originality). For example, in this sample performance, the learner captures and maintains the audience's attention through organization (grouping similar ideas together, such as the setting and describing the breakfast) and adding descriptive details such as adjectives (*My fav!*) and prepositional phrases (*to eat*). Learners are *Exceeding* expectations when they can attend to organization, details, and originality in their performance. For example, in this sample performance, in addition to organization and additional descriptive details (*big, with bacon*), the learner demonstrates originality by not only using a rejoinder (*So yummy!*) to add interest but also including a question (*What you eat this morning?*) to engage the audience in the social media post.

Table 8.4

Impact Performance Domain Indicators (PDIs) for Learners Performing Within the Intermediate Level

	INTERMEDIATE			
Sublevels	BEGINNING	DEVELOPING	MEETING	EXCEEDING
Context	familiar, informal, formal, straight-forward			
Content	familiar, concrete, at times researched			
Performance Domain Indicator	I can present my ideas, but do not maintain my audience's attention.	I can present my ideas in a way that, at times, captures and maintains the attention of my audience by using organization, descriptive details, and/or originality.	I can present my ideas in a way that captures and maintains the attention of my audience by using organization, descriptive details, and/or originality.	I can present my ideas in a way that captures and maintains the attention of my audience by using organization, descriptive details, and originality.

Intermediate Task: Post a reply to your friend's breakfast photo message on social media and compare your breakfasts.

Sample Learner Responses: Notice that all four sample responses exhibit **Intermediate Mid** characteristics and therefore are similar, if not almost exact responses. This is intentional so as to highlight how learners use organization, descriptive details, and/or originality as they progress through the levels (*Beginning* to *Exceeding*).

INTERMEDIATE			
BEGINNING	**DEVELOPING**	**MEETING**	**EXCEEDING**
I eated eggs this morning because they are healthy. But I prefer cereal because of the sugar. I see that eggs is your favorite meal! Lol. My dad says that eggs are good.	Lol. I eated eggs this morning because they are very healthy. But I had with rice and beans. But I prefer cereal because lots of the sugar. I see that eggs is your favorite meal! Lol. My dad says that eggs are good.	Lol. I see that bacon and eggs is your favorite meal for breakfast! I also eated eggs this morning, but I had with rice and beans. My dad says that eggs are good to us because they are very healthy But, I prefer cereal because of all the sugar. Lol.	Lol. Again? I see that bacon and eggs is your favorite meal for breakfast! LOVE IT! I also eated eggs this morning, but I had with rice and beans. My dad says that eggs are good to us because they are very healthy. But, I prefer cereal like FruitySquares, because of all the sugar. YUM! Lol. Well, enjoy!

Description of Learner Responses: At the *Beginning* level, the learner performing within the Intermediate level presents their ideas, but in a way that does not maintain the attention of the audience. At the *Developing* level, they are able to capture, and at times maintain their audience's attention by using organization, descriptive details, and/or originality. In this sample performance, the learner captures (*Lol*), and at times maintains the audience's attention by adding some descriptive details (*very, But I had with rice and beans, lots of*). Learners are *Meeting* expectations when they are able to capture and maintain the audience's attention by using some, but not all, elements of Impact (organization, details, and/or originality). For example, in this sample performance, the learner captures and maintains the audience's attention by presenting their ideas in an organized way (grouping similar ideas together) and adding additional descriptive details (*for breakfast, also, to us, because of all the sugar*). Learners are *Exceeding* expectations when they can attend to organization, details, and originality in their performance. For example, in this sample performance, in addition to organization and descriptive details, the learner illustrates originality by incorporating a rhetorical question (*Again?*) and adding points of emphasis (*LOVE IT! YUM!*).

Table 8.5
Impact Performance Domain Indicators (PDIs) for Learners Performing Within the Advanced Level

	ADVANCED			
Sublevels	BEGINNING	DEVELOPING	MEETING	EXCEEDING
Context	familiar, unfamiliar, informal, formal, complex			
Content	familiar, academic, social, professional, concrete, abstract			
Performance Domain Indicator	I can present my ideas, but do not maintain my audience's attention.	I can present my ideas in a way that, at times, captures and maintains the attention of my audience by using organization, descriptive details, and/or originality.	I can present my ideas in a way that captures and maintains the attention of my audience by using organization, descriptive details, and/or originality.	I can present my ideas in a way that captures and maintains the attention of my audience by using organization, descriptive details, and originality.

Advanced Task: Create a podcast episode for your listeners that brings awareness to how nutrition impacts the human body.

Sample Learner Responses: Notice that all four sample responses exhibit **Advanced Low** characteristics and therefore are similar, if not almost exact responses. This is intentional so as to highlight how learners use organization, descriptive details, and/or originality as they progress through the levels (*Beginning* to *Exceeding*).

ADVANCED			
BEGINNING	**DEVELOPING**	**MEETING**	**EXCEEDING**
This episode is about artificial sweeteners. A recent health study found that artificial sweeteners are linked to health problems. More research is needed. Artificial sweeteners taste like sugar but have no calories, which is why they are popular. These are for people who want to lose weight. But, a health study finded that artificial sweeteners is linked to heart problems and also increase in weight At the grocery store, think twice about diet products. Good-bye and thanks!	Hello listeners! This episode is about artificial sweeteners. The artificial sweeteners taste like sugar but have no calories, which is why they are popular for peoples want to lose weight. They are in many products. However, a health study finded that artificial sweeteners are linked to heart problems and also increase in weight. More research is needed, but you may you think twice about diet products. Good-bye!	Hello to all my listeners! This episode is about artificial sweeteners, like SweArtif and Azcufal. The artificial sweeteners taste like sugar but have zero calories, which is why they are so popular for peoples want to lose weight. The products that are popular is soda, cereals, chips, and cookies! However, a recent health study finded that artificial sweeteners are linked to heart problems and also increase in weight. More research is needed in the future. So, the next time when you are in the grocery store, you think twice about diet products. Thanks for listen. Good-bye!	Hello to all my listeners! This episode of <u>The Body and Our Nutrition</u> is about artificial sweeteners, like SweArtif and Azcufal. The artificial sweeteners taste like sugar but have zero calories, which is why they are super popular for peoples want to lose weight. The products that are popular is soda, cereals, chips, and cookies! However, did you know a health study finded that artificial sweeteners is linked to heart problems and also increase in weight? More research is needed in the future. So, the next time when you are in the grocery store, you can think twice about diet products. Is it worth it? Until then, thanks for listen and "Be well."

Description of Learner Responses: At the *Beginning* level, the learner performing within the Advanced level presents their ideas, but in a way that does not maintain the attention of the audience (for example, one big paragraph of ideas). At the *Developing* level, they are able to capture, and at times maintain their audience's attention by using organization, descriptive details, and/or originality. This learner communicates in an organized way: an introduction (*Hello listeners! This episode is about...*), main content with supporting details (*taste like sugar, no calories*, and *linked to heart problems*) and conclusion (*more research is needed* and *Good-bye!*). Learners are *Meeting* expectations when they are able use some, but not all, elements of Impact (organization, details, and/or originality). This learner uses the above organization as well as descriptive details to elaborate on and illustrate their ideas. They do this through their use of adjectives (*zero, recent, grocery, diet*) and examples (*soda, cereals, chips, and cookies*), including proper nouns (*SweArtif* and *Azcufal*). Learners are *Exceeding* expectations when they can attend to all three elements of organization, details, and originality in their performance. For example, in this sample performance, in addition to organization and descriptive details, the learner illustrates originality by creating a name for the podcast (*The Body and Our Nutrition*) and a sign-off (*"Be well"*), as well as uses rhetorical questions that capture and maintain audience attention (*did you know...?* and *Is it worth it?*).

YOUR TURN

LEARNING TARGETS CHECK:	
I can	☐ describe the Impact performance domain. ☐ describe how Impact shows up in learners' performance at various levels.

Pause and reflect:

How would you describe Impact to your learners? Consider any explanations, examples, and/or visuals you might use to describe the performance domain:

Impact in learner work:

The following exercise includes a sample task for the Intermediate performance level. Write a learner response that includes the characteristics of Impact for learners performing within each level. Use the provided *Developing* sample to guide you.

Intermediate task:

In a social media post, tell your friends about a trip you recently took.

Learner sample responses exhibiting Intermediate Mid characteristics:

INTERMEDIATE			
BEGINNING	DEVELOPING	MEETING	EXCEEDING
	Hey friends! I went to Texas where I did a river walk. While there, I did river cruise and afterwards I did river tour walk. When I was there, I saw @alamo. BTW, it was the most old church. During the afternoon on Saturday, I went to museum. I went to tea gardens, which from Japanese, and I saw have water pool and fish. #YOLO! It was hot.		

The Performance Domain Indicators (PDIs) Assessment and Feedback Guide

The *Performance Domain Indicators (PDIs) Assessment and Feedback Guide* is a resource for both learners and educators to use when assessing learner performance. The information within this guide is based on the PDIs of Impact: *Beginning, Developing, Meeting,* and *Exceeding* (Table 8.6). This guide can be used at each proficiency level: Novice, Intermediate, and Advanced. It is important to note that a performance assessment evaluates a learner's *performance*, and not *the learner*. Therefore, a learner is not *at* a level, but rather a learner's performance may be consistent *with* a level.

The purpose of the *Performance Domain Indicators (PDIs) Assessment and Feedback Guide* is to provide a visual pathway for evaluating the Impact of a learner's performance. The left-hand column provides guiding questions that lead us to identify the Impact consistent with a learner's performance. These guiding questions are based upon the performance levels' PDIs, which are presented lowest to highest. Starting at the *Beginning* level, evaluators progress through each question, responding "yes" or "no." If evaluators reply "yes" to all questions in the *Beginning* level, they continue to the next level (*Developing*), repeating the process, and continuing through the levels. If evaluators reply "no" to a question, they go back to the previous level, in which all their replies for the level's guiding questions are "yes." At the last level where all questions are answered "yes," evaluators continue across the chart. They can then refer to the second column labeled *Performance Domain Indicator* for the PDI that best aligns with the learner's performance. Based on this evaluation, the following two columns provide example GLOW and GROW comments. GLOW feedback states what the learner achieved and GROW feedback directs learners how to develop their language skills. This feedback is not unit specific, but rather supports overarching language performance goals that learners can work towards throughout a course. Including evidence from learner performance within the GLOW/GROW feedback is most effective.

Table 8.6
Performance Domain Indicators (PDIs) Assessment and Feedback Guide

<table>
<tr><th colspan="3">IMPACT
Target performance level: **Meeting**</th></tr>
<tr><td rowspan="3">*The context and content corresponds to the proficiency level a learner is working within.*</td><td>NOVICE</td><td>Context: familiar, informal, formal, predictable
Content: familiar, everyday</td></tr>
<tr><td>INTERMEDIATE</td><td>Context: familiar, informal, formal, straight-forward
Content: familiar, concrete, at times researched</td></tr>
<tr><td>ADVANCED</td><td>Context: familiar, unfamiliar, informal, formal, complex
Content: familiar, academic, social, professional, concrete, abstract</td></tr>
</table>

Guiding questions	Performance Domain Indicator	GLOW	GROW
Beginning Can the learner • present their ideas?	I can present my ideas, but do not maintain my audience's attention.	• You present your ideas.	• What organizational structure (*cause/effect, chronological, compare/contrast, description, problem and solution, pros/cons, sequential, or storytelling*) might help you organize your ideas more effectively? • How might you organize your ideas by grouping similar ideas together? • What other descriptive details might you add to maintain the attention of your audience?
Developing Can the learner capture and maintain the audience's attention at times by: • presenting ideas in an organized way? • and/or using descriptive details? • and/or presenting ideas in a novel and imaginative manner?	I can present my ideas in a way that, at times, captures and maintains the attention of my audience by using organization, descriptive details, and/or originality.	At times you capture and maintain the attention of your audience: • through organization (*grouping similar ideas together, using an organizational structure, etc.*). • by adding descriptive details to illustrate your ideas. • by presenting your ideas in a novel or imaginative manner to show originality.	• How might you organize your ideas differently to maintain the attention of your audience? • What organizational structure (*cause/effect, chronological, compare/contrast, description, problem and solution, pros/cons, sequential, or storytelling*) might help you organize your ideas more effectively? • What additional descriptive details might you add to maintain the attention of your audience? • How could you add originality by presenting your ideas in a novel, new, or imaginative manner?
Meeting Can the learner capture and maintain the audience's attention by using one or more of the following: • presenting ideas in an organized way? • using descriptive details? • presenting ideas in a novel and imaginative manner?	I can present my ideas in a way that captures and maintains the attention of my audience by using organization, descriptive details, and/or originality.	You capture and maintain the attention of your audience: • through organization (*grouping similar ideas together, using an organizational structure, etc.*). • by adding descriptive details to illustrate your ideas. • by presenting your ideas in a novel or imaginative manner to show originality.	• How might you organize your ideas differently to maintain the attention of your audience? • What additional descriptive details might you add to maintain the attention of your audience? • How could you add originality by presenting your ideas in a novel, new, or imaginative manner? • What might make someone remember your presentation? • How could your presentation elicit the desired effects in your audience?

Exceeding Can the learner capture and maintain the audience's attention by using all of the following: • presenting ideas in an organized way? • using descriptive details? • presenting ideas in a novel and imaginative manner?	I can present my ideas in a way that captures and maintains the attention of my audience by using organization, descriptive details, and originality.	You capture and maintain the attention of your audience: • through organization (*grouping similar ideas together, using an organizational structure, etc.*). • by adding descriptive details to illustrate your ideas. • by presenting your ideas in a novel or imaginative manner to show originality.	• What would happen if you took or added another perspective? • What might you add or adjust to help your audience relate to your ideas? • Is there a different way to share your ideas that would be more intriguing or evoke a reaction from your audience? • How might your audience be compelled to feel or act as a result of your presentation?

Performance Domain Indicators within a Rubric

In order to evaluate learners' performances, the PDIs are placed within a rubric with four performance level labels: *Beginning, Developing, Meeting,* and *Exceeding.* The *Meeting* level aligns with the target performance level for the learners. These labels communicate to learners how their performance compares to the standard; learners are *Beginning* to meet, *Developing* towards, *Meeting,* or *Exceeding* their target performance level. It is important to highlight that, similar to other ACTFL publications, when placed within a rubric, these four performance levels are arranged high to low, beginning with the highest on the left. This is so that learners read the highest level of performance first. Table 8.7 illustrates the rubric alignment and arrangement for the Impact performance domain for the presentational mode of communication.

Table 8.7
Aligning the Impact Performance Domain Indicators (PDIs) in a Rubric

Target performance level: **Meeting** Context: familiar, informal, formal, predictable Content: very familiar, familiar, everyday				
NOVICE				
	EXCEEDING	**MEETING**	**DEVELOPING**	**BEGINNING**
Performance level description	I can present my ideas in a way that captures and maintains the attention of my audience by using organization, descriptive details, and originality.	I can present my ideas in a way that captures and maintains the attention of my audience by using organization, descriptive details, and/or originality.	I can present my ideas in a way that, at times, captures and maintains the attention of my audience by using organization, descriptive details, and/or originality.	I can present my ideas, but do not maintain my audience's attention.

Target performance level: **Meeting** Context: familiar, informal, formal, straight-forward Content: familiar, concrete, at times researched				
INTERMEDIATE				
	EXCEEDING	**MEETING**	**DEVELOPING**	**BEGINNING**
Performance level description	I can present my ideas in a way that captures and maintains the attention of my audience by using organization, descriptive details, and originality.	I can present my ideas in a way that captures and maintains the attention of my audience by using organization, descriptive details, and/or originality.	I can present my ideas in a way that, at times, captures and maintains the attention of my audience by using organization, descriptive details, and/or originality.	I can present my ideas, but do not maintain my audience's attention.

Target performance level: **Meeting** Context: familiar, unfamiliar, informal, formal, complex Content: familiar, academic, social, professional, concrete, abstract				
ADVANCED				
	EXCEEDING	**MEETING**	**DEVELOPING**	**BEGINNING**
Performance level description	I can present my ideas in a way that captures and maintains the attention of my audience by using organization, descriptive details, and originality.	I can present my ideas in a way that captures and maintains the attention of my audience by using organization, descriptive details, and/or originality.	I can present my ideas in a way that, at times, captures and maintains the attention of my audience by using organization, descriptive details, and/or originality.	I can present my ideas, but do not maintain my audience's attention.

Performance Assessment in Action

As educators our understanding of the PDIs is critical to providing effective feedback that promotes language growth in our learners. Therefore, it is important to build our capacity to use the PDIs. Here, the goal is to model how to use the Impact PDIs to evaluate learner work, which is the basis of the GLOW and GROW feedback that is provided. The focus of this section is to evaluate learner work and provide feedback, *not* to determine a learner's proficiency level. In other words, the evaluation indicates the learner's performance is consistent with a level and provides feedback to indicate next steps for language growth.

This section demonstrates how to use these rubrics to evaluate sample presentational learner performances within the Novice, Intermediate, and Advanced level. These learner samples exemplify products of a summative assessment. They show evidence from learners after exposure to and practice within a unit of study. That is, learners complete these tasks following classroom instruction and multiple opportunities for formative practice on these topics. After the evaluation of each learner sample there is a model of how to provide GLOW and GROW feedback using examples from the *Performance Domain Indicators (PDIs) Assessment and Feedback Guide.*

Each learner sample:

- indicates the PDI that best aligns with the performance in the rubric.
- uses the evaluation to explain what the learner can do in this performance sample.
- models how to provide GLOW and GROW feedback using examples from the *Performance Domain Indicators (PDIs) Assessment and Feedback Guide.*

LEARNERS PERFORMING WITHIN THE NOVICE LEVEL

Mode of communication: *Presentational*
Target performance level: **Meeting**
Context: familiar, formal, predictable
Content: familiar, everyday

Novice Task: For the hallway display, select one of the people we have studied in this unit. Create a descriptive writing in which you compare how you are similar in order to highlight what you have in common, and contrast how you are different in order to feature how you each make use of your attributes in our diverse world.

LEARNER SAMPLE RESPONSE

Hey! My name is Pari. I 12 years old. I am Persian.
Ingrid is sports. Ingrid like to dance. I am not to dance. I am to swim.
I is shy. Ingrid is shy. I is play sports.
I am to read. Ingrid like to dance.
I am to draw. Ingrid like to dance. Well, see ya later!

Evaluation & Explanation

IMPACT			
NOVICE			
EXCEEDING	**MEETING**	**DEVELOPING**	**BEGINNING**
I can present my ideas in a way that captures and maintains the attention of my audience by using organization, descriptive details, and originality.	I can present my ideas in a way that captures and maintains the attention of my audience by using organization, descriptive details, and/or originality.	I can present my ideas in a way that, at times, captures and maintains the attention of my audience by using organization, descriptive details, and/or originality.	I can present my ideas, but do not maintain my audience's attention.

Evaluation: In this performance sample, the learner presents their ideas in a way that, at times, captures (*Hey*!) and maintains the attention of their audience. At times the learner uses organization to maintain the attention of their audience. The learner compares their attributes to Ingrid's, largely relying on describing the likes/dislikes and personality traits of each person. At times the learner organizes their ideas by grouping similar ideas together (*Ingrid like to dance. I am not to dance* and *I is shy. Ingrid is shy*).

Feedback:

- GLOW: At times you capture and maintain the attention of your audience through organization by grouping some similar ideas together.
- GROW: What additional descriptive details could you add to strengthen the connections between you and Ingrid and maintain the attention of your audience?

LEARNERS PERFORMING WITHIN THE INTERMEDIATE LEVEL

Mode of communication: *Presentational*
Target performance level: **Meeting**
Context: familiar, formal, straight-forward
Content: familiar, researched

Intermediate Task: As part of an Earth Day campaign in your community, write a formal letter to an influential leader advocating for change that would address an environmental issue that you have learned about.

LEARNER SAMPLE RESPONSE

Honorable Mayor Wilson,

Help! My name is Kai Meyer. I live in Elmdale now. I like to live in Elmdale We have strong engaged for community here. Since 3 years, Elmdale won the "Best city in the USA". We try to win that again and we could. We could to do more of to clean up and beautify our city. Maybe have like the BUGA garden show in Germany. Different cities host and make big gardens. And plant trees. Like big plant show at the fair.

A lot in Elmdale is full of garbage. When I run on hiking trails I see a lot of garbage. Nature reserves, like Forest Park, have more garbage. It is not pretty. I remember you to since 3 years. It would be great if mentality to our city. Run people need clean trails. They are impacted.

Here are things do. We could the volunteers clean up the parks. This would also help the people in the city do it. Other volunteers could the large places. The city could have event. The event would be "Consciousness about Garbage in Plymouth"

We could say, plant more trees in the niehgborhoods. This would give back the trees we take for construction. Maybe be a tree hugger? Plants and gardens too but for now trees. When we plant more trees, this make our community a better place. Plant now! Act now!

Sincerely,
Kai Meyer

Evaluation & Explanation

IMPACT			
INTERMEDIATE			
EXCEEDING	MEETING	DEVELOPING	BEGINNING
I can present my ideas in a way that captures and maintains the attention of my audience by using organization, descriptive details, and originality.	I can present my ideas in a way that captures and maintains the attention of my audience by using organization, descriptive details, and/or originality.	I can present my ideas in a way that, at times, captures and maintains the attention of my audience by using organization, descriptive details, and/or originality.	I can present my ideas, but do not maintain my audience's attention.

Evaluation: In this sample performance, the learner maintains the attention of their audience through descriptive details and originality. At times the learner organizes their ideas: sometimes the learner groups similar statements together, and at other times the learner makes use of an organizational structure (problem and solution). Throughout the performance, the learner uses descriptive details such as adjectives (*strong, Best, different, big, clean, large, better*), examples (*Maybe have like the BUGA garden show in Germany, When I run on hiking trails I see a lot of garbage, like Forest Park, We could the volunteers clean up the parks, The event would be "Consciousness about Garbage in Plymouth"*), reasons (*They are impacted, This would also help the people in the city do it, this make our community a better place, This would give back the trees we take for construction*), and a comparison (*BUGA...Like big plant show*). The learner adds originality through the use of a rhetorical question (*Maybe be a tree hugger?*) and commands (*Plant now! Act now!*).

Feedback:

- GLOW: You capture and maintain the attention of your audience by adding descriptive details to illustrate your ideas and presenting your ideas in a novel or imaginative manner (*Maybe be a tree hugger?, Plant now! Act now!*) to show originality.
- GROW: How might you organize your ideas differently to maintain the attention of your audience?

LEARNERS PERFORMING WITHIN THE ADVANCED LEVEL

Mode of communication: *Presentational*
Target performance level: **Meeting**
Context: familiar, informal, complex
Content: familiar, academic, social, professional, concrete

Advanced Task: Based on the movie, write a diary entry from the perspective of one of the baseball players that includes their reflections of the recruitment practices of professional baseball leagues.

LEARNER SAMPLE RESPONSE

Dear diary,

I cannot believe that this investigation about my age is still going on! It is just not fair! I am not a liar! How much analyses have I to do? Because of this, I did not get the chance to sign when I turned 16 years. In the Professional Baseball League they think that all us players are liars. There are some that lies, but there are a lot of us who tells the truth.

But what are they suppose to do, if only one year older means you are worth $1 million less? Seriously, one year? The PBL uses us for our poverty. It's not fair that they treat us differently, pay us differently just because we live in poorer country. Why I don't make money because I am a great baseball player? Why am I the cheap export? If I am in power, I would talks with the representatives to work for changes in recruiting regulations, like age restrictions and equal pay.

Yet I know that if I work hard, I will get a contract of any price which, for me, is the way out of poverty. It is also my family's way out of poverty because they are depending on me. The first thing I take on is buy my parents a house so they never have to worry about housing ever again! I just have to be patient. All I want to do is play baseball- it's what I love, it's what I borned to do, it's all I have ever done.

Let's play ball!
-Mike

Evaluation & Explanation

IMPACT			
ADVANCED			
EXCEEDING	MEETING	DEVELOPING	BEGINNING
I can present my ideas in a way that captures and maintains the attention of my audience by using organization, descriptive details, and originality.	I can present my ideas in a way that captures and maintains the attention of my audience by using organization, descriptive details, and/or originality.	I can present my ideas in a way that, at times, captures and maintains the attention of my audience by using organization, descriptive details, and/or originality.	I can present my ideas, but do not maintain my audience's attention.

Evaluation: In this sample performance, the learner presents their ideas in a way that captures and maintains the attention of their audience by using all of the following: organization, descriptive details, and originality. First, the learner presents their ideas within three developed paragraphs: ball players as liars, discrimination in pay, and then baseball as a way out of poverty. Second, the learner uses descriptive details that support their central focus. The learner includes the process to verify age (*analyses*); the age at which baseball players can receive contracts (*16*); the pay gap (*$1 million less*) and its reason (*one year*); perceived treatment (*cheap export*); personal motivation to sign (*way out of poverty*) and external pressure (*they* [family] *are depending on me* and *buy my parents a house*). All of these details combined provide the reader a complete idea of the injustices felt by a ballplayer in the recruiting process for the professional leagues. Additionally, the learner illustrates originality through their subjective tone and reliance on feelings over fact to deliver a personalized message. The learner uses exclamatory statements to convey emotion (*It is just not fair! I am not a liar!*) as well as rhetorical questions for dramatic effect (*How much analyses have I to do?; Seriously, one year?*; and *Why I don't make money because I am a great baseball player? Why am I the cheap export?*).

Feedback:

- GLOW: You capture and maintain the attention of your audience by presenting your ideas in a novel and imaginative manner. You illustrate originality in how you convey the emotions experienced by you as a ballplayer.
- GROW: What might you add or adjust to help your audience relate to your ideas?

YOUR TURN

LEARNING TARGETS CHECK:	
I can	☐ evaluate learner work using the Performance Domain Indicators (PDIs). ☐ give effective feedback using the Impact PDIs.

Now it is your turn to practice evaluating learner performances and providing feedback. Remember, learners complete these performance tasks following classroom instruction and multiple opportunities for formative practice on these topics. In this section, use the Impact PDIs to indicate the level of performance that best corresponds with the following presentational learner performance samples. Then provide each learner GLOW and GROW feedback. You may want to use the *Performance Domain Indicators (PDIs) Assessment and Feedback Guide* to help guide your evaluation and feedback of the learner's performance in the Impact performance domain.

Then, turn to APPENDIX D | Impact (p.443-445) to compare your evaluation and feedback to one provided by the authors. Reflect on how your evaluation and feedback was similar and/or different, and why. You can do this individually and/or with your colleagues (for example, with a Professional Learning Community (PLC)). This exercise can be an opportunity for rich discussion to help increase inter-rater reliability among educators.

LEARNERS PERFORMING WITHIN THE NOVICE LEVEL

Mode of communication: *Presentational*
Target performance level: **Meeting**
Context: familiar, formal, predictable
Content: familiar, everyday

Novice Task: For the hallway display, select one of the people we have studied in this unit. Create a descriptive writing in which you compare how you are similar in order to highlight what you have in common, and contrast how you are different in order to feature how you each make use of your attributes in our diverse world.

LEARNER SAMPLE RESPONSE

Greetings! My name is Leo. I am 12 years old.

Naiomi is 24 years old. She is Diné (Navajo).

Naiomi & I is similar. Naiomi is sports-minded because to skateboard. I do not like to skateboard. I like hockey but no skateboarding. I like hockey in the winter with my friends.

Naiomi is hard-working. Naiomi really likes to practice skateboarding. How interesting! I like hockey.

Naiomi not is lazy. She likes to work for more skate parks. How important! Many people to need more skate parks. Many people to need more hockey parks too. Is a problem. How important!

Naiomi and I is different but equal. Thank you for read!

Evaluation & Explanation

IMPACT			
NOVICE			
EXCEEDING	**MEETING**	**DEVELOPING**	**BEGINNING**
I can present my ideas in a way that captures and maintains the attention of my audience by using organization, descriptive details, and originality.	I can present my ideas in a way that captures and maintains the attention of my audience by using organization, descriptive details, and/or originality.	I can present my ideas in a way that, at times, captures and maintains the attention of my audience by using organization, descriptive details, and/or originality.	I can present my ideas, but do not maintain my audience's attention.

Evaluation:

Feedback:

- GLOW:
- GROW:

Turn to APPENDIX D | Impact (p.443) to compare your evaluation and explanation to one provided by the authors.

LEARNERS PERFORMING WITHIN THE INTERMEDIATE LEVEL

Mode of communication: *Presentational*
Target performance level: **Meeting**
Context: familiar, formal, straight-forward
Content: familiar, researched

Intermediate Task: As part of an Earth Day campaign in your community, write a formal letter to an influential leader advocating for change that would address an environmental issue that you have learned about.

LEARNER SAMPLE RESPONSE

Dear Mr. President,

Did you heared, one of the major problems environmental in the world is the increase of the ocean level as result of global warming. The increase of the ocean level is a problem Many Carribean countries are sinking and that is destroying the work or life of many people.

People are constructing sea barriers for flooding. One other thing Carribean countries are doing is transport help now, not help in the future. For the future, it's important that the world, specifically the United States, reduce the greenhouse gas emissions because a rise in greenhouse gases cause more global warming. As a result, the icebergs melt and the sea level rise. The problem is very important for you.

One example of this problem is of a little country in the Pacific Ocean. The country is Tuvalu. Tuvalu is home for 11,000 people and increase of sea level is a very big problem for this country. In the last decade, Tuvalu lost 2 islands a the ocean. This is very bad for that many people would have eliminate outside of their house and in 50 years, the whole country absent.

A protect millions of people and the health of our environments, I would think that is important you reduce the emissions greenhouse gas for the future of the world. Also, I would think that a good solution for now is do construct many sea barriers and raise to support for people and families close to the coast.

Thanks,
Avery

Evaluation & Explanation

IMPACT			
INTERMEDIATE			
EXCEEDING	**MEETING**	**DEVELOPING**	**BEGINNING**
I can present my ideas in a way that captures and maintains the attention of my audience by using organization, descriptive details, and originality.	I can present my ideas in a way that captures and maintains the attention of my audience by using organization, descriptive details, and/or originality.	I can present my ideas in a way that, at times, captures and maintains the attention of my audience by using organization, descriptive details, and/or originality.	I can present my ideas, but do not maintain my audience's attention.

Evaluation:

Feedback:

- GLOW:
- GROW:

Turn to APPENDIX D | Impact (p.444) to compare your evaluation and explanation to one provided by the authors.

LEARNERS PERFORMING WITHIN THE ADVANCED LEVEL

Mode of communication: *Presentational*
Target performance level: **Meeting**
Context: familiar, informal, complex
Content: familiar, academic, social, professional, concrete

Advanced Task: Based on the movie, write a diary entry from the perspective of one of the baseball players that includes their reflections of the recruitment practices of professional baseball leagues.

LEARNER SAMPLE RESPONSE

Dear Diary

I am angry! Even that my results are conclusive, I still have to do more tests. This means that I can lose my chance to sign with a professional baseball team. Out of all the 105 players, I have the best chance. It was to be a dream come true! However, because my tests are no decided, it is a controversy for teams to sign with me. I dreamed this my whole life. It's what I sacrificed so many years. What the Professional Baseball League has did to me, I think it an injustice. I did all those tests that show that I am 16 years and I did not lie. In fact my family gived the PBL all the documents that they needed. The PBL did no need the same documents or the same tests of the other baseball players. It's not fair that we give you more information. And because of this, no one wants to sign me.

If I were a different baseball player, I would no have to take the tests. I just want to be baseball player. I can help my family too. I wants to try to be as good as the other players, even better. I hope some team signs me. I won't accept that I've lost the opportunity. I will fight for my opportunity. I will not back down. Someday I will win the World Series.

Hugs,
Mikey

Evaluation & Explanation

IMPACT			
ADVANCED			
EXCEEDING	MEETING	DEVELOPING	BEGINNING
I can present my ideas in a way that captures and maintains the attention of my audience by using organization, descriptive details, and originality.	I can present my ideas in a way that captures and maintains the attention of my audience by using organization, descriptive details, and/or originality.	I can present my ideas in a way that, at times, captures and maintains the attention of my audience by using organization, descriptive details, and/or originality.	I can present my ideas, but do not maintain my audience's attention.

Evaluation:

Feedback:

- GLOW:
- GROW:

Turn to APPENDIX D | Impact (p.445) to compare your evaluation and explanation to one provided by the authors.

Learning Experiences to Facilitate Learner Growth

Once educators have clarified for learners the goals of performance and provided feedback, learners need learning experiences to help them *understand* the Impact performance domain and PDIs as well as *develop* their language performance. Learning experiences to *understand* the performance domain are listed first, followed by learning experiences to *develop* learner performance. Each learning experience includes *Learner outcomes* (what learners can do upon successful completion of the experience) and an outline of logistical components (*time, preparation, materials, instructions*). *Alternatives* and *Differentiation* offer ways to personalize the experience for a variety of learners. Each learning experience includes short examples, often including learners' work, to help educators visualize each learning experience. The learning experiences can be used with an entire class of learners as a way to introduce and focus learner work on a particular performance domain. Learning experiences can also be assigned to learners by educators or self-selected by learners themselves for further practice within a performance domain. These examples can serve as a springboard for educators to develop their own learning experiences for each performance domain when working with their learners.

CLARIFYING EXPECTATIONS

Domain: Impact

Focus: Understanding how Impact is evaluated

Note: This learning experience can be replicated in multiple performance domains.

Learner outcomes	Time	Materials	Prep
I can identify how Impact is evaluated by: • evaluating my own work using self-assessment questions. • determining the PDI that best aligns with my work. • using the GROW guiding questions to revise and/or add to my work.	• Prep time: 5 minutes • Implementation time: 30 minutes • Debrief time: 5 minutes	• The performance task • Learners' presentational performance such as a draft • The Impact PDIs • Self-assessment questions • GROW guiding questions	• Prepare to display the PDIs, self-assessment questions, and the GROW guiding questions. • Be sure learners have access to their performance.

Instructions

1. (PURPOSE) Tell learners that they will learn how to self-assess their work and make changes in order to reach the next performance level.
2. (SET UP) Remind learners about the performance task for this presentational performance.
3. Display the PDIs and instruct learners to use the self-assessment questions to evaluate their work.
4. (GUIDANCE) Go through a few of the self-assessment questions with the learners, directing learners to reflect on their own performance to identify if it best aligns to the *Beginning, Developing, Meeting,* or *Exceeding* PDIs.
5. (ENGAGEMENT) Release the lesson to have learners continue reflecting on the self- assessment questions and have them mark which PDI best aligns to their work.
6. (GUIDANCE) When learners have identified the PDI that best aligns to their work, point them toward the GROW guiding questions for that level.
7. (ENGAGEMENT) Learners use the GROW guiding questions for that level to guide them to improve their work.
8. (DEBRIEF) Learners could share their reflections and improvements with a partner.
9. Ask learners to reflect on:
    a. What did you notice about your Impact before and after you reflected on the self-assessment and used the GROW guiding questions?
    b. How might you apply what you learned to your future work when completing a summative task?

Alternatives	Differentiation
Learners could complete this learning experience multiple times with multiple presentational tasks throughout a unit. As learners engage in this learning experience, it eventually can be done more independently and does not need to be guided by the educator.	Learners could work together to give and get feedback from each other. After exchanging drafts, each learner could complete the "self" assessment questions as feedback for their partner, turning it into a peer assessment. Learners could then discuss the assessment of each other's work and brainstorm changes to level up their work. Learners could assess an example of work from an anonymous learner individually or in a group discussion.

EXAMPLE

Target performance level: **Meeting**
Context: familiar, informal, predictable
Content: familiar, everyday

Task: *Flip the Stereotype*: Create a flipchart that describes things that are easily seen by other people on the outside. Under each description, in parentheses, write what people might think based on what stereotypes they may think or see (*I am*. . .). Then, on the inside of the paper, write things that others might not easily see or know about you (personality, likes/dislikes. . .) to "flip" the stereotype.

Learner's draft:

OUTSIDE

I red hair.
(I am different.)

I not smile.
(I am unfriendly.)

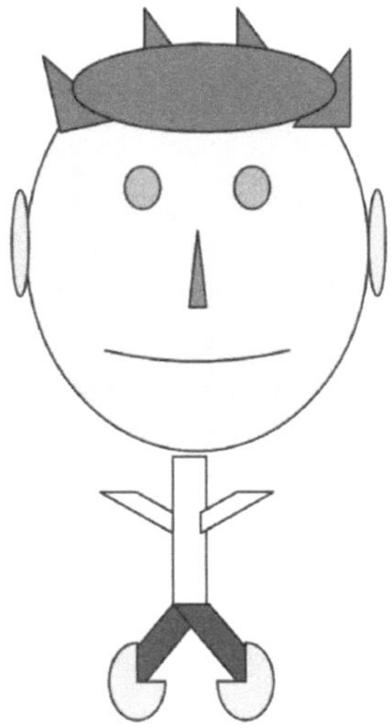

I small short.
(I am weak.)

I have shoes nice
(I am rich.)

INSIDE

I athlete.	*I like my hair.*
I am strong.	*I student good.*
I am friend.	*I helps brothers.*
I am some worry.	

Note: Adapted from Sherrow (2018).

Example of how a learner might fill out the sections of the guided self-assessment (Table 8.10) and identify their GROW guiding questions (from Table 8.6).

TARGET PERFORMANCE LEVEL	Meeting	**CONTEXT**	Corresponds to the proficiency level a learner is working with
PERFORMANCE DOMAIN	Impact	**CONTENT**	Corresponds to the proficiency level a learner is working with

Option 1: Select ways you organized your ideas:	**Option 2: How did you organize your ideas?**
☐ I grouped similar ideas together ☐ I organized my ideas around importance ☐ Cause and effect ☐ Chronological (in some kind of numerical order: First, second, third; Beginning to end…) ☐ Compare and contrast ☑ Description ☐ Problem and solution ☐ Pros and cons ☐ Sequential ☐ Storytelling ☐ Other:____________	
Option 1: Select which descriptive details you included:	**Option 2: What descriptive details did you include?**
Adverbs ☐ How (*slowly, quickly…*) ☐ Where (*here, outside, below…*) ☐ When (*yesterday, now, last year…*) ☐ How much (*almost, just, very…*) ☐ How often (*always, never, sometimes…*) ☐ Contrast (*but…*) Descriptions ☑ Feelings/Emotions ☑ Adjectives ☐ Imagery (visually descriptive or figurative language) ☐ Metaphors (a word or phrase that takes on the meaning of something else) ☐ Analogies (comparison of two things to help explain an idea) ☐ Examples (*for example, like, such as…)* ☐ Prepositional phrases (*from, in, of, with/without…*) ☐ Reasons (*because…*) Setting ☐ Weather and Seasons ☐ Locations Timing ☐ Months/Days of the week ☐ Time of day	

<table>
<tr><td colspan="2">How did you maintain the attention of your audience?

I described myself and my feelings.</td></tr>
<tr><td>Option 1: Describe how you presented your ideas in a novel or imaginative manner to show originality today:

How I look. What I do. How I am. I did 3 ways of descriptions.</td><td>Option 2: How might you present your ideas in a novel or imaginative manner to show originality?</td></tr>
<tr><td colspan="2">Evaluate how you think you performed in Impact today:
☐ Beginning: I can present my ideas, but do not maintain my audience's attention.
☑ Developing: I can present my ideas in a way that, at times, captures and maintains the attention of my audience by using organization, descriptive details, and/or originality.
☐ Meeting: I can present my ideas in a way that captures and maintains the attention of my audience by using organization, descriptive details, and/or originality.
☐ Exceeding: I can present my ideas in a way that captures and maintains the attention of my audience by using organization, descriptive details, and originality.</td></tr>
<tr><td colspan="2">Think about your own experience and what you have done to improve in Impact. What advice would you give other learners to help them develop impact?

Remember to put more different things in to make it interesting.</td></tr>
</table>

Learner directions: Use the GROW guiding questions for the level that best matches your performance. Reflect on the questions, then make changes to your work to reach the next level of performance.

GROW GUIDING QUESTIONS:

EXCEEDING	MEETING	DEVELOPING	BEGINNING
• What would happen if you took or added another perspective? • What might you add or adjust to help your audience relate to your ideas? • Is there a different way to share your ideas that would be more intriguing or evoke a reaction from your audience? • How might your audience be compelled to feel or act as a result of your presentation?	• How might you organize your ideas differently to maintain the attention of your audience? • What additional descriptive details might you add to maintain the attention of your audience? • How could you add originality by presenting your ideas in a novel, new, or imaginative manner? • What might make someone remember your presentation? • How could your presentation elicit the desired effects in your audience?	• How might you organize your ideas differently to maintain the attention of your audience? • What organizational structure (*cause/effect, chronological, compare/contrast, description, problem and solution, pros/cons, sequential, or storytelling*) might help you organize your ideas more effectively? • What additional descriptive details might you add to maintain the attention of your audience? • How could you add originality by presenting your ideas in a novel, new, or imaginative manner?	• What organizational structure (*cause/effect, chronological, compare/contrast, description, problem and solution, pros/cons, sequential, or storytelling*) might help you organize your ideas more effectively? • How might you organize your ideas by grouping similar ideas together? • What other descriptive details might you add to maintain the attention of your audience?

Example of what a learner engaged in this process might think and rewrite based on clarifying expectations. This example shows how the learner went from brainstorming ideas to writing them in a text.

Learner's thinking:

I have some details. How can I organize my writing? I'll take the ideas on the inside and match them to what people see and stereotypes they may have of me. Then I'll put the sentences together using phrases like "people think" and "really."

Matching descriptions from the inside of the flipchart to the outside of the flipchart:

OUTSIDE

~~I red hair.~~
~~(I am different.)~~
I like my red hair.

I am sometimes worry.
~~I not smile.~~
~~(I am unfriendly.)~~

I am friend.
I helps brothers.

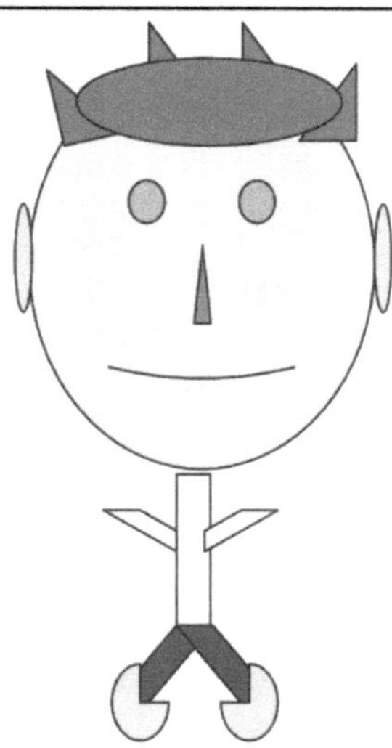

I am strong.
I am athlete.

~~I small short.~~
~~(I am weak.)~~

~~I have shoes nice~~
~~(I am rich.)~~

INSIDE

I athlete.	*I like my hair.*
I am strong.	*I student good.*
I am friend.	*I helps brothers.*
I am some worry.	

Note: Adapted from Sherrow (2018).

Rewrite:

I red hair, but I like my red hair.
I small short. People think I am weak. Not good on team. I am athlete. I am strong.
I not always smile. I am sometimes worry. Really I am friend. I helps brothers.

FOSTERING ORIGINALITY

<table>
<tr><td colspan="4">Domain: Impact
Focus: <u>Understanding</u> how originality maintains the audience's attention</td></tr>
<tr><th>Learner outcomes</th><th>Time</th><th>Materials</th><th>Prep</th></tr>
<tr><td>I can understand Impact by identifying originality in a text.</td><td>• Prep time: 10 minutes
• Implementation time: 30 minutes
• Debrief time: 5 minutes</td><td>• Written text in the target language (Optional: include a video or audio version)
• List of the ways originality can be featured in a text (in base language or target language)
• Paper/pencil or digital writing tools</td><td>• Find a text that features originality in multiple ways.
• Prepare a list of the ways originality can be featured in a text (see example).</td></tr>
<tr><td colspan="4">Instructions
1. (PURPOSE) Tell learners that they will be the audience so that they can feel how originality impacts them by capturing and maintaining their interest.
2. (SET UP) Read the selected text out loud, or play an audio recording/video that reads the selected text out loud for learners. Ask learners to listen and observe how the selected text impacts them.
3. Pass out or display the examples of originality (see example) and a copy of the selected text.
4. (GUIDANCE) Reread the first line(s) together with learners. As a class, identify one example of originality in the text. Have the learners write it down on a piece of paper or a digital device.
5. (ENGAGEMENT) Instruct learners to listen to the next few lines as you reread them outloud. Together, note any examples of originality and write them down.
6. Learners will then continue to re-read the text to find examples of originality and write them down.
7. (GUIDANCE) You may want to interrupt to point out or give examples to illustrate specific literary devices with which the learners may not be as familiar.
8. (DEBRIEF) Learners could share their favorite findings.
9. (ENGAGEMENT) Ask learners to add to the selected text or write their own version of the text, incorporating some of the examples of originality found in the selected text.
10. (ENGAGEMENT) Ask learners to share their writings in small groups. When sharing, ask learners to identify what examples of originality they hear.
11. Ask learners to reflect on:
a. What did you learn about originality?
b. How might you apply what you learned to future work when completing a performance task?</td></tr>
<tr><td colspan="2">Alternatives
Learners could be divided into groups to look for specific examples of originality. As they listen to the text and hear a question, the group assigned to questions could stand. As the text continues and there is an example of a metaphor, the metaphor group stands.
The educator may want to stop the audio and discuss the various literary devices when they first appear and are identified.</td><td colspan="2">Differentiation
Learners could be given only a portion of the text or a small number of examples of originality.
Learners could work in pairs or small groups to add to the selected text or write their own version of the text, incorporating some of the literary devices found in the selected text.</td></tr>
</table>

EXAMPLE

Learners were given three poems and a list of examples of originality that might be found in the texts. Learners highlighted and identified examples of originality in the poems. Then, learners wrote their own poem, incorporating examples of originality.

Examples of originality found in texts

- word play
- rhymes
- alliteration
- rich descriptions
- multiple example, ideas, or solutions
- connections to some things you know well
- descriptions that evoke feelings
- questions
- unexpected ideas
- ideas presented in a novel and imaginative manner
- metaphors, similes, personification
- others...

Learner work:

Example of how a learner underlined and identified, in bold, examples of originality in the poems.

SUMMER

We race our bikes to the lake. — *connections to some things you know well*
Jump in making ripples that carry us through
to hot nights with ice cream melting, — *rich descriptions*
fireflies and butterflies emerging,
Until we come dripping from the water — *descriptions that evoke feelings*
refreshed and exhausted. — *ideas presented in a novel and imaginative manner*

What now? — *question*

SPRING

Blooming tulips, holding hands, chirping birds, — *multiple examples, ideas or solutions*
Spring has sprung and the Jack-in the-box
is out of the box.

AUTUMN

As the leaves leave the trees and — *word play*
the sun peers through the branches, — *personification*
the shadows become arms that will — *unexpected ideas, personification*
embrace me as Fall falls upon the earth. — *word play*
Autumn oughta be awesome! — *alliteration*

WINTER

Your Turn!

Winter poem written by the learner that includes examples of orginality.

WINTER	
Winter withers	**alliteration**
grass, trees, plants	**multiple examples**
Cold calls out	**alliteration, personification**
frostbite, ice, stalled car batteries	**multiple examples, novel and imaginative**
Wind weaves	**alliteration**
blizzards, downed power lines, wind chill	**multiple examples, familiar**
but...	
Snow swells	**alliteration**
sledding hills, hot cocoa, hope of snow days	**multiple examples, evoke feelings**

GRAPHIC ORGANIZER MATCH

Domain: Impact

Focus: Understanding how organization improves Impact

Learner outcomes	Time	Materials	Prep
I can understand how organization improves my Impact by identifying which organizational structure best communicates a message.	• Prep time: 10 minutes • Implementation time: 30 minutes • Debrief time: 5 minutes	• List of tasks (in target language or base language) that elicit different organization structures • List and examples of graphic organizers (in target language, base language, or visual representations) for a variety of texts	• Prepare a list of performance tasks. • Prepare a list and examples of graphic organizers that match the anticipated performance of the tasks.

Instructions

1. (PURPOSE) Tell learners that they will see visual representations of how a text can be organized. They will look at some performance tasks and imagine how they could be completed. Then they will match the performance tasks to the appropriate graphic organizer that best communicates the message.
2. (SET UP) Present some graphic organizers and ask learners what type of information they would anticipate being represented by a few of the organizers.
3. Give learners one performance task as an example (*Create a social media post that describes what you do to get ready for class each morning*). Ask learners to discuss how they might complete that task (*I would list the things I do first, second... until I am ready*).
4. Ask learners to match the performance task to a graphic organizer representation (example: timeline). Discuss how and why the chosen graphic organizer matches (example – *It is a list of things that happen one after another in a span of time*).
5. Divide the learners into groups of 3-5 learners each.
6. (ENGAGEMENT) Instruct learners to read each of the performance tasks, think about how they would perform that performance task, and match the performance to a graphic organizer.
7. (DEBRIEF) Learners could share their matches and discuss additional ways to organize a performance task.
8. Ask learners to reflect on:
    a. What did you notice about how texts can be organized?
    b. How might you apply what you learned to your future work when completing a performance task?

Alternatives	Differentiation
Learners could be given examples of performances, instead of the performance tasks to elicit them, and match those performances to graphic organizers.	Educators could limit the number of graphic organizers given to learners. Learners could map out ideas for each performance task by adding keywords and/or ideas to one, or more, graphic organizers. Learners could write their own tasks to fit various graphic organizers and see if other learners agree.

EXAMPLE

Learners match the performance tasks (1-5) with a graphic organizer (A-E) that shows how a performance could be organized.

Performance tasks:

1. Describe to an exchange student what is similar and different in the cultures of England and Canada.
2. Create a social media post that describes what you do to get ready for class each morning.
3. Describe the character's ancestry to your small group in class.
4. Present to the class what led to the colonization of South Africa and how that has impacted the inhabitants.
5. Tell a friend how to make dumplings.

Graphic organizers:

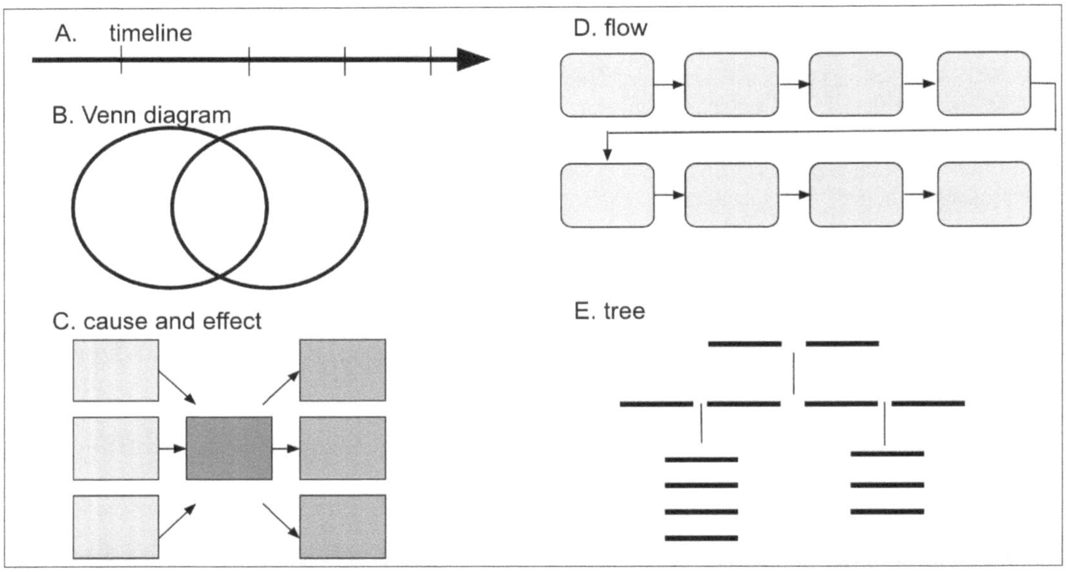

Note: From Customizable Graphic Organizers Templates, by the Center for Advanced Research on Language Acquisition (CARLA), 2018, (https://carla.umn.edu/cobaltt/modules/strategies/gorganizers/EDITABLE.HTML). Copyright 2023 by Regents of the University of Minnesota. Adapted with permission. More organizers found at: https://carla.umn.edu/cobaltt/modules/strategies/gorganizers/EDITABLE.HTML

Learner work:

Example of how one learner matched the performance tasks with the appropriate graphic organizer:

1. *B*
2. *A*
3. *E*
4. *C*
5. *D*

BRAINSTORM BUILDING

Domain: Impact **Focus:** <u>Developing</u> Impact by brainstorming details *Note:* This learning experience can be replicated in multiple performance domains.			
Learner outcomes	**Time**	**Materials**	**Prep**
I can develop Impact to maintain my audience's attention by: • brainstorming various ways to add details. • describing one idea in multiple ways.	• Prep time: 5-15 minutes • Implementation time: 20 minutes • Debrief time: 5 minutes	• Sentence starters • Ideas for descriptive details to add (displayed or copied for each learner)	• Prepare sentence starters. • Prepare lists of possible descriptive details.

Instructions

1. (PURPOSE) Tell learners that they will brainstorm descriptive details to add impact to a sentence.
2. (SET UP) Give learners an example sentence starter (*I feel successful…*). Show learners possible ways to add descriptive details (*because…, when…,*). See example for a list of possible descriptive details.
3. (ENGAGEMENT) As a class, brainstorm ideas of how learners might add to the sentence (see examples in the chart below).
4. Divide learners into groups of 3-5 learners each.
5. Display or hand out a sentence starter and ideas for descriptive details (see example of the sentence starter below).
6. (ENGAGEMENT) Learners brainstorm in their groups and write how they might add descriptive details to complete the sentence starter.
7. Optional (GUIDANCE) Learners can see the variety of details they are using if they color-code their details to correspond with the chart.
8. (DEBRIEF) Learners could share their ideas with the class or between groups.
9. Ask learners to reflect on:
    a. What did you notice about adding details to the sentence starter?
    b. How might you apply what you learned to your future work when completing a performance task?

Alternatives	**Differentiation**
Learners can use the same descriptive details over and over for various performance tasks, and add more descriptive details when they are ready. Learners could do this individually instead of in groups, then share in small groups.	Learners could add more categories of ideas for descriptive details (*where: in school, at home, at work,…*). Learners could add ideas to the existing groups of descriptive details (*because it's: rewarding, fun, …*).

EXAMPLE:

Learners complete this sentence starter using the descriptive details handout below:

I help others ______________________________.

Descriptive details handout

Because it's...

- important
- helpful
- nice
- easy
- difficult
- interesting

When...

Other ideas:

- but...
- with/without...
- for...
- I have...
- I need...
- I can...

When I feel...

In...

Learner work:

Additions from the chart above are underlined.

I help others in the summer because I have time.
I help others when I feel sad.

LEVEL UP

Domain: Impact

Focus: Developing Impact by creating progressions

Note: This learning experience can be replicated in multiple performance domains.

Learner outcomes	Time	Materials	Prep
I can develop Impact by building progressions of Impact to "level up."	• Prep time: 5 minutes • Implementation time: 30 minutes • Debrief time: 5 minutes	• PDIs for Impact to display • Presentational performance task • Paper/pencil or digital writing tools for each learner	• Prepare to display PDIs. • Have a performance task ready for learners to write or speak about.

Instructions

1. (PURPOSE) Tell learners that they will develop their Impact by working with a group to write/say an example performance at each level (*Beginning, Developing, Meeting,* and *Exceeding*).
2. (SET UP) Display and remind learners of the targeted PDIs for Impact.
3. Divide learners into groups of 3-5 learners each and ask them to take out paper/pencil or digital writing tools.
4. Give learners an example presentational task.
5. Optional (GUIDANCE) Provide or do an example together as a whole class, writing one performance level together.
6. (ENGAGEMENT) Release the lesson to have learners work in groups to write one example of each level (*Beginning, Developing, Meeting,* and *Exceeding*) using the given task.
7. (GUIDANCE) Remind learners to look at the PDIs to be sure of what level they are aiming for with each example.
8. (DEBRIEF) Learners share their reflections and improvements with a partner, another group, or the class.
9. Ask learners to reflect on:
    a. What did you notice about each example as you progressed through the performance levels of Impact?
    b. How might you apply what you learned to your future work when completing a performance task?

Alternatives

Learners could do this individually instead of in groups,then share in small groups.

Learners could take turns writing an example for each level (*Beginning, Developing, Meeting, Exceeding*). Groups of students could write a presentational example for each PDI, or groups could be assigned to write a presentational example for one assigned PDI.

One group could share their "leveled up" examples with another group to see if they identify what level each example is meant to be.

Differentiation

After writing examples for each level about one task together as a class and another in groups, learners could each individually write an example for one level, perhaps on a new task, and then share it out with their group. The group can decide which performance level it best matches.

Learners could evaluate example texts that have already been created as *Beginning, Developing, Meeting,* or *Exceeding.*

EXAMPLE

Target performance level: **Meeting**
Context: familiar, informal, straight-forward
Content: familiar, concrete,researched

Task: Write a blog post on how music can act as protest.

Learner instructions: Based on the PDIs, write an example of each level of performance.

PDIs displayed:

TARGET PERFORMANCE LEVEL: MEETING				
	EXCEEDING	**MEETING**	**DEVELOPING**	**BEGINNING**
Performance Domain Indicators	I can present my ideas in a way that captures and maintains the attention of my audience by using organization, descriptive details, and originality.	I can present my ideas in a way that captures and maintains the attention of my audience by using organization, descriptive details, and/or originality.	I can present my ideas in a way that, at times, captures and maintains the attention of my audience by using organization, descriptive details, and/or originality.	I can present my ideas, but do not maintain my audience's attention.

Learner work:

Learners were given the performance task. As a class, they brainstormed a written example for the *Beginning* level.

BEGINNING

Midnight Oil uses songs to work for good. Midnight Oil, from Australia, is a band. They advocated for rights of Indigenous People and climate protection.

In small groups, learners worked together to write "leveled up" examples for *Developing, Meeting,* and *Exceeding.*

EXCEEDING

Can a song make a difference?

Songs from Midnight Oil, a band from Australia whose songs bring attention to the rights of Indigenous People and climate protection. Their songs became famous for advocating giving native Australian lands back to the Pintupi. Midnight Oil recorded an album. The Uluru rock was given back to the local Pitjantjatjara people. These songs remind us that there are still many sites to be given back to the Indiginous People in Australia and around the world.

MEETING

Songs from Midnight Oil. They are a band from Australia whose songs bring attention to the rights of Indigenous People and climate protection. Their songs advocated for giving native Australian lands back to the Pintupi.

DEVELOPING

Midnight Oil, from Australia, is a band whose songs bring attention to the rights of Indigenous People and climate protecion. They advocated for things like giving land back.

Note: In this example the longest text is in fact the *Exceeding*, but that will not always be the case.

IMPACT CLOUD

<table>
<tr><td colspan="4">Domain: Impact
Focus: <u>Developing</u> Impact by adding descriptive details</td></tr>
<tr><th>Learner outcomes</th><th>Time</th><th>Materials</th><th>Prep</th></tr>
<tr>
<td>I can develop Impact by
• highlighting the descriptive details I have included.
• adding more descriptive details to elaborate on my ideas.</td>
<td>• Prep time: 5 minutes
• Implementation time: 20 minutes
• Debrief time: 5 minutes</td>
<td>• Presentational task
• Learners' written drafts in target language
• Impact Cloud graphic (in target language)
• Highlighters/pens/ markers in the colors of the Impact Cloud (paper and pens, or digital tools)</td>
<td>• Make copies or display the Impact Cloud. graphic for all learners.
• Be sure learners can access their drafts.</td>
</tr>
<tr><td colspan="4">Instructions
1. (PURPOSE) Tell learners that they will improve their writing by adding more descriptive details to elaborate on their ideas and maintain the attention of their audience.
2. (SET UP) Have learners take out a draft of target language writing that they have already begun and highlighters/ pens/markers.
3. Show learners the Impact Cloud (see example). Explain to learners that they will be highlighting the descriptive details they used in their draft. If they have a rich rainbow of colors, they have achieved a variety of descriptive details. If they do not have a lot of colors or often repeat the same colors, they will have time to add more descriptive details to achieve a "rainbow effect" of descriptive details in their writing.
4. (GUIDANCE) Instruct learners to look at the "frequency" line from the Impact Cloud in purple (see example below).
5. Ask learners how and where they might add a descriptive detail about frequency in their writing. Give them an example: I swim <u>every day</u>.
6. Instruct learners to highlight, in purple, every example of frequency in their draft. If they don't have any examples of frequency, they can add details about frequency to their draft and then highlight it.
7. (ENGAGEMENT) Learners look at each part of the Impact Cloud for specific types of details, then find and highlight them using the corresponding color(s) in their writing drafts.
8. Encourage learners to add additional descriptive details and highlight them, so that they have an array of colors in their final highlighted draft.
9. (DEBRIEF) Learners could show their colorful drafts to each other.
10. Ask learners to reflect on:
a. What did you learn about adding descriptive details? How might descriptive details maintain the attention of your audience?
b. How might you apply what you learned to your future work when completing a performance task?</td></tr>
<tr><td colspan="2">Alternatives
The educator could have an example text to which all learners could add descriptive details. Divide learners into small groups with 2-3 learners each. Each group has a copy of the example text. Learner groups can rotate to different stations around the classroom. Each station features one of the spokes on the Impact Cloud. Learners discuss the descriptive details featured at that station and add that descriptive detail to their joint writing. Suggestions could be posted at each station to support learners to add specific examples of details (when: in the summer, when I am hungry,...). At the end, although all groups began with the same example text, each finalized text will be different and can be shared with all learners.</td>
<td colspan="2">Differentiation
Learners could first brainstorm ways to add each type of descriptive detail and post these in the Impact Cloud colors at designated stations around the room.
Learners could ask each other questions based on the Impact Cloud (where, when, why, with whom...) and see if their partner has the answers in their writing.</td></tr>
</table>

EXAMPLE

Target performance level: **Meeting**
Context: familiar, informal, predictable
Content: familiar, everyday

Task: Introduce yourself to your classmates through a digital post. You and your classmates will read each others' posts in order to determine who might make good partners.

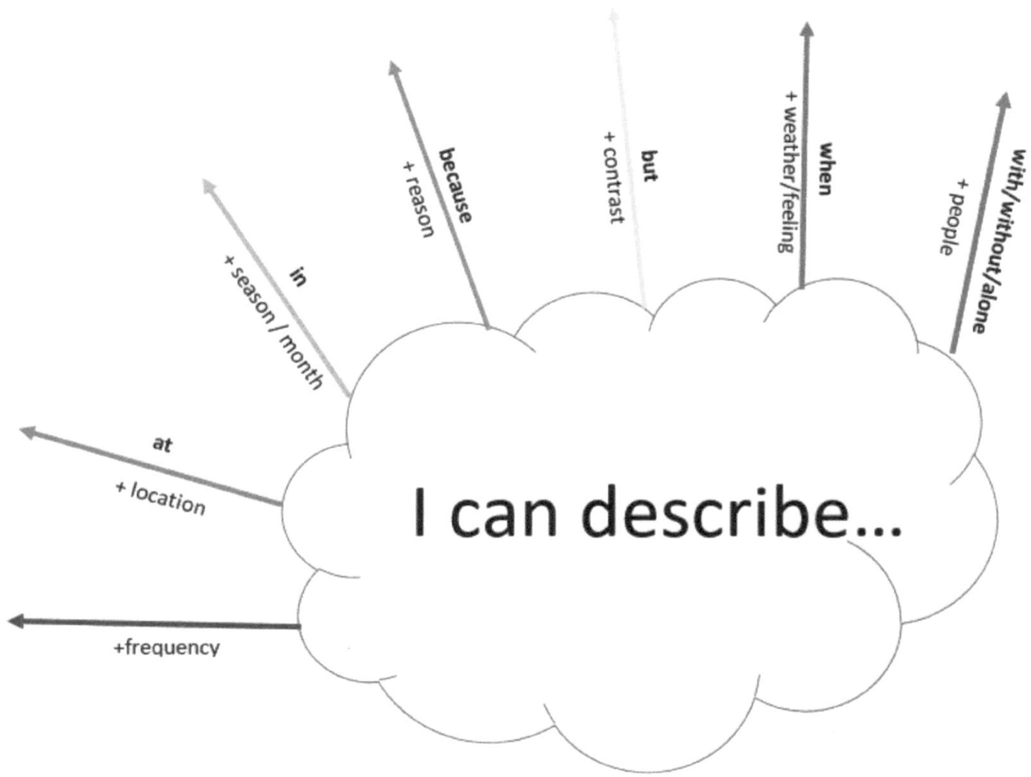

Learner work:

Example of what a finished piece of learner's work might look like:

Hello, my name is Shriya. I like read with family. I like videogames with friends. In summer. I don't I like sometimes music. Impatient when sick.

Note: From Wayzata Public Schools, Minnesota (2017). Reprinted with permission.

LOOK AGAIN... AND AGAIN

Domain: Impact

Focus: Developing Impact by elaborating with descriptive details

Learner outcomes	Time	Materials	Prep
I can develop Impact by: • elaborating on my original ideas. • adding additional descriptive details that maintain the attention of my audience. • looking at something multiple times to see more possibilities.	• Prep time: 15 minutes • Implementation time: 15 minutes • Debrief time: 5 minutes	• A photo for each learner (choose public domain or select photos that connect to the unit theme, elicit interest, and present multiple possibilities) • A graphic organizer for each learner (see below)	• Find photos. • Make a copy of the graphic organizer for each learner.

Instructions

1. (PURPOSE) Tell learners that they will elaborate on their ideas to develop a narrative about a photo. This will maintain the attention of their audience.
2. (SET UP) Hand out a photo and a graphic organizer to each learner.
3. (ENGAGEMENT) Instruct learners to write down their first impressions of what is happening in the photo.
4. Instruct learners to "look again" to look deeply into the photo and elaborate on their ideas to add more descriptive details.
5. Instruct learners to look yet again ("look again and again"), group ideas, add more descriptive details, and clarify to polish up the text.
6. (DEBRIEF) Learners could share their photos and texts with each other.
7. Ask learners to reflect on:
    a. What did you learn about elaborating and adding descriptive details?
    b. How might you apply what you learned to your future work when completing a performance task?

Alternatives	Differentiation
The instructions show the educator guiding the learners step-by-step. Learners could be allowed more choice and freedom to move through the steps at their own pace. Learners could be placed into groups of three learners each and then pass their photo and organizer to the second learner in their group, who will complete the *Look again* part. The third learner in the group will complete the *Look again and again* part. Although learners are doing each step individually, together they would create 3 different narratives about three different photos.	Learners could be given a photo and guided through the writing by only being shown a portion of the photo at a time. Learners write only about what they see in the first portion of the photo. Then another section is uncovered and learners write about that. Continue until the complete photo can be seen at the end. Learners could use more than one, or a series of, photos and tell a longer story.

EXAMPLE

Graphic organizer provided to learners in the target language:

First impressions	**Look again** Add more details	**Look again and again** Group ideas, add more details, and clarify

Note: From [People by a sea landscape], by R. Lach, 2023, Pexels (https://www.pexels.com/photo/sea-landscape-man-person-9626362/)

Learner work:

Example of how a learner's graphic organizer might look when finished:

First impressions	**Look again** Add more details	**Look again and again** Group ideas, add more details, and clarify
Taylor draws natures. *Taylor is in art class.* *Students all draw naturues.*	*Tayor draws waters of nature.* *It is first period art class.* *Students all draw nature. They draw beautiful nature. One photos river.* *It is a river and waves.*	*SPEAK OUT for NATURE* *It is first period art class.* *Students go to the river. Students all draw nature.* *Taylor draws waters of nature. It is a poster. It is beautiful. The poster says "Keep Nature Beautiful!"*

YOUR TURN

LEARNING TARGET CHECK:	
I can	☐ select learning experiences that support learners' growth with Impact.

Complete the chart by identifying specific learning experiences from the *Learning Experiences to Facilitate Learner Growth* section (p. 291-310) that you could use in an upcoming unit to help learners *understand* or *develop* Impact. Note any materials or prep needed to implement the learning experience in your upcoming unit. Consider any alternatives or differentiation that would better align the learning experience to your unit, the targeted level of performance, and/or your learners.

UNIT:			
PERFORMANCE DOMAIN: IMPACT			
Learning experience	**What type of learning experience is it?** (Circle one)	**Materials/Prep**	**Alternatives/ Differentiation**
	Understanding/ Developing		
	Understanding/ Developing		
	Understanding/ Developing		

Learners' Self-Assessments

Self-assessment provides an opportunity for learners to reflect on their performance, set goals, and ultimately to own their learning. This section features three ways learners can self-assess their work: *Make It Visible, Glow and Grow Self-Assessment*, and *Guided Self-Assessments*. Each is educator-designed but learner-driven. That is, the self-assessment is designed by the educator around the PDIs but it is the learner who must reflect on their performance to complete it. The same self-assessments are used in each performance domain chapter to build consistency for learners. Each can be used for learner self-assessment after a formative or summative task. Educators might select self-assessments that have more scaffolding, such as the *Guided Self-Assessment* and *Make It Visible*, after formative tasks where learners may need more support to self-assess their performance, such as the beginning of a unit or a course. The *Glow and Grow Self-Assessment*, which is more open-ended, can be used when learners feel more comfortable reflecting on the PDIs and summarizing their work, such as after formative tasks that occur at the end of the unit or after a summative task. Overall, educators can make adjustments to any of these self-assessments and use them with intentionality based on their learners, their pacing within a unit or course, and the performance task.

Make It Visible

This self-assessment provides an opportunity for learners to visibly see their Impact in a given formative or summative task. Learners might circle, highlight, color-code, or note the ways in which they used language in a given presentational performance (see Figure 8.1). Or learners can self-assess by marking yes/no and providing evidence (see Table 8.8 and Figure 8.2). Educators can provide opportunities for revisions and/or additions for learners who may find they are not yet *Meeting* expectations, so learners have opportunities for language growth.

The learner samples in this section demonstrate how each self-assessment can be used at one performance level. However, these self-assessments can be used at any level: Novice, Intermediate, or Advanced.

Figure 8.1

Presentational Self-Assessment #1 Using the "Make It Visible" Approach

Directions: Read over your presentational work and mark it accordingly:

- Organization: Put **(**parentheses**)** around similar ideas that you grouped together
- Details: Underline details (setting, timing, feelings, adverbs, prepositional phrases, reasons, contrast)
- Originality: Highlight novel or imaginative ways you presented your ideas

Example of how the learner, performing within the Novice level, completes this self-assessment:

> Hey! My name is Pari. I 12 years old. I am Persian.
>
> Ingrid is sports. **(**Ingrid like to dance. I am not to dance.**)** I am to swim.
>
> **(**I is shy. Ingrid is shy.**)** I is play sports.
>
> I am to read. Ingrid like to dance.
>
> I am to draw. Ingrid like to dance. Well, see ya later!

Note: In this example, the learner only demonstrates evidence of organization in **(**parentheses**)**.

Table 8.8

Presentational Self-Assessment #2 Using the "Make It Visible" Approach

Impact Reflection Guide How do I organize my work?			
	YES	**NO**	**COMMENTS/EXAMPLES**
Cause/Effect			
Chronological			
Compare/Contrast			
Description			
Problem and Solution			
Pros/Cons			
Sequential			
Storytelling			

Figure 8.2

Example of a Completed Presentational Self-Assessment Using the "Make It Visible" Approach

Directions: Read over your presentational performance. Complete the *Impact Reflection Guide* and list examples where the audience can see how you organized your performance.

Honorable Mayor Wilson,

Help! My name is Kai Meyer. I live in Elmdale now. I like to live in Elmdale We have strong engaged for community here. Since 3 years, Elmdale won the "Best city in the USA". We try to win that again and we could. We could to do more of to clean up and beautify our city. Maybe have like the BUGA garden show in Germany. Different cities host and make big gardens. And plant trees. Like big plant show at the fair.

A lot in Elmdale is full of garbage. When I run on hiking trailsl see a lot of garbage. Nature reserves, like Forest Park, have more garbage. It is not pretty. I remember you to since 3 years. It would be great if mentality to our city. Run people need clean trails. They are impacted.

Here are things do. We could the volunteers clean up the parks. This would also help the people in the city do it. Other volunteers could the large places. -The city could have event. The event would be "Consciousness about Garbage in Plymouth"

We could say, plant more trees in the niehgborhoods. This would give back the trees we take for construction. Maybe be a tree hugger? Plants and gardens too but for now trees. When we plant more trees, this make our community a better place, if we plant more trees. Plant now! Act now!

Sincerely,
Kai Meyer

Example of how the learner, performing within the Intermediate level, completes this self-assessment:

Impact Reflection Guide

How do I organize my work?

	YES	NO	COMMENTS/EXAMPLES
Cause/Effect	X		• *...have more garbage. It is not pretty.* • *This would give back the trees we take for construction.* • *When we plant more trees, this make our community a better place.*
Chronological		X	
Compare/Contrast	X		• *BUGA...Like big plant show at the fair.*
Description	X		• *strong engaged for community* • *big gardens* • *clean trails* • *Best city in the USA*
Problem and Solution	X		• *Solution: We could to do more of to clean up and beautify our city. Maybe have like the BUNGA garden show in Germany.* • *Problem: A lot in Elmdale is full of garbage.* • *Solution: We could the volunteers clean up the parks. The city could have event.* • *Solution: Plant now! Act now!*
Pros/Cons		X	
Sequential		X	
Storytelling		X	

GLOW and GROW Self Assessment

Using the *Meeting* Performance Domain Indicator, learners can self-assess their work on a one-point rubric after a formative or summative task. In Table 8.9, learners would complete the *Where I GLOW (What are my strengths?)* and *How I can GROW (What can I do to improve?)* sections by citing evidence from their own presentational performance for each performance domain. The *GLOW/GROW Ideas* are given as prompts so that learners are reminded of what to look for or work toward.

Table 8.9
GLOW and GROW Self-Assessment

Impact Target performance level: **Meeting**		
The context and content corresponds to the proficiency level a learner is working within.	NOVICE	Context: familiar, informal, formal, predictable Content: familiar, everyday
	INTERMEDIATE	Context: familiar, informal, formal, straight-forward Content: familiar, concrete, at times researched
	ADVANCED	Context: familiar, unfamiliar, informal, formal, complex Content: familiar, academic, social, professional, concrete, abstract

Instructions: Complete the following reflection by writing where you GLOW and where you can GROW in each area. Make sure to include evidence from your work to support your reasoning.		
Where I GLOW: What are my strengths?	**Performance Domain Indicator**	**How can I GROW What can I do to improve?**
	I can present my ideas in a way that captures and maintains the attention of my audience by using organization, descriptive details, and/or originality.	

GLOW IDEAS	**GROW IDEAS**
How did you capture and maintain the attention of your audience: • through organization (*grouping similar ideas together, using an organizational structure, etc.*)? • by adding descriptive details to illustrate your ideas? • by presenting your ideas in a novel or imaginative manner to show originality?	• How might you organize your ideas differently to maintain the attention of your audience? • What additional descriptive details might you add to maintain the attention of your audience? • How could you add originality by presenting your ideas in a novel, new, or imaginative manner? • What might make someone remember your presentation? • How could your presentation elicit the desired effects in your audience?

Guided Self-Assessments

This self-assessment includes guiding questions to help learners evaluate their own performance after a formative or summative task (see Table 8.10). Options are included to help educators personalize the self-assessment for their learners, or learners can self-select which options to answer.

Table 8.10

Presentational Guided Self-Assessment

<table>
<tr><td>TARGET PERFORMANCE LEVEL</td><td>Meeting</td><td>CONTEXT</td><td>Corresponds to the proficiency level a learner is working with</td></tr>
<tr><td>PERFORMANCE DOMAIN</td><td>Impact</td><td>CONTENT</td><td>Corresponds to the proficiency level a learner is working with</td></tr>
<tr><td colspan="2">Option 1: Select ways you organized your ideas:
☐ I grouped similar ideas together
☐ I organized my ideas around importance
☐ Cause and effect
☐ Chronological (in some kind of numerical order: First, second, third; Beginning to end…)
☐ Compare and contrast
☐ Description
☐ Problem and solution
☐ Pros and cons
☐ Sequential
☐ Storytelling
☐ Other: ____________</td><td colspan="2">Option 2: How did you organize your ideas?</td></tr>
<tr><td colspan="2">Option 1: Select which descriptive details you included:
Adverbs
☐ How (slowly, quickly…)
☐ Where (here, outside, below…)
☐ When (yesterday, now, last year…)
☐ How much (almost, just, very…)
☐ How often (always, never, sometimes…)
☐ Contrast (but…)
Descriptions
☐ Feelings/Emotions
☐ Adjectives
☐ Imagery (visually descriptive or figurative language)
☐ Metaphors (a word or phrase that takes on the meaning of something else)
☐ Analogies (comparison of two things to help explain an idea)
☐ Examples (for example, like, such as…)
☐ Prepositional phrases (from, in, of, with/without…)
☐ Reasons (because…)
Setting
☐ Weather and Seasons
☐ Locations
Timing
☐ Months/Days of the week
☐ Time of day</td><td colspan="2">Option 2: What descriptive details did you include?</td></tr>
</table>

<table>
<tr><td colspan="2">How did you maintain the attention of your audience?</td></tr>
<tr><td>Option 1: Describe how you presented your ideas in a novel or imaginative manner to show originality today:</td><td>Option 2: How might you present your ideas in a novel or imaginative manner to show originality?</td></tr>
<tr><td colspan="2">Evaluate how you think you performed in the your use of Impact today:
☐ Beginning: I can present my ideas, but do not maintain my audience's attention.
☐ Developing: I can present my ideas in a way that, at times, captures and maintains the attention of my audience by using organization, descriptive details, and/or originality.
☐ Meeting: I can present my ideas in a way that captures and maintains the attention of my audience by using organization, descriptive details, and/or originality.
☐ Exceeding: I can present my ideas in a way that captures and maintains the attention of my audience by using organization, descriptive details, and originality.</td></tr>
<tr><td colspan="2">Think about your own experience and what you have done to improve in Impact. What advice would you give other learners to help them develop Impact?</td></tr>
</table>

YOUR TURN

LEARNING TARGET CHECK:	
I can	☐ provide learners with self-assessments to evaluate their work.

Complete the chart by identifying specific self-assessments from the *Learners' Self-Assessments* section (p. 312-317) that could be used in an upcoming unit to help learners evaluate their own work. Next, describe a formative or summative performance task in your upcoming unit that learners could complete and then self-assess using the chosen-self-assessment. Finally, list any additional materials or preparation that might be needed to implement this self-assessment in the *Notes* section of the chart.

UNIT:		
PERFORMANCE DOMAIN: IMPACT		
Learner self-assessments	**Performance task** Formative or summative	**Notes**

Advice From Learners

As a purposeful way for learners to become aware of their own learning, we asked learners to reflect on what worked for them to improve their performance in various performance domains. Sharing advice can build learner metacognitive skills, or awareness of one's own learning, which has been linked to improved learning outcomes (Hattie, 2017). Together learners build a bank of suggestions and advice that they can access when looking to improve in a specific performance domain. This is a way for learners to realize what they have learned about a performance domain, monitor their own understanding of the performance domain, suggest and choose which advice to employ, and evaluate whether particular choices are successful. Here is what some learners said, when asked to share their insights on Impact and give advice.

Novice

- *Make it logical so your audience can follow along.*
- *Use your imagination to give it a kick.*
- *What is going to make your presentational [performance] unique?*
- *Have fun with this part!*
- *Don't put [the audience] to sleep. Keep it interesting and easy to follow.*
- *Use all your tools.*

Intermediate

- *What does your audience care about?*
- *Why are you giving this presentational [performance] to this audience – do they know why? – tell them!*
- *What is going to make this a success with your audience?*
- *Read it to someone and find out what they ask, then put those answers in.*
- *You know the story, they don't – keep it organized so you don't lose them.*
- *Put in enough details to be super interesting, but not so many that it gets boring.*

Advanced

- *Who is listening or reading this and how can you connect to them?*
- *Be sure you find a real audience.*
- *What do you want the audience to do after they read/hear your presentational [performance]?*
- *Think about what you want your audience to feel.*
- *Fire up your audience.*
- *Mark where you want what reaction from your audience (laugh, groan…).*
- *Hook them, lull them, then surprise them!*

References

Adair-Hauck, B., Glisan, E. W., & Troyan, F. J. (2013). *Implementing integrated performance assessment.* ACTFL

Center for Advanced Research on Language Acquisition (CARLA). (2018). *Customizable graphic organizers templates.* Regents of the University of Minnesota. https://carla.umn.edu/cobaltt/modules/strategies/gorganizers/EDITABLE.HTML

Elisondo, R., Rinaudo, M.C., & Donolo, D. (2013). The unexpected and education: Curriculums for creativity. *Creative Education, 4*(12), 11–15. https://doi.org/10.4236/ce.2013.412a2002.

Hattie, J. (2017). *250+ influences on student achievement.* Visible Learning Plus. https://visible-learning.org/wp-content/uploads/2018/03/VLPLUS-252-Influences-Hattie-ranking-DEC-2017.pdf

Lach, R. (2023). *People by a sea landscape* [Photograph]. Pexels. https://www.pexels.com/photo/sea-landscape-man-person-9626362/

Myers, T. (1994-2023). *Using descriptive detail.* The WAC Clearinghouse. https://wac.colostate.edu/repository/resources/writing/guides/.

National Council of State Supervisors for Languages (NCSSFL) – ACTFL. (2017). *NCSSFL-ACTFL Can-Do Statements: Performance Indicators for Language Learners.* ACTFL. https://www.actfl.org/educator-resources/ncssfl-actfl-can-do-statements

Serravallo, J. (2017). *The writing strategies book.* Heinemann.

Sherrow, H. (2018). *Soy yo: Bringing life, purpose, and meaning to your Novice descriptions unit* [Conference session]. ACTFL Convention, New Orleans, LA.

Troyan, F. J., Adair-Hauck, B., & Glisan, E. W. (2023). *The integrated performance assessment: Twenty years and counting.* ACTFL.

Wiggins, G. (1998). *Educative assessment: Designing assessments to inform and improve student performance.* Jossey-Bass.

Wiggins, G. (2012, February 3). On assessing for creativity: Yes you can, and yes you should. *Authentic Education.* http://grantwiggins.wordpress.com/2012/02/03/on-assessing-for-creativity-yes-you-can-and-yes-you-should/

CHAPTER 9 | COMMUNICATION STRATEGIES
Performance Domain

LEARNING TARGETS:	
I can	☐ describe the Communication Strategies performance domain. ☐ describe how Communication Strategies shows up in learners' performance at various levels. ☐ evaluate learner work using the Performance Domain Indicators (PDIs). ☐ give effective feedback based on the Communication Strategies PDIs. ☐ select learning experiences that support learners' growth with Communication Strategies. ☐ provide learners with self-assessments to evaluate their work.

What do we mean by *Communication Strategies*?

Communication Strategies are the ways learners maintain and advance communication in the target language. This happens in all modes of communication, however, the focus for this performance domain is only for the interpersonal performance assessments. This is in part due to the reliance on interlocutors for immediate, spontaneous feedback. When performing interpersonal tasks, learners participate by asking and answering questions, exchanging information, and eventually cooperating in conversations. This performance domain also refers to the variety of ways learners problem solve in order to overcome communication breakdowns. This happens when a learner experiences their own linguistic limitation and/or when there is a gap in understanding with their partner. In both instances, a learner can either modify their language or their message to improve the effectiveness of communication.

How do *Communication Strategies* develop in learner performance?

A learner's use of Communication Strategies depends on their language resources. First, learners may begin by answering, and then later asking simple questions. As they develop more language resources, they exchange information and use appropriate follow–up questions, and then eventually cooperate in conversations. As learners encounter communication breakdowns, they first learn to overcome these by using gestures or facial cues, as well as appeals for help. With greater language resources, learners begin to problem solve in the target language by using similar words, using circumlocution, and eventually paraphrasing and illustrating.

What do *Communication Strategies* look like in learner performance?

The sample learner performances in Table 9.1 illustrate how learners use Communication Strategies. Within the Novice level, learners advance conversation by asking and answering simple questions (*Do you like to...? And you?*). Additionally, when confronted with a gap in understanding, Learner 1 problem-solves by repeating (*Do you like to sing...in group?*) and gestures (*brings arms together to form a circle*). Within the Intermediate level, these learners advance communication through questioning, but they now also use follow-up questions (*When do you practice? Do I have to audition?*). In order to overcome a gap in understanding around the term *audition*, Learner 2 asks for help by repeating a word (*Audition?*) to which Learner 1 clarifies by using a similar word (*try-out*) and then rephrasing (*Sing before the director first?*). Within the Advanced level, learners advance conversation through cooperation [co-operation] (Warren, 2006), meaning learners fully share the responsibility of negotiating meaning; both learners develop topics and initiate topic changes (p. 223). Learner 2 changes the topic from professional singer to community choir (*I think the content has shifted over time too*). Additionally, Learner 1 uses a probing question (*What do you mean?*) to gather more information. As a way to overcome their linguistic limitation, Learner 2 uses circumlocution (*styles of music*) to communicate the term *genres*.

Table 9.1
Sample Learner Performances

NOVICE	INTERMEDIATE	ADVANCED
Task: Talk with your partner to find an activity you both like to do.	**Task:** Persuade your friend to participate in an activity you like to do.	**Task:** Discuss how musical preferences of young people have changed from generation to generation with a friend.
Learner 1: Do you like to dance? **Learner 2:** No. **Learner 1:** Do you like to sing, um… group? **Learner 2: …** **Learner 1:** Do you like to sing… in group? **Learner 2:** Um…repeat? **Learner 1:** Do you like to sing… um, lalala…in group (*brings arms together to form a circle*)? **Learner 2:** Um…yes. I like to sing. In…in group. And you? **Learner 1:** Good. Me also.	**Learner 1:** You like to sing? **Learner 2:** Yes! Well, I am in community choir. **Learner 1:** Really? That sounds fun! When do you practice? **Learner 2:** We practice every Tuesday and Thursday, from 4pm. Do you want to join? **Learner 1:** Yeah. Do I have to audition? **Learner 2:** Audition? **Learner 1:** Um… try-out? Sing before the director first? **Learner 2:** Oh! No, no audition. It's community choir, so anyone can participate. I give you my director's email and you can write him. You should! **Learner 1:** Fantastic!	**Learner 1:** Have you noticed how different our musical preferences are compared to our parents? **Learner 2:** Yeah, the styles of music have really changed. It's interesting how technology and the internet have influenced our musical preferences. With access to streaming and social media, we are exposed to a wider variety of music from all over the world. **Learner 1:** Absolutely! It's so easy to discover new music and explore different genres. We have access to hundreds of songs at our fingertips, which definitely influences our musical preferences. **Learner 2:** Totally. Digital access makes it so much easier to discover new music. But I think the content has shifted over time too. **Learner 1:** What do you mean? **Learner 2:** Like, our parents had a lot of songs related to politics and social issues, ya know? We have songs about that too, but also we have a lot of songs about personal experiences and relationships. **Learner 1:** True. I think our generation really values individuality, so our music reflects that. I wonder what future music will be like? **Learner 2:** I can only imagine! With technology and new artists, who knows what kind of music we'll be listening to!

The Performance Domain Indicators and Descriptions

The following section presents the Performance Domain Indicators (PDIs) for Communication Strategies by performance level: Novice (Table 9.2), Intermediate (Table 9.3), and Advanced (Table 9.4). The Communication Strategies PDIs are primarily a combination of language from both the *NCSSFL-ACTFL Can-Do Statements: Performance Indicators for Language Learners* (NCSSFL-ACTFL, 2017) and the *ACTFL Proficiency Guidelines* (ACTFL, 2012b). The PDIs for this performance domain are applied to the interpersonal mode of communication. In order to illustrate Communication Strategies, the PDIs are accompanied by a learner task and sample learner responses. In addition, the PDIs are accompanied by a description that is meant to deepen our understanding of how Communication Strategies develop across the sublevels (Low, Mid, and High) in learner performance at each performance level (Novice, Intermediate, and Advanced).

Table 9.2

Communication Strategies Performance Domain Indicators (PDIs) for Learners Performing Within the Novice Level

	NOVICE		
Sublevels	LOW	MID	HIGH
Context	familiar, informal, formal, predictable		
Content	very familiar	very familiar, everyday	familiar, everyday
Performance Domain Indicator	**I can answer simple questions**. If there is a breakdown, **I can use gestures**, use facial cues, and/or *use my base language*.	**I can answer**, and at times **ask simple questions**. If there is a breakdown, **I can** use gestures/facial cues, use *my base language, and/or repeat word(s)*.	**I can answer and ask** simple **questions**. If there is a breakdown, **I can use gestures**/facial cues, *repeat word(s)*, and/or use similar word(s).

- The language in bold indicates the source is the *NCSSFL-ACTFL Can-Do Statements: Performance Indicators for Language Learners* (NCSSFL-ACTFL, 2017).
- The language in italics indicates that the source is the *ACTFL Proficiency Guidelines* (ACTFL, 2012b).
- The underlined language indicates the source is Troyan et al. (2023).
- Some language may appear in additional levels to provide scaffolding, consistency and/or clarity.
- For classroom purposes, some language has been modified to be learner-friendly (ie. *repetition* to *repeat words* and *substitute different words* to *similar words*).

Novice Task: Discuss and compare what you and your friend prefer to eat for lunch at school.

Sample Learner Responses: (**Learner 2** demonstrates the PDIs)

NOVICE LOW	NOVICE MID	NOVICE HIGH
Learner 1: Hi! **Learner 2:** Hey! Eat? **Learner 1:** Sure! What do you like to eat? **Learner 2:** Um… (*raises eyebrow*)? **Learner 1:** What do you like to eat (*mimics eating food with hands*)? **Learner 2:** Ah (*nods*), Pizza. **Learner 1:** Cool! I like pizza too! What do you prefer, cheese or sausage? **Learner 2:** Cheese. Yum (*rubs stomach*)! **Learner 1:** I like cheese sometimes too. **Learner 2:** (*Nods*)	**Learner 1:** Hi! **Learner 2:** Hey! I so hungry! Eat time? **Learner 1:** Sure! What do you like to eat? **Learner 2:** Repeat (*raises eyebrow*)? **Learner 1:** What do you like to eat (*mimics eating food with hands*)? **Learner 2:** Ah, yes (*nods*). I like pizza. **Learner 1:** Cool! I like pizza too! What do you prefer, cheese or sausage? **Learner 2:** Prefer cheese. Yum (*rubs stomach*)! And you? **Learner 1:** I like cheese sometimes too. **Learner 2:** No way! Do you like sausage? **Learner 1:**… **Learner 2:** Do you like sausage? **Learner 1:** Um, I don't know (*shrugs*). **Learner 2:** Do you like, um (*thumbs up*), sausage? **Learner 1:** Oh! No way! Gross! **Learner 2:** I like (*nods*).	**Learner 1:** Hi! **Learner 2:** Hey! I'm starving. Let's eat! **Learner 1:** Sure! What do you like to eat? **Learner 2:** I don't understand (*shrugs*). **Learner 1:** What do you like to eat (*mimics eating food with hands*)? **Learner 2:** Ah, gotcha (*nods*). I like pizza. **Learner 1:** Cool! I like pizza too! What do you prefer, cheese or sausage? **Learner 2:** I prefer cheese. So yummy (*rubs stomach*)! What do you prefer? **Learner 1:** I like cheese sometimes too. **Learner 2:** How delish! Do you like sausage? **Learner 1:**… **Learner 2:** Do you like sausage? **Learner 1:** Um, I don't know (*shrugs*). **Learner 2:** Do you like, um, do you like (*thumbs up*), you know… meat? **Learner 1:** Oh! No way! Gross! **Learner 2:** Seriously? I love sausage! Is my meat favorite.

Description of Learner Responses: At first, learners performing within the Novice level may only participate by responding to their interlocutor (*Ah, pizza. Cheese.*). As their responses expand, they may include rejoinders (*Yum! No way! How delish! Seriously?*), which are quick replies or responses made in reaction to what a partner said. This can demonstrate a learner is listening to their partner. With more practice, these learners become able to ask simple questions. Simple questions are formulaic, or follow a pattern (*And you? Do you like…?*). Learners performing within the Novice level often begin with direct questions (*yes/no* and *either/or*). Eventually, they begin to ask for information using highly practiced and predictable *who, what, when, where, why, how* questions (*What do you prefer?*). These questions tend to be closed questions that require only a short answer. For learners performing within the Novice level, the asking and answering of questions is their primary strategy to engage with their interlocutor and advance the conversation.

In the classroom setting, it is important to model and scaffold strategies that learners performing within the Novice level can use to overcome communication barriers. This includes the use of gestures (*nods, mimics eating food with hands, shrugs*), facial cues (*raises eyebrow*), and repetition (*Do you like sausage?*). These learners can also appeal for help (*Um?* and *I don't understand*) from their interlocutor as a strategy to negotiate meaning. Learners may also use their base language (the language from which the learner operates), and *foreignize* words, pronouncing it as if it were the target language. Eventually, with more linguistic resources, they are able to use repetition and become more able to substitute, or use similar, words (*meat* for *sausage*).

Table 9.3

Communication Strategies Performance Domain Indicators (PDIs) for Learners Performing Within the Intermediate Level

	INTERMEDIATE		
Sublevels	**LOW**	**MID**	**HIGH**
Context	familiar, informal, formal, straight-forward		
Content	familiar	familiar, at times researched	familiar, concrete, at times researched
Performance Domain Indicator	**I can exchange information** by **answering and asking follow-up questions**. If there is a breakdown, **I can** *repeat word(s)*, <u>use similar word(s)</u>, *rephrase*, and/or <u>ask for help</u>.	**I can exchange information by answering and asking a variety of follow-up questions.** If there is a breakdown, **I can** *rephrase*, <u>ask for help</u>, and/or *correct myself*.	**I can exchange information by answering and asking a variety of appropriate questions,** and at times <u>cooperate in a conversation</u>. If there is a breakdown, **I can** *rephrase, correct myself*, and/or *use circumlocution*.

- The language in bold indicates the source is the *NCSSFL-ACTFL Can-Do Statements: Performance Indicators for Language Learners* (NCSSFL-ACTFL, 2017).
- The language in italics indicates that the source is the *ACTFL Proficiency Guidelines* (ACTFL, 2012b).
- The underlined language indicates the source is Adair-Hauck et al. (2013) (*use similar words*), the *ACTFL Performance Descriptors for Language Learners* (ACTFL, 2012a) (*ask for help*), or Warren (2006) (*cooperate in a conversation*).
- Some language may appear in additional levels to provide scaffolding, consistency and/or clarity.
- For classroom purposes, some language has been modified to be learner-friendly (ie. *self-correction* to *correct myself, ask for clarification* to *ask for help*).

Intermediate Task: You and your friend discuss and decide where to eat lunch together.

Sample Learner Responses: (**Learner 2** demonstrates the PDIs)

INTERMEDIATE LOW	INTERMEDIATE MID	INTERMEDIATE HIGH
Learner 1: Hey you! Are you hungry? **Learner 2:** Hi! Yes, I'm hungry. **Learner 1:** Good! May we eat lunch now? **Learner 2:** Yes. Where do you want to go? **Learner 1:** I like the restaurant over there (*points in that direction*). **Learner 2:** Where? **Learner 1:** Um, at the end (*points in that direction*). **Learner 2:** At the end? I don't understand "at the end." **Learner 1:** The pizza restaurant. At the end. They have a lot of different pizzas. **Learner 2:** Oh, yes! The pizza restaurant over there. You like pizza? **Learner 1:** I love pizza! Yummy! **Learners 2:** Awesome! Me too! What type of pizza do you like? **Learner 1:** I prefer pepperoni pizza. **Learner 2:** Um, you like thick crust? **Learner 1:** What do you mean? **Learner 2:** You know, the pizza with thick crust? **Learner 1:** Oh yeah (*nods*). It's ok (*shrugs*). **Learner 2:** Yeah! They have pizza with thick crust? **Learner 1:** I'm not sure. May we go and see? **Learner 2:** Let's go.	**Learner 1:** Hey you! Are you hungry? **Learner 2:** OMG, I'm SO (*said with emphasis*) hungry (*rubs stomach*). I could eat a horse (*laughs*)! **Learner 1:** Good! May we eat lunch now? **Learner 2:** Of course! Yes, please (*laughs*)! Where do you want to go? **Learner 1:** I like the restaurant over there (*points in that direction*). **Learner 2:** The restaurant over there...which restaurant? **Learner 1:** Um, the one at the end (*points in that direction*). **Learner 2:** The one at the end? What kind of food do they have? I like BLTs. **Learner 1:** The pizza restaurant. At the end. They have a lot of different pizzas. **Learner 2:** Ah, I see. The pizza restaurant on the corner. Do you like pizza? **Learner 1:** I love pizza! Yummy! **Learners 2:** Awesome (*smiles*)! Me too! It's my fav. What kind of pizza do you like? **Learner 1:** I prefer pepperoni pizza. **Learner 2:** No kidding?! Do they have, um, the pizza from Chicago... **Learner 1:** What do you mean? **Learner 2:** You know, with very thick crust? **Learner 1:** Oh yeah (*nods*). It's ok (*shrugs*). **Learner 2:** Yeah! Do they have that?	**Learner 1:** Hey you! Are you hungry? **Learner 2:** OMG! Yes, I'm starving. In fact, I'm so hungry I could eat a horse (*laughs*)! How about you? **Learner 1:** Good! May we eat lunch now? **Learner 2:** Of course! Absolutely! Do you have any suggestions? Where is a good place to go? **Learner 1:** I like the restaurant over there (*points in that direction*). **Learner 2:** Which one? Is it the restaurant with the patio in the sun? **Learner 1:** Um, the one at the end (*points in that direction*). **Learner 2:** Yeah. It's a nice day, but is there some...um, some tables not in the sun? I don't want to sit in the sun. Maybe we can ask for a table with an umbrella. What kind of restaurant is it? **Learner 1:** A pizza restaurant. At the end. They have a lot of different pizzas. **Learner 2:** Ah, alright, the pizza restaurant with the patio. Yeah, I think it will be a good place to eat. Are you a pizza lover? **Learner 1:** I love pizza! Yummy! **Learner 2:** Right (*smiles*)? I love a good pizza too. So, what's your favorite kind of pizza to order? **Learner 1:** I prefer pepperoni pizza. **Learner 2:** For real?! That's one of my favorites as well. Will they have that type of pizza...you know...the one from Chicago...

	Learner 1: I'm not sure. May we go and see? **Learner 2:** Of course! Come on, let's go (*waves Learner 2 toward themselves and starts walking*)!	**Learner 1:** What do you mean? **Learner 2:** You know, it's that Chicago style that has the thick crust. What is it called? **Learner 1:** Oh yeah (*nods*). It's ok (*shrugs*). **Learner 2:** Seriously? Are you sure (*raises eyebrows*)? Because it's really tasty! If they have that we will have to try it out. **Learner 1:** I'm not sure. May we go and see? **Learner 2:** Of course! Come on! Let's go check it out. You can choose the pizza (*waves Learner 2 toward themselves and starts walking*)!

Description of Learner Responses: Learners performing within the Intermediate level continue to use questions to engage with their interlocutor and advance the conversation, but they do so with more variety and flexibility. These learners can respond to and ask appropriate follow-up questions. Their responses and questions are relevant and responsive to the information (a restaurant for lunch, type of food) and/or interlocutor. Learners may continue to use rejoinders (*Awesome! Me too! Ah, I see. No kidding?! Absolutely!*) to react to and affirm what their partner said. Their questions further gather (*Where do you want to go? Do you have any suggestions? Where is a good place to go?*), reinforce (*The one at the end?*), and/or evaluate (*Are you sure?*) the information exchanged. As they continue to develop their linguistic resources, they begin to cooperate in conversations. That is, each learner equally shares responsibility to initiate and develop topics.

While engaging in interpersonal tasks, these learners can use the target language to overcome and even prevent communication breakdowns. Learners may restate (*The restaurant over there...* and *The one at the end?*), rephrase (*Oh yes! The pizza restaurant over there..., You know, with very thick crust?*), and/or express their need for help (*I don't understand "at the end"*). As their linguistic resources further develop, learners may be able to circumlocute, or use language they do know to talk around words they don't know (*um, some tables not in the sun?* instead of *shade*, and *you know, it's that Chicago style that has the thick crust* instead of *deep dish pizza*).

Table 9.4

Communication Strategies Performance Domain Indicators (PDIs) for Learners Performing Within the Advanced Level

	ADVANCED		
Sublevels	**LOW**	**MID**	**HIGH**
Context	familiar, unfamiliar, informal, formal, complex		
Content	familiar, academic, social, concrete	academic, social, professional, concrete	academic, social, professional, concrete, abstract
Performance Domain Indicator	**I can** cooperate in a conversation by initiating and developing topics and topic changes. If there is a breakdown, **I can** *rephrase* and/or *use circumlocution.*	**I can** cooperate in a conversation and **ask probing questions**. At times **I can** transition among topic changes in a **cohesive** manner. If there is a breakdown, **I can** *rephrase, paraphrase idea(s),* and/or *use circumlocution.*	**I can** cooperate in a conversation and transition among topics in a **cohesive** manner. If there is a breakdown, **I can** *paraphrase, use circumlocution,* and/or *illustrate idea(s).*

- The language in bold indicates the source is the *NCSSFL-ACTFL Can-Do Statements: Performance Indicators for Language Learners* (NCSSFL-ACTFL, 2017).
- The language in italics indicates that the source is the *ACTFL Proficiency Guidelines* (ACTFL, 2012b).
- The underlined language indicates the source is Warren (2006).
- Some language may appear in additional levels to provide scaffolding, consistency and/or clarity.

Advanced Task: After watching a news report about locally grown food, discuss with a friend if you think it is a sustainable option.

Sample Learner Responses: (**Learner 2** demonstrates the PDIs)

ADVANCED LOW	ADVANCED MID	ADVANCED HIGH
Learner 1: Well, that was interesting. I doesn't know that we have these local farms in our community. **Learner 2:** Same here. It's kinda sad that I have not hear of them until now. **Learner 1:** After watch that, I feel I am more motivated to help and buy from these farms. **Learner 2:** For sure (*nods head*)! I think to eat locally grown food is healthier, especially since the produce does no travel long distances. Therefore, it tastes better.	**Learner 1:** Well, that news segment was interesting. I didn't even know we have these local farms in our community. **Learner 2:** I know! It's kind of sad that I've haven't' heard of them until now. **Learner 1:** Yeah. After watching that news report, I'm motivated to support our local farmers. **Learner 2:** For sure (*nods head*)! Eating locally grown food is definitely better for your overall health. In fact, I think the food tastes better, too.	**Learner 1:** Well, that was interesting. Who knew we had these local farms right here in our community? **Learner 2:** I know, right (*raises eyebrows*)?! Yeah, it's sorta sad that I've lived here my entire life and I wasn't aware. **Learner 1:** I swear I'd never even heard about them until now. It makes me want to support our local farmers, ya know (*squints eyes*)?

Learner 1: Yeah (*nods head*). I appreciate the freshness of the food when I buy from the farmer's market..., which I think it has more nutrients, meaning that is healthier too.

Learner 2: Is that weird (*tilts head*)? Like, we know that eating locally grown is better, but we don't do it so often. Why is that?

Learner 1: Well, I think because it cost more than to buy at the grocery store.

Learner 2: Yeah (*nods head*), like the reporter said... that, that the, um, steep cost of groceries is impacting many families.

Learner 1: Right. I mean, for a family that can no make ends meet, there's no question why they shop at wholesale market. Because they buy in bulk, they offer much low prices.

Learner 2: That makes perfect sense (*leans back*). For example, there's a co-op near to my house, but I think we shopped there a handful of times. I will ask my mom..., but probably it's the cost, especially since we are a large family. What do your family?

Learner 1: Like I said, sometimes we go to the farmer's market, which is pretty fun!

Learner 2: I totally forgot about that (*leans forward*)! You know what (*tilts head*)? Maybe I will plant a vegetable garden this spring.

Learner 1: I like your idea. Maybe I do it too.

Learner 1: Yeah (*nods head*). I appreciate how fresh the food is when I buy it at the farmer's market (*shakes head*). It's not like the processed foods that contain preservatives added to them (*frowns*).

Learner 2: Yeah, well, they do this so that produce can artificially mature while transport, in those refrigerated trucks. It also gives products a longer shelf life.

Learner 1: Well, my family has a small garden where we grow different kinds of vegetables. In this way, we don't have to buy in grocery stores.

Learner 2: That sounds great! I bet it's also much cheaper option. I mean, it's like free produce. Well, besides the cost of the seeds and water. But, tell me, is it a lot of work?

Learner 1: Sort of (*looks to the right*). You do have to water it if it doesn't rain. And we weed it every so often. So, yeah. I guess it is work. But, it's free and fresh! So, it's a win-win!

Learner 2: I'll have to look into that. My family is a member of, like, a co-op service, where every month a local farm delivers a box of their seasonal produce to us.

Learner 1: That's nice. How expensive is that?

Learner 2: Good question. I'm not sure (*strokes chin*). I think it depends on the produce and season. Obviously though, it is more expensive than to buy it from a wholesale market.

Learner 1: That's why I think that eating locally grown can be out of people's reach. The cost is too much.

Learner 2: Yeah. I think we all just do what we can, ya know? Hey (*raises eyebrows*), maybe I'll plant a garden!

Learner 2: For sure (*nods head*)! And it's a win-win because it's so much healthier than buying processed foods. Just imagine all the preservatives that they are added so it be shipped across the country in refrigerated trucks. In some cases, the fruits or vegetables ripen artificially.

Learner 1: That sounds gross (*leans back*)! Now I'm definitely going to buy more locally grown foods!

Learner 2: Right (*raises eyebrows*)? I would even dare to say that the produce tastes better, so you can actually taste the flavor of, like, carrots and celery.

Learner 1: Just think of all the natural nutrients you be feeding your body! On the surface it looks like an easy choice. But like the reporter said, it often comes down to cost. I think it's probably not sustainable for families who is, are trying to make ends meet.

Learner 2: Oh really? Why not (*tilts head*)?

Learner 1: Well, think of the prices at the wholesale market stores..., where, because they buy in bulk, offer deep discounts in pricing. The result is then that families with a limited budget can only afford shopping there.

Learner 2: You make a good point (*nods head*). Eating locally grown is not exactly cheap. Obviously, you get what you pay for, but for some peoples, it's just not a sustainable option.

Learner 1: Yeah, although, for me at least, it feels good to buy local because I am supporting a family, a family business instead of a corporation.

Learner 2: That being said, then there are both advantages and disadvantages to eating locally grown food. Whenever I can, I try to support my community by eating locally grown.

Learner 1: Same here (*nods head*).

Description of Learner Responses: Learners performing within the Advanced level develop the capacity to participate as equal partners in a conversation, which Warren (2006) terms [co-operation] cooperation. According to Warren, cooperation is achieved when the conversation partner fully shares the responsibility to initiate topics, develop, and close topics as they shift and change. In this sample, Learner 2 participates equally in both turns and length of responses within the conversation. Learner 2 initiates topics: benefits of eating locally grown (*healthier* and *tastes better*) and growing a garden (*Maybe I will plant a vegetable garden*); Learner 2 develops topics: high food cost (*reporter said* and *for example, there's a co-op...*); and Learner 2 closes and shifts to a new topic: the benefits of eating locally grown (*Like, we know that eating locally grown is better, but we don't do it so often. Why is that?*).

As learners progress they begin to use probing questions (*But, tell me, is it a lot of work?, Why not?*) as a communication strategy to further advance the topic (*vegetable garden, sustainability*). Additionally, they become increasingly more able to adapt to shifts and/or changes in topics cohesively. This is evidenced in how Learner 2 uses rejoinders to affirm their partner's responses (*I know!, For sure!, That sounds great!, Good question*) as well as subordinating conjunctions (*where, what, that*) and discourse markers (*In fact, besides, Obviously, That being said*) to transition among topic shifts.

Learners performing within the Advanced level can use the target language to overcome and even prevent breakdowns in communication. For example, both learners use circumlocution, or words that a learner knows well in order to explain a word that they do not know (*long distances* instead of *far; cost more* instead of *more expensive*). As learners progress through the Advanced level, they are able to paraphrase, or communicate a similar message in a different way (*I bet it's also much cheaper option. I mean, it's like free produce* and *You make a good point. Eating locally grown is not exactly cheap*). This allows learners to check for understanding. Learners are also able to use illustration as a communicative strategy, describing aspects in detail to create further clarity in a message (to illustrate the impact of shipping foods: *Just imagine all the preservatives that they are added so it be shipped across the country in refrigerated trucks*).

YOUR TURN

LEARNING TARGETS CHECK:	
I can	☐ describe the Communication Strategies performance domain. ☐ describe how Communication Strategies shows up in learners' performance at various levels.

Pause and reflect:
How would you describe Communication Strategies to your learners? Consider any explanations, examples, and/or visuals you might use to describe the performance domain:

Communication Strategies in learner work:
The following exercise includes a sample task for each of the performance levels. Write a learner response that includes the characteristics of Communication Strategies for learners performing within each level. Use the provided Intermediate sample to guide you.

Novice	Intermediate	Advanced
Task: Talk with your partner to decide on which activity you both like to do in your Physical Education class today.	**Task:** Compare activities you are planning to do on the weekend and consider their health benefits. Add plans if you feel you need to be more active or health minded.	**Task:** Discuss the pros and cons of athlete activism and determine if athletes should use their platform to take social action on issues that impact them and others in society.
	Learner 1: What is on your calendar in Saturday? **Learner 2:** Saturday. Um, I have to run…a race. **Learner 1:** Oh, I can't race (*shakes head*). But we can be healthy. In Saturday, can you go to a restaurant? **Learner 2:** What type of restaurant? **Learner 1:** It's a healthy. They have all plant-based foods. **Learner 2:** What? **Learner 1:** It's all plant-based. **Learner 2:** What type is…? **Learner 1:** Oh, it's all food from plants. Plants like vegetables, not animals. **Learner 2:** Ah (*nods*). Ok, I like vegetables. When time is the dinner? No wait (*shakes head*), when… I mean, what time is the dinner? **Learner 1:** At four in the night. **Learner 2:** Four…at night (*raises eyebrows*)? **Learner 1:** Sorry (*shakes head*). Four in the afternoon. **Learner 2:** Ok. I don't have any activities at four. My race is done. And restaurants are fun. Let's go! **Learner 1:** Great (*smiles*)! I'll see you on Saturday! Maybe I come see you race before.	

The Performance Domain Indicators (PDIs) Assessment and Feedback Guide

The *Performance Domain Indicators (PDIs) Assessment and Feedback Guide* is a resource for both learners and educators to use when assessing learner performance. The information within each guide is based on PDIs of the following performance level targets: Novice High (Table 9.5), Intermediate Mid (Table 9.6), Intermediate High (Table 9.7), and Advanced Low (Table 9.8). However, these guides can serve as a template for other performance level targets. It is important to note that a performance assessment evaluates a learner's *performance*, and not *the learner*. Therefore, a learner is not *at* a level, but rather a learner's performance may be consistent *with* a level.

The purpose of the *Performance Domain Indicators (PDIs) Assessment and Feedback Guide* is to provide a visual pathway for evaluating the Communication Strategies of a learner's performance. The left-hand column provides guiding questions that lead us to identify the Communication Strategies consistent with a learner's performance. These guiding questions are based upon the performance levels' PDIs, which are presented lowest to highest. Starting at the *Beginning* level, evaluators progress through each question, responding "yes" or "no." If evaluators reply "yes" to all questions in the *Beginning* level, they continue to the next level (*Developing*), repeating the process, and continuing through the levels. If evaluators reply "no" to a question, they go back to the previous level, in which all their replies for the level's guiding questions are "yes." At the last level where all questions are answered "yes," evaluators continue across the chart. They can then refer to the second column labeled *Performance Domain Indicator* for the PDI that best aligns with the learner's performance. Based on this evaluation, the following two columns provide example GLOW and GROW comments. GLOW feedback states what the learner achieved and GROW feedback directs learners how to develop their language skills. This feedback is not unit specific, but rather supports overarching language performance goals that learners can work towards throughout a course. Including evidence from learner performance within the GLOW/GROW feedback is most effective.

Table 9.5

Performance Domain Indicators (PDIs) Assessment and Feedback Guide

Communication Strategies Target performance level: **Novice High** Context: familiar, informal, formal, predictable Content: familiar, everyday			
Guiding questions	**Performance Domain Indicator**	**GLOW**	**GROW**
Novice Low Beginning Can the learner: • maintain communication by answering simple questions? • overcome a breakdown in communication (if it occurs) by using: - gestures? - facial cues? - their base language?	I can answer simple questions. If there is a breakdown, I can use gestures, use facial cues, and/ or use my base language.	**Maintain communication:** • You maintain communication by responding to simple questions. • You demonstrate that you were listening to your partner through (*gestures, facial cues, appropriate eye contact, rejoinders…*). **Overcome breakdowns in communication:** • You use (*gestures, facial cues*) to communicate your ideas while remaining in the target language. • You help your partner understand your ideas by using (*gestures and/or facial cues*). • You indicate to your partner that you need help by using (*gestures and/or facial cues*).	**Maintain and advance communication:** • What questions could you ask in order to maintain and advance communication? • What strategies (*gestures, facial cues, appropriate eye contact, rejoinders…*) might you use to demonstrate you are listening to your partner? **Overcome breakdowns in communication:** • What strategies (*gestures, facial cues, and/or repeating words*) might you use to communicate ideas to your partner while remaining in the target language? • How could you use (*gestures, facial expressions, and/or repeating words*) to clarify in the target language, rather than using your base language? • How could you use the target language to indicate to your partner that you need help?

Novice Mid Developing Can the learner: • maintain and advance communication by - answering simple questions? - at times asking simple questions? • overcome a breakdown in communication (if it occurs) by: - using gestures? - using facial cues? - using their base language? - repeating word(s)?	I can answer, and at times ask simple questions. If there is a breakdown, I can use gestures/ facial cues, use my base language, and/or repeat word(s).	**Maintain and advance communication:** • You maintain communication by responding to simple questions. • At times you ask simple questions to maintain and advance communication. • You demonstrate that you were listening to your partner through (*gestures, facial cues, appropriate eye contact, rejoinders...*). **Overcome breakdowns in communication:** • You use (*gestures, facial cues*) to communicate your ideas while remaining in the target language. • You help your partner understand your ideas by (*using gestures, using facial cues, and/or repeating words*). • You indicate to your partner that you need help by using (*gestures, facial cues, and/ or a specific word/phrase like "repeat?"*).	**Maintain and advance communication:** • What additional questions could you ask in order to maintain and advance communication? • What strategies (*gestures, facial cues, appropriate eye contact, rejoinders...*) might you use to demonstrate you are listening to your partner? **Overcome breakdowns in communication:** • What strategies (*gestures, facial cues, repeating words, and/or using similar words*) might you use to communicate ideas to your partner while remaining in the target language? • How could you use (*gestures, facial cues, repeating words, and/or similar words*) to clarify in the target language, rather than using your base language? • How could you use the target language to indicate to your partner that you need help?

<table>
<tr>
<td>Novice High Meeting
Can the learner:
• maintain and advance communication by
- answering simple questions?
- asking simple questions?
• overcome a breakdown in communication (if it occurs) by:
- using gestures?
- using facial cues?
- repeating word(s)?
- using similar word(s)?</td>
<td>I can answer and ask simple questions. If there is a breakdown, I can use gestures/ facial cues, repeat word(s), and/ or use similar word(s).</td>
<td>Maintain and advance communication:
• You maintain communication by responding to simple questions.
• You ask simple questions to maintain and advance communication.
• You demonstrate that you were listening to your partner through (gestures, facial cues, appropriate eye contact, rejoinders...).
Overcome breakdowns in communication:
• You help your partner understand your ideas by (using gestures, using facial cues, repeating words, and/or using similar words) to make your message clearer.
• You indicate to your partner that you need help by using (gestures, facial cues, and/ or a specific word/phrase like "repeat?").</td>
<td>Maintain and advance communication:
• How could you invite your partner to share their opinions and ideas so you don't dominate the conversation?
• How could you comment on what your partner said before moving on to the next idea?
• How might your questions follow-up on ideas that your partner mentions, rather than asking random questions on different topics?
• What strategies (gestures, facial cues, appropriate eye contact, rejoinders...) might you use to demonstrate you are listening to your partner?
Overcome breakdowns in communication:
• What strategies (repeating words, using similar words, and/or rephrasing) might you use to help your partner when they don't understand?
• What strategies (repeating words/phrases, using similar words, rephrasing, and/or asking follow-up questions) might you use to check that you understand your partner's ideas?
• How could you use the target language to indicate to your partner that you need help?</td>
</tr>
</table>

<table>
<tr>
<td>Intermediate Low Exceeding
Can the learner:<ul><li>maintain and advance communication by
- answering questions?
- asking follow-up questions?</li><li>overcome a breakdown in communication (if it occurs) by:
- repeating word(s)?
- using similar word(s)?
- rephrasing?
- asking for help?</li></ul></td>
<td>I can exchange information by answering and asking follow-up questions. If there is a breakdown, I can repeat word(s), use similar word(s), rephrase, and/or ask for help.</td>
<td>Maintain and advance communication:<ul><li>You maintain communication by responding to your partner's questions.</li><li>You advance communication by asking appropriate questions that follow-up on ideas that your partner mentions.</li><li>You demonstrate that you were listening to your partner through (gestures, facial cues, appropriate eye contact, rejoinders, responses, follow-up questions...).</li></ul>Overcome breakdowns in communication:<ul><li>You help your partner understand your ideas by (repeating words, using similar words, and/or rephrasing) to make your message clearer.</li><li>You check that you understand your partner's ideas by (repeating words, using similar words, rephrasing, and/or asking follow-up questions).</li><li>You use the target language to ask your partner for help when you don't understand something.</li></ul></td>
<td>Maintain and advance communication:<ul><li>How could you invite your partner to share their opinions and ideas so you don't dominate the conversation?</li><li>How could you comment on what your partner said before moving on to the next idea?</li><li>How might you increase the variety of questions you use to follow-up on ideas that your partner mentions?</li><li>How could you demonstrate you are listening to your partner?</li></ul>Overcome breakdowns in communication:<ul><li>What strategies (repeating words, using similar words, rephrasing, and/ or correcting yourself) might you use to help your partner when they don't understand?</li><li>What strategies (repeating, using similar words, rephrasing, and/or asking follow-up questions) might you use to check that you understand your partner's ideas?</li><li>What are additional ways you could use to indicate to your partner that you need help?</li></ul></td>
</tr>
</table>

Table 9.6
Performance Domain Indicators (PDIs) Assessment and Feedback Guide

Communication Strategies Target performance level: **Intermediate Mid** Context: familiar, informal, formal, straight-forward Content: familiar, at times researched			
Guiding questions	**Performance Domain Indicator**	**GLOW**	**GROW**
Novice High Beginning Can the learner: • maintain and advance communication by - answering simple questions? - asking simple questions? • overcome a breakdown in communication (if it occurs) by: - using gestures? - using facial cues? - repeating word(s)? - using similar word(s)?	I can answer and ask simple questions. If there is a breakdown, I can use gestures/facial cues, repeat word(s), and/or use similar word(s).	**Maintain and advance communication:** • You maintain communication by responding to simple questions. • You ask simple questions to maintain and advance communication. • You demonstrate that you were listening to your partner through (*gestures, facial cues, appropriate eye contact, rejoinders…*). **Overcome breakdowns in communication:** • You help your partner understand your ideas by (*using gestures, using facial cues, repeating words, and/or using similar words*) to make your message clearer. • You indicate to your partner that you need help by using (*gestures, facial cues, and/or a specific word/phrase like "repeat?"*).	**Maintain and advance communication:** • How could you invite your partner to share their opinions and ideas so you don't dominate the conversation? • How could you comment on what your partner said before moving on to the next idea? • How might your questions follow-up on ideas that your partner mentions, rather than asking random questions on different topics? • What strategies (*gestures, facial cues, appropriate eye contact, rejoinders…*) might you use to demonstrate you are listening to your partner? **Overcome breakdowns in communication:** • What strategies (*repeating words, using similar words, and/or rephrasing*) might you use to help your partner when they don't understand? • What strategies (*repeating words/phrases, using similar words, rephrasing, and/or asking follow-up questions*) might you use to check that you understand your partner's ideas? • How could you use the target language to indicate to your partner that you need help?

<table>
<tr>
<td>Intermediate Low Developing
Can the learner:
• maintain and advance communication by
- answering questions?
- asking follow-up questions?
• overcome a breakdown in communication (if it occurs) by:
- repeating word(s)?
- using similar word(s)?
- rephrasing?
- asking for help?</td>
<td>I can exchange information by answering and asking follow-up questions. If there is a breakdown, I can repeat word(s), use similar word(s), rephrase, and/or ask for help.</td>
<td>Maintain and advance communication:
• You maintain communication by responding to your partner's questions.
• You advance communication by asking appropriate questions that follow-up on ideas that your partner mentions.
• You demonstrate that you were listening to your partner through (gestures, facial cues, appropriate eye contact, rejoinders, responses, follow-up questions. . .).

Overcome breakdowns in communication:
• You help your partner understand your ideas by (repeating words, using similar words, and/or rephrasing) to make your message clearer.
• You check that you understand your partner's ideas by (repeating words, using similar words, rephrasing, and/or asking follow-up questions).
• You use the target language to ask your partner for help when you don't understand something.</td>
<td>Maintain and advance communication:
• How could you invite your partner to share their opinions and ideas so you don't dominate the conversation?
• How could you comment on what your partner said before moving on to the next idea?
• How might you increase the variety of questions you use to follow-up on ideas that your partner mentions?
• How could you demonstrate you are listening to your partner?

Overcome breakdowns in communication:
• What strategies (repeating words, using similar words, rephrasing, and/ or correcting yourself) might you use to help your partner when they don't understand?
• What strategies (repeating, using similar words, rephrasing, and/or asking follow-up questions) might you use to check that you understand your partner's ideas?
• What are additional ways you could use to indicate to your partner that you need help?</td>
</tr>
</table>

Intermediate Mid Meeting Can the learner: • maintain and advance communication by - answering a variety of questions? - asking a variety of follow-up questions? • overcome a breakdown in communication (if it occurs) by: - rephrasing? - asking for help? - correcting themselves?	I can exchange information by answering and asking a variety of follow-up questions. If there is a breakdown, I can rephrase, ask for help, and/or correct myself.	**Maintain and advance communication:** • You maintain communication by responding to your partner's questions. • You advance communication by asking a variety of questions that follow-up on ideas that your partner mentions. • You demonstrate that you were listening to your partner through (*rejoinders, affirming responses, follow-up questions...*). **Overcome breakdowns in communication:** • You help your partner understand your ideas by (*rephrasing and/or correcting yourself*) to make your message clearer. • You check that you understand your partner's ideas by (*rephrasing and/or asking follow-up questions*). • You use the target language to ask your partner for help when you don't understand something.	**Maintain and advance communication:** • Think about the communication as a whole. What might have been a more appropriate way to start, progress, or end communication? • What additional questions would have been appropriate to maintain and advance communication? • How might you more fully cooperate with your partner by sharing the responsibility to initiate and develop topics? • How could you demonstrate you are listening to your partner? **Overcome breakdowns in communication:** • What strategies could you use to help your partner when they don't understand? • How could you use circumlocution, or use language that you know well in order to explain a word/phrase you don't know, to get your message across? • What strategies (*rephrasing and/or asking follow-up questions*) might you use to check that you understand your partner's ideas? • What are additional ways you could indicate to your partner that you need help?

Intermediate High Exceeding Can the learner: • maintain and advance communication by - answering a variety of appropriate questions? - asking a variety of appropriate questions? - at times sharing the responsibility to initiate and develop topics? • overcome a breakdown in communication (if it occurs) by: - rephrasing? - correcting themselves? - using circumlocution?	I can exchange information by answering and asking a variety of appropriate questions, and at times cooperate in a conversation. If there is a breakdown, I can rephrase, correct myself, and/or use circumlocution.	**Maintain and advance communication:** • You maintain communication by responding to your partner's questions. • You advance communication by using a variety of open-ended questions to invite your partner to share their opinions and ideas. • You advance communication by asking a variety of questions that follow-up on ideas that your partner mentions. • Your responses show that you are interested in what your partner is saying. • You are beginning to cooperate with your partner by sharing the responsibility to initiate and develop topics. **Overcome breakdowns in communication:** • You help your partner understand your ideas by (*rephrasing, correcting yourself, and/or using circumlocution*) to make your message clearer. • You check that you understand your partner's ideas. • When you don't understand something your partner says, you clarify by (*rephrasing and/or asking appropriate questions*).	**Maintain and advance communication:** • How might you more fully cooperate with your partner by equally sharing the responsibility to initiate and develop topics? • How might you more fully develop topics through explanations and/or comparisons of preferences, opinions, and advice? • How might you maintain and advance communication by initiating topic changes? • How might you move beyond using questions to maintain and advance communication? • What are additional ways you can invite your partner to share their opinions and ideas? • How could you demonstrate you are listening to your partner? **Overcome breakdowns in communication:** • What strategies could you use to help your partner when they don't understand? • How could you use circumlocution, or use language that you know well in order to explain a word/phrase you don't know, to get your message across? • How might you check that you understand your partner, or that your partner understands you? • What are additional ways you could use to indicate to your partner that you need help?

Table 9.7

Performance Domain Indicators (PDIs) Assessment and Feedback Guide

Communication Strategies Target performance level: **Intermediate High** Context: familiar, informal, formal, straight-forward Content: familiar, concrete, at times researched			
Guiding questions	**Performance Domain Indicator**	**GLOW**	**GROW**
Intermediate Low Beginning Can the learner: • maintain and advance communication by - answering questions? - asking follow-up questions? • overcome a breakdown in communication (if it occurs) by: - repeating word(s)? - using similar word(s)? - rephrasing? - asking for help?	I can exchange information by answering and asking follow-up questions. If there is a breakdown, I can repeat word(s), use similar word(s), rephrase, and/or ask for help.	**Maintain and advance communication:** • You maintain communication by responding to your partner's questions. • You advance communication by asking appropriate questions that follow-up on ideas that your partner mentions. • You demonstrate that you were listening to your partner through (*gestures, facial cues, appropriate eye contact, rejoinders, responses, follow-up questions...*). **Overcome breakdowns in communication:** • You help your partner understand your ideas by (*repeating words, using similar words, and/or rephrasing*) to make you message clearer. • You check that you understand your partner's ideas by (*repeating words, using similar words, rephrasing, and/or asking follow-up questions*). • You use the target language to ask your partner for help when you don't understand something.	**Maintain and advance communication:** • How could you invite your partner to share their opinions and ideas so you don't dominate the conversation? • How could you comment on what your partner said before moving on to the next idea? • How might you increase the variety of questions you use to follow-up on ideas that your partner mentions? • How could you demonstrate you are listening to your partner? **Overcome breakdowns in communication:** • What strategies (*repeating words, using similar words, rephrasing, and/ or correcting yourself*) might you use to help your partner when they don't understand? • What strategies (*repeating, using similar words, rephrasing, and/or asking follow-up questions*) might you use to check that you understand your partner's ideas? • What are additional ways you could use to indicate to your partner that you need help?

<table>
<tr>
<td>Intermediate Mid
Developing
Can the learner:
• maintain and advance communication by
- answering a variety of questions?
- asking a variety of follow-up questions?
• overcome a breakdown in communication (if it occurs) by:
- rephrasing?
- asking for help?
- correcting themselves?</td>
<td>I can exchange information by answering and asking a variety of follow-up questions. If there is a breakdown, I can rephrase, ask for help, and/or correct myself.</td>
<td>Maintain and advance communication:
• You maintain communication by responding to your partner's questions.
• You advance communication by asking a variety of questions that follow-up on ideas that your partner mentions.
• You demonstrate that you were listening to your partner through (rejoinders, affirming responses, follow-up questions. . .).
Overcome breakdowns in communication:
• You help your partner understand your ideas by (rephrasing and/ or correcting yourself) to make your message clearer.
• You check that you understand your partner's ideas by (rephrasing and/or asking follow-up questions).
• You use the target language to ask your partner for help when you don't understand something.</td>
<td>Maintain and advance communication:
• Think about the communication as a whole. What might have been a more appropriate way to start, progress, or end communication?
• What additional questions would have been appropriate to maintain and advance communication?
• How might you more fully cooperate with your partner by sharing the responsibility to initiate and develop topics?
• How could you demonstrate you are listening to your partner?
Overcome breakdowns in communication:
• What strategies could you use to help your partner when they don't understand?
• How could you use circumlocution, or use language that you know well in order to explain a word/phrase you don't know, to get your message across?
• What strategies (rephrasing and/or asking follow-up questions) might you use to check that you understand your partner's ideas?
• What are additional ways you could indicate to your partner that you need help?</td>
</tr>
</table>

<table>
<tr>
<td>Intermediate High Meeting
Can the learner:
• maintain and advance communication by
- answering a variety of appropriate questions?
- asking a variety of appropriate questions?
- at times sharing the responsibility to initiate and develop topics?
• overcome a breakdown in communication (if it occurs) by:
- rephrasing?
- correcting themselves?
- using circumlocution?</td>
<td>I can exchange information by answering and asking a variety of appropriate questions, and at times cooperate in a conversation. If there is a breakdown, I can rephrase, correct myself, and/or use circumlocution.</td>
<td>Maintain and advance communication:
• You maintain communication by responding to your partner's questions.
• You advance communication by using a variety of open-ended questions to invite your partner to share their opinions and ideas.
• You advance communication by asking a variety of questions that follow-up on ideas that your partner mentions.
• Your responses show that you are interested in what your partner is saying.
• You are beginning to cooperate with your partner by sharing the responsibility to initiate and develop topics.
Overcome breakdowns in communication:
• You help your partner understand your ideas by (rephrasing, correcting yourself, and/or using circumlocution) to make your message clearer.
• You check that you understand your partner's ideas.
• When you don't understand something your partner says, you clarify by (rephrasing and/or asking appropriate questions).</td>
<td>Maintain and advance communication:
• How might you more fully cooperate with your partner by equally sharing the responsibility to initiate and develop topics?
• How might you more fully develop topics through explanations and/or comparisons of preferences, opinions, and advice?
• How might you maintain and advance communication by initiating topic changes?
• How might you move beyond using questions to maintain and advance communication?
• What are additional ways you can invite your partner to share their opinions and ideas?
• How could you demonstrate you are listening to your partner?
Overcome breakdowns in communication:
• What strategies could you use to help your partner when they don't understand?
• How could you use circumlocution, or use language that you know well in order to explain a word/phrase you don't know, to get your message across?
• How might you check that you understand your partner, or that your partner understands you?
• What are additional ways you could use to indicate to your partner that you need help?</td>
</tr>
</table>

Advanced Low Exceeding Can the learner: • maintain and advance communication by - equally sharing the responsibility with their partner to initiate and develop topics? • overcome a breakdown in communication (if it occurs) by: - rephrasing? - using circumlocution?	I can cooperate in a conversation by initiating and developing topics and topic changes. If there is a breakdown, I can rephrase and/or use circumlocution.	**Maintain and advance communication:** • You cooperate with your partner by equally sharing the responsibility to initiate and develop topics. • You maintain and advance communication, developing topics through (*explanations and/or comparisons of preferences, opinions, and advice*). • You maintain and advance communication by initiating topic changes. • You advance communication by using a variety of ways to invite your partner to share their opinions and ideas. • You use a variety of ways to show that you are interested in what your partner was saying. **Overcome breakdowns in communication:** • You (*rephrase and/or use circumlocution*) to successfully communicate your ideas. • You help your partner understand your ideas by (*rephrasing and/or using circumlocution*). • You check that you understand your partner's ideas. • When you don't understand something your partner says, you clarify by (*rephrasing, and/or asking appropriate questions*).	**Maintain and advance communication:** • How might you more fully develop topics and show interest in what your partner said by supporting, reacting to, and comparing preferences and opinions? • How could you close a topic before initiating a new topic? • How might you more cohesively transition among topic changes? • How might you incorporate probing questions elicit more information from your partner? **Overcome breakdowns in communication:** • What strategies could you use to help your partner when they don't understand? • How could you paraphrase to get your message across and/or clarify? • How might you check that you understand your partner, or that your partner understands you?

Table 9.8
Performance Domain Indicators (PDIs) Assessment and Feedback Guide

<table>
<tr><th colspan="4">Communication Strategies
Target performance level: Advanced Low
Context: familiar, unfamiliar, informal, formal, complex
Content: familiar, academic, social, concrete</th></tr>
<tr><th>Guiding questions</th><th>Performance Domain Indicator</th><th>GLOW</th><th>GROW</th></tr>
<tr>
<td>Intermediate Mid Beginning
Can the learner:
• maintain and advance communication by
- answering a variety of questions?
- asking a variety of follow-up questions?
• overcome a breakdown in communication (if it occurs) by:
- rephrasing?
- asking for help?
- correcting themselves?</td>
<td>I can exchange information by answering and asking a variety of follow-up questions. If there is a breakdown, I can rephrase, ask for help, and/or correct myself.</td>
<td>Maintain and advance communication:
• You maintain communication by responding to your partner's questions.
• You advance communication by asking a variety of questions that follow-up on ideas that your partner mentions.
• You demonstrate that you were listening to your partner through (rejoinders, affirming responses, follow-up questions. . .).
Overcome breakdowns in communication:
• You help your partner understand your ideas by (rephrasing and/ or correcting yourself) to make your message clearer.
• You check that you understand your partner's ideas by (rephrasing and/or asking follow-up questions).
• You use the target language to ask your partner for help when you don't understand something.</td>
<td>Maintain and advance communication:
• Think about the communication as a whole. What might have been a more appropriate way to start, progress, or end communication?
• What additional questions would have been appropriate to maintain and advance communication?
• How might you more fully cooperate with your partner by sharing the responsibility to initiate and develop topics?
• How could you demonstrate you are listening to your partner?
Overcome breakdowns in communication:
• What strategies could you use to help your partner when they don't understand?
• How could you use circumlocution, or use language that you know well in order to explain a word/phrase you don't know, to get your message across?
• What strategies (rephrasing and/or asking follow-up questions) might you use to check that you understand your partner's ideas?
• What are additional ways you could indicate to your partner that you need help?</td>
</tr>
</table>

Intermediate High Developing Can the learner: • maintain and advance communication by - answering a variety of appropriate questions? - asking a variety of appropriate questions? - at times sharing the responsibility to initiate and develop topics? • overcome a breakdown in communication (if it occurs) by: - rephrasing? - correcting themselves? - using circumlocution?	I can exchange information by answering and asking a variety of appropriate questions, and at times cooperate in a conversation. If there is a breakdown, I can rephrase, correct myself, and/or use circumlocution.	**Maintain and advance communication:** • You maintain communication by responding to your partner's questions. • You advance communication by using a variety of open-ended questions to invite your partner to share their opinions and ideas. • You advance communication by asking a variety of questions that follow-up on ideas that your partner mentions. • Your responses show that you are interested in what your partner is saying. • You are beginning to cooperate with your partner by sharing the responsibility to initiate and develop topics. **Overcome breakdowns in communication:** • You help your partner understand your ideas by (*rephrasing, correcting yourself, and/or using circumlocution*) to make your message clearer. • You check that you understand your partner's ideas. • When you don't understand something your partner says, you clarify by (*rephrasing and/or asking appropriate questions*).	**Maintain and advance communication:** • How might you more fully cooperate with your partner by equally sharing the responsibility to initiate and develop topics? • How might you more fully develop topics through explanations and/or comparisons of preferences, opinions, and advice? • How might you maintain and advance communication by initiating topic changes? • How might you move beyond using questions to maintain and advance communication? • What are additional ways you can invite your partner to share their opinions and ideas? • How could you demonstrate you are listening to your partner? **Overcome breakdowns in communication:** • What strategies could you use to help your partner when they don't understand? • How could you use circumlocution, or use language that you know well in order to explain a word/phrase you don't know, to get your message across? • How might you check that you understand your partner, or that your partner understands you? • What are additional ways you could use to indicate to your partner that you need help?

Advanced Low Meeting Can the learner: • maintain and advance communication by - equally sharing the responsibility with their partner to initiate and develop topics? • overcome a breakdown in communication (if it occurs) by: - rephrasing? - using circumlocution?	I can cooperate in a conversation by initiating and developing topics and topic changes. If there is a breakdown, I can rephrase and/or use circumlocution.	**Maintain and advance communication:** • You cooperate with your partner by equally sharing the responsibility to initiate and develop topics. • You maintain and advance communication, developing topics through (*explanations and/or comparisons of preferences, opinions, and advice*). • You maintain and advance communication by initiating topic changes. • You advance communication by using a variety of ways to invite your partner to share their opinions and ideas. • You use a variety of ways to show that you are interested in what your partner was saying. **Overcome breakdowns in communication:** • You (*rephrase and/or use circumlocution*) to successfully communicate your ideas. • You help your partner understand your ideas by (*rephrasing and/or using circumlocution*). • You check that you understand your partner's ideas. • When you don't understand something your partner says, you clarify by (*rephrasing, and/or asking appropriate questions*).	**Maintain and advance communication:** • How might you more fully develop topics and show interest in what your partner said by supporting, reacting to, and comparing preferences and opinions? • How could you close a topic before initiating a new topic? • How might you more cohesively transition among topic changes? • How might you incorporate probing questions to elicit more information from your partner? **Overcome breakdowns in communication:** • What strategies could you use to help your partner when they don't understand? • How could you paraphrase to get your message across and/or clarify? • How might you check that you understand your partner, or that your partner understands you?

<table>
<tr>
<td>

Advanced Mid Exceeding

Can the learner:

- maintain and advance communication by
  - equally sharing the responsibility with their partner to initiate, develop, and close topics?
  - asking probing questions?
  - at times transitioning among topic changes in a cohesive manner?
- overcome a breakdown in communication (if it occurs) by:
  - rephrasing?
  - paraphrasing?
  - using circumlocution?

</td>
<td>I can cooperate in a conversation and ask probing questions. At times I can transition among topic changes in a cohesive manner. If there is a breakdown, I can rephrase, paraphrase idea(s), and/or use circumlocution.</td>
<td>

Maintain and advance communication:

- You cooperate with your partner by equally sharing the responsibility to initiate, develop, and close topics.
- You maintain communication by (*offering advice and expressing emotions in detail*).
- You maintain and advance communication, developing topics and showing interest in what your partner says by (*supporting, reacting to, and comparing preferences and opinions*).
- You maintain and advance communication by transitioning among topic changes in a cohesive manner.
- You advance communication by asking probing questions to elicit additional information.

Overcome breakdowns in communication:

- You help your partner understand your ideas by (*rephrasing, paraphrasing, and/or using circumlocution*).
- You check that you understand the ideas expressed by your partner.
- When you don't understand something your partner says, you clarify by (*paraphrasing and/or asking probing questions*).

</td>
<td>

Maintain and advance communication:

- How might you maintain and advance communication by discussing, supporting, and debating opinions and advice?
- How might you more cohesively transition among topic changes?
- How can you ask questions with precision to elicit specific information?

Overcome breakdowns in communication:

- What strategies could you use to help your partner when they don't understand?
- How might you use illustration to further your meaning?
- How might you check that you understand your partner, or that your partner understands you?

</td>
</tr>
</table>

Performance Domain Indicators within a Rubric

In order to evaluate learners' performances, the PDIs are placed within a rubric with four performance level labels: *Beginning, Developing, Meeting,* and *Exceeding* (see Table 9.9). The *Meeting* level aligns with the target performance level for the learners. These labels communicate to learners how their performance compares to the standard; learners are *Beginning* to meet, *Developing* towards, *Meeting,* or *Exceeding* their target performance level. It is important to highlight that, similar to other ACTFL publications, when placed into a rubric, these four performance levels are arranged high to low, beginning with the highest on the left. This is so that learners read the highest level of performance first. Table 9.9 illustrates this rubric alignment and arrangement for the Communication Strategies performance domain for interpersonal communication.

Table 9.9

Aligning the Communications Strategies Performance Domain Indicators (PDIs) in a Rubric

Target performance level: **Novice High** Context: familiar, informal, formal, predictable Content: familiar, everyday				
	INTERMEDIATE LOW	NOVICE HIGH	NOVICE MID	NOVICE LOW
	EXCEEDING	MEETING	DEVELOPING	BEGINNING
Performance level description	I can exchange information by answering and asking follow-up questions. If there is a breakdown, I can repeat word(s), use similar word(s), rephrase, and/or ask for help.	I can answer and ask simple questions. If there is a breakdown, I can use gestures/facial cues, repeat word(s), and/or use similar word(s).	I can answer, and at times ask simple questions. If there is a breakdown, I can use gestures/facial cues, use my base language, and/or repeat word(s).	I can answer simple questions. If there is a breakdown, I can use gestures, facial cues, and/or use my base language.

Target performance level: **Intermediate Mid** Context: familiar, informal, formal, straight-forward Content: familiar, at times researched				
	INTERMEDIATE HIGH	**INTERMEDIATE MID**	**INTERMEDIATE LOW**	**NOVICE HIGH**
	EXCEEDING	**MEETING**	**DEVELOPING**	**BEGINNING**
Performance level description	I can exchange information by answering and asking a variety of appropriate questions, and at times cooperate in a conversation. If there is a breakdown, I can rephrase, correct myself, and/or use circumlocution.	I can exchange information by answering and asking a variety of follow-up questions. If there is a breakdown, I can rephrase, ask for help, and/or correct myself.	I can exchange information by answering and asking follow-up questions. If there is a breakdown, I can repeat word(s), use similar word(s), rephrase, and/or ask for help.	I can answer and ask simple questions. If there is a breakdown, I can use gestures/facial cues, repeat word(s), and/or use similar word(s).

Target performance level: **Advanced Low** Context: familiar, unfamiliar, informal, formal, complex Content: familiar, academic, social, concrete				
	ADVANCED MID	**ADVANCED LOW**	**INTERMEDIATE HIGH**	**INTERMEDIATE MID**
	EXCEEDING	**MEETING**	**DEVELOPING**	**BEGINNING**
Performance level description	I can cooperate in a conversation and ask probing questions. At times I can transition among topic changes in a cohesive manner. If there is a breakdown, I can rephrase, paraphrase idea(s), and/or use circumlocution.	I can cooperate in a conversation by initiating and developing topics and topic changes. If there is a breakdown, I can rephrase and/or use circumlocution.	I can exchange information by answering and asking a variety of appropriate questions, and at times cooperate in a conversation. If there is a breakdown, I can rephrase, correct myself, and/or use circumlocution.	I can exchange information by answering and asking a variety of follow-up questions. If there is a breakdown, I can rephrase, ask for help, and/or correct myself.

Performance Assessment in Action

As educators our understanding of the PDIs is critical to providing effective feedback that promotes language growth in our learners. Therefore, it is important to build our capacity to use the PDIs. Here, the goal is to model how to use the Communication Strategies PDIs to evaluate learner work, which is the basis of the GLOW and GROW feedback that is provided. The focus of this section is to evaluate learner work and provide feedback, *not* to determine a learner's proficiency level. In other words, the evaluation indicates the learner's performance is consistent with a level and provides feedback to indicate next steps for language growth.

This section demonstrates how to use these rubrics to evaluate sample interpersonal learner performances within the Novice, Intermediate, and Advanced level. These learner samples exemplify products of a summative assessment. They show evidence from learners after exposure to and practice within a unit of study. That is, learners complete these tasks following classroom instruction and multiple opportunities for formative practice on these topics. After the evaluation of each learner sample there is a model of how to provide GLOW and GROW feedback using examples from the *Performance Domain Indicators (PDIs) Assessment and Feedback Guide*.

Each learner sample:

- indicates the PDI that best aligns with the performance in the rubric.
- uses the evaluation to explain what the learner can do in this performance sample.
- models how to provide GLOW and GROW feedback using examples from the *Performance Domain Indicators (PDIs) Assessment and Feedback Guide*.

LEARNERS PERFORMING WITHIN THE NOVICE LEVEL

Mode of communication: *Interpersonal*
Target performance level: **Novice High**
Context: familiar, informal, predictable
Content: familiar, everyday

Novice Task: Chat with your new classmate to find out how you both may be similar to and/or different from each other.

LEARNER SAMPLE RESPONSE

Learner 1: Hello.

Learner 2: Hey! How's it going?

Learner 1: Good. And you?

Learner 2: Very good. What do you like more, sports or ski?

Learner 1: Ski.

Learner 2: Me too (*points to self*)! I like to ski. A lot. Um, my favorite...my favorite sport...in the...in the winter. Um, do you like to sing?

Learner 1: I don't like to sing.

Learner 2: Do you like to do...soccer in it's hot or it's cold?

Learner 1: Um...repeat?

Learner 2: Do you like to do soccer in it's hot or it's cold?

Learner 1: ...

Learner 2: Do you like to do soccer... (*kicks leg*)...in it's hot or it's cold?

Learner 1: No...comprehend (*shrugs*).

Learner 2: Do you like...soccer (*kicks leg*)...in it's hot (*fans face*) or um... it's cold, brrr (*shivers and rubs arms*)?

Learner 1: Oh! Um, yes. I like...um, hot?

Learner 2: (*Nods*)

Learner 1: Yes. Hot.

Learner 2: Cool! Me...me too!

Learner 1: Ride bike?

Learner 2: Well, sometimes. Yes, I like to ride a bike. Sometimes. In the...in the summer?

Learner 1: Ok, bye.

Learner 2: See ya later!

Evaluation & Explanation

COMMUNICATION STRATEGIES | LEARNER 1			
EXCEEDING	**MEETING**	**DEVELOPING**	**BEGINNING**
I can exchange information by answering and asking follow-up questions. If there is a breakdown, I can repeat word(s), use similar word(s), rephrase, and/or ask for help.	I can answer and ask simple questions. If there is a breakdown, I can use gestures/facial cues, repeat word(s), and/or use similar word(s).	I can answer, and at times ask simple questions. If there is a breakdown, I can use gestures/ facial cues, use my base language, and/or repeat word(s).	I can answer simple questions. If there is a breakdown, I can use gestures, facial cues, and/ or use my base language.

Evaluation: In this performance sample, Learner 1 primarily relies on answering questions to maintain the conversation. At times the learner uses memorized phrases (*And you? Ride bike?*) as simple questions to advance the conversation. When a breakdown occurs, the learner indicates a need for help in the target language (*Um...repeat?, No...comprehend*).

Feedback:

- GLOW: When a breakdown in communication occurs, you indicate a need for help using the target language.
- GROW: What questions could you ask in order to maintain and advance communication?

COMMUNICATION STRATEGIES | LEARNER 2			
EXCEEDING	**MEETING**	**DEVELOPING**	**BEGINNING**
I can exchange information by answering and asking follow-up questions. If there is a breakdown, I can repeat word(s), use similar word(s), rephrase, and/or ask for help.	I can answer and ask simple questions. If there is a breakdown, I can use gestures/facial cues, repeat word(s), and/or use similar word(s).	I can answer, and at times ask simple questions. If there is a breakdown, I can use gestures/ facial cues, use my base language, and/or repeat word(s).	I can answer simple questions. If there is a breakdown, I can use gestures, facial cues, and/ or use my base language.

Evaluation: In this performance sample, Learner 2 maintains and advances the conversation by asking and answering simple, direct questions. Although the learner is able to add more details to their questions (adding *in it's hot or it's cold*), the questions are still formulaic, or patterned, structures (*What do you like more...? Do you like...?*). The learner is able to show they are listening to what their partner says by using some rejoinders (*Me too! Cool!*) to affirm their partner's responses. When a breakdown occurs, the learner repeats the question (*Do you like to do soccer...in it's hot or it's cold?*) and uses gestures (*kicks leg, fans face, shivers and rubs arms*) to overcome the breakdown while remaining in the target language.

Feedback:

- GLOW: When a breakdown in communication occurs, you remain in the target language and help your partner understand by repeating the question and using gestures.
- GROW: How might your questions follow-up on ideas that your partner mentions, rather than asking random questions on different activities?

LEARNERS PERFORMING WITHIN THE INTERMEDIATE LEVEL

Mode of communication: *Interpersonal*
Target performance level: **Intermediate Mid**
Context: familiar, informal, straight-forward
Content: familiar, researched

Intermediate Task: After reading and viewing texts to learn about ways we can implement change, select an organization that works to better their community. Discuss your organization with a partner to learn more about the organizations you have each selected, why you selected yours, and how your organizations implement change for others.

LEARNER SAMPLE RESPONSE

Learner 1: Hi Paz!

Learner 2: Hi! How are you?

Learner 1: I'm alright. What is your organization called?

Learner 2: My organization is called the Family Stay House...But no place like home.

Learner 1: How interesting (*nods*)!

Learner 2: What is your organization called?

Learner 1: The organization...er, sorry...my organization favorite is called Renewing the Countryside.

Learner 2: Oh, how fantastic! What does it do? Renew, reuse, recycle (*laughs*)?

Learner 1: Renewing the Countryside gives money for the...for the farmers and help the children of poor families in rural communities.

Learner 2: Great! Great (*nods*)!

Learner 1: What does your organization try to do (*tilts head*)?

Learner 2: The Family Stay House tries to support and help families, families that need the help economically paying for pro-proced... when the children are sick. Where is the organization?

Learner 1: The organization...er, sorry...my organization favorite is called Renewing the Countryside.

Learner 2: My organization, um, is in the city.

Learner 1: Great! Did it do something in the past?

Learner 2: Every year, the Race for the Kids, um remember money for organization, um, to pay for the, um, pro-proced-procedures.

Learner 1: How cool (*smiles*)!

Learner 2: Um, yes, yes, yes (*nods*). Um, How many people serves the organization?

Learner 1: Many people serves the organization in the city because everyone wants to help the, the rural communities.

Learner 2: Yes, great!

Learner 1: I like your organization a lot. How can I help your organization? I pitch in?

Learner 2: Oh, how fantastic (*eyes widen*)! You can work as a volunteer – reading books to children, playing sports with the children, donating money and getting money for the organization.

Learner 1: How fun! Why should I help?

Learner 2: Um, because ...because, in my opinion, it is important to help the people-.

Learner 1: Great, great, yes (*nods*)!

Learner 2: What they do for your organization?

Learner 1: Um you can get money for the organization or you can donate. A little bit goes a long way!

Learner 2: I think so.

Learner 1: Bye (*waves*)!

Learner 2: Bye (*waves*)!

Learner 1: Thanks for talking with me.

Learner 2: I'll see you laters. Thanks for talking with me.

Evaluation & Explanation

COMMUNICATION STRATEGIES | LEARNER 1			
EXCEEDING	**MEETING**	**DEVELOPING**	**BEGINNING**
I can exchange information by answering and asking a variety of appropriate questions, and at times cooperate in a conversation. If there is a breakdown, I can rephrase, correct myself, and/or use circumlocution.	I can exchange information by answering and asking a variety of follow-up questions. If there is a breakdown, I can rephrase, ask for help, and/or correct myself.	I can exchange information by answering and asking follow-up questions. If there is a breakdown, I can repeat word(s), use similar word(s), rephrase, and/or ask for help.	I can answer and ask simple questions. If there is a breakdown, I can use gestures/facial cues, repeat word(s), and/or use similar word(s).

Evaluation: In this performance sample, Learner 1 exchanges information primarily by asking and answering follow-up questions. These questions move beyond highly practiced, ritualized questions. Rather, the questions appropriately ask for more information and follow-up on the topic at hand: their partner's organization (*Did it do something in the past? How can I help your organization? Why should I help?*). There is a variety of open-ended questions used to further the conversation (*What...? Did...? How...? Why...?*). Learner 1 demonstrates they are listening to their partner by using rejoinders (*How interesting! How cool! How fun! Great, great, yes!*). The learner also problem-solves by self-correcting (*The organization...er, sorry... my organization...*). When Learner 2 asks *Where is the organization?,* Learner 1 responds by repeating the name of the organization rather than the location. However, it does not result in a breakdown in communication. Overall, Learner 1 relies primarily on questions to maintain and advance the conversation, but there is no evidence of real cooperation beyond asking and responding.

Feedback:

- GLOW: You help your partner understand your ideas by correcting yourself to make your message clearer.
- GROW: How might you more fully develop topics before moving on to the next question?

COMMUNICATION STRATEGIES | LEARNER 2			
EXCEEDING	**MEETING**	**DEVELOPING**	**BEGINNING**
I can exchange information by answering and asking a variety of appropriate questions, and at times cooperate in a conversation. If there is a breakdown, I can rephrase, correct myself, and/or use circumlocution.	I can exchange information by answering and asking a variety of follow-up questions. If there is a breakdown, I can rephrase, ask for help, and/or correct myself.	I can exchange information by answering and asking follow-up questions. If there is a breakdown, I can repeat word(s), use similar word(s), rephrase, and/or ask for help.	I can answer and ask simple questions. If there is a breakdown, I can use gestures/facial cues, repeat word(s), and/or use similar word(s).

Evaluation: In this performance sample, Learner 2 maintains and advances the conversation by asking and answering follow-up questions. The learner asks a variety of simple questions to elicit more information about their partner's organization (*What is your organization called? What does it do? How many people serves the organization?*). The questions are appropriate to the topic (the partner's organization), although some of the questions are asked out of context (*Where is the organization? What they do for your organization?*). Learner 2 maintains the conversation by showing they are listening and responding to their partner (*How fantastic! Great!*). When Learner 2 asks *Where is the organization?*, Learner 1 responds with the name instead of the location. While this does not result in breakdown in communication, Learner 2 does model how to best answer the question with a location (*My organization, um, is in the city*). In addition, Learner 2 often gives examples to clarify (*Renew, reuse, recycle?* and *reading books to children, playing sports...*). Overall, Learner 2 primarily uses questions to advance the conversation.

Feedback:

- GLOW: You advance communication by using a variety of open-ended questions to invite your partner to share their opinions and ideas.
- GROW: How might you more fully develop topics before moving on to the next question?

LEARNERS PERFORMING WITHIN THE ADVANCED LEVEL

Mode of communication: Presentational
Target performance level: **Advanced Low**
Context: familiar, informal, complex
Content: familiar, academic, social, concrete

Advanced Task: After visiting a Monarch butterfly sanctuary, you and a friend discuss your reactions to learning about the monarch butterfly migrations and how it's being threatened.

LEARNER SAMPLE RESPONSE

Learner 1: So, what did ya think?... of the butterfly sanctuary?

Learner 2: I think that... um, the butterflies, the monarch butterflies are incredible. And these places, these sanctuaries, well, they are magical. I don´t know much things about the butterflies and their migrations before now.

Learner 1: Uhm... Same here. What fascinates me is how millions of butterflies, these tiny insects, come from all over the continent..., and to end up in these sanctuaries in Mexico, ya know?

Learner 2: Yeah, it is incredible. These places, they are so important to, to their migration process. They need these sanctuaries for, um.., this is where they sleep during the winter months.

Learner 1: Exactly. These sanctuaries are where the monarchs hibernate, so they are vital to this natural phenomenon. What's more, is the monarch's cultural influence on, like, the festival for Day of the Dead. For them, the butterflies represent the souls of their loved ones, like the butterflies (*air quotes*) are their loved ones coming back.

Learner 2: It's interesting how, how nature can influence cultural practices, like, what you said, about Day of the Dead. (...)

Learner 1: RIght. This is why I am glad to have learned that they are taking measures to, um, conserve these spaces, um, these spaces that are their habitats. Right?

Learner 2: Yes. They are protecting against destruction because of people cutting down trees illegally. But, I understand why they have to do it.

Learner 1: How so? What do you mean by that?

Learner 2: Well, some peoples depends on cutting down the trees, because they need that money to buy food and clothes for their family.

Learner 1: Ah ha (*nods head*). Now I understand. Yeah, they are between a rock and a hard place. Ya know? I don't know what I would do if... if I was in that situation where, where my family depended on the income from illegal logging. What would you do?

Learner 2: It's difficult to say what I would do too, especially because there are no other good options for them, to have, to have different jobs.

Learner 1: And, on the other hand, it's not just about to conserve the sanctuaries. For example, the use of chemicals... or pesticides in fields kills butterflies along the migration routes. It's kind of gotten out of hand. I'm not sure what can be done.

Learner 2: Well, one thing we can do is plant more milkweed, which is a flower that the butterflies depend on for food.

Evaluation & Explanation

COMMUNICATION STRATEGIES | LEARNER 1			
EXCEEDING	**MEETING**	**DEVELOPING**	**BEGINNING**
I can cooperate in a conversation and ask probing questions. At times I can transition among topic changes in a cohesive manner. If there is a breakdown, I can rephrase, paraphrase idea(s), and/or use circumlocution.	I can cooperate in a conversation by initiating and developing topics and topic changes. If there is a breakdown, I can rephrase and/or use circumlocution	I can exchange information by answering and asking a variety of appropriate questions, and at times cooperate in a conversation. If there is a breakdown, I can rephrase, correct myself, and/or use circumlocution.	I can exchange information by answering and asking a variety of follow-up questions. If there is a breakdown, I can rephrase, ask for help, and/or correct myself.

Evaluation: In this performance sample, Learner 1 is able to cooperate in the conversation; they share in the responsibility to initiate, develop, and/or close topic shifts and changes. Learner 1 further develops the topic of butterfly migration (*millions of butterflies, these tiny insects, come from all over the continent... and to end up in these sanctuaries in Mexico*). Learner 1 shifts the topic from the migration process to its cultural influence (*What's more, is the monarch's cultural influence on, like, the festival for Day of the Dead*). Learner 1 does so cohesively by using a discourse marker (*What's more*). Another example is when Learner 1 shifts the topic from the conservation of the sanctuaries to the fields along the migration routes (*And, on the other hand, it's not just about to conserve the sanctuaries*). Again, Learner 1 does this cohesively by using a discourse marker (*on the other hand*). Additionally, Learner 1 uses a probing question that asks for Learner 2 to further develop their idea (*How so? What do you mean by that?*). Finally, Learner 1 paraphrases Learner 2 (*These sanctuaries are where the monarchs hibernate, so they are vital to this natural phenomenon*). Learner 1 uses rephrasing to be more specific with vocabulary (*chemicals... or pesticides*).

Feedback:

- GLOW: You maintain and advance communication by transitioning among topic changes in a cohesive manner.
- GROW: How might you illustrate the monarch butterfly migration or the Day of the Dead cultural practices?

COMMUNICATION STRATEGIES | LEARNER 2			
EXCEEDING	**MEETING**	**DEVELOPING**	**BEGINNING**
I can cooperate in a conversation and ask probing questions. At times I can transition among topic changes in a cohesive manner. If there is a breakdown, I can rephrase, paraphrase idea(s) and/or use circumlocution.	I can cooperate in a conversation by initiating and developing topics and topic changes. If there is a breakdown, I can rephrase and/or use circumlocution.	I can exchange information by answering and asking a variety of appropriate questions, and at times cooperate in a conversation. If there is a breakdown, I can rephrase, correct myself, and/or use circumlocution.	I can exchange information by answering and asking a variety of follow-up questions. If there is a breakdown, I can rephrase, ask for help, and/or correct myself.

Evaluation: In this performance sample, Learner 2 can at times cooperate in a conversation. Learner 2 primarily responds to questions (*I think that... um, the butterflies, the monarch butterflies are incredible* and *Well, some peoples depends on cutting down the trees...*). Learner 2 also responds to topic shifts (*Yes. They are protecting against destruction...*). However, at times Learner 2 initiates topic shifts (*They need these sanctuaries for, um.., this is where they sleep during the winter months* and *But, I understand why they have to do it*). In addition, Learner 2 successfully circumlocution (*sleep during the winter* for *hibernate; cutting down trees* for *logging;* and *money to buy food and clothes for their family* for *income*) as a communication strategy.

Feedback:

- GLOW: You use circumlocution to successfully communicate your ideas.
- GROW: How might you more fully develop the topics discussed; for example, cultural practices referring to Day of the Dead or conservation measures?

YOUR TURN

LEARNING TARGETS CHECK:	
I can	☐ evaluate learner work using the Performance Domain Indicators (PDIs). ☐ give effective feedback using the Communication Strategies PDIs.

Now it is your turn to practice evaluating learner performances and providing feedback. Remember, learners complete these performance tasks following classroom instruction and multiple opportunities for formative practice on these topics. In this section, use the Communication Strategies PDIs to indicate the level of performance that best corresponds with the following interpersonal learner performance samples. Then provide each learner GLOW and GROW feedback. You may want to use the *Performance Domain Indicators (PDIs) Assessment and Feedback Guide* to help guide your evaluation and feedback of the learner's performance in the Communication Strategies performance domain.

Then, turn to APPENDIX E | Communication Strategies (p.447-p.451) to compare your evaluation and feedback to one provided by the authors. Reflect on how your evaluation and feedback was similar and/or different, and why. You can do this individually and/or with your colleagues (for example, with a Professional Learning Community (PLC)). This exercise can be an opportunity for rich discussion to help increase inter-rater reliability among educators.

LEARNERS PERFORMING WITHIN THE NOVICE LEVEL

Mode of communication: *Interpersonal*
Target performance level: **Novice High**
Context: familiar, informal, predictable
Content: familiar, everyday

Novice Task: Chat with your new classmate to find out how you both may be similar and/or different.

LEARNER SAMPLE RESPONSE

Learner 1: Um...Sports?

Learner 2: Yes (*nods*), I like sports a LOT (*smiles*). My favorite! And you?

Learner 1: Yes (*nods*).

Learner 2: What do you like more, baseball or football?

Learner 1: Baseball. I...mmm...baseball...yes. And you, sir?

Learner 2: I like baseball AND I like football! I like to play baseball in the summer. I like to watch football in the fall.

Learner 1: Ok. Um, television?

Learner 2: Yes, I like TV. I really like to watch sports on TV. And you?

Learner 1: Very good (*nods*).

Learner 2: Ok. Do you like to read?

Learner 1: Um...repeat?

Learner 2: Do you...do you like...to read?

Learner 1: ...

Learner 2: Do you like...to read?

Learner 1: Um... (*shrugs shoulders*)

Learner 2: Um, do you like to read? Um (*gestures with hands*) read...read. Um, books?

Learner 1: Oh! Yes (*nods*). I...I...yes.

Learner 2: Ok. I...um...I...too (*points to self, nods*)! I like read books. Um, do you like to swim?

Learner 1: Repeat?

Learner 2: Do you like to swim (*gestures swimming movements with arms*)?

Learner 1: Oh, yes (*nods*)! Yes, swim...yes! And you, sir?

Learner 2: Cool! I too. I like to swim in the summer. Sometimes I like to swim in the winter in the...um...in the...yeah.

Learner 1: ...

Learner 2: Ok, well, thanks! Bye (*waves*)!

Learner 1: Bye (*waves*)!

Evaluation & Explanation

COMMUNICATION STRATEGIES | LEARNER 1			
EXCEEDING	MEETING	DEVELOPING	BEGINNING
I can exchange information by answering and asking follow-up questions. If there is a breakdown, I can repeat word(s), use similar word(s), rephrase, and/or ask for help.	I can answer and ask simple questions. If there is a breakdown, I can use gestures/facial cues, repeat word(s), and/or use similar word(s).	I can answer, and at times ask simple questions. If there is a breakdown, I can use gestures/ facial cues, use my base language, and/or repeat word(s).	I can answer simple questions. If there is a breakdown, I can use gestures, facial cues, and/or use my base language.

Evaluation:

Feedback:

- GLOW:
- GROW:

COMMUNICATION STRATEGIES | LEARNER 2			
EXCEEDING	MEETING	DEVELOPING	BEGINNING
I can exchange information by answering and asking follow-up questions. If there is a breakdown, I can repeat word(s), use similar word(s), rephrase, and/or ask for help.	I can answer and ask simple questions. If there is a breakdown, I can use gestures/facial cues, repeat word(s), and/or use similar word(s).	I can answer, and at times ask simple questions. If there is a breakdown, I can use gestures/ facial cues, use my base language, and/or repeat word(s).	I can answer simple questions. If there is a breakdown, I can use gestures, facial cues, and/or use my base language.

Evaluation:

Feedback:

- GLOW:
- GROW:

Turn to APPENDIX E | Communication Strategies (p. 447-448) to compare your evaluation and explanation to one provided by the authors.

LEARNERS PERFORMING WITHIN THE INTERMEDIATE LEVEL

Mode of communication: *Interpersonal*
Target performance level: **Intermediate Mid**
Context: familiar, informal, straight-forward
Content: familiar, researched

Intermediate Task: After reading and viewing texts to learn about ways we can implement change, select an organization that works to better their community. Discuss your organization with a partner to learn more about the organizations you have each selected, why you selected yours, and how your organizations implement change for others.

LEARNER SAMPLE RESPONSE

Learner 1: Hi Kim (*waves*)!

Learner 2: Hi Hai (*waves*)!

Learner 1: What's up?

Learner 2: Um, not a lot (*shrugs shoulders*). And you?

Learner 1: Not a lot, not a lot. What is the name of your organization?

Learner 2: My organization is called Special Olympics.

Learner 1: Yes (*nods*) and what does that organization do?

Learner 2: Repeat please?

Learner 1: What does that organization do?

Learner 2: Me organization to try, um, to play sports with people with special you need...people with special needs.

Learner 1: How fantastic (*smiles*)!

Learner 2: What organization you work a volunteer?

Learner 1: My organization is called the Blizzard Foundation.

Learner 2: Very well (*nods*). Where is the organization?

Learner 1: My organization is in North Minneapolis. And...but it tries to work in all parts of Minnesota.

Learner 2: Very well (*nods*).

Learner 1: What did organization do in the past?

Learner 2: In the past, the Special Olympics to play sports...baseball, soccer, and basketball with a lot of people with special you need and...puts on the Polar Plunge.

Learner 1: Yes (*nods*).

Learner 2: What did your organization do in the past year?

Learner 1: My organization works as help people that want to play baseball but I can't buy. In the past, my organization worked with Miracle League. The children of Miracle League love baseball and it was very fun.

Learner 2: Very well. What is the priorities of the organization?

Learner 1: The first priority of my organization is donates money to children and families that can't buy baseball. And you, what is the priority?

Learner 2: Me priorities organization is helps people with special you need...did...no...has very fun.

Learner 1: And you volunteered with your organization in the past?

Learner 2: Ah no (*shakes head*), but I am going helps in the future.

Learner 1: Yes.

Learner 2: Bye (*waves*).

Learner 1: Ah, hold on.

Learner 2: Sorry.

Learner 1: How can I help your organization?

Learner 2: Repeat please?

Learner 1: How can I help your organization?

Learner 2: You work a volunteer to play sports with people with special you need and to donate money.

Learner 1: That's great! Thanks for talking with me!

Learner 2: Thanks, sir.

Evaluation & Explanation

COMMUNICATION STRATEGIES | LEARNER 1			
EXCEEDING	**MEETING**	**DEVELOPING**	**BEGINNING**
I can exchange information by answering and asking a variety of appropriate questions, and at times cooperate in a conversation. If there is a breakdown, I can rephrase, correct myself, and/or use circumlocution.	I can exchange information by answering and asking a variety of follow-up questions. If there is a breakdown, I can rephrase, ask for help, and/or correct myself.	I can exchange information by answering and asking follow-up questions. If there is a breakdown, I can repeat word(s), use similar word(s), rephrase, and/or ask for help.	I can answer and ask simple questions. If there is a breakdown, I can use gestures/facial cues, repeat word(s), and/or use similar word(s).

Evaluation:

Feedback:

- GLOW:
- GROW:

COMMUNICATION STRATEGIES | LEARNER 2			
EXCEEDING	**MEETING**	**DEVELOPING**	**BEGINNING**
I can exchange information by answering and asking a variety of appropriate questions, and at times cooperate in a conversation. If there is a breakdown, I can rephrase, correct myself, and/or use circumlocution.	I can exchange information by answering and asking a variety of follow-up questions. If there is a breakdown, I can rephrase, ask for help, and/or correct myself.	I can exchange information by answering and asking follow-up questions. If there is a breakdown, I can repeat word(s), use similar word(s), rephrase, and/or ask for help.	I can answer and ask simple questions. If there is a breakdown, I can use gestures/facial cues, repeat word(s), and/or use similar word(s).

Evaluation:

Feedback:

- GLOW:
- GROW:

Turn to APPENDIX E | Communication Strategies (p. 449-450) to compare your evaluation and explanation to one provided by the authors.

LEARNERS PERFORMING WITHIN THE ADVANCED LEVEL

Mode of communication: *Interpersonal*
Target performance level: **Advanced Low**
Context: familiar, informal, complex
Content: familiar, academic, social, concrete

Advanced Task: After visiting a Monarch butterfly sanctuary, you and a friend discuss your reactions to learning about the monarch butterfly migrations and how it's being threatened.

LEARNER SAMPLE RESPONSE

Learner 1: Hey (*waves hand*).

Learner 2: Hey.

Learner 1: So, what do you think about what we learned, um, about the sanctuaries?

Learner 2: Well, to be honest, I didn't even know of them. I had no idea that there are places like these where millions of butterflies goes to, to hibernate, like clusters of them. It was incredible to see.

Learner 1: Agreed (*widens eyes*). It blew my mind to see them togethers on only a tree branch. And that there are too many that their weight may... may... break the tree branch! It's a place that I want to go..., to, like, to experience it.

Learner 2: Yeah, I wonder how it would be (*tilts head*)? I think that I might be scared, because of these tiny insects, ya know? I don't know how I could feel. You?

Learner 1: Huh. Yeah (*shrugs shoulders*). It makes me nervous, I guess... Um, well, the sanctuaries are importants to the lifecycle of these butterflies. With no reserves, there would no be butterflies.

Learner 2: Uh huh. It was interesting to learn that only here in this specific places does it have the perfect temperature, the perfect humidity and everything. Like everything is done only for the butterflies in this place and that is why they all come every year to spend the winter.

Learner 1: I know (*raises eyebrows*)! It's a perfect ecosystem, which me.., which makes me sad that peoples cut down the trees not legally in those areas, meaning they destroy their habitat.

Learner 2: I wonder if they do not knows about how these sanctuaries are important. Or, maybe they have no choice because they need to earn a living (*shrugs and raises hands*). But it's not just this. There is also climate change and the use of pesticides that, that contribute to the destruction of the habitats.

Learner 1: Oh, for sure (*nods head*)! For example, when the farmers there use pesticides in the fields for the migratory routes, the butterflies get, um... um..., sick (*looks at Learner 2*)?

Learner 2: Sick (*tilts head*)?

Learner 1: Yeah, they get sicks because the pesticides on their food.

Learner 2: Ah! You mean poison.

Learner 1: Yes, poison. They get poisons when they eat the flower, the, um... the milkweed.

Learner 2: Yes, there are many threats to this species. Well (*sighs*), I only hope that they can protect it so one day in the future I can travel there and visit the sanctuaries.

Learner 1: Ha (*laughs*)! Yes, of course.

Evaluation & Explanation

COMMUNICATION STRATEGIES | LEARNER 1			
EXCEEDING	**MEETING**	**DEVELOPING**	**BEGINNING**
I can cooperate in a conversation and ask probing questions. At times I can transition among topic changes in a cohesive manner. If there is a breakdown, I can rephrase, paraphrase idea(s), and/or use circumlocution.	I can cooperate in a conversation by initiating and developing topics and topic changes. If there is a breakdown, I can rephrase and/or use circumlocution.	I can exchange information by answering and asking a variety of appropriate questions, and at times cooperate in a conversation. If there is a breakdown, I can rephrase, correct myself, and/or use circumlocution.	I can exchange information by answering and asking a variety of follow-up questions. If there is a breakdown, I can rephrase, ask for help, and/or correct myself.

Evaluation:

Feedback:

- GLOW:
- GROW:

COMMUNICATION STRATEGIES | LEARNER 2			
EXCEEDING	**MEETING**	**DEVELOPING**	**BEGINNING**
I can cooperate in a conversation and ask probing questions. At times I can transition among topic changes in a cohesive manner. If there is a breakdown, I can rephrase, paraphrase idea(s), and/or use circumlocution.	I can cooperate in a conversation by initiating and developing topics and topic changes. If there is a breakdown, I can rephrase and/or use circumlocution.	I can exchange information by answering and asking a variety of appropriate questions, and at times cooperate in a conversation. If there is a breakdown, I can rephrase, correct myself, and/or use circumlocution.	I can exchange information by answering and asking a variety of follow-up questions. If there is a breakdown, I can rephrase, ask for help, and/or correct myself.

Evaluation:

Feedback:

- GLOW:
- GROW:

Turn to APPENDIX E | Communication Strategies (p. 451) to compare your evaluation and explanation to one provided by the authors.

Learning Experiences to Facilitate Learner Growth

Once educators have clarified for learners the goals of performance and provided feedback, learners need learning experiences to help them *understand* the Communication Strategies performance domain and PDIs as well as *develop* their language performance. Learning experiences to *understand* the performance domain are listed first, followed by learning experiences to *develop* learner performance. Each learning experience includes *Learner outcomes* (what learners can do upon successful completion of the experience) and an outline of logistical components (*time, preparation, materials, instructions*). *Alternatives* and *Differentiation* offer ways to personalize the experience for a variety of learners. Each learning experience includes short examples, often including learners' work, to help educators visualize each learning experience. The learning experiences can be used with an entire class of learners as a way to introduce and focus learner work on a particular performance domain. Learning experiences can also be assigned to learners by educators or self-selected by learners themselves for further practice within a performance domain. These examples can serve as a springboard for educators to develop their own learning experiences for each performance domain when working with their learners.

CLARIFYING EXPECTATIONS

Domain: Communication Strategies

Focus: <u>Understanding</u> how Communication Strategies is evaluated

Note: This learning experience can be replicated in multiple performance domains.

<table>
<tr><th>Learner outcomes</th><th>Time</th><th>Materials</th><th>Prep</th></tr>
<tr>
<td>I can identify how Communication Strategies is evaluated by:<ul><li>evaluating my own work using self-assessment questions.</li><li>determining the PDI that best aligns with my work.</li><li>using the GROW guiding questions to revise and/or add to my work.</li></ul></td>
<td><ul><li>Prep time: 5 minutes</li><li>Implementation time: 30 minutes</li><li>Debrief time: 5 minutes</li></ul></td>
<td><ul><li>The performance task</li><li>Learners' interpersonal performance, such as a recording</li><li>The Communication Strategies PDIs</li><li>Self-assessment questions</li><li>GROW guiding questions</li></ul></td>
<td><ul><li>Prepare to display the PDIs, self-assessment questions, and the GROW guiding questions.</li><li>Be sure learners have access to their performance.</li></ul></td>
</tr>
</table>

Instructions

1. (PURPOSE) Tell learners that they will learn how to self-assess their work and make changes in order to reach the next performance level.
2. (SET UP) Remind learners about the task for this interpersonal performance.
3. Display the PDIs and instruct learners to use the self-assessment questions to evaluate their interpersonal work, such as a recording.
4. (GUIDANCE) Go through a few of the self-assessment questions with the learners, directing the learners to reflect on their own performance to identify if it best aligns to the *Beginning, Developing, Meeting*, or *Exceeding* PDIs.
5. (ENGAGEMENT) Release the lesson to have learners continue reflecting on the self-assessment questions and have them mark which PDIs best aligns to their work.
6. (GUIDANCE) When learners have identified the PDI that best aligns to their work, point them toward the GROW guiding questions for that level.
7. (ENGAGEMENT) Learners use the GROW guiding questions for that level to guide them to improve their work.
8. (DEBRIEF) Learners could share their reflections and improvements with a partner.
9. Ask learners to reflect on:
    a. What did you notice about your Communication Strategies before and after you reflected on the self-assessment and used the GROW guiding questions?
    b. How might you apply what you learned to your future work when completing a summative task?

<table>
<tr><th>Alternatives</th><th>Differentiation</th></tr>
<tr>
<td>Learners could complete this learning experience multiple times with multiple interpersonal tasks throughout a unit.

As learners engage in this learning experience, it eventually can be done more independently and does not need to be guided by the educator.</td>
<td>Learners could work together to give and get feedback from each other. After exchanging drafts, each learner could complete the "self" assessment questions as feedback for their partner, turning it into a peer assessment. Learners could then discuss the assessment of each other's work and brainstorm changes to level up their work.

Learners could assess an example of work from an anonymous learner individually or in a group discussion.</td>
</tr>
</table>

EXAMPLE

Target performance level: **Novice High**
Context: familiar, informal, predictable
Content: familiar, everyday

Task: To celebrate our differences, investigate which of the given profiles would add the most diversity to a group with you and your partner. Ask and answer questions about likes and dislikes to determine which of the profiles would be the most diverse.

LEARNER SAMPLE RESPONSE

Learner 1: Sports?

Learner 2: Yes, I like sports. And you?

Learner 1: Yes, sometimes.

Learner 2: What do you like more, skateboard or dancing?

Learner 1: To dance. I…to dance…many. And you?

Learner 2: I don't like to dance. Or skateboard. I don't like…um…don't like…yeah.

Learner 1: Ok. Um, you…you to dance. And Ingrid…Ingrid dance.

Learner 2: Yes, no…no Ingrid. No…no group.

Learner 1: No group.

Learner 2: Nicolas…Nicolas like…like to read. Do you like to read?

Learner 1: Um…repeat?

Learner 2: Do you…do you like…to read?

Learner 1: …

Learner 2: Do you like…to read?

Learner 1: No…comprehend.

Learner 2: Um, do you like to read? Um (*gestures with hands*) read…read, um, books? Um, Harry Potter, books?

Learner 1: Oh! Yes. Like…like…yes.

Learner 2: Ok. I like to read. And Nicolas read. No group Nicolas.

Learner 1: Naiomi?

Learner 2: Yes, Naiomi. Group of 3 – you, I, Naiomi.

Learner 1: Yes.

<table>
<tr><td colspan="4">Example of how Learner 1 might fill out the sections of the guided self-assessment (Table 9.15) and identify their GROW guiding questions (from Table 9.2).</td></tr>
<tr><td>TARGET PERFORMANCE LEVEL</td><td>Novice High</td><td>CONTEXT</td><td>Familiar, informal, formal, predictable</td></tr>
<tr><td>PERFORMANCE DOMAIN</td><td>Communication Strategies</td><td>CONTENT</td><td>Familiar, everyday</td></tr>
<tr><td colspan="4">What description(s) best matches your performance today?
☑ I used strategies to maintain and advance communication (keep the communication going).
☑ I used strategies to overcome a breakdown in communication (when my partner or I did not understand something).</td></tr>
<tr><td colspan="2">Option 1: What types of Communication Strategies did you use to maintain and advance communication today?
☑ I responded to my partner's questions.
☐ I asked my partner simple questions that followed a pattern (Do you like...? What do you like more...?).
☐ I asked questions to follow-up on an idea that my partner said.
☐ I demonstrated I was listening to my partner through gestures (nodding), facial cues (appropriate eye contact, raise eyebrows, smile...) and/or rejoinders (Really? Wow? Me too!).</td><td colspan="2">Option 2: List ways that you maintained and advanced communication today:</td></tr>
<tr><td colspan="2">Option 1: What types of Communication Strategies did you use to overcome a breakdown in communication?
☐ I gestured.
☐ I repeated.
☐ I used similar words.
☑ I indicated that I didn't understand.
☐ I modeled an answer for my partner.
☐ I asked follow-up questions to clarify when I didn't understand my partner.
☐ I rephrased my message by stating it in a different way.
☐ I asked for help to get my point across.</td><td colspan="2">Option 2: List the Communication Strategies you used to overcome a breakdown in communication:</td></tr>
<tr><td colspan="4">Evaluate how you think you performed in the your use of Communication Strategies today:
☑ Beginning: I can answer simple questions. If there is a breakdown, I can use gestures, facial cues, and/or use my base language.
☐ Developing: I can answer, and at times ask simple questions. If there is a breakdown, I can use gestures/facial cues, use my base language, and/or repeat word(s).
☐ Meeting: I can answer and ask simple questions. If there is a breakdown, I can use gestures/facial cues, repeat word(s), and/or use similar word(s).
☐ Exceeding: I can exchange information by answering and asking follow-up questions. If there is a breakdown, I can repeat word(s), use similar word(s), rephrase, and/or ask for help.</td></tr>
<tr><td colspan="4">Think about your own experience and what you have done to improve in your use of Communication Strategies. What advice would you give other learners to help them develop Communication Strategies?
Ask more questions that follow a pattern.</td></tr>
</table>

Learner directions: Use the GROW guiding questions for the level that best matches your performance. Reflect on the questions, then make changes to your work in order to reach the next level of performance.

GROW GUIDING QUESTIONS:			
EXCEEDING	**MEETING**	**DEVELOPING**	**BEGINNING**
Maintain and advance communication: • How could you invite your partner to share their opinions and ideas so you don't dominate the conversation? • How could you comment on what your partner said before moving on to the next idea? • How might you increase the variety of questions you use to follow-up on ideas that your partner mentions? • How could you demonstrate you are listening to your partner? **Overcome breakdowns in communication:** • What strategies (*repeating words, using similar words, rephrasing, and/or correcting yourself*) might you use to help your partner when they don't understand? • What strategies (*repeating, using similar words, rephrasing, and/ or asking follow-up questions*) might you use to check that you understand your partner's ideas? • What are additional ways you could use to indicate to your partner that you need help?	**Maintain and advance communication:** • How could you invite your partner to share their opinions and ideas so you don't dominate the conversation? • How could you comment on what your partner said before moving on to the next idea? • How might your questions follow-up on ideas that your partner mentions, rather than asking random questions on different topics? • What strategies (*gestures, facial cues, appropriate eye contact, rejoinders…*) might you use to demonstrate you are listening to your partner? **Overcome breakdowns in communication:** • What strategies (*repeating words, using similar words, and/ or rephrasing*) might you use to help your partner when they don't understand? • What strategies (*repeating words/ phrases, using similar words, rephrasing, and/or asking follow-up questions*) might you use to check that you understand your partner's ideas? • How could you use the target language to indicate to your partner that you need help?	**Maintain and advance communication:** • What additional questions could you ask in order to maintain and advance communication? • What strategies (*gestures, facial cues, appropriate eye contact, rejoinders…*) might you use to demonstrate you are listening to your partner? **Overcome breakdowns in communication:** • What strategies (*gestures, facial cues, repeating words, and/or using similar words*) might you use to communicate ideas to your partner while remaining in the target language? • How could you use (*gestures, facial cues, repeating words, and/ or similar words*) to clarify in the target language, rather than using your base language? • How could you use the target language to indicate to your partner that you need help?	**Maintain and advance communication:** • What questions could you ask in order to maintain and advance communication? • What strategies (*gestures, facial cues, appropriate eye contact, rejoinders…*) might you use to demonstrate you are listening to your partner? **Overcome breakdowns in communication:** • What strategies (*gestures, facial cues, and/or repeating words*) might you use to communicate ideas to your partner while remaining in the target language? • How could you use (*gestures, facial expressions, and/or repeating words*) to clarify in the target language, rather than using your base language?

Example of what a learner engaged in this process might think and rewrite based on clarifying expectations. This example shows how the learner went from brainstorming ideas to writing them in the transcript.

Learner's thinking:

Hmm, none of my questions follow a pattern.

Instead I could say:

- *Do you like sports?*
- *Do you like to dance or skateboard more?*
- *Do Naomi like to read?*

Rewrite:

Transcript of learner sample. Learner's revisions are underlined.

Learner 1: ~~Sports?~~ *Do you like sports?*

Learner 2: Yes, I like sports. And you?

Learner 1: Yes, sometimes.

Learner 2: What do you like more, skateboard or dancing?

Learner 1: To dance. I...to dance...many. ~~And you?~~ *Do you like to dance or skateboard more?*

Learner 2: I don't like to dance. Or skateboard. I don't like...um...don't like...yeah.

Learner 1: Ok. Um, you...you to dance. And Ingrid... Ingrid dance.

Learner 2: Yes, no...no Ingrid. No...no group.

Learner 1: No group.

Learner 2: Nicolas...Nicolas like...like to read. Do you like to read?

Learner 1: Um...repeat?

Learner 2: Do you...do you like...to read?

Learner 1: ...

Learner 2: Do you like...to read?

Learner 1: No...comprehend.

Learner 2: Um, do you like to read? Um (*gestures with hands*) read...read, um, books? Um, Harry Potter, books?

Learner 1: Oh! Yes. Like...like...yes.

Learner 2: Ok. I like to read. And Nicolas read. No group Nicolas.

Learner 1: ~~Naomi?~~ *Do Naomi like to read?*

Learner 2: Yes, Naomi. Group of 3 – you, I, Naomi.

Learner 1: Yes.

BRAINSTORM BUILDING

Domain: Communication Strategies

Focus: Developing Communication Strategies by brainstorming ways to maintain/advance a conversation and overcome communication breakdowns

Note: This learning experience can be replicated in multiple performance domains.

Learner outcomes	Time	Materials	Prep
I can develop Communication Strategies by brainstorming specific questions/statements to maintain or advance a conversation and to overcome breakdown in communication.	• Prep time: 5-15 minutes • Implementation time: 20 minutes • Debrief time: 5 minutes	• Transcripts of conversations: these could be short conversations or excerpts from conversations • Paper/pencil or digital writing tools for each learner	• Prepare transcripts of conversations.

Instructions

1. (PURPOSE) Tell learners that they will brainstorming ways to maintain and advance a conversation as well as overcome possible breakdowns in communication.
2. (SET UP) Brainstorm together as a class some things they could say to maintain and advance the conversation or overcome a breakdown in communication (see example).
3. Pair learners.
4. Display or hand out example conversations which learners will add to using their brainstormed Communication Strategies (see example).
5. (ENGAGEMENT) Learners brainstorm additional things they could say to maintain the conversation or a overcome breakdown in the conversation they are given.
6. Learners write their additions and note what type of strategy it is (see example).
7. (DEBRIEF) Learners could share their ideas with the class, between pairs, and/or add to the previously brainstormed class chart of ideas.
8. Ask learners to reflect on:
    a. How did you decide what you need to add?
    b. How might you apply what you learned to your future work when completing a performance task?

Alternatives	Differentiation
Learners could be given specific phrases that exemplify types of Communication Strategies and place them into the conversations. Learners can use the same Communication Strategies over and over for various performance tasks, and build on more strategies when they are ready.	Learners could add more categories of strategies that they might use. Learners could create their own interactions that elicit various types of Communication Strategies.

EXAMPLE

Chart generated by initial brainstorming as a class:

Maintain & advance the conversation:	Overcome or prevent a breakdown in communication:
• Really?! • Tell me more. • (Ask questions)	• Do you understand? • An example is… • (Give my answer to my question, then ask again)

Learner work:

Learners were given the sheet on the left and wrote *possible responses*, seen here on the right.

Example: Overcoming breakdown

Task: Compare a food pantry and a school meal program with a friend. Fill in the next line in the conversation.

Conversation 1

Learner 1: A food pantry has food, cans, but need a… a…

Learner 2: Need a kitchen or hot.

Learner 1: Yes. and cans, need a open.

Learner 2: A can opener?

Learner 1: Yes.

Learner 2: The (?) is good too.

Learner 1: ______________________________

↙

Possible responses for Learner 1:

- *Please repeat that.*
- *I did not understand.*
- *What is good?*

(overcoming breakdown)

Example: Advancing the conversation

Task: Compare a food pantry and a school meal program with a friend. Fill in the next line in the conversation.

Conversation 2

Learner 1: A food pantry is a building like a store. A program is not a store.

Learner 2: ______________________________

↙

Possible responses for Learner 2:

- *What is a program?*
- *How is a food pantry like a store?*
- *What is a program like?*

(asking for more info to advance the conversation)

As a class, learners shared out additional questions and statements they brainstormed with their partner. Additions have been added to the chart and highlighted.

Maintain & advance the conversation:	Overcome or prevent a breakdown in communication:
• Really?! • Tell me more. • (Ask questions) • What is a…? • How is … like…? • What is a … like?	• Do you understand? • An example is… • (give my answer to my question, then ask again) • Please repeat that. • I did not understand. • What is…?

LEVEL UP

Domain: Communication Strategies

Focus: Developing Communication Strategies by creating progressions

Note: This learning experience can be replicated in multiple performance domains.

Learner outcomes	Time	Materials	Prep
I can develop Communication Strategies by building progressions of Communication Strategies to "level up."	• Prep time: 20 minutes • Implementation time: 30 minutes • Debrief time: 5 minutes	• PDIs for Communication Strategies to display at the appropriate level (Novice, Intermediate, Advanced) • Interpersonal performance task • One set of transcriptions to use as a model • Paper/pencil, digital writing tools, or digital recording tools for each learner	• Prepare to display PDIs. • Have a task ready for learners to write or speak about. • Have all transcriptions available.

Instructions

1. (PURPOSE) Tell learners that they will develop their Communication Strategies by working with a group to write/speak an example performance at each level (*Beginning, Developing, Meeting,* and *Exceeding*).
2. (SET UP) Display and remind learners of the targeted PDIs for Communication Strategies.
3. Divide learners into groups of 3-5 learners each and ask them to take out paper/pencil, digital writing tools, or digital recording tools.
4. Give learners an interpersonal task with a transcript of one side of the interpersonal conversation.
5. Optional (GUIDANCE) Provide or do an example together as a whole class and write the other part of the interpersonal conversation for one performance level.
6. (ENGAGEMENT) Release the lesson to have learners work in groups to write/record one example of each level (*Beginning, Developing, Meeting,* and *Exceeding*) using the given task.
7. (GUIDANCE) Remind learners to look at the PDIs to be sure of what level they are aiming for with each example.
8. (DEBRIEF) Learners share their reflections and improvements with a partner, another group, or the class
9. Ask learners to reflect on:
   a. What did you notice about each example as you progressed through the performance levels of Communication Strategies?
   b. How might you apply what you learned to your future work when completing a performance task?

Alternatives

Learners could do this individually instead of in groups, then share in small groups.

Learners could take turns writing an example for each level (*Beginning, Developing, Meeting, Exceeding*). Groups of students could write an example interpersonal script for each PDI, or groups could be assigned to write an example interpersonal script for one assigned PDI.

One group could share their "leveled up" examples with another group to see if they identify what level each sample is meant to be.

Differentiation

After creating samples for each level about one task together as a class and another in groups, learners could each individually write an example for one level and then share it out with their group. The group can decide which performance level it best matches.

Learners could evaluate example texts that have already been created as *Beginning, Developing, Meeting,* or *Exceeding.*

EXAMPLE

Target performance level: **Intermediate Mid**
Context: familiar, informal, straight-forward
Content: familiar, researched

Task: With a classmate, discuss who has access to education.

Learner instructions: Based on the PDIs, write an example of each level of performance.

PDIs displayed:

TARGET PERFORMANCE LEVEL: INTERMEDIATE MID				
	EXCEEDING	**MEETING**	**DEVELOPING**	**BEGINNING**
Performance Domain Indicators	I can exchange information by answering and asking a variety of appropriate questions, and at times cooperate in a conversation. If there is a breakdown, I can rephrase, correct myself, and/or use circumlocution.	I can exchange information by answering and asking a variety of follow-up questions. If there is a breakdown, I can rephrase, ask for help, and/or correct myself.	I can exchange information by answering and asking follow-up questions. If there is a breakdown, I can repeat word(s), use similar word(s), rephrase, and/or ask for help.	I can answer and ask simple questions. If there is a breakdown, I can use gestures/ facial cues, repeat word(s), and/ or use similar word(s).

Learner work:

Learners were given the performance task and scripted responses from Learner 2 for all performance levels. As a class, they brainstormed example questions and responses for Learner 1 for the *Beginning* level.

BEGINNING

Learner 1: Do boys or girls go to school?

Learner 2: What?

Learner 1: Do boys or girls go to school?

Learner 2: Only boys go to school.

Learner 1: Only boys? And girls?

Learner 2: ...have money (*gestures*)?

Learner 1: Yes, girls with money go to school.

Learner 2: I don't think that.

Learner 1: Repeat?

Learner 2: No.

Learner 1: Ok.

In small groups, learners then worked together to write "leveled up" questions and responses for Learner 1 for *Developing, Meeting,* and *Exceeding.*

EXCEEDING

Learner 1: Who gets access to education?

Learner 2: What?

Learner 1: Education, like… Who gets to go to school?

Learner 2: Only boys go to school.

Learner 1: Really? When do girls go to school?

Learner 2:..have money (*gestures*)?

Learner 1: Yes with money. Can rich girls go to school and get education?

Learner 2: I don't think that.

Learner 1: Tell me more about that. Is that just your opinion?

Learner 2: No.

Learner 1: Wait, no what? Only boys go to school. Girls not allowed education. Right? But, I am not sure if you agree or disagree with that.

MEETING

Learner 1: Who gets education?

Learner 2: What?

Learner 1: Who gets education? Boys or girls?

Learner 2: Only boys go to school.

Learner 1: Only boys? What about girls?

Learner 2:..have money (*gestures*)?

Learner 1: Yes with money. Do girls with money go to school?

Learner 2: I don't think that.

Learner 1: Girls not allowed education?

Learner 2: No.

Learner 1: So only boys can go to school. Even rich girls can't. And you agree or disagree?

DEVELOPING

Learner 1: Who goes to school?

Learner 2: What?

Learner 1: Who goes to school? Boys or girls?

Learner 2: Only boys go to school.

Learner 1: Only boys? What about girls?

Learner 2:..have money (*gestures*)?

Learner 1: Yes, girls with money go to school.

Learner 2: I don't think that.

Learner 1: They can't?

Learner 2: No.

Learner 1: So only boys can go to school. Girls with money can't?

CHAT MATS

<table>
<tr><td colspan="4">Domain: Communication Strategies
Focus: Developing a repertoire of Communication Strategies</td></tr>
<tr><th>Learner outcomes</th><th>Time</th><th>Materials</th><th>Prep</th></tr>
<tr><td>I can develop my Communication Strategies by practicing specific phrases to use when appropriate to maintain and advance the conversation, as well as overcome a breakdown in communication.</td><td>• Prep time: 20 minutes
• Implementation time: 10 minutes or lesson length
• Debrief time: 5 minutes</td><td>• Interpersonal performance task
• Chat mat for each learner with useful phrases that are generic enough to be used with various content topics</td><td>• Prepare the performance task.
• Prepare chat mats.</td></tr>
<tr><td colspan="4">Instructions
1. (PURPOSE) Tell learners that they will experience how to use specific phrases while interacting with their partners. This will provide them with a repertoire of Communication Strategies they can use in conversations.
2. (SET UP) Present the interpersonal performance task for this lesson. Pass out the chat mats.
3. Review a few types of Communication Strategies with examples on the chat mat.
4. (GUIDANCE) Point out how the strategies are organized into categories (maintaining & advancing the conversion, overcoming a breakdown in communication) on the chat mat to help learners identify when to best use each strategy.
5. (SET UP) Divide learners into groups of two.
6. (ENGAGEMENT) Learners practice performing an interpersonal task together, referring to their chat mats to support their conversation.
7. (DEBRIEF) Learners share out the phrases they used most, or found most effective.
a. What did you learn about using Communication Strategies?
b. How might you apply what you learned to your future work when completing a performance task?</td></tr>
<tr><th colspan="2">Alternatives</th><th colspan="2">Differentiation</th></tr>
<tr><td colspan="2">Make poster versions of chat mats and hang them around the room. Color-code chat mat posters with strategies that might best fit learners performing within the Novice, Intermediate, and/or Advanced level.

Learners could reuse the same chat mat each time they perform an interpersonal task.</td><td colspan="2">After learners use the chat mats, they could add more ideas to them. Once new additions have been added, learners could switch chat mats with another group to see other possible phrases.

Phrases on the chat mats could be divided into two categories: Maintain and advance the conversation and overcome a breakdown in communication. Or learners could take phrases from a chat mat and categorize them themselves.</td></tr>
</table>

EXAMPLE

Examples of chat mats that could be used with learners:

Maintaining	Advancing – Adding something
How interesting! Really! Wow! 	Wait! I want to add... Yes, but... 
Advancing – Asking questions	**Overcoming Barriers**
Can you repeat that? Tell me more. What?	I don't know. I need help.

MAINTAINING & ADVANCING		OVERCOMING BARRIERS
• Awesome! • I agree! • Yes • Really?! • No way!	• Who • What • Where • When • Why • How • Do you mean...? • Is it like...?	• Say that again please. • I don't understand. • An example maybe? • It is like... • How do I say...

PASS THE PHRASE

Domain: Communication Strategies **Focus:** Developing a repertoire of Communication Strategies			
Learner outcomes	**Time**	**Materials**	**Prep**
I can develop my Communication Strategies by practicing specific phrases when appropriate to the context to maintain and advance the conversation, as well as overcome a breakdown in communication.	• Prep time: 30 minutes • Implementation time: 30 minutes or lesson length • Debrief time: 5 minutes	• Performance task(s) • Various phrases used as Communication Strategies on cards that learners can pass around (see examples)	• Make cards with various phrases used as Communication Strategies (see examples). Optional: You can color-code each type of strategy.

Instructions

1. (PURPOSE) Tell learners that they will experience using specific phrases in a conversation. They will receive a card with a phrase on it. When they use the phrase appropriately in the conversation, they can pass the card on to someone else. That learner must now use the phrase appropriately in the conversation and pass it on again. The intention is to provide learners a repertoire of Communication Strategies that they can use in their conversations.
2. (SET UP) Prime learners for a conversation on a performance task.
3. Pass out the cards with phrases to learners.
4. Encourage learners to speak in complete thoughts and use phrases appropriately within the context of the conversation.
5. Also encourage them to create opportunities for other learners to use their phrases.
6. (GUIDANCE) Instruct learners that they can always call for a time out in the conversation to ask about the meaning of a phrase, or when they might use a card.
7. (ENGAGEMENT) One learner volunteers to start the conversation.
8. Learners then continue to discuss, using the phrases on the cards and adding more information when appropriate. When they appropriately use the phrase on the card, they pass it on to another learner.
9. (GUIDANCE) You may want to watch that one learner does not get overwhelmed with too many cards.
10. (DEBRIEF) Learners could write from memory their favorite phrases in each category.
11. Ask learners to reflect on:
    a. What did you learn about using Communication Strategies?
    b. How might you apply what you learned to your future work when completing a performance task?

Alternatives	**Differentiation**
Consider using a talking stick or other discussion device that can be passed around the class. Only the person who holds the stick/device can talk, the rest must listen. Educators can indicate that the stick/device must be passed in a specific direction. This encourages all learners to participate and listen to the others. Learners could be divided into smaller groups to give voice to more learners.	Learners could focus on one type of strategy and only use phrases from that category (see chart of phrases and categories below). Learners could be allowed to "steal" a card by using the phrase on a card that another learner currently has.

EXAMPLE

Cards could be made, in the target language, with some of the phrases below. Each card would display one phrase. Phrases could be organized (and/or color-coded) into categories of types of Communication Strategies.

MAINTAINING & ADVANCING THE CONVERSATION	OVERCOMING BREAKDOWN IN COMMUNICATION
Ways to show you are listening to your partner • Wow! Really? • How fun!/That does not sound like fun! • Oh no! I'm sorry! • How interesting! • Me too!/Me neither!... • Ah, yes! I know what you mean... **Asking for more information** • What? • Is it like...? • Can you tell me more? **Asking follow-up questions** • With whom? • At what time?/when? • Why? • Where/where from? • What else? • How? **Interrupting, connecting and getting the floor** • Excuse me,... • Wait a minute,... • Hold on, ... • Let me tell you...	**Asking for help** • I need help with... • I don't know how to say it, but... • It might be like... **Asking for clarification** • Could you repeat that please? • I'm confused. • What do you mean by...? • Can you say that more slowly? • Could you be more specific? • Can you give an example? • I don't understand the question. • I didn't understand what you said.

Learner work:

Example excerpt of two learners in a conversation about what compensation people receive for various jobs. Learner 2 uses the phrase on the card, then passes it on.

(Phrase Card)

Could you be more specific?

Learner 1:

So is it fair? Who say what job gets more money?

↙

Learner 2:

Could you be more specific?

→

Learner 1:

More dangerous, more money.

More help others, maybe.

More education, yes more money.

↙

Learner 2:

Like teacher have education, so maybe more money?

INSIDE – OUTSIDE CIRCLES (OR MOVING LINES)

Domain: Communication Strategies

Focus: Developing conversation with Communication Strategies

Learner outcomes	Time	Materials	Prep
I can: • maintain and advance communication. • overcome a breakdown in communication.	• Prep time: 5 minutes • Implementation time: 20-30 minutes • Debrief time: 5 minutes	• Performance tasks • Examples of phrases used as Communication Strategies	• Prep questions and examples to display or prepare a copy so that each learner can access them.

Instructions

1. (PURPOSE) Tell learners they will practice using multiple Communication Strategies to maintain and advance the conversation. In this lesson, they will have lots of opportunities to converse with multiple partners.
2. (SET UP) Ask learners for ways they might express Communication Strategies to maintain and advance the conversation and overcome a breakdown in communication. List learner's ideas and review Communication Strategies with learners.
3. Divide the learners into two groups (group 1 and group 2) and have the learners in group 1 form a circle facing outward. Have the learners in group 2 each find a partner from group 1 and face that partner. This will mean group 2 will form an outer circle that faces inward (see the diagram in the example below).
4. (GUIDANCE) Instruct learners from group 1 (the inner circle) to begin the conversation using the given performance task. Group 2 learners (the outer circle) will advance the conversation using Communication Strategies. They will have two minutes to discuss the topic back and forth, with both partners using multiple Communication Strategies.
5. (ENGAGEMENT) Learners are given the performance task and all pairs begin to discuss. They may use their notes or reference the display of Communication Strategies.
6. (GUIDANCE) At the end of two minutes, stop the discussions. Give learners an opportunity to reflect about any Communication Strategies they used and how they used them.
7. Have learners in the inner circle move left, so that everyone has a new partner.
8. Repeat the process with a new performance task. Continue the rotation and new performance tasks every two minutes.
9. (ENGAGEMENT) Learners hear and use various Communication Strategies with each new partner and prompt.
10. (DEBRIEF) Learners could reflect on their favorite phrases, their most successful phrases, the phrases they used the most often, or the phrases they did not use as much and why.
11. Ask learners to reflect on:
    a. What did you learn about using Communication Strategies?
    b. How might you apply what you learned to your future work when completing a performance task?

Alternatives	Differentiation
Learners could discuss the same performance task for each round. Learners could form two equal lines facing each other, instead of circles. After each round, one line moves left so each learner has a new partner. If there are an uneven number of learners, the odd one out for that round could listen and possibly circle the Communication Strategies used by a pair of learners. Moving faster or more slowly allows for various types of interactions in inside/outside circles. You could have a set of lighting rounds at the end for quick responses. Learners could use a chat mat with Communication Strategies to reference while participating in the inside-outside circle.	Educators could assign a specific type of Communication Strategy for a round to practice more deliberately. For example, "With this partner, I want you both to ask for clarification." Learners can track the number of Communication Strategies they use by circling them. They could try to use more strategies than their partner, or count up their strategies over the course of a round or several rounds. Learners could challenge themselves to use every Communication Strategy displayed.

EXAMPLE

An example display of Communication Strategies in the target language (modify as appropriate for learners):

MAINTAINING & ADVANCING THE CONVERSATION

Way to show that I am listening to my partner:

- Wow! Really?
- How fun!/That does not sound like fun!
- Oh no! I'm sorry!
- How interesting!
- Me too!/Me neither!...
- Ah, yes! I know what you mean...

Asking for more information

- What?
- Is it like...?
- Can you tell me more?

Asking follow-up questions

- With whom?
- At what time?/when?
- Why?
- Where/where from?
- What else?
- How?

Interrupting, connecting and getting the floor

- Excuse me,...
- Wait a minute,...
- Hold on,...
- Let me tell you...

OVERCOMING BREAKDOWN IN COMMUNICATION

Asking for help

- I need help with...
- I don't know how to say it, but...
- It might be like...

Asking for clarification

- Could you repeat that please?
- I'm confused.
- What do you mean by...?
- Can you say that more slowly?
- Could you be more specific?
- Can you give an example?
- I don't understand the question.
- I didn't understand what you said.

Learner work:

Example excerpt of two learners in a conversation using Communication Strategies in *Inside-Outside Circles*. The Communication Strategies used are underlined.

Task: Interview a friend about a holiday or something they celebrate.

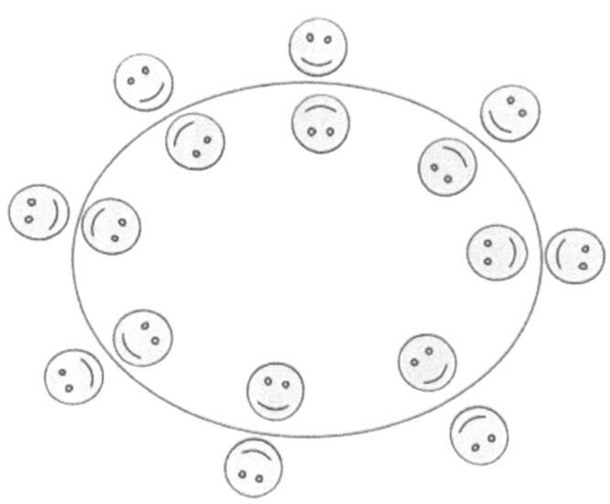

Learner 1: *Juneteenth is holiday. I celebrate with my family.*

→

Learner 2: *How interesting!* *Do you eat special?* *What do you?*

↙

Learner 1: *Could you repeat that please?*

→

Learner 2: *What do you eat or drink?*

↙

Learner 1: *Red drink.*

PYRAMID OF CATEGORIES

Domain: Communication Strategies

Focus: Developing the Communication Strategy of giving examples

Learner outcomes	Time	Materials	Prep
I can communicate unfamiliar ideas by: • using words I know well to express ideas. • describing something instead of using the exact word for it. • giving examples using words that I am familiar with.	• Prep time: 20 min • Implementation time: 5 minutes per situation, depends on how many rounds you choose to do. • Debrief time: 5 minutes	• A list of 6 categories in which learners will be able to name examples • Timer(s) • Paper/pencil or digital writing tools for each learner who is observing	• Make pyramids with 6 categories and coverings for each.

Instructions

1. (PURPOSE) Learner 1 will try to get Learner 2 to guess each block on the pyramid. Each block is a category, like *Things at the Grocery Store*. Learner 1 will see what is under each block on the pyramid. Learner 1 will try to get Learner 2 to name the category by giving examples of things that fall into that category, like *cookies, milk, lettuce, soap, ice cream, cashiers*... This will help learners practice the Communication Strategy of giving examples. For the purposes of this experience, pairs will be given a time limit to guess all of the categories.
2. (SET UP) Have learners pair up and decide who will be Learner 1 (reading/acting) and Learner 2 (guessing the category).
3. Give Learner 1 a pyramid with covered categories. Learner 1 looks at the first category (bottom left of pyramid) but Learner 2 does not see it.
4. Tell Learner 1 that they must give examples of the category, but cannot name the category. Learner 2 will try to guess what the category is.
5. (ENGAGEMENT) Learner 1 begins by giving examples of things in that category. Learner 2 guesses what the category is. As categories are correctly guessed, Learner 1 acknowledges they are correct. Learner 1 then reads the next category/block on the pyramid and gives examples of the new category. The pair try to guess all categories within the time limit.
6. (GUIDANCE) Learner 1 can decide to pass and go back to a category if there is enough time.
7. (GUIDANCE) Encourage learners to begin with one word clues. Depending on the level of performance, learners could develop longer descriptive phrases like *a package of cookies, lettuce wrapped in plastic*.
8. (DEBRIEF) Learners reflect on how this strategy could help them communicate, especially if they don't know the exact word they wish to express.
9. Ask learners to reflect on:
   a. What did you learn about giving examples to communicate an idea?
   b. How might you apply what you learned to your future work when completing a performance task?

Alternatives

Each block on the pyramid could be given a score so pairs of learners could tally how many points they earned after each round.

Instead of categories and examples, learners could use circumlocution to describe the blocks on the pyramid to get their partners to understand and say what is on the pyramid. For example,

Learner 1 says: *I ride it to school.*	**Learner 2** responds: *car,...bike*
Then **Learner 1** says: *It is yellow.*	**Learner 2** responds: *What?*
Then **Learner 1** says: *It stops at the corner.*	Then **Learner 2** responds: *A school bus!*

Differentiation

Learners could be given lists of words to divide among the categories.

Learners could come up with their own categories and trade them with other pairs.

EXAMPLE

STEP 1:
Learner 1 sees the category under each block of the pyramid, one a time:

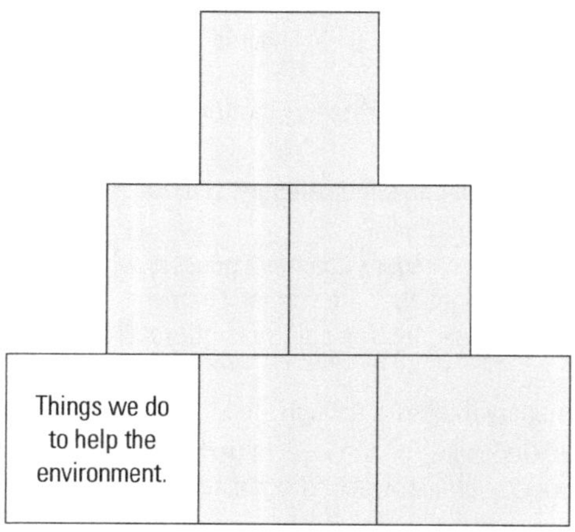

STEP 2:

Learner 1 says: *recycling no eat meat* → **Learner 2** says: *Garbage, no... um. Things to help the environment.*

STEP 3:

The next square is revealed and **Learner 1** gives clues for it. → **Learner 2** guesses the next category.

YOUR TURN

LEARNING TARGET CHECK:	
I can	☐ select learning experiences that support learners' growth with Communication Strategies.

Complete the chart by identifying specific learning experiences from the *Learning Experiences to Facilitate Learner Growth* section (p. 366-384) that you could use in an upcoming unit to help learners *understand* or *develop* Communication Strategies. Note any materials or prep needed to implement the learning experience in your upcoming unit. Consider any alternatives or differentiation that would better align the learning experience to your unit, the targeted level of performance, and/or your learners.

UNIT:			
PERFORMANCE DOMAIN: COMMUNICATION STRATEGIES			
Learning experience	**What type of learning experience is it?** (Circle one)	**Materials/Prep**	**Alternatives / Differentiation**
	Understanding/ Developing		
	Understanding/ Developing		
	Understanding/ Developing		

Learners' Self-Assessments

Self-assessment provides an opportunity for learners to reflect on their performance, set goals, and ultimately to own their learning. This section features three ways learners can self-assess their work: *Make It Visible, Glow and Grow Self-Assessment*, and *Guided Self-Assessments*. Each is educator-designed but learner-driven. That is, the self-assessment is designed by the educator around the PDIs but it is the learner who must reflect on their performance to complete it. The same self-assessments are used in each performance domain chapter to build consistency for learners. Each can be used for learner self-assessment after a formative or summative task. Educators might select self-assessments that have more scaffolding, such as the *Guided Self-Assessment* and *Make It Visible*, after formative tasks where learners may need more support to self-assess their performance, such as the beginning of a unit or a course. The *Glow and Grow Self-Assessment*, which is more open-ended, can be used when learners feel more comfortable reflecting on the PDIs and summarizing their work, such as after formative tasks that occur at the end of the unit or after a summative task. Overall, educators can make adjustments to any of these self-assessments and use them with intentionality based on their learners, their pacing within a unit or course, and the performance task.

Make It Visible

This self-assessment provides an opportunity for learners to visibly see their Communication Strategies in a given formative or summative task. Learners might circle, highlight, color-code, or note the ways in which they used language in a given interpersonal performance (see Table 9.10 and Figure 9.1). Or learners can self-assess by marking yes/no and providing evidence (see Table 9.11, Figure 9.2, Table 9.12, and Figure 9.3). Educators can provide opportunities for revisions and/or additions for learners who may find they are not yet *Meeting* expectations, so learners have opportunities for language growth.

The learner samples in this section demonstrate how each self-assessment can be used at one performance level. However, these self-assessments can be used at any level: Novice, Intermediate, or Advanced.

Table 9.10

Interpersonal Self-Assessment #1 Using the "Make It Visible" Approach

Communication Strategies Reflection Guide: How do I maintain and advance the conversation?		
MOVE TO:	**CIRCLE YOUR LEVEL OF PERFORMANCE**	**MOVE FROM:**
Uses the target language all the time	**4 3 2 1**	Uses non-target language frequently
Volunteers comments related to discussion	**4 3 2 1**	Only responds when asked
Asks appropriate/ follow-up questions related to what someone else said	**4 3 2 1**	Asks random questions
Asks clarifying questions when something is not understood	**4 3 2 1** I understood everything my partner said	Moves on without addressing misunderstandings
Gives responses with details, reasons, explanations	**4 3 2 1**	Gives short responses
Invites others to give their opinions, ideas	**4 3 2 1**	Dominates the discussion
Adds ideas, insights additional information to make the discussion more interesting	**4 3 2 1**	Repeats ideas that others already contributed
Actively listens to what others are saying	**4 3 2 1**	Does not pay attention during the discussion

Note: Adapted from "Interpersonal Communication: Focus on Feedback," by Sandrock, P. & Clementi, D., 2018. Adapted with permission.

Figure 9.1
Example of a Completed Interpersonal Self-Assessment Using the "Make It Visible" Approach

Directions: Listen to the recording of your interpersonal conversation. Complete the *Communication Strategies Reflection Guide* by circling your level of performance.

LEARNER SAMPLE

Learner 1: Hello.

Learner 2: Hey! How's it going?

Learner 1: Good. And you?

Learner 2: Very good. What do you like more, sports or ski?

Learner 1: Ski.

Learner 2: Me too (*points to self*)! I like to ski. A lot. Um, my favorite...my favorite sport...in the...in the winter. Um...do you like to sing?

Learner 1: I don't like to sing.

Learner 2: Do you like to do...soccer in it's hot or it's cold?

Learner 1: Um...repeat?

Learner 2: Do you like to do soccer in it's hot or it's cold?

Learner 1:...

Learner 2: Do you like to do soccer...(*kicks leg*)...in it's hot or it's cold?

Learner 1: No...comprehend (*shrugs*).

Learner 2: Do you like...soccer (*kicks leg*)... in it's hot (*fans face*) or um... it's cold, brrr (*shivers and rubs arms*)?

Learner 1: Oh! Um, yes. I like...um, hot?

Learner 2: (*Nods*)

Learner 1: Yes. Hot.

Learner 2: Cool! Me...me too!

Learner 1: Ride bike?

Learner 2: Well, sometimes. Yes, I like to ride a bike. Sometimes. In the...in the summer?

Learner 1: Ok, bye.

Learner 2: See ya later!

Example of how Learner 2, performing at the Novice level, completes this self-assessment:

Communication Strategies Reflection Guide: How do I maintain and advance the conversation?		
CIRCLE YOUR LEVEL OF PERFORMANCE	**CIRCLE YOUR LEVEL OF PERFORMANCE**	**CIRCLE YOUR LEVEL OF PERFORMANCE**
Uses the target language all the time	(4) 3 2 1	Uses non-target language frequently
Volunteers comments related to discussion	(4) 3 2 1	Only responds when asked
Asks appropriate/ follow-up questions related to what someone else said	4 (3) 2 1	Asks random questions
Asks clarifying questions when something is not understood	4 3 2 1 (I understood everything my partner said)	Moves on without addressing misunderstandings
Gives responses with details, reasons, explanations	4 (3) 2 1	Gives short responses
Invites others to give their opinions, ideas	4 (3) 2 1	Dominates the discussion
Adds ideas, insights additional information to make the discussion more interesting	4 (3) 2 1	Repeats ideas that others already contributed
Actively listens to what others are saying	(4) 3 2 1	Does not pay attention during the discussion

Note: Adapted from "Interpersonal Communication: Focus on Feedback," by Sandrock, P. & Clementi, D., 2018. Adapted with permission.

Table 9.11

Interpersonal Self-Assessment #2 Using the "Make It Visible" Approach

Note: The ways in which someone can show they are listening to their partner are highly dependent on the social and cultural context they are operating within. These strategies should be adapted so they are appropriate to the social and cultural context of the performance task.

Communication Strategies Reflection Guide: How do I show my partner that I am listening?			
WAYS TO SHOW I AM LISTENING TO MY PARTNER	**YES**	**NO**	**COMMENTS/EXAMPLES**
Show you are listening – nodding your head, rejoinders (*Great! Really? Oh my!*)			
Keep an open mind, avoid interrupting			
Ask clarifying questions after speaker pauses			
Paraphrase something the speaker said (*You said that..., You think that...*)			
Ask appropriate follow-up questions that probe what the speaker said			
Give your opinion after follow-up questions, clarifications, paraphrasing			

Note: Adapted from "Interpersonal Communication: Focus on Feedback," by Sandrock, P. & Clementi, D., 2018. Adapted with permission.

Figure 9.2

Example of a Completed Interpersonal Self-Assessment Using the "Make It Visible" Approach

Directions: Watch a video recording of your interpersonal conversation. Complete the *Communication Strategies Reflection Guide* and list examples of how you showed your partner that you were listening.

LEARNER SAMPLE

Learner 1: Hi Paz!

Learner 2: Hi! How are you?

Learner 1: I'm alright. What is your organization called?

Learner 2: My organization is called the Family Stay House...But no place like home.

Learner 1: How interesting (*nods*)!

Learner 2: What is your organization called?

Learner 1: The organization...er, sorry...my organization favorite is called Renewing the Countryside.

Learner 2: Oh, how fantastic! What does it do? Renew, reuse, recycle (*laughs*)?

Learner 1: Renewing the Countryside gives money for the...for the farmers and help the children of poor families in rural communities.

Learner 2: Great! Great (*nods*)!

Learner 1: What does your organization try to do (*tilts head*)?

Learner 2: The Family Stay House tries to support and help families, families that need the help economically paying for pro-proced... when the children are sick. Where is the organization?

Learner 1: The organization...er, sorry...my organization favorite is called Renewing the Countryside.

Learner 2: My organization, um, is in the city.

Learner 1: Great! Did it do something in the past?

Learner 2: Every year, the Race for the Kids, um remember money for organization, um, to pay for the, um, pro-proced-procedures.

Learner 1: How cool (*smiles*)!

Learner 2: Um, yes, yes, yes (*nods*). Um, How many people serves the organization?

Learner 1: Many people serves the organization in the city because everyone wants to help the, the rural communities.

Learner 2: Yes, great!

Learner 1: I like your organization a lot. How can I help your organization? I pitch in?

Learner 2: Oh, how fantastic (*eyes widen*)! You can work as a volunteer – reading books to children, playing sports with the children, donating money and getting money for the organization.

Learner 1: How fun! Why should I help?

Learner 2: Um, because...because, in my opinion, it is important to help the people.

Learner 1: Great, great, yes (*nods*)!

Learner 2: What they do for your organization?

Learner 1: Um you can get money for the organization or you can donate. A little bit goes a long way!

Learner 2: I think so.

Learner 1: Bye (*waves*)!

Learner 2: Bye (*waves*)!

Learner 1: Thanks for talking with me.

Learner 2: I'll see you laters. Thanks for talking with me.

Example of how Learner 1, performing within the Intermediate level, completes this self-assessment:

Communication Strategies Reflection Guide: How do I show my partner that I am listening?			
WAYS TO SHOW I AM LISTENING TO MY PARTNER	**YES**	**NO**	**COMMENTS/EXAMPLES**
Show you are listening – nodding your head, rejoinders (*Great! Really? Oh my!*)	X		*How interesting.* *Great!* *How cool!* *How fun!*
Keep an open mind, avoid interrupting	X		
Ask clarifying questions after speaker pauses		X	
Paraphrase something the speaker said (*You said that…, You think that…*)		X	
Ask appropriate follow-up questions that probe what the speaker said	X		*How can I help your organization?* *Why should I help?*
Give your opinion after follow-up questions, clarifications, paraphrasing		X	

Note: Adapted from "Interpersonal Communication: Focus on Feedback," by Sandrock, P. & Clementi, D., 2018. Adapted with permission.

Table 9.12

Interpersonal Self-Assessment #3 Using the "Make It Visible" Approach

Communication Strategies Reflection Guide: How do I overcome a breakdown in communication?			
Negotiating of meaning	**Yes**	**No**	**Comments/Examples**
Use gestures or facial cues			
Repeat words or phrases			
Use similar words to communicate my message			
Help my partner using the target language			
Rephrase my message			
Ask follow-up questions to clarify when I don't understand your partner			
Ask for help using the target language			
Correct myself			
Use circumlocution, or use language that I know well in order to explain a word/phrase I don't know			
Paraphrase			
Ask probing questions to clarify when I don't understand your partner			
Give examples to illustrate my message			

Figure 9.3

Example of a Completed Interpersonal Self-Assessment Using the "Make It Visible" Approach

Directions: Watch a video recording of your interpersonal conversation. Complete the *Communication Strategies Reflection Guide* and list examples of how you overcame a breakdown in communication.

LEARNER SAMPLE

Learner 1: So, what did ya think?... of the butterfly sanctuary?

Learner 2: I think that... um, the butterflies, the monarch butterflies are incredible. And these places, these sanctuaries, well, they are magical. I don´t know much things about the butterflies and their migrations before now.

Learner 1: Uhm... Same here. What fascinates me is how millions of butterflies, these tiny insects, come from all over the continent..., and to end up in these sanctuaries in Mexico, ya know?

Learner 2: Yeah, it is incredible. These places, they are so important to, to their migration process. They need these sanctuaries for, um.., this is where they sleep during the winter months.

Learner 1: Exactly. These sanctuaries are where the monarchs hibernate, so they are vital to this natural phenomenon. What's more, is the monarch's cultural influence on, like, the festival for Day of the Dead. For them, the butterflies represent the souls of their loved ones, like the butterflies (*air quotes*) are their loved ones coming back.

Learner 2: It's interesting how, how nature can influence cultural practices, like, what you said, about Day of the Dead. (...)

Learner 1: RIght. This is why I am glad to have learned that they are taking measures to, um, conserve these spaces, um, these spaces that are their habitats. Right?

Learner 2: Yes. They are protecting against destruction because of people cutting down trees illegally. But, I understand why they have to do it.

Learner 1: How so? What do you mean by that?

Learner 2: Well, some peoples depends on cutting down the trees, because they need that money to buy food and clothes for their family.

Learner 1: Ah ha (*nods head*). Now I understand. Yeah, they are between a rock and a hard place. Ya know? I don't know what I would do if... if I was in that situation where, where my family depended on the income from illegal logging. What would you do?

Learner 2: It's difficult to say what I would do too, especially because there are no other good options for them, to have, to have different jobs.

Learner 1: And, on the other hand, it's not just about to conserve the sanctuaries. For example, the use of chemicals... or pesticides in fields kills butterflies along the migration routes. It's kind of gotten out of hand. I'm not sure what can be done.

Learner 2: Well, one thing we can do is plant more milkweed, which is a flower that the butterflies depend on for food.

Example of how Learner 1, performing within the Advanced level, completes this self-assessment:

Communication Strategies Reflection Guide:
How do I overcome a breakdown in communication?

NEGOTIATING OF MEANING	YES	NO	COMMENTS/EXAMPLES
Use gestures or facial cues	X		*air quotes, nods*
Repeat words or phrases		X	
Use similar words to communicate my message		X	
Help my partner using the target language		X	
Rephrase my message	X		*millions of butterflies, these tiny insects*
Ask follow-up questions to clarify when I don't understand your partner		X	
Ask for help using the target language		X	
Correct myself		X	
Use circumlocution, or use language that I know well in order to explain a word/phrase I don't know		X	
Paraphrase	X		*These sanctuaries are where the monarchs hibernate, so they are vital to this natural phenomenon.*
Ask probing questions to clarify when I don't understand your partner	X		*How so? What do you mean by that?*
Give examples to illustrate my message	X		*For example, the use of chemicals... or pesticides in fields kills butterflies along the migration routes.*

GLOW and GROW Self Assessment

Using the *Meeting* Performance Domain Indicator for each level, learners can self-assess their work on a one-point rubric after a formative or summative task. In Tables 9.12, 9.13, and 9.14, learners would complete the *Where I GLOW (What are my strengths?)* and *How I can GROW (What can I do to improve?)* sections by citing evidence from their own interpersonal performance for each performance domain. The *GLOW/GROW Ideas* are given as prompts so that learners are reminded of what to look for or work toward.

Table 9.12
GLOW and GROW Self-Assessment

Communication Strategies Target performance level: **Novice High** Context: familiar, informal, formal, predictable Content: familiar, everyday		
Instructions: Complete the following reflection by writing where you GLOW and where you can GROW in each area. Make sure to include evidence from your work to support your reasoning.		
Where I GLOW: What are my strengths?	**Performance Domain Indicator**	**How can I GROW? What can I do to improve?**
	I can answer and ask simple questions. If there is a breakdown, I can use gestures/facial cues, repeat word(s), and/or use similar word(s).	

GLOW IDEAS	**GROW IDEAS**
Maintain and advance communication: • How did you maintain communication by responding to simple questions? • What simple questions did you ask to maintain and advance communication? • How did you demonstrate you were listening to your partner through (*gestures, facial cues, appropriate eye contact, rejoinders…*)? **Overcome breakdowns in communication:** • How did you help your partner understand your ideas by (*using gestures, using facial cues, repeating words, and/or using similar words*) to make your message clearer? • Were you able to stay in the target language and indicate to your partner if you needed help by using (*gestures, facial cues, and/or a specific word/phrase like "repeat?"*)?	**Maintain and advance communication:** • How could you invite your partner to share their opinions and ideas so you don't dominate the conversation? • How could you comment on what your partner said before moving on to the next idea? • How might your questions follow-up on ideas that your partner mentioned, rather than asking random questions on different topics? • What strategies (*gestures, facial cues, appropriate eye contact, rejoinders…*) might you use to demonstrate you are listening to your partner? **Overcome breakdowns in communication:** • What strategies (*repeating words, using similar words, and/or rephrasing*) might you use to help your partner when they don't understand? • What strategies (*repeating words/phrases, using similar words, rephrasing, and/or asking follow-up questions*) might you use to check that you understand the ideas your partner expressed? • How could you use the target language to indicate to your partner that you need help?

Table 9.13
GLOW and GROW Self-Assessment

<table>
<tr><th colspan="3">Communication Strategies
Target performance level: Intermediate Mid
Context: familiar, informal, formal, straight-forward
Content: familiar, at times researched</th></tr>
<tr><td colspan="3">Instructions: Complete the following reflection by writing where you GLOW and where you can GROW in each area. Make sure to include <u>evidence</u> from your work to support your reasoning.</td></tr>
<tr><td>Where I GLOW:
What are my strengths?</td><td>Performance
Domain Indicator</td><td>How can I GROW?
What can I do to improve?</td></tr>
<tr><td></td><td>I can exchange information by answering and asking a variety of follow-up questions. If there is a breakdown, I can rephrase, ask for help, and/or correct myself.</td><td></td></tr>
</table>

<table>
<tr><th>GLOW IDEAS</th><th>GROW IDEAS</th></tr>
<tr><td>Maintain and advance communication:
• How did you respond to your partner's questions to maintain communication?
• What questions did you ask that followed-up on ideas that your partner mentioned? Did you use a variety of questions?
• How did you demonstrate that you were listening to your partner through (rejoinders, affirming responses, follow-up questions…)?

Overcome breakdowns in communication:
• How did you help your partner understand your ideas by (rephrasing and/or correcting yourself) to make your message clearer?
• How did you check that you understood the ideas expressed by your partner by (rephrasing and/or asking follow-up questions)?
• How did you use the target language to ask your partner for help if you didn't understand something?</td><td>Maintain and advance communication:
• Think about the communication as a whole. What might have been a more appropriate way to start, progress, or end communication?
• What additional questions would have been appropriate to maintain and advance communication?
• How might you more fully cooperate with your partner by sharing the responsibility to initiate and develop topics?
• How could you demonstrate you are listening to your partner?

Overcome breakdowns in communication:
• What strategies could you use to help your partner when they don't understand?
• How could you use circumlocution, or use language that you know well in order to explain a word/phrase you don't know, to get your message across?
• What strategies (rephrasing and/or asking follow-up questions) might you use to check that you understand your partner's ideas?
• What are additional ways you could indicate to your partner that you need help?</td></tr>
</table>

Table 9.14
GLOW and GROW Self-Assessment

Communication Strategies Target performance level: **Advanced Low** Context: familiar, unfamiliar, informal, formal, complex Content: familiar, academic, social, concrete		
Instructions: Complete the following reflection by writing where you GLOW and where you can GROW in each area. Make sure to include evidence from your work to support your reasoning.		
Where I GLOW: **What are my strengths?**	**Performance** **Domain Indicator**	**How can I GROW?** **What can I do to improve?**
	I can cooperate in a conversation by initiating and developing topics and topic changes. If there is a breakdown, I can rephrase and/or use circumlocution.	

GLOW IDEAS	GROW IDEAS
Maintain and advance communication: • How did you cooperate with your partner by equally sharing the responsibility to initiate and develop topics? • How did you maintain and advance communication, developing topics through (*explanations and/or comparisons of preferences, opinions, and advice*)? • How did you maintain and advance communication by initiating topic changes? • How did you advance communication and use a variety of ways to invite your partner to share their opinions and ideas? • In what ways did you show that you were interested in what your partner was saying? **Overcome breakdowns in communication:** • How did you (*rephrase and/or use circumlocution*) to successfully communicate your ideas? • How did you help your partner understand your ideas by (*rephrasing and/or using circumlocution*) in the target language? • How did you check that you understood the ideas expressed by your partner? • How did you clarify if you didn't understand something your partner said (*rephrasing and/or asking appropriate questions*)?	**Maintain and advance communication:** • How might you more fully develop topics and show interest in what your partner said by supporting, reacting to, and comparing preferences and opinions? • How could you close a topic before initiating a new topic? • How might you more cohesively transition among topic changes? • How might you incorporate probing questions to elicit more information from your partner? **Overcome breakdowns in communication:** • What strategies could you use to help your partner when they don't understand? • How could you paraphrase to get your message across and/or clarify? • How might you check that you understand your partner, or that your partner understands you?

Guided Self-Assessments

This self-assessment includes guiding questions to help learners evaluate their own performance after a formative or summative task (see Tables 9.15, 9.16, and 9.17). Options are included to help educators personalize the self-assessment for their learners, or learners can self-select which options to answer.

Table 9.15
Interpersonal Guided Self-Assessment

<table>
<tr><td>TARGET PERFORMANCE LEVEL</td><td>Novice High</td><td>CONTEXT</td><td>Familiar, informal, formal, predictable</td></tr>
<tr><td>PERFORMANCE DOMAIN</td><td>Communication Strategies</td><td>CONTENT</td><td>Familiar, everyday</td></tr>
<tr><td colspan="4">What description(s) best matches your performance today?
☐ I used strategies to maintain and advance communication (keep the communication going).
☐ I used strategies to overcome a breakdown in communication (when my partner or I did not understand something).</td></tr>
<tr><td colspan="2">Option 1: What types of Communication Strategies did you use to maintain and advance communication today?
☐ I responded to my partner's questions.
☐ I asked my partner simple questions that followed a pattern (Do you like…? What do you like more…?).
☐ I asked questions to follow-up on an idea that my partner said.
☐ I demonstrated I was listening to my partner through gestures (nodding), facial cues (appropriate eye contact, raise eyebrows, smile…) and/or rejoinders (Really? Wow? Me too!).</td><td colspan="2">Option 2: List ways that you maintained and advanced communication today:</td></tr>
<tr><td colspan="2">Option 1: What types of Communication Strategies did you use to overcome a breakdown in communication?
☐ I gestured.
☐ I repeated.
☐ I used similar words.
☐ I indicated that I didn't understand.
☐ I modeled an answer for my partner.
☐ I asked follow-up questions to clarify when I didn't understand my partner.
☐ I rephrased my message by stating it in a different way.
☐ I asked for help to get my point across.</td><td colspan="2">Option 2: List the Communication Strategies you used to overcome a breakdown in communication:</td></tr>
<tr><td colspan="4">Evaluate how you think you performed in the your use of Communication Strategies today:
☐ Beginning: I can answer simple questions. If there is a breakdown, I can use gestures, facial cues, and/or use my base language.
☐ Developing: I can answer, and at times ask simple questions. If there is a breakdown, I can use gestures/facial cues, use my base language, and/or repeat word(s).
☐ Meeting: I can answer and ask simple questions. If there is a breakdown, I can use gestures/facial cues, repeat word(s), and/or use similar word(s).
☐ Exceeding: I can exchange information by answering and asking follow-up questions. If there is a breakdown, I can repeat word(s), use similar word(s), rephrase, and/or ask for help.</td></tr>
<tr><td colspan="4">Think about your own experience and what you have done to improve in your use of Communication Strategies. What advice would you give other learners to help them develop Communication Strategies?</td></tr>
</table>

Table 9.16
Interpersonal Guided Self-Assessment

<table>
<tr><td>TARGET PERFORMANCE LEVEL</td><td>Intermediate Mid</td><td>CONTEXT</td><td>Familiar, informal, formal, straight-forward</td></tr>
<tr><td>PERFORMANCE DOMAIN</td><td>Communication Strategies</td><td>CONTENT</td><td>Familiar, at times researched</td></tr>
<tr><td colspan="4">What types of Communication Strategies did you use today?
☐ Strategies to maintain and advance communication (keep the communication going).
☐ Strategies to overcome a breakdown in communication (when my partner or I did not understand something).</td></tr>
<tr><td colspan="2">Option 1: What types of Communication Strategies did you use to maintain and advance communication today?
☐ I responded to my partner's questions.
☐ I asked my partner simple questions that followed a pattern (Do you like…? What do you like more…?).
☐ I asked questions to follow-up on an idea that my partner said.
☐ I asked a variety of questions to follow-up on ideas that my partner said.
☐ I cooperated in the conversation: I shared equal responsibility to introduce and develop topics.
☐ I demonstrated I was listening to my partner through gestures (nodding), facial cues (appropriate eye contact, raise eyebrows, smile…), rejoinders (Really? Wow? Me too!), affirming responses (I agree that…I can understand how you think…I'm sorry to hear that you feel that way…), and/or follow-up questions.</td><td colspan="2">Option 2: List ways that you maintained and advanced communication today:</td></tr>
<tr><td colspan="2">Option 1: What types of Communication Strategies did you use to overcome a breakdown in communication?
☐ I gestured.
☐ I repeated.
☐ I used similar words.
☐ I modeled an answer for my partner.
☐ I asked follow-up questions to clarify when I didn't understand my partner.
☐ I rephrased my message by stating it in a different way.
☐ I asked for help to get my point across.
☐ I corrected myself.
☐ I used circumlocution: I used language that I know well in order to explain a word/phrase that I didn't know.</td><td colspan="2">Option 2: List the Communication Strategies you used to overcome a breakdown in communication:</td></tr>
<tr><td colspan="4">Evaluate how you think you performed in Communication Strategies today:
☐ Beginning: I can answer and ask simple questions. If there is a breakdown, I can use gestures/facial cues, repeat word(s), and/or use similar word(s).
☐ Developing: I can exchange information by answering and asking follow-up questions. If there is a breakdown, I can repeat word(s), use similar word(s), rephrase, and/or ask for help.
☐ Meeting: I can exchange information by answering and asking a variety of follow-up questions. If there is a breakdown, I can rephrase, ask for help, and/or correct myself.
☐ Exceeding: I can exchange information by answering and asking a variety of appropriate questions, and at times cooperate in a conversation. If there is a breakdown, I can rephrase, correct myself, and/or use circumlocution.</td></tr>
<tr><td colspan="4">Think about your own experience and what you have done to improve in your use of Communication Strategies. What advice would you give other learners to help them develop Communication Strategies?</td></tr>
</table>

Table 9.17

Interpersonal Guided Self-Assessment

TARGET PERFORMANCE LEVEL	Advanced Low	CONTEXT	Familiar, unfamiliar, informal, formal, complex
PERFORMANCE DOMAIN	Communication Strategies	CONTENT	Familiar, academic, social, concrete

What types of Communication Strategies did you use today?

- ☐ Strategies to maintain and advance communication (keep the communication going).
- ☐ Strategies to overcome a breakdown in communication (when my partner or I did not understand something).

Option 1: What types of Communication Strategies did you use to maintain and advance communication today?	Option 2: List ways that you maintained and advanced communication today:
☐ I responded to my partner's questions. ☐ I asked questions to follow-up on an idea that my partner said. ☐ I asked a variety of questions to follow-up on ideas that my partner said. ☐ I asked probing questions that went beyond basic details. ☐ I cooperated in the conversation: I shared equal responsibility to introduce and develop topics. ☐ I used a variety of ways to show that I was interested in what my partner was saying.	

Option 1: What types of Communication Strategies did you use to overcome a breakdown in communication?	Option 2: List the Communication Strategies you used to overcome a breakdown in communication:
☐ I asked follow-up questions to clarify when I didn't understand my partner. ☐ I rephrased my message by stating it in a different way. ☐ I asked for help to get my point across. ☐ I corrected myself. ☐ I used circumlocution: I used language that I know well in order to explain a word/phrase that I didnt' know. ☐ I paraphrased to clarify understanding.	

Evaluate how you think you performed in Communication Strategies today:

- ☐ **Beginning:** I can exchange information by answering and asking a variety of follow-up questions. If there is a breakdown, I can rephrase, ask for help, and/or correct myself.
- ☐ **Developing:** I can exchange information by answering and asking a variety of appropriate questions, and at times cooperate in a conversation. If there is a breakdown, I can rephrase, correct myself, and/or use circumlocution.
- ☐ **Meeting:** I can cooperate in a conversation by initiating and developing topics and topic changes. If there is a breakdown, I can rephrase and/or use circumlocution.
- ☐ **Exceeding:** I can cooperate in a conversation and ask probing questions. At times I can transition among topic changes in a cohesive manner. If there is a breakdown, I can rephrase, paraphrase idea(s), and/or use circumlocution.

Think about your own experience and what you have done to improve in your use of Communication Strategies. What advice would you give other learners to help them develop Communication Strategies?

YOUR TURN

LEARNING TARGET CHECK:	
I can	☐ provide learners with self-assessments to evaluate their work.

Complete the chart by identifying specific self-assessments from the *Learners' Self-Assessments* section (p. 385-400) that could be used in an upcoming unit to help learners evaluate their own work. Next, describe a formative or summative performance task in your upcoming unit that learners could complete and then self-assess using the chosen-self-assessment. Finally, list any additional materials or preparation that might be needed to implement this self-assessment in the *Notes* section of the chart.

UNIT:		
PERFORMANCE DOMAIN: COMMUNICATION STRATEGIES		
Learner self-assessments	**Performance task** Formative or summative	**Notes**

Advice From Learners

As a purposeful way for learners to become aware of their own learning, we asked learners to reflect on what worked for them to improve their performance in various performance domains. Sharing advice can build learner metacognitive skills, or awareness of one's own learning, which has been linked to improved learning outcomes (Hattie, 2017). Together learners build a bank of suggestions and advice that they can access when looking to improve in a specific performance domain. This is a way for learners to realize what they have learned about a performance domain, monitor their own understanding of the performance domain, suggest and choose which advice to employ, and evaluate whether particular choices are successful. Here is what some learners said, when asked to share their insights on Communication Strategies and give advice.

Novice Interpersonal:

- *Be ready, but listen to your partner, don't just talk at them, ask stuff.*
- *Have a way to ask for help if you get stuck.*
- *Give your answer if your partner doesn't. Then they know what to do.*

Intermediate Interpersonal

- *Think about questions you could ask, including follow-up questions – be ready.*
- *Be ready with several ways to say the same thing, in case your partner doesn't understand something. Like examples, or answering your own question.*
- *Give your partner enough time to talk, and say more than one thing at a time – go in-depth.*
- *Make it interesting and be curious to have a real conversation. But don't ask your partner something weird.*

Advanced Interpersonal:

- *Prepare, but be willing to shift with your partner to make the conversation together.*
- *Listen for opportunities to ask more.*
- *Keep talking and recover if things get messed up.*
- *Know enough to have enough to say, then let it flow.*

References

Adair-Hauck, B., Glisan, E. W., & Troyan, F. J. (2013). *Implementing integrated performance assessment.* ACTFL.

ACTFL. (2012a). *ACTFL performance descriptors for language learners.* https://www.actfl.org/educator-resources/actfl-performance-descriptors

ACTFL. (2012b). *ACTFL proficiency guidelines – Speaking, writing, listening, and reading* (3rd ed.). https://www.actfl.org/educator-resources/actfl-proficiency-guidelines

Hattie, J. (2017). *250+ influences on student achievement.* Visible Learning Plus. https://visible-learning.org/wp-content/uploads/2018/03/VLPLUS-252-Influences-Hattie-ranking-DEC-2017.pdf

National Council of State Supervisors for Languages (NCSSFL) – ACTFL. (2017). *NCSSFL-ACTFL Can-Do Statements: Performance Indicators for Language Learners.* ACTFL. https://www.actfl.org/educator-resources/ncssfl-actfl-can-do-statements

Sandrock, P. & Clementi, D. (2018). *Interpersonal communication: Focus on feedback* [Conference session]. ACTFL Convention, New Orleans, LA.

Troyan, F. J., Adair-Hauck, B., & Glisan, E. W. (2023). *The integrated performance assessment: Twenty years and counting.* ACTFL.

Warren, M. (2006). *Features of naturalness in conversation.* John Benjamins Publishing Company. https://doi.org/10.1075/pbns.152

CHAPTER 10 | GRADING AND REPORTING

LEARNING TARGETS:	
I can	☐ describe how to align gradebooks with Performance Domain Indicators. ☐ describe how to use Performance Domain Indicators to create grading opportunities that promote continued language growth for all learners. ☐ describe ways to track classroom behavior and report it separately from learners' language performance.

This book is meant to serve as a guide for educators to evaluate learner work using the Performance Domain Indicators (PDIs) within each performance domain and provide feedback to promote learners' language growth. However, since both assessment and grading are realities in world language classrooms, educators need to consider how their grading practices support effective feedback for language growth. This chapter provides guidance on how to take a standards-based approach towards grading focusing on performance expectations, assessment, and feedback. Aligning grading and reporting practices with the PDIs provides opportunities to evaluate learner work and support language growth. When the PDIs are placed into a scoring rubric, a framework for evaluation and grading is created. By matching the PDIs with learners' evidence, scores can be assigned that show where a learner is as well as their pathway towards growth. Consistent use and placement of the PDIs within these scoring rubrics creates alignment across languages and levels within a department. That is, scoring rubrics with aligned PDIs ensure that the learner will be assessed and scored with consistency, regardless of what teacher, which language, or what level a learner is working within.

Educators are invited to consider these three questions to align grading and reporting practices with performance domains and their indicators:

- How can gradebooks be aligned with the PDIs?
- How can the PDIs be used to create grading opportunities for continued language growth for all learners?
- How can classroom behaviors be separated from language performance to ensure that grades accurately reflect what the learner *can do*?

How can gradebooks be aligned with the PDIs?

A grade is intended to convey an accurate reflection of what a learner knows and can do in relation to performance criteria: "The primary goal of grading and reporting is communication. …Grading and reporting certify the attainment of learning goals, identify where additional work is needed and provide a basis for improvement efforts" (Guskey & Bailey, 2001, p. 2). The PDIs for a course can be placed within a scoring rubric to clearly communicate performance expectations to learners. Once placed in a scoring rubric, the PDIs can be paired with a number or score. What number/score is used will depend upon and should correspond to a department's and/or building's grading agreements. Tables 10.1 and 10.2 offer examples of how a number/score can be paired with a range of PDIs.

Table 10.1
Example Using a Standards-Based 4-Point Grading Scale

	Target Performance Level: **Intermediate High** Context: familiar, informal, formal, straight-forward Content: familiar, concrete, at times researched			
	4 **Exceeding**	**3** **Meeting**	**2** **Developing**	**1** **Beginning**
Language Use	I can create with language by (re)combining a variety of vocabulary and structures in various time frames.	I can create with language by (re)combining a variety of vocabulary and structures, and at times in various time frames.	I can create with language by (re)combining vocabulary and structures.	I can use practiced vocabulary and formulaic structures, and at times (re)combine vocabulary and structures to create with language.

Note: In this grading scale, each performance domain is aligned to number (1-4), which represents a performance level (*Exceeding, Meeting, Developing, Beginning*).

Table 10.2
Example Using a 10-Point Grading Scale

	Target Performance Level: **Intermediate High** Context: familiar, informal, formal, straight-forward Content: familiar, concrete, at times researched			
	10 **EXCEEDING**	**9** **MEETING**	**7** **DEVELOPING**	**6** **BEGINNING**
Language Use ___/10	I can create with language by (re)combining a variety of vocabulary and structures in various time frames.	I can create with language by (re)combining a variety of vocabulary and structures, and at times in various time frames.	I can create with language by (re)combining vocabulary and structures.	I can use practiced vocabulary and formulaic structures, and at times (re)combine vocabulary and structures to create with language.

Note: In this grading scale, each performance domain is worth 10 points and can be converted to a percentage using a 100-point percentage scale (10/10 = 100%; 9/10 = 90%; 7/10 = 70%; 6/10 = 60%).

Educators across a language department create alignment by routinely using scoring rubrics that outline the expected range of the PDIs for a course. This alignment is realized horizontally: that is, courses with the same target performance level, regardless of language, use the same scoring rubric with consistent PDIs to evaluate learner work. For example, all level 1 courses could use the range of the PDIs from Novice Low (*Beginning*) to Intermediate Low (*Exceeding*), aligning their performance target to the *Meeting*, or Novice High, performance level. Alignment can also be realized vertically, as progressions of the PDIs on a continuum can be aligned throughout an entire language pathway. For example, level 1 courses could use a range of the PDIs from Novice Low (*Beginning*) to Intermediate Low (*Exceeding*), aligning their performance target to the *Meeting*, or Novice High, performance level. Level 3 courses could use a range of the PDIs from Novice High (*Beginning*) to Intermediate High (*Exceeding*), aligning their performance target to the *Meeting*, or Intermediate Mid, performance level. The progression of a department's vertical alignment will depend on multiple factors, such as the number of instructional hours completed in each course and/or how the target language corresponds to a learner's base language (example: logographic languages, such as Chinese and Japanese, may take longer to learn for learners whose base language uses the Roman alphabet). However, once grades are aligned to scoring rubrics based on the PDIs, transparency is created for all stakeholders. Educators, learners, and families are better able to understand the expectations and learning outcomes of the course, track progress, and apply feedback for language growth.

When evaluating a learner's work, educators mark the PDIs that best describe the characteristics of a learner's performance within the targeted range in which they are performing. Table 10.3 shows how a learner is performing within a range of the PDIs, where the target performance level (Intermediate High) is designated as the *Meeting* level. On this particular performance, the learner is meeting expectations in Language Use and Communication Strategies, exceeding expectations in Text Type, and is at the *Developing* level in Intercultural Communication. By marking learners' performance in this way, educators can communicate to learners "information about the discrepancy between where they are and where they need to be" (Erkens et al., 2017, p. 41). Each field on the scoring rubric describes what the learner can do, rather than just providing a numeric score. The PDIs, formatted into a narrative rubric such as this, clarify performance expectations for learners, provide opportunities to self-assess, and allow educators to evaluate and comment on learner work. Note that in this example, numeric scoring examples were provided on the rubric for educators. However, educators are encouraged to provide numeric scores in a separate place, such as a gradebook, rather than on a scoring rubric. As Wiliam (2011) notes, "As soon as students get a grade, the learning stops" (p. 123). Providing scoring rubrics without numeric scores attached allows learners to focus on their performance, what they can do, and provide opportunities for reflection and next steps without the influence of a numeric score. Once reflection has been completed, educators can direct learners to a gradebook to see a numeric representation of their overall grade.

Table 10.3

Evaluation of a Learner's Interpersonal Performance Using a Range of the PDIs from Intermediate Low to Advanced Low.

Target Performance Level: **Intermediate High** Context: familiar, informal, formal, straight-forward Content: familiar, concrete, at times researched				
	EXCEEDING	**MEETING**	**DEVELOPING**	**BEGINNING**
Scoring using a 4-point scale	**4**	**3**	**2**	**1**
Scoring using a 10-point scale	**10**	**9**	**7**	**6**
Language Use How do I use language to complete the performance task?	I can create with language by (re)combining a variety of vocabulary and structures in various time frames.	I can create with language by (re)combining a variety of vocabulary and structures, and at times in various time frames.	I can create with language by (re)combining vocabulary and structures.	I can use practiced vocabulary and formulaic structures and at times (re)combine vocabulary and structures to create with language.
Text Type How extensive and complex is the language I use and how do I organize it?	I can create simple paragraphs and/or paragraph-length discourse.	I can form (a) series of connected and complex sentences that may combine to create a simple paragraph(s) and/or paragraph-length discourse.	I can form a series of connected sentences, and at times complex sentences.	I can form simple sentences, and at times series of sentences.
Intercultural Communication How well does my language and behavior match the social and cultural context of the performance task?	I can use a variety of language and/or behaviors that are appropriate to the social/cultural context.	I can use language and/or behaviors that are appropriate to the social/cultural context.	I can, at times, use language and/or behaviors that are appropriate to the social/cultural context.	I use language and/or behaviors that are not appropriate to the social/cultural context.
Communication Strategies How do I maintain and advance communication?	I can cooperate in a conversation by initiating and developing topics and topic changes. If there is a breakdown, I can rephrase and/or use circumlocution.	I can exchange information by answering and asking a variety of appropriate questions, and at times cooperate in a conversation. If there is a breakdown, I can rephrase, correct myself, and/or use circumlocution.	I can exchange information by answering and asking a variety of follow-up questions. If there is a breakdown, I can rephrase, ask for help, and correct myself.	I can exchange information by answering and asking follow-up questions. If there is a breakdown, I can repeat word(s), use similar word(s), rephrase, and/or ask for help.

Note: The boxes outlined in bold indicate how the learner's performance was evaluated.

For each assessment, educators are encouraged to report separate scores for each performance domain in the gradebook, rather than a cumulative total, to clearly align gradebooks to the PDIs. Similar to a standards-based approach to grading, "teachers plan each assessment to provide direct evidence of student proficiency on specific learning outcomes/goals and then record this evidence by goal, dedicating columns or blocks of space in their gradebook to each learning goal" (O'Connor, 2011, p. 59). For example, for the learner's performance on Table 10.3, the educator would report separate scores for each of the performance domains of Language Use, Text Type, Intercultural Communication, and Communication Strategies. Scoring each performance domain separately gives a transparent and more detailed picture of where the learner is meeting expectations and areas for improvement. In this way, learner progress and achievement of the PDIs is accurately represented in a way that growth within each performance domain can be clearly documented and tracked.

Table 10.4 demonstrates how this might appear in a gradebook. In this example, the educator has divided the gradebook into three categories: Interpretive, Interpersonal, and Presentational. Aligning a grade book with the three modes of communication reflects the learning outcomes of a language course. Although all of the World-Readiness Standards for Learning Languages (National Standards Collaborative Board, 2015) are part of the curriculum, evidence of learning within each standard can be exhibited through the three modes of communication. Scores in these three categories will make up the learner's summative grade. Each category is weighted to demonstrate to learners that all three modes are needed for successful communication. Scores for each performance domain are reported separately to reflect learner achievement in each mode of communication. In Table 10.4, the learner has completed one interpersonal and one presentational assessment.

Table 10.4
Example of a Gradebook Reporting Out Scores for Assessments in the Interpersonal and Presentational Modes

Communication modes and performance domains that are being scored:		**Assessment 1**	**Assessment 2**	**Assessment 3**
Category 1: 33% INTERPRETIVE MODE *				
Category 2: 34% INTERPERSONAL MODE	Language Use	3		
	Text Type	4		
	Intercultural Communication	3		
	Communication Strategies	2		
Category 3: 33% PRESENTATIONAL MODE	Language Use	3		
	Text Type	3		
	Intercultural Communication	2		
	Impact	2		

* *Note:* The interpretive mode is not presented in this book.

When performance domain scores are recorded separately, all stakeholders can see a clearer picture of learner performance. Unfortunately, grading systems may ultimately average performance domain scores from an assessment, or educators may be required to report an overall grade in each communication mode. Wherever possible, provide separate scores for each performance domain within each mode of communication. This provides the clearest picture of learner performance and tracks learner language growth in relation to the PDIs within each performance domain.

Although the 100-point scale and percentage grading has long been used in education, it is not the most accurate way to assign scores. "Percentage grading systems that attempt to identify a hundred distinct levels of performance distort the precision, objectivity, and reliability of grades" (Guskey, 2015, p.33). For example, Feldman (2019) notes that the 100-point grading system often assigns a 10- or 11-point interval to the letter grades A, B, C, and D, but assigns a 60-point interval for an F (see Table 10.5), creating a system that is not equivalent.

Table 10.5
100-Point Grading Scale and Corresponding Point Intervals

LETTER GRADE	PERCENTAGE	INTERVAL
A	90-100	11 points
B	80-89	10 points
C	70-79	10 points
D	60-69	10 points
F	0-59	60 points

Note: Adapted from *Grading for Equity*, by J. Feldman, 2019, Corwin. Adapted with permission.

However, educators can apply a standards-based grading approach to a 100-point grading scale by using integer grading, a system through which integers 0-4 or 0-5 are each assigned to a letter grade. "By limiting the number of grade categories to four or five through an integer grading system, educators can offer more honest, sensible, and reliable evaluation of students' performance" (Guskey, 2015, p.33). If a grading system requires a 100-point scale, educators can determine the numeric grade and interval to assign to each level of the PDIs. One example of this is from Marzano Academies, where they applied the integer grading to a letter grade (see Table 10.6) as well as a 4-point proficiency scale (see Table 10.7). School districts have also created their own grading systems, like the examples from Wayzata Public Schools (Wayzata, MN) (see Table 10.8) and from Spotsylvania County Public Schools (Spotsylvania, VA) (Table 10.9). All of these examples show how the 100-point grading scale can be aligned using integers for each level of the PDIs. Integer grading requires support so that all stakeholders understand how scores, translated into percentages, align with grades. It is important to understand that a 50% does not equate to getting 50 out of 100 questions correct, but instead is a numerical measure associated with where a learner is at in their learning. Setting the score for *Meeting* expectations as well as what letter grade represents that performance, is a discussion for a department, program or district. Once determined, it provides the starting point for all other scores, percentages, and grades.

Table 10.6
Integer Grading Applied to Letter Grades

AVERAGE PROFICIENCY SCALE SCORE	LETTER GRADE
3.75 – 4.00	A+
3.26 – 3.74	A
3.00 – 3.25	A-
2.84 – 2.99	B+
2.67 – 2.83	B
2.50 – 2.66	B-
2.34 – 2.49	C+
2.17 – 2.33	C
2.00 – 2.16	C-
1.76 – 1.99	D+
1.26 – 1.75	D
1.00 – 1.25	D-
Below 1.00	F

Note: From "Reporting & Grading," by Marzano Academies, 2023 https://marzanoacademies.org/reporting-and-grading/. Reprinted with permission.

Table 10.7
Integer Grading Applied to 4-point Proficiency Scale

AVERAGE PROFICIENCY SCALE SCORE	ONE HUNDRED-POINT SCALE SCORE
4.0	100
3.5	95
3.0	90
2.5	80
2.0	70
1.5	65
1.0	60
Below 1.0	50

Note: From "Reporting & Grading," by Marzano Academies, 2023 https://marzanoacademies.org/reporting-and-grading/. Reprinted with permission.

Table 10.8
Integer Grading Scale

SCORE	DESCRIPTION	LETTER GRADE	PERCENTAGE
3.5 – 4	Exceeding	A	87.5-100%
3.25 – 3.49		A-	81.25-87.49%
3 – 3.24		B+	75-81.24%
2.75 – 2.99	Meeting	B	68.75-74.99%
2.5 – 2.74		B-	62.50-68.74%
2.25 – 2.49		C+	56.25-62.49%
2 – 2.24	Developing	C	50-56.24%
1.75 – 1.99		C-	43.75-49.99%
1.5 – 1.74		D+	37.5-43.74%
1.25 – 1.49	Approaching	D	31.25-37.49%
1 – 1.24		D-	25-31.24%
Below 1	Incomplete Not attempted	F	Below 25%

Note: From Wayzata Public Schools, 2015. Reprinted with permission.

Table 10.9
Integer Grading Scale

MASTERY PROGRESS CHECK AND ASSESSMENT

5 = **Advanced** (approaching next sub-level of proficiency)
4 = **Proficient** (meets ends of unit standards)
3 = **Developing** (approaching end of unit standards)
2 = **Emerging** (below end of unit standards but making progress)
1 = **Foundational** (below end of unit standards and needs reinforcement on previous level material)
0 = **No submission** or relied on outside resource to complete (online translator/dictionary; other person)

INTERPERSONAL TASK

	Total points	%		Total points	%
5	30	100%	2	12	70%
	29	98%		11	68%
	28	97%		10	67%
	27	95%		9	65%
	26	93%		8	63%
	25	92%		7	62%
4	24	90%	1	6	60%
	23	88%		5	58%
	22	87%		4	57%
	21	85%		3	55%
	20	83%		2	53%
	19	82%		1	52%
3	18	80%			
	17	78%			
	16	77%			
	15	75%			
	14	75%			
	13	72%			

PRESENTATIONAL TASK

	Total points	%		Total points	%
5	25	100%	2	10	70%
	24	98%		9	68%
	23	96%		8	66%
	22	94%		7	64%
	21	92%		6	62%
4	20	90%	1	5	60%
	19	88%			
	18	86%			
	17	84%			
	16	82%			
3	15	80%			
	14	78%			
	13	76%			
	12	74%			
	11	72%			

Note: From *Instructional Revolution: Equipping Educators in Proficiency-Based Grading* [Conference Presentation], by A. Jones & P. Prudencio, 2023, ACTFL 2023 Convention, Chicago, IL, United States. https://docs.google.com/presentation/d/1Gd6Ld5MD8IFT-6waDektDadGUMQobXZFR/present?slide=id.p1. Copyright 2023 by Spotsylvania County Public Schools. Reprinted with permission.

It is important to note that in some of these examples, the *Exceeding* level is the equivalent of an A. Some districts/departments may choose to set the *Meeting* level as an A, and the *Exceeding* level as an A+. Regardless of the letter grade assigned, the levels communicate to learners how their performance compares to the standard: learners are *Beginning* to meet, *Developing* towards, *Meeting*, or *Exceeding* their target performance level. Districts/departments will need to determine what letter grade best fits each level, as well as clearly communicate to learners what each level indicates.

Aligning a gradebook to the PDIs supports aligned expectations for learners' performances with the PDIs of each domain. This creates a transparent process that provides a consistent reflection of what a learner knows and can do. In this way, the PDIs help educators take a standards-based approach resulting in consistent and meaningful grading and reporting practices.

YOUR TURN

LEARNING TARGET CHECK:	
I can	☐ describe how to align gradebooks with Performance Domain Indicators.

Pause and reflect:

- How might your gradebook align with the PDIs?
- How might each performance domain be reported separately in your gradebook so all stakeholders can see strengths and areas for improvements?
- What scores best align with each level of performance (*Exceeding, Meeting, Developing, Approaching*)?
- In what ways could your department vertically and horizontally align their grading and reporting practices? How would this alignment benefit educators and learners?

How can the PDIs be used to create grading opportunities for continued language growth for all learners?

Assessments that are evaluated using the PDIs offer the opportunity for meaningful feedback as well as measures of evaluation such as grades. Although a summative grade reflects what a learner knows and can do at the end of a period of learning, feedback with the opportunity to improve is the driving force to nurture hope, spark motivation, and promote continued learning. Learners may showcase their skills multiple times throughout a unit, in both formative and summative assessments. Using the PDIs as guides, learners can self-assess their work to understand where they are and what next steps they can take for language growth. Even after a learning sequence is over, learners can see the pathway to continue their growth when the PDIs remain consistent throughout multiple units in a course.

Unfortunately, learner language growth is not always recognized in a learner's grade. Summative grades, given after each learning sequence is complete, are often averaged together. That is, previous scores are averaged with current scores, regardless of a learner's current level of performance. According to Guskey (2015)

> Averaging can...have detrimental effects on student motivation. Suppose, for example, that a student does poorly on one or two major assessments administered early in the marking period...Even if they perform at the highest level from that time on, the practice of averaging gives them virtually no chance of attaining a high grade. (p. 98)

If feedback is to matter, a learner must be given opportunities to apply that feedback and receive recognition for improvement. Some educators provide opportunities for reassessment after each assessment is complete. However, when the PDIs are used consistently throughout multiple units, educators have the unique opportunity to replace previous assessment scores with more current assessment scores. In this way, learners do not need to retake assessments within each unit. Rather, reassessment is part of the practice. Learners are provided feedback on each assessment. Learners then have the opportunity to apply that feedback on the next performance task, which might occur in the same unit or in the next unit of study. Learners' performance on the next performance task is an opportunity for them to demonstrate growth from their previous performance. Rather than averaging scores from learners' previous work, only scores from learners' most current work make up a learner's grade. In this way, learners are recognized for their growth and their grade is a more accurate reflection of what they can do. "If students demonstrate that past assessment results no longer accurately reflect their learning, then that information must be discarded and replaced by the new information" (Guskey, 2015, p. 98). Replacing previous assessment scores with current assessment scores encourages risk-taking, celebrates learning from mistakes, recognizes growth and accomplishment, and makes practice without penalization the norm. The focus is on learning and feedback, creating a cycle that recognizes growth. Each performance provides an opportunity for feedback until learners ultimately reach the end of the course and a final grade must be assigned.

In the gradebook, this can be shown by replacing previous assessment scores with the most current assessment scores. Each time a learner performs a summative task, their current work is evaluated using the PDIs. In Table 10.9, assessment 1 is moved into a "no count" category and assessment 2 now determines the learner's grade. In the example, this learner made growth in the interpersonal mode within the performance domain of Intercultural Communication, scoring a 2 (or *Developing*) on the first assessment, but scored a 3 (or *Meeting*) on the second assessment. The current scores are not a combination, or average, of what the learner used to be able to do combined with what they can do now. Rather, the scores reflect the learner's current performance. If the learner completes a third assessment, those scores will replace the scores from the second assessment. The grade is composed of the most recent assessment scores, showing evidence of the learner's most current abilities in each mode of communication.

It is important to note that there may be times when a learner's most recent score is lower than their previous score. For example, in Table 10.10, in the presentational mode within the performance domain of Language Use, the learner scored a 3 (or *Meeting*) on the first assessment, but scored a 2 (or *Developing*) on the second assessment. This might be due to increasing complexity with content, vocabulary or structures. Or, it might reflect that a learner has taken risks with the language but is unable to sustain performance. Consistency is a critical element in evaluating learner work and providing meaningful feedback. The most recent performance, even if it scores lower than the previous performance, is the best indicator of the learner's current language skills. Educators are encouraged to report the scores for most recent performance, provide feedback for language growth, and offer opportunities for reassessment. Reassessment opportunities might occur with the next performance assessment (for example, assessment 3). Or, if the lower score occurs on the final assessment of the course, educators can offer a retake opportunity. Regardless, both options provide the learner an opportunity to apply the feedback for language growth.

Table 10.10
An Example of a Gradebook Showing Grade Replacement

Communication modes and performance domains that are being scored:		Assessment 1 NO COUNT	Assessment 2	Assessment 3
Category 1: 33% INTERPRETIVE MODE *				
Category 2: 34% INTERPERSONAL MODE	Language Use	3	3	
	Text Type	4	4	
	Communication Strategies	3	4	
	Intercultural Communication	2	3	
Category 3: 33% PRESENTATIONAL MODE	Language Use	3	2	
	Text Type	3	4	
	Impact	2	3	
	Intercultural Communication	2	2	

* *Note:* The interpretive mode is not presented in this book.

As learners show evidence of progress, the most recent PDIs better characterize their work. By providing opportunities for learners to act upon the feedback they are given, educators nurture hope. According to Erkens et al. (2017)

> Even in their most frustrating moments, learners must believe success is possible if not imminent; otherwise, they will abandon the task before them. It is imperative that teachers help learners build a repertoire of success – a history filled with evidence of capabilities – so that when learners do have difficult tasks, their hopefulness can fuel their stamina, and they can persevere in the face of a challenge. (p. 18)

Consistent use of the PDIs for each assessment within a course provides the opportunity for learner language growth. Learner motivation increases when learners are able to see their progress. Replacing previous assessment scores with the most current assessment scores is one way educators can recognize language learner growth and progress within a gradebook.

Another way to recognize language learner growth and progress in grading and reporting practices is to remove penalties on formative work. As learners work through a unit of study, they need ample opportunities to practice their skills in each performance domain, receive feedback, and apply new learning towards the targeted level of performance. "Grading when students are still learning sends the message that if you don't learn quickly, you must not be very smart" (Vatterott, 2015, p.66). Learners need a way to track their progress and growth in their formative work, but within an environment that provides time, feedback, and a focus on learning – not grades – so they feel safe enough to take risks. Aligning the PDIs to formative work creates a system that tracks growth and progress of learner performance within each performance domain.

To create a risk-free environment for formative work, educators can weight the formative category in the gradebook as a 0% category. This allows the educator to score and report formative work in relation to the PDIs so all stakeholders can track progress and growth. However, because the formative work is reported in a 0% category, learners are not penalized for mistakes they may make during the learning process. This encourages risk-taking and celebrates learning from mistakes. Learner language growth can be documented throughout a unit without fear of penalty. In Table 10.10, all formative learner work is tracked using a weight of 0%, so learners have opportunities to practice their performance within each performance domain without it impacting their overall grade

Depending on the goal of the formative work, educators may choose to evaluate learner work using a single performance domain, or multiple performance domains. For example, learners might be asked to complete the following formative performance task: *Write a note to your new instructor describing an activity you like to do.* Educators might evaluate this formative work using only the PDIs for the Text Type performance domain and record the learner's score, aligned to the Text Type PDI, in the gradebook in a 0% category. Or, educators might evaluate this formative work using the PDIs for multiple performance domains (Language Use, Text Type, and Intercultural Communication) and record each score, aligned to the PDI of each performance domain, in the gradebook in a 0% category. Learners may also contribute towards tracking their formative work by completing self-assessments aligned to the PDIs. Learners might self-assess the Text Type performance domain in their work using the *Guided Self-Assessment* approach (see Table 6.14, Table 6.15, and Table 6.16 in Chapter 6). The self-assessment score, aligned to the Text Type PDI, for each learner could be reviewed by the educator and recorded in the gradebook in a 0% category. Or, learners might rotate to three different stations, using a *Guided Self-Assessment* at each station to evaluate a different performance domain (example: Language Use, Text Type, and Intercultural Communication) in their work. Upon review, educators can record each self-assessment score, aligned to the PDIs of each corresponding performance domain, in the gradebook in a 0% category.

Table 10.11 demonstrates how formative work, aligned to the PDIs, can be tracked throughout a unit of study. In this example, note that some formative tasks were evaluated using a single performance domain (example: Unit 2 Task 2 – Text Type), while others were evaluated using multiple performance domains (Unit 2 Task 4 reports scores for Language Use, Text Type, and Intercultural Communication). The scores reported out included evaluations by both the educator and the learner.

Table 10.11
Gradebook Reporting Formative Interpersonal and Presentational Learner Work

DATE	FORMATIVE INTERPERSONAL COMMUNICATION – 0%	SCORE	COMMENT
3/31	Unit 2 Task 4 – Communication Strategies	4	
3/31	Unit 2 Task 4 – Text Type	3	Learner self-assessment
3/31	Unit 2 Task 4 – Language Use	3	
3/25	Unit 2 Task 3 – Communication Strategies	3	Learner self-assessment
3/20	Unit 2 Task 3 – Intercultural Communication	2	
3/15	Unit 2 Task 2 – Text Type	3	
3/02	Unit 2 Task 1 – Language Use	2	
DATE	**FORMATIVE PRESENTATIONAL COMMUNICATION – 0%**	**SCORE**	**COMMENT**
3/27	Unit 2 Task 4 – Intercultural Communication	4	Learner self-assessment
3/27	Unit 2 Task 4 – Text Type	3	Learner self-assessment
3/27	Unit 2 Task 4 – Language Use	3	Learner self-assessment
3/24	Unit 2 Task 3 – Intercultural Communication	3	
3/23	Unit 2 Task 3 – Impact	3	Learner self-assessment
3/12	Unit 2 Task 2 – Text Type	3	
3/03	Unit 2 Task 1 – Language Use	2	

YOUR TURN

LEARNING TARGET CHECK:	
I can	☐ describe how to use Performance Domain Indicators to create grading opportunities that promote continued language growth for all learners.

Pause and reflect:

- How do your current grading and reporting practices encourage opportunities for language learner growth? What additional practices could be adopted to track progress and growth?
- How might you consistently use performance domains and the PDIs with learners' summative and formative work to positively impact learners?
- What reassessment opportunities can you provide to learners? How will reassessments be reported out in the gradebook?

How can classroom behaviors be separated from language performance to ensure that grades accurately reflect what the learner *can do*?

A grade is intended to clearly communicate learner performance in reference to the standards. When learner behavior, effort, and/or timeliness are included in the grade, the grade no longer communicates a clear message of how the learner is progressing in reference to the established evaluation criteria. As Schimmer (2016) states:

> We most often use grades to indicate student proficiency as it relates to standards or learning outcomes for a subject, and since most curricular standards make no reference to behavioral attributes (like punctuality), we compromise accuracy when we combine achievement (curricular standards) and nonachievement (anything else) factors. (p. 94)

Therefore, in order for a learner's grade to accurately represent their language knowledge and skill, behaviors are reported separately. This ensures that the reporting of a learner's achievement and progress towards the targeted performance level of a course is not penalized or rewarded by the learner's perceived behavior, effort, or timeliness.

According to Feldman (2019), separating behavior from language performance is an important step in promoting bias-resistant grades. Bias-resistant grades means "that we must limit the impact of our biases by limiting elements of a grade that are judgments of our students' behaviors" (p. 120). An educator's cultural values and preferences, the learning environment, and/or school district all impact bias and how someone might define "successful" learner behaviors:

> Rewarding certain behaviors is meant to support student learning but it forces students to fit within a set of behaviors anchored to the teacher's subjective, implicitly biased idea of what a successful student is – behaviors that more often than not are the behaviors that their teacher has and/or values, embedded within that teacher's specific culture, upbringing, and learning styles. In truth, we often superimpose the behavior we engaged in that made us successful. In doing so, we often ignore the diversity of learning styles, contexts, culture and needs among our students. (p. 122)

Separating behavior from language performance limits the amount of bias that can influence a grade. Bias-free grading focuses on learner knowledge and skills rather than behavior. This shift can create confidence among all stakeholders because a learner's grade is an accurate representation of the learner's achievement of the target performance level of a course.

In order to achieve bias-resistant grades, school districts can report learner behavior separately; for example: weekly narrative communication to parents/guardians, frequent student/teacher surveys as screening instruments, or tracking behaviors in a management system. We invite educators to explore the following resources as they consider equitable grading practices: *Grading for Equity* (Feldman, 2019), *Rethinking Grading* (Vatterott, 2015), and *A Repair Kit for Grading: 15 Fixes for Broken Grades* (O'Connor, 2007).

Educators play a direct role in establishing culturally responsive and inclusive approaches that address/promote classroom behaviors for all learners. It is important to reflect upon the impact of our own teaching and classroom management practices, and how they can influence learner behavior. Consider the following reflection questions:

- How do I encourage each learner to participate in their own, individual way?
- What classroom procedure(s)/activities/etc. promote/hinder my learner's best?
- Does my student show up differently in other environments? How? Why?
- How are my learner's behaviors impacting their achievement scores? Or not?
- How do my learner's behaviors align/challenge my own ideas of behavior?
- Why is this behavior presenting itself this way? What are other factors to consider?

In addition, educators can help to promote ownership of learner behaviors in the classroom. Like self-assessment of language performance, learners can engage in regular, ongoing, and consistent self-assessment of classroom behaviors and how they contribute to *their* learning and performance. Feldman (2019) suggests creating student trackers because as he notes "trackers promote a sense of ownership and agency." Doing so can help learners reflect on their performance and "make connections between their actions and their performance outcomes" (p. 220). Table 10.12 provides an example of what a student tracker might look like in a world language classroom.

Table 10.12
Student Tracker for Interpersonal Performance

<table>
<tr><th>PERFORMANCE DOMAIN</th><th>GOAL FOR INTERPERSONAL ASSESSMENT</th><th>SCORE FOR INTERPERSONAL ASSESSMENT</th><th>REFLECTION</th></tr>
<tr><td>Language Use</td><td></td><td></td><td rowspan="4">GLOW (What are my strengths?):

GROW (What can I do to improve)?

Factors that contributed to my success:
Strategies:

Classroom behaviors:

Next steps:</td></tr>
<tr><td>Text Type</td><td></td><td></td></tr>
<tr><td>Intercultural Communication</td><td></td><td></td></tr>
<tr><td>Communication Strategies</td><td></td><td></td></tr>
</table>

This shift in grading practice allows for learners to reflect on how *their* behaviors influence *their* results. Using a student tracker, as illustrated in Table 10.12, provides learners an opportunity to set goals, identify the level of their performance, reflect on what they did well and areas for improvement, make connections between academic performance and behaviors that led to success, and take next steps. This develops learners' self-regulation, in which learners control their own learning process (Brookhart, 2008), and learners' metacognition, or thinking about their thinking to become aware of their own learning (Fisher et al., 2021). Student trackers enable learners to become empowered, independent learners who are able to decide on their own learning goals and select the tools, strategies, or behaviors to successfully reach those goals.

In all, separating classroom behaviors from learners' language performance can create an environment that encourages learners to both learn and master content *and* develop behaviors that positively contribute towards their learning experience. Learners have the opportunity to reflect on what went well, what could be improved, and how next steps in language performance and/or behavior positively impact their success. The focus is on learner reflection and growth.

YOUR TURN

LEARNING TARGET CHECK:	
I can	☐ describe ways to track classroom behavior and report it separately from learners' language performance.

Pause and reflect:

- In your current gradebook, how is learner language performance reported? In what ways is classroom behavior (learner behavior, effort, timeliness) reported?
- In what ways could you separate classroom behavior from a learner's language performance?
- How might student trackers be used to encourage learner self-regulation and metacognition?

Conclusion

The grading practices presented in this chapter are but one way to recognize learner achievement, growth, and progress. Teams are encouraged to discuss ways they can work within their district grading and reporting guidelines to align the PDIs with grading practices that recognize continuous learner language growth, as well as advocate to create more equitable grading practices. Grading practices that are consistent and meaningful create positive learning environments where learners feel safe and able to take risks, learn from mistakes, and ultimately take ownership of the learning. "A 21st century approach to education must be less about rigor and more about deeper learning, less about enticing students with the currency of grades and more about building engaged and vibrant communities" (Dueck, 2014, p.167). We hope the guiding questions provided in this chapter will facilitate further discussions around how to use the PDIs, assessment, and grading practices to build vibrant learning communities.

References

Brookhart, S. M. (2008). *How to give effective feedback to your students.* ASCD.

Dueck, M. (2014). *Grading smarter not harder: Assessment strategies that motivate kids and help them learn.* ASCD.

Erkens, C., Schimmer, T., & Vagle, D. N. (2017). *Essential assessment: Six tenets for bringing hope, efficacy, and achievement to the classroom.* Solution Tree Press.

Fisher, D., Frey, N., & Almarode, J. (2021). *Student learning communities: A springboard for academic and social-emotional development.* ASCD.

Feldman, J. (2019). *Grading for equity: What it is, why it matters, and how it can transform schools and classrooms* (1st ed.). Corwin.

Guskey, T. R., & Bailey, J. M. (2001). *Developing grading and reporting systems for student learning.* Corwin.

Guskey, T. R. (2015). *On your mark: Challenging the conventions of grading and reporting* (1st ed.). Solution Tree Press.

Jones, A. & Prudencio, P. (2023). *Instructional Revolution: Equipping Educators in Proficiency-Based Grading* [Conference Presentation]. ACTFL 2023 Convention, Chicago, IL, United States. https://docs.google.com/presentation/d/1Gd6Ld5MD8lFT6waDektDadGUMQobXZFR/present?slide=id.p1

Marzano Academies. (2023). *Reporting & Grading.* https://marzanoacademies.org/reporting-and-grading/

National Standards Collaborative Board. (2015). *World-readiness standards for learning languages* (4th ed.). ACTFL.

O'Connor, K. (2011). *A repair kit for grading.* Pearson.

Schimmer, T. (2016). *Grading from the inside out: Bringing accuracy to student assessment through a standards-based mindset.* Solution Tree Press.

Vatterott, C. (2015). *Rethinking grading: Meaningful assessment for standards-based learning.* ASCD.

Wiliam, D. (2011). *Embedded formative assessment.* Solution Tree Press.

APPENDIX A | Language Use

LEARNERS' SAMPLE EVALUATION

Presentational | **Novice High** | p. 89
Context: familiar, formal, predictable
Content: familiar, everyday

Evaluation & Explanation

LANGUAGE USE			
EXCEEDING	**MEETING**	**DEVELOPING**	**BEGINNING**
I can create with language by (re)combining vocabulary and structures.	I can use practiced vocabulary and formulaic structures, and at times (re)combine vocabulary and structures to create with language.	I can use isolated, memorized and practiced vocabulary and formulaic structures.	I can use isolated, memorized and practiced vocabulary.

Evaluation: In this performance sample, the learner uses practiced vocabulary and formulaic structures to communicate their message. The learner uses practiced vocabulary to name activities (*skateboarding, hockey, work*), personality descriptions (*sports-minded, hard-working, not lazy*), rejoinders (*How interesting! How important!*), and a season (*in the winter*). At times the learner combines vocabulary using practiced patterns (*practice skateboarding, skate parks, hockey parks*). The learner uses formulaic structures (*I like/I do not like, Naiomi is...*) to craft their message.

Feedback:

- GLOW: You use practiced vocabulary and formulaic structures to communicate your message.
- GROW: How might you create with language by combining and recombining vocabulary and structures more consistently throughout your performance?

Interpersonal | **Novice High** | p. 91
Context: familiar, informal, predictable
Content: familiar, everyday

Evaluation & Explanation

LANGUAGE USE | LEARNER 1			
EXCEEDING	**MEETING**	**DEVELOPING**	**BEGINNING**
I can create with language by (re)combining vocabulary and structures.	I can use practiced vocabulary and formulaic structures, and at times (re)combine vocabulary and structures to create with language.	I can use isolated, memorized and practiced vocabulary and formulaic structures.	I can use isolated, memorized and practiced vocabulary.

Evaluation: In this performance sample, Learner 1 uses isolated, memorized and practiced vocabulary to communicate their message. That is, the learner largely relies on using practiced vocabulary in isolation, using isolated vocabulary to ask questions (*Sports?*) and provide responses (*Yes. Baseball. Very good.*). At times the learner attempts to extend their responses (*I...mmm...baseball...yes*), but falls back to relying on using isolated words to communicate their message.

Feedback:
- GLOW: You use memorized and practiced vocabulary in isolation to communicate your message.
- GROW: How could you use the formulaic, or patterned, structure of *I like* to give more information to your partner?

LANGUAGE USE | LEARNER 2			
EXCEEDING	**MEETING**	**DEVELOPING**	**BEGINNING**
I can create with language by (re)combining vocabulary and structures.	I can use practiced vocabulary and formulaic structures, and at times (re)combine vocabulary and structures to create with language.	I can use isolated, memorized and practiced vocabulary and formulaic structures.	I can use isolated, memorized and practiced vocabulary.

Evaluation: In this performance sample, Learner 2 creates with language by (re)combining vocabulary and structures to communicate their message. Learner 2 uses practiced vocabulary to name activities (*sports, baseball, football, read, swim*), rejoinders (*I too! Cool!*), and seasons (*in the summer, in the winter*). Learner 2 uses formulaic structures (*What do you like more...? Do you like...? I like...*) to craft their questions and responses. Throughout the performance, Learner 2 combines vocabulary in different ways (*play baseball, watch football, watch sports on TV, read books, swim in the summer, swim in the winter*).

Feedback:
- GLOW: You create with language by combining & recombining vocabulary and structures.
- GROW: How might you expand your language by combining and recombining a variety of vocabulary and structures?

Presentational | **Intermediate Mid** | p. 92
Context: familiar, formal, straight-forward
Content: familiar, researched

Evaluation & Explanation

LANGUAGE USE			
EXCEEDING	**MEETING**	**DEVELOPING**	**BEGINNING**
I can create with language by (re)combining a variety of vocabulary and structures, at times across various time frames.	I can create with language by (re)combining a variety of vocabulary and structures, and at times use various time frames.	I can create with language by (re)combining vocabulary and structures.	I can use practiced vocabulary and formulaic structures, and at times (re)combine vocabulary and structures to create with language.

Evaluation: In this performance sample, the learner creates with language and at times uses various time frames. The learner combines and recombines a variety of vocabulary (*major problems, sea barriers, gas emissions, greenhouse gasses*). The learner mainly uses the present time frame (*the increase of the ocean level is a problem…, people are constructing, the icebergs melt and the sea level rise*). At times the learner uses other time frames, such as two examples of the past (*Did you heared, lost*). The learner is able to use phrases to refer to the future time frame (*for the future, in 50 years*) but often reverts back to the present tense structures (*for the future, it's important…, in 50 years, the whole country absent*). Overall, in this performance the learner creates with a variety of language and at times in various time frames.

Feedback:
- GLOW: You create with language by combining & recombining a variety of vocabulary and structures.
- GROW: How might you use various, or multiple, time frames throughout your performance?

Interpersonal | **Intermediate Mid** | p. 94
Context: familiar, informal, straight-forward
Content: familiar, researched

Evaluation & Explanation

LANGUAGE USE | LEARNER 1			
EXCEEDING	**MEETING**	**DEVELOPING**	**BEGINNING**
I can create with language by (re)combining a variety of vocabulary and structures, at times across various time frames.	I can create with language by (re)combining a variety of vocabulary and structures, and at times use various time frames.	I can create with language by (re)combining vocabulary and structures.	I can use practiced vocabulary and formulaic structures, and at times (re)combine vocabulary and structures to create with language.

Evaluation: In this performance sample, Learner 1 creates with language in various time frames. The learner combines vocabulary (*play baseball, first priority, donates money, buy baseball, volunteered with your organization*), and structures (*...but it tries to work in all parts of Minnesota, my organization worked with Miracle League..., children and families that can't buy baseball*). Additionally, Learner 1 is able to use an empty subject pronoun (*it*) and possessive pronouns (*my, your*) to demonstrate flexibility in how they use and apply grammatical structures when clarifying the word *organization.* The learner uses multiple time frames: present (*is called, tries, works*), and past (*What did organization do in the past?, My organization worked with Miracle League. ...it was very fun, And you volunteered...*). Overall Learner 1 is able to combine and recombine a variety of vocabulary and structures in various time frames to communicate their message.

Feedback:
- GLOW: You create with language by combining & recombining a variety of vocabulary and structures.
- GROW: How might you communicate across various time frames (past, present, future) throughout your message?

LANGUAGE USE | LEARNER 2			
EXCEEDING	**MEETING**	**DEVELOPING**	**BEGINNING**
I can create with language by (re)combining a variety of vocabulary and structures, at times across various time frames.	I can create with language by (re)combining a variety of vocabulary and structures, and at times use various time frames.	I can create with language by (re)combining vocabulary and structures.	I can use practiced vocabulary and formulaic structures, and at times (re)combine vocabulary and structures to create with language.

Evaluation: In this performance sample Learner 2 creates with language and at times uses various time frames. Learner 2 combines vocabulary (*people with special needs, priorities of the organization, helps people*) and some structures (*to try, um, to play sports, puts on the Polar Plunge, What did your organization do in the past year?*) to create with language. At times the learner is able to use possessive pronouns (*my, your*) to clarify the word *organization.* The learner primarily relies on the present time frame (*is called, is, puts on*) but, at times uses the past time frame (*In the past, the Special Olympics..., What did your organization do in the past year?*) and attempts a future time frame (*I am going helps in the future*). Overall the learner creates with a variety of language and at times uses various time frames.

Feedback:
- GLOW: You create with language by combining & recombining a variety of vocabulary and structures.
- GROW: How might you use various, or multiple, time frames throughout your performance?

Presentational | **Advanced Low** | p. 95
Context: familiar, informal, complex
Content: familiar, academic, social, professional, concrete

Evaluation & Explanation

LANGUAGE USE			
EXCEEDING	**MEETING**	**DEVELOPING**	**BEGINNING**
I can use a wide range of vocabulary and structures that are, at times, precise across various time frames.	I can use a range of vocabulary and structures across various time frames.	I can create with language by (re)combining a variety of vocabulary and structures, at times across various time frames.	I can create with language by (re)combining a variety of vocabulary and structures, and at times use various time frames.

Evaluation: In this performance sample, the learner uses a range of vocabulary, such as *conclusive, professional, sacrificed, controversy, to sign, injustice, documents, opportunity*. The learner uses structures such as prepositional phrases (*of all 105 players, of the other ballplayers*), auxiliary verbs (*have to* and *can*), the hypothetical "if" clause (*If I were*), and the passive voice (*are no decided*). The learner creates with language in various time frames: the present (*I am, This means, I have, It's* and *I want*); the past (*It was, I dreamed, I did, my family gived, they needed*); and the future (*I would no have to, I won't accept, I will fight, I will not back down, I will win*).

Feedback:
- GLOW: You use a range of vocabulary and structures throughout your message.
- GROW: How might you use more precise vocabulary to communicate your message?

Interpersonal | **Advanced Low** | p. 97
Context: familiar, informal, complex
Content: familiar, academic, social, concrete

Evaluation & Explanation

LANGUAGE USE | LEARNER 1			
EXCEEDING	**MEETING**	**DEVELOPING**	**BEGINNING**
I can use a wide range of vocabulary and structures that are, at times, precise across various time frames.	I can use a range of vocabulary and structures across various time frames.	I can create with language by (re)combining a variety of vocabulary and structures, at times across various time frames.	I can create with language by (re)combining a variety of vocabulary and structures, and at times use various time frames.

Evaluation: In this performance sample, Learner 1 uses a range of vocabulary such as *sanctuaries, tree branch, lifecycle, butterflies, reserves, ecosystem.* The learner also uses a range of structures, such as direct and indirect object pronouns (*to see them togethers, it makes me nervous, makes me sad*). The learner is able to communicate across various time frames: the present (*there are, I want, they destroy*), the past (*we learned, it blew*), and the future (*may break, there would no be*).

Feedback:
- GLOW: You use a range of vocabulary and structures throughout your performance.
- GROW: What structures might help you communicate your message more precisely within a time frame?

LANGUAGE USE | LEARNER 2			
EXCEEDING	**MEETING**	**DEVELOPING**	**BEGINNING**
I can use a wide range of vocabulary and structures that are, at times, precise across various time frames.	I can use a range of vocabulary and structures across various time frames.	I can create with language by (re)combining a variety of vocabulary and structures, at times across various time frames.	I can create with language by (re)combining a variety of vocabulary and structures, and at times use various time frames.

Evaluation: In this performance sample, Learner 2 uses a range of vocabulary, such as *butterflies, insects, humidity, sanctuaries, climate change, pesticides, destruction, habitats, threats, poison.* The learner is able to use structures across various time frames: the present (*there are places, they do not knows, there is*), the past (*I didn't, it was*), and the future (*it would be, might be scared, I can travel*). Additionally, the learner uses structures to hypothesize such as *I wonder, I could, maybe.*

Feedback:
- GLOW: You communicate across various time frames (past, present, future) throughout your message.
- GROW: How might you use more precise vocabulary for words such as *place* or *everything*?

APPENDIX B | Text Type

LEARNERS' SAMPLE EVALUATION

Presentational | **Novice High** | p. 158
Context: familiar, formal, predictable
Content: familiar, everyday

Evaluation & Explanation

TEXT TYPE			
EXCEEDING	**MEETING**	**DEVELOPING**	**BEGINNING**
I can form simple sentences, and at times series of sentences.	I can use simple sentences most of the time.	I can use practiced and memorized words and phrases, and at times use simple sentences.	I can use practiced and memorized words and phrases.

Evaluation: In this performance sample, the learner uses simple sentences, and at times series of sentences. The learner uses formulaic structures to form simple sentences (*I like…, Naiomi likes…, Naiomi is…*). Additionally, the learner, at times, writes multiple sentences on the same topic to create a series of sentences. For example, the learner writes multiple sentences about their likes (skateboarding and hockey) and groups the sentences together to create a series of sentences on the same topic. The learner is able to demonstrate this again with the topic of skate and hockey parks.

Feedback:
- GLOW: At times you use multiple sentences on a related topic to create series of sentences.
- GROW: What coordinators (*and, but, or, for, so*) could you add to better connect your ideas?

Interpersonal | **Novice High** | p. 160
Context: familiar, informal, predictable
Content: familiar, everyday

Evaluation & Explanation

TEXT TYPE | LEARNER 1			
EXCEEDING	**MEETING**	**DEVELOPING**	**BEGINNING**
I can form simple sentences, and at times series of sentences.	I can use simple sentences most of the time.	I can use practiced and memorized words and phrases, and at times use simple sentences.	I can use practiced and memorized words and phrases.

Evaluation: In this performance sample, Learner 1 uses practiced, memorized words and phrases to communicate their message. The learner largely relies on memorized words (*Sports? Yes. Baseball. Um, television?*) to ask and respond to questions. At times the learner is able to use practiced phrases (*Very good, And you, sir?*) to communicate to their partner.

Feedback:
- GLOW: You use words/phrases to communicate your message.
- GROW: How might you use *I like* to create complete sentences?

TEXT TYPE | LEARNER 2			
EXCEEDING	**MEETING**	**DEVELOPING**	**BEGINNING**
I can form simple sentences, and at times series of sentences.	I can use simple sentences most of the time.	I can use practiced and memorized words and phrases, and at times use simple sentences.	I can use practiced and memorized words and phrases.

Evaluation: In this performance sample, Learner 2 uses simple sentences, and at times series of sentences to communicate their message. That is, the learner is able to say multiple sentences on a related topic, such as baseball (*I like baseball AND I like football! I like to play baseball in the summer...*), television (*Yes, I like TV. I really like to watch sports on TV*), and swimming (*I like to swim in the summer. Sometimes I like to swim in the winter...*). The learner is able to use one coordinator (*and*) to connect their ideas.

Feedback:
- GLOW: At times you use multiple sentences on a related topic to create series of sentences.
- GROW: What coordinators (*and, but, or, for, so*) could you add to better connect your ideas?